AFRICANS IN AMERICA

SERIES ADVISORS

Charles Johnson
Patricia Smith
WGBH Series Research Team

AFRICANS IN AMERICA

America's Journey through Slavery

HARCOURT BRACE & COMPANY
New York San Diego London

ISBN 0-15-100339-4

Text set in Fournier
Designed by Linda Lockowitz

Printed in the United States of America
First edition
E D C B A

CONTENTS

Charles Johnson's short stories are listed in italics.

PREFACE

CREATING THIS BOOK and the PBS series *Africans in America: America's Journey through Slavery* has been a transformative process, an excursion back in time to the origins of our nation and its experience with slavery. It has been a search for answers to questions that continue to trouble us today. Over the past three years we have traveled to different parts of the world researching and filming the programs. We've tried to understand how our history of enslavement has defined who we are and what we believe today. We've attempted to weave into one narrative a story of our national identity and our racial identity: a story of the birth of our nation, as witnessed and recorded by people free and unfree, rich and poor, master and slave, proslavery and antislavery. This history is a story about the meaning of freedom. It is a uniquely American story, a story whose legacy we encounter daily when we pass one another on the streets, in the halls, and on the playing fields and we see race.

During the production of the films we traveled to three continents and engaged the scholarship of academic advisors from around the world. We've researched hundreds of journals, letters, narratives, and inventories for evidence and witnesses to this history. In the spring of 1996 we began filming on location throughout the United States, in England, and in Ghana. One of the first locations we photographed was El Mina castle, situated on the west coast of Africa, on a rocky knoll, with the raging Atlantic on three sides.

Built by the Portuguese in 1482, El Mina was the first of forty-five forts and castles constructed to sustain an ever-expanding slave trade between Europeans and Africans—a trade that within one hundred years would be dominated by a European desire for human labor. While filming at El Mina castle, I recognized the awesome task we were undertaking as we began slowly reconstructing our nation's story and, in doing so, experiencing the history firsthand. While filming in Ghana, I kept a diary.

> JOURNAL ENTRY
> OCTOBER 10, 1996, 4:45 A.M., GHANA, WEST AFRICA
> I was awakened by the roar of the Atlantic breaking on the western horizon. We rose in the darkness to film along its shores. There, emerging from the thick palm trees, was the early morning's endless march of women and young girls. Heavy with baskets, buckets, and large metal bowls filled to capacity with fresh fruit, yams, and laundry, they glided across the sands on their way to the El Mina market. There was a dignity in their straight bodies, their heavy loads balanced on their heads, and their purposeful walk. Off in the distance, fishing boats fought the unrelenting currents and crashing waves and paddled out to the rolling seas.

> As I watched the brisk business I was reminded that once again I would be forced this day to confront moments in my people's history I had learned to forget. Within El Mina castle I would come face-to-face with my history of enslavement. I wouldn't be able to hide in my family's tales of accomplishments—stories told and retold so often by grandparents and great aunts and uncles, reminders of who we really are and the kind of people we come from. Today I would confront that part of me my elders seemed so reluctant to acknowledge or accept. Today I had to work in the place where so many thousands spent their last days on the soil of their homeland. El Mina was the point of departure, the place where thousands of captured Africans would begin their journey toward becoming American. The place where ship captains and their crews would begin the long death march to the Americas. Today we would begin our filming in the dungeons of El Mina castle.

I am asked often as I travel around the country presenting *Africans in America*, Why should we revisit a past wrought with pain, anguish, guilt, and embarrassment? Why should we study a history filled with such tragedy?

David Blight, a historian at Amherst College, reminded me once during a moment of doubt that we "have to face the story of slavery as a part of our past because it is part of who we are." He urged that the story of slavery is as much a part of who we are as the victory in World War II or great inventions or the Union victory in the Civil War or the American Revolution. He went on to say that "our history as a nation is like the history of other people and other nations. We have a history of contradictions. We have a history fraught with tragedy as well as some triumph." He impressed on me that it is our responsibility not only to study and understand our heroes and heroines, our triumphs and victories, but it is also essential that we study our mistakes and tragedies and learn the lessons, or we risk failing again. With this purpose in mind, I found the strength to confront my discomfort, my emotions, and my ambivalence toward the history.

> JOURNAL ENTRY
> OCTOBER 11, 1996, 9:00 A.M., EL MINA CASTLE
> I am hurried and anxious this morning. We are outside the fort waiting for our government escort. The town of El Mina is an old fishing town on the tip of the West African Horn.
>
> I had visited El Mina and its dungeons before when we came to do research. I had sensed the spirits in the dark dampness of the large underground caverns. I had touched the cold stone walls and felt on my skin the clammy moss that covered them. I had shed tears, experienced swells of anger and feelings of loss. And as I waited to enter its dungeons again, I dreaded the day before me. I was unsure that I could face once again a place where the most painful part of my history began. Was it the fear of confronting the horror it so vividly represented? Or was it my reluctance to face the feelings of anger, guilt, and shame that I knew would well up again? All I knew was that I wanted to find within me a way toward understanding, toward closure, a way toward the future.

Legal enslavement lasted in this land until the passage of the Thirteenth Amendment in 1865. For almost one hundred years after the American Revolution, slavery and freedom stood side by side. How could a nation that believed in "the right to life, liberty and the pursuit of happiness" justify the unfree status of millions of people within its boundaries?

This ambiguity even today clouds our vision of our nation as a land of one people and one history. Historian Nathan Huggins writes that "the challenge of the paradox is that there can be no white history or black history, nor can there be an integrated history that does not begin to comprehend that slavery and freedom, white and black, are joined at the hip."

Somewhere in the past we learned to accept inequality in our society, we developed a tolerance for notions of superiority and inferiority, and we began to subscribe to notions of racial distinctions. It is during this stage of our history that we began to lose sight of our common humanity. In the black communities for many years after emancipation there was great shame and embarrassment about the memory of enslavement. Rather than admit and accept the past, children were raised to deny their slave bloodlines. And in the white community there was often a fear and hatred of black freedom that expressed itself through racism, or there was a total denial of any family, financial, or circumstantial relationship to slavery entirely. I hear so often, "It was someone else's history." "My mother or father or grandparents didn't do it." "At least our ancestors couldn't have been enslaved or enslavers because our family comes from the North." It was as if we all arrived in America after slavery was abolished—untouched, unfettered, unblemished by its existence.

How deep are the scars of slavery? Are we responsible for the sins of our ancestors? Should we be accountable today for past injustices and pains? How much has our history of slavery informed, defined, the American character?

JOURNAL ENTRY
OCTOBER 11, 1996, 9:00 P.M., EL MINA CASTLE
As we worked in silence most of the day, a tour of visitors came through and we met a couple from Iowa. They seemed glad to see other Americans in this place, so far from home. As they moved through the darkness, I could hear their tears. Suddenly I felt no longer alone.

Today, at El Mina castle I saw other people from other countries walk through the dungeons but none responded like those from my country. Master and slave, enslaved and enslaver, we have all been changed and molded by this shared past. Here, there was something we shared. Clearly there was anguish in the past, that could be felt in this place. But for those of us from the Americas, white and black, there were even more questions that this place conjured up. Maybe we, or our ancestors, came from the same town or county? Maybe we had the same friends? Maybe we even shared family, possibly even blood? Our story of slavery is so complicated and complex. . . . In the dungeons of El Mina, we all cried.

Who is an American? What is an American freedom?

These questions have been repeatedly asked around the *Africans in America* production table as the staff struggled to understand how we've become a nation, separate and unequal. How has race become an accepted marker of character, a measurement of potential, and a determinant of opportunity and privilege? At first we were cautious in our conversations and debates, obviously aware of our differences and sensitivities. I suspected that we wouldn't be able to overcome the lessons from the past that we carried as men and women, young and old, white and black, into this production. I was concerned that we, too, might find ourselves overwhelmed by a past we all shared yet felt and understood so differently.

Our journey forced us to confront ideas of racial discrimination and racial attitudes we for so long considered a part of human nature. What we discovered is that race itself and racism were constructions born out of our need to maintain an economy and a social order dependent on human bondage. We learned that although many in the country recognized enslavement as morally corrupt and socially hazardous, people tried to find ways to justify its continuation and ultimately devised ideas of inferiority and superiority. The story of our nation's approval of slavery is a tragic story. It is a story of ambition and greed overcoming justice and humanity. It is a lesson that should tell us, "Never again."

> JOURNAL ENTRY
> OCTOBER 11, 1996, 9:00 P.M., EL MINA CASTLE
> I tried to maintain a businesslike manner and attitude—for my camera crew, and myself, but the smell . . . I had forgotten the smell. It was pungent and ancient, damp and thick. It surrounded me, penetrated every sense, and every thought, and would not let me escape or forget. It forced me to think of the many, maybe just like me, who dwelled in this darkness, unsure of what lay before them, unable to imagine what would happen next. It forced me to marvel at the person whose blood I share. A captive, who saw a future even in this dark tomb. It was that survivor's commitment to a future, his or her hope for tomorrow, that has given me life.

Our long struggle in this country to make America be America for all its people has been an inspiration and model for other nations and oppressed people. The women's movement, the labor movement, and the civil rights movement all have their roots in the movement for equality and justice inspired by abolitionists. We have a long legacy of activism in this country. It is a legacy of mass movements that are nudging us ever closer to a more perfect union. They represent the actions of many individuals who believe in the promises of the language in our nation's freedom documents—the unalienable right to the pursuit of happiness and the self-evident truth that all men, women, and children are created equal.

There is a quote on the wall above my desk. It reads, "History belongs to everyone and to no one." This book and the films that will accompany it are meant for everyone. On these pages and in the films, you will hear the voices, learn the stories, and witness the lives of many different people responsible for the creation of our nation, and in these lives you will see yourself.

> JOURNAL ENTRY
> OCTOBER 20, 1996, 7:00 P.M., ACCRA AIRPORT, GHANA
> Today we finished filming the dungeons. We started the day with a sense of an awesome responsibility. We knew we had to photograph these chambers and make them real for those who had never seen them before, make them real for those who don't want to believe in the horror, for those who do not care to admit to the holocaust that began in these dark holds.
>
> As I leave West Africa, I am forced to consider how young we Americans are, compared to people from other parts of the world. We have ancestral roots in so many distant places. We are such a recent phenomenon. We are a rare nation on this earth and our unique quality lies in the diversity of our people. We must nurture

our special place on the globe. We should appreciate our unique nationality. . . . I'm looking forward to getting back home.

—ORLANDO BAGWELL, Executive Producer, *Africans in America*

AFRICANS IN AMERICA

PROLOGUE

THE GODPOP OF THUNDER rattled lush landscape. Bullet rain washed the warm from tree leaves, sent jungle life scurrying for cover. Lightning, brighter than any sun, illuminated one moment. Within the circle of that moment, a wooden stool descended and floated earthward, unaffected by the rain's push, the wind's whip and rattle, the sky's promise of yet more violence. Flashes of lightning marked the stool's gentle descent, illuminating its gold inlays as they dotted the restless sky with eerie pinpoints of light.

This seemingly inanimate stool beat with the pulse of a people. For over three hundred years, the African nation known as the Asante had treasured this heavensent thing. It served as a harbor for their dreams. It became a part of their story.

It was there when the drums found their language and opened their throats to sing, heralding the arrival of the Asantehene, ruler of the Asante nation. He perched regally as the world vied for his attention and spun purely for his pleasure. Women with hips like water danced heatedly, brightly colored raiment clinging to their motion. Men popped their torsos, pounded their flat feet into the earth, and whirled, chanting tribute that was deep and guttural, their hands coaxing the drums to fever. Excited children, driven to near delirium by the pace of the ceremony, cluttered the celebration's edges and gulped it all, their eyes wide and too full of everything.

The Asante, lovers of the land, embraced its bounties. They danced in victory, in unchallenged glee, because they were soon to be the undisputed rulers of an ever-expanding territory along Africa's Gold Coast. To attain that land they warred with and conquered people whose faces mirrored their own, faces black and tinged blacker by the unrelenting sunshower. In fact, the Asante frequently battled with the Fanti to gain access to the coast.

Voracious traders, the Asante bartered what they could—gold, glossy cowrie shells, cloth dyed bright like a scream from the sun. Or their prisoners of war. These captives were used to work the land, for household labor, as servants, as soldiers, as employees of the state, and, in some African societies, for religious sacrifice. Their will was no longer their own. They were slaves.

The white man did not introduce slavery to Africa. The bowing of one human being before another was an accepted notion from the moment man first sensed frailty on the part of a rival. And by the fifteenth century, men with dark skin had become quite comfortable with the concept of man as property.

These were the forefathers of Samuel Sulemana Fuseini, a Ghanaian teacher and politician descended from African slave drivers. "Before the white man came we were fighting among ourselves," he said.

> Fighting started because of hunger and want of food and animals. Sometimes people fought to get more cowrie shells. We had no money then; the currency they used was the cowrie. Prisoners of war were taken to be sold in a great market like Salaga—the most famous of the markets in all of Ghana.
>
> When these people fought, men and women and children were arrested and taken to the slave market where the great wealth of the Asante was created. When we fought a war, we had to pay tribute—and slaves are what the Asante wanted.

The development of slavery in Africa was tied to the complexities of social caste and the unwieldy forces of nature. There was no early moment when the decision was made, no defining moment that bellows, "This is where it began, and why." Weaker tribes succumbed and the hierarchy shifted, shifted, shifted again—and it was understood, according to the ever-askew rules of war, that the vanquished would serve. It was the price to be paid for weakness.

But slavery in Africa was not rooted in the horrid squalor the word suggests to us today. Those three wretched syllables, heavy with so much history, routinely conjure up painful images of once-proud men and women with their spirits sheared away. Slave ships crammed with writhing cargo. Backs crisscrossed with welts and gleaming scars. The ripped fabric of families. Shoulders slumped. The auction block. Midnight runs with guns popping staccato in the distance. Men as machines. Chains, rattling and rusted. Innocents cursed by a skin's hue.

In many African societies, enslavement had rules that dictated how the slaves were to be treated. They were required to be part of the family, either through adoption or marriage. Every slave was entitled to food, clothing, shelter. Slave owners had to be responsive and accessible. Slaves were to be trained and disciplined as children were trained and disciplined.

And although tradition spoke of punishing the slave for wrongdoing, a slave owner seldom had the power of life and death over his slave.

In Africa, a rigid societal structure provided for aristocracy and monarchy, but there was also a complex layering of commoners, tradespeople, and lesser landowners. Slaves were used to facilitate the development and distribution of goods. However, these "domestic" slaves could own and manage property, take a husband or wife, own slaves themselves, or inherit substantial bounty at the discretion or death of the master. Almost immediately upon enslavement, captives could set their sights on the possibilities of eventual freedom.

Wealth meant much more than the accumulation of money. It meant being surrounded by people, being a part of a far-reaching extended family. Money and material goods were only good for buying allegiance from people and for purchasing slaves.

So domestic slaves, far from being considered faceless property, were often adopted into the family, ultimately enjoying privileges afforded their owners' offspring. The families of slave and owner often commingled and intermarried, leading to a further blurring of anticipated roles. Tradition and time could garner new freedoms. In a striking correlation to the customs of feudal Europe, these African slaves often felt harbored and secure in their bond to someone who, in the process of overseeing an investment, was duty bound to protect them.

Slavery that existed in Africa before the arrival of European traders drew a very thin line between the free and the captive. While slaves in generations to come would be doomed by their color and chained to their fate, in medieval times they lived lives similar to many western Europeans. They were tied to the fruits of the land and tended to consider themselves only temporarily enslaved. In other words, they were still human, still capably in charge of their own destinies, still with their self-esteem and ability to dream intact.

Long before the arrival of Europeans on West Africa's coast, the two continents shared a common acceptance of slavery as an unavoidable and necessary—perhaps even desirable—fact of existence. The commerce between the two continents, as tragic as it would become, developed upon familiar territory. Slavery was not a twisted European manipulation, although Europe capitalized on a mutual understanding and greedily expanded the slave trade into what would become a horrific enterprise.

Initially, the process of African enslavement by Europeans was a ragged, disorganized undertaking.

Prince Henry of Portugal, born in 1394 to King John and his English wife, the princess Phillippa, was a natural explorer. Early in his life, he participated in his country's first foray into Africa, at the Moroccan port of Ceuta. By twenty-five, he was governor of the southern coasts of Portugal as well as Master of the Order of Christ. As explorer, missionary, and politician, he was understandably anxious to discover what mysteries and riches Africa had to offer. He wanted to test the strength of Africa's Muslim presence, investigate rumors of gold, and perhaps establish colonies that would strengthen Portugal's niche as an imperialistic power. Tempting chronicles of profitable adventures piqued the Portuguese appetite for exploration.

Prince Henry recruited Portuguese captains who shared his vision, and the slow but relentless exploration of Africa began. Arguin Island, off the West African coast, was reached by Nuno Tristão in 1444 and later became the first processing area for the country's slave trade. Once Pope Nicholas V issued a document legalizing the enslavement of heathens and atheists, the way was paved for Portuguese-operated slaving stations all along Africa's western coast. Dinis Dias reached Cape Verde in 1444; two years later, Nuno Tristão reached the portal of the Gambia River.

After the 1453 fall of Constantinople to the "infidel" Turks, the politically and economically restless Portuguese ached for a trade route to the East circumventing the Moslem-controlled overland routes through northern Africa. Portugal was a determined defender of Christian Europe. A viable route along the West African coast might reveal a vulnerability in staunch Moslem defenses.

In 1460, the death of the ambitious prince slowed the frenetic pace of Portuguese exploration. However, in 1469, Fernão Gomes of Lisbon rounded Africa's western outcrop, daring the steamy Niger to reach what were later named the Slave, Ivory, and Gold Coasts.

In 1482 on the Gold Coast, a stunning fort rose from the dust to the sky. Men who dreamed burnished dreams erected São Jorge da Mina—"St. George of the Mine"—in the region where gold had been mined over many years by the natives. The first-known European structure south of the Sahara, El Mina faced the sea to offer a measure of protection from other European interlopers. It also functioned as the first of many slaving centers that would eventually pepper the West African coastline. It took the Portuguese two years to build. In the course of the slave trade, the castle would be controlled by the Portuguese, the Dutch, and the British.

But the construction of El Mina was by no means a sign that the Portuguese had challenged and conquered the inhabitants of the region. The elaborate fort did not flaunt military or strategic superiority. In fact, in a nod to diplomacy and collaboration, it was built with the full knowledge and required consent of the native African chief.

A sixteenth-century Portuguese traveler noted:

> The gold mines were seven in number . . . divided among seven kings. . . . The mines are dug very deeply into the ground. The kings have slaves whom they put in the mines and to whom they gave wives . . . and they bear and rear children in these mines. The kings, also, furnish them with food and drink.

During this era, Africans and Europeans stood together as equals, companions in commerce and profit. Kings exchanged respectful letters across color lines and addressed each other as colleagues. Natives of the two continents were tied into a common economy—their survival and sense of worth was locked to the land, and their economic structure was dependent upon trade with distant merchants who provided spices and other necessities such as cloth.

In that time of shared freedoms, new worlds opened for both Europeans and Africans. There was much to be learned. But lurking beneath the glossy surface of camaraderie were questions and suspicions—the seeds of events that would destroy a relationship never based on black or white.

It was a thunder that had no sound. Tribe stalked tribe, and eventually more than 20 million Africans would be kidnapped in their own homeland. Half died before reaching the coast.

Europe's initial involvement in the business of human being as product was curiously minimal. But a growing need for labor strained, then fractured, a tenuous relationship that was based on healthy trade and mutual respect. The Portuguese established successful trading posts along the coastline, filled maritime coffers with gold; and other Europeans, most pointedly the Spaniards, began to take note of the burgeoning market in slaves. By the start of the sixteenth century, almost 200,000 Africans had been taken from their homes and transported to Europe, São Tomé, and the Atlantic islands.

Columbus's voyages unlocked a whole new dimension for such trade. Following exploratory ventures into Brazil, a haven the Portuguese happened upon in 1500, they forged a permanent settlement to head off French intervention. The sparsely but enthusiastically settled Brazilian territory—with Jesuit missionaries and rough-hewn Indians living side by side—turned increasingly to the quick, highly profitable cultivation of sugar, a crop that required constant vigilance and bouts of intensive, bone-wearying labor.

There was not nearly enough local manpower in Portugal, Brazil, or the early Spanish Caribbean. Indians, alienated by the unfamiliar intricacies of sugar cultivation, wouldn't volunteer for duty—and efforts to enslave them were not always successful. Unlike the imported African slaves, they could flee and disappear into familiar countryside or the waiting arms of family.

Accustomed to cooperative hunting and land cultivation, the Indians withered beneath the white man's irrational demands for constant product from the mines, farms, plantations, and fields. When the Indians failed to meet those demands, they were abused, tortured, even murdered.

And their ranks were decimated by European maladies such as the pox, diphtheria, and tuberculosis, which meant certain death to a population that had lived in isolation for centuries. In Europe, these diseases would typically strike children who then, if they survived, were immune as adults. But the Indians had no such defense. Adults died by the thousands, which stunned the clockwork of the community. Suddenly there was no one to gather food, farm, tend to the ill or dead, formulate the rules for a society to live by. Not only could the Indians not be counted on as a labor supply—in many areas, within two generations, they were almost extinct.

During the resultant labor shortage, everyone recognized the power wielded by the sugar crop. The Spaniards saw it as the answer to the finicky economy of their Central American and Caribbean settlements. But a sugar plantation could not operate efficiently without a hugely dedicated, unquestioning workforce.

The answer was in African captives. By the mid–sixteenth century, black slaves were already used in the island colonies of Madeira and the Canaries for similar labor-intensive work. A cargo of seventeen Africans arrived in Hispaniola in 1505. Soon the Antilles sugar plantations were manned by African slaves.

A heavy influx of European capital fed more and more Africans into the burgeoning sugar economy, changing the complexion of the colonies. The die had been cast. It was the beginning of major European involvement in the trafficking of slaves. Since the Portuguese had the longest experience and the most connections along the coastline, they controlled the initial outward flow of slaves, forcing upward the price of Africans in the New World. That prompted more vigorous competition.

Enter the Atlantic slave traders. Based in Europe, flush with West African contacts, they began to satisfy the European hunger for labor by exchanging European goods such as guns and textiles for growing numbers of African captives, who they shipped to the New World. Some were tempted to operate without official sanction.

After the papal arbitration of 1493 excluded Spain from Africa, the country had to count on companies and individuals of other countries to transport slaves to Spanish colonies. That privilege of transport was called asiento.

In 1562, English adventurer John Hawkins sailed to what is now Sierra Leone. His voyage was funded by enthusiastic London merchants, with no real support from the government. The three ships he commanded—the *Salamon*, the *Swallow*, and the *Jonas*—flew no colors and had no asiento. Hawkins was officially an outlaw.

A wily and ambitious swashbuckler, Hawkins hailed from Plymouth, England, and his father, William, had been involved in maritime trade. John Hawkins had established contacts in Africa and Brazil. He'd spent time in the Canary Islands where he realized how much money there was to be made in buying Africans and trading them in the New World.

In Sierra Leone, Hawkins claims that he "got into his possession, partly by the sworde and partly by other meanes, to the number of 300 Negroes at the least, besides other merchandises which that countrey yeeldeth." This notation suggests that he may have used force to round up the slaves, maybe even capturing some himself. Perhaps he bargained for others. The slaves were transported to Hispaniola, where they were traded for ginger, pearls, sugar. Hawkins realized a profit of approximately 12 percent.

On a second voyage two years later—financed by Queen Elizabeth, who overcame her initial antipathy to slavery—Hawkins transported more than four hundred slaves to Panama, claiming a net profit of 60 percent.

Hawkins had entered a European Atlantic slaving system

that already existed along the west coast of Africa. Although he was an English interloper, he capitalized fully on his familiarity with transatlantic trade.

His dispassionate, matter-of-fact descriptions of the Negroes he encountered mirrored the racial attitudes of the day. "These people are all black," he said of Cape Verde natives,

> and are called Negroes, without any apparel, saving before their privities: of stature goodly men, and well liking by reason of their food, which passeth all other Guineans for kine, goats, pullen, rice, fruits and fish. . . . These men also are more civil than any other, because of their daily traffic with the Frenchmen, and are of nature very gentle and loving.

Hawkins faced no moral dilemma—the humans he captured for barter were merely commodities. Hawkins's contemporaries did not see slavery as the ritual and heartless suppression of a race of men. The captives were just one leg of a simple and profitable system of trade.

Although it was quite some time before England was gripped by the fever to explore, a few subjects of the crown urged the country to wake up and pay attention to the exploratory exploits of Spain and Portugal. Geographer Richard Hakluyt wrote in 1587:

> Reveal to us the Courts of China and the unknown straits which still lie hid: throw back the portals which have been closed since the world's beginning at the dawn of time. There yet remain for you new lands, ample realms, unknown peoples, they wait yet, I say, to be discovered and subdued, quickly and easily, under the happy auspices of your arms and enterprise and the sceptre of our most serene Elizabeth.

Although the time was one of intellectual light, day-to-day existence in Elizabethan England was often horrid. The population grew from approximately 3.25 million in 1570 to more than 4 million in 1600—farming villages could no longer provide sufficient resources, and many farm inhabitants became migrants in desperate pursuit of work. The burgeoning number of migrants and vagrants worried the general populace since poverty was seen as a sure sign of moral decay.

Some nobles advocated sending the unemployed across the Atlantic, leaving them to fend for themselves. And citizens weary of England's dangers began to wonder if there were perhaps more welcoming vistas in other parts of the world.

So Queen Elizabeth created a hero to inspire other heroes: Sir John Hawkins. His coat of arms was an African in chains.

Hawkins sailed to Africa on three occasions, and his blatant intervention infuriated the Spaniards. In the fall of 1568, a Spanish force overwhelmed Hawkins's fleet and confiscated his cargo. Hawkins fled, and England was kept out of the slaving business for the next hundred years. The Spaniards had drawn a very clear line in the sand—there were profits to be made, and there was no room for interlopers.

But the stage had been set. England would send settlers to the New World to seek opportunities which seemed out of their reach at home. And once the settlers had touched new ground, they had to decide whether the plantations of British America would be slave or free.

Slave. Or free.

PART ONE

Terrible Transformation

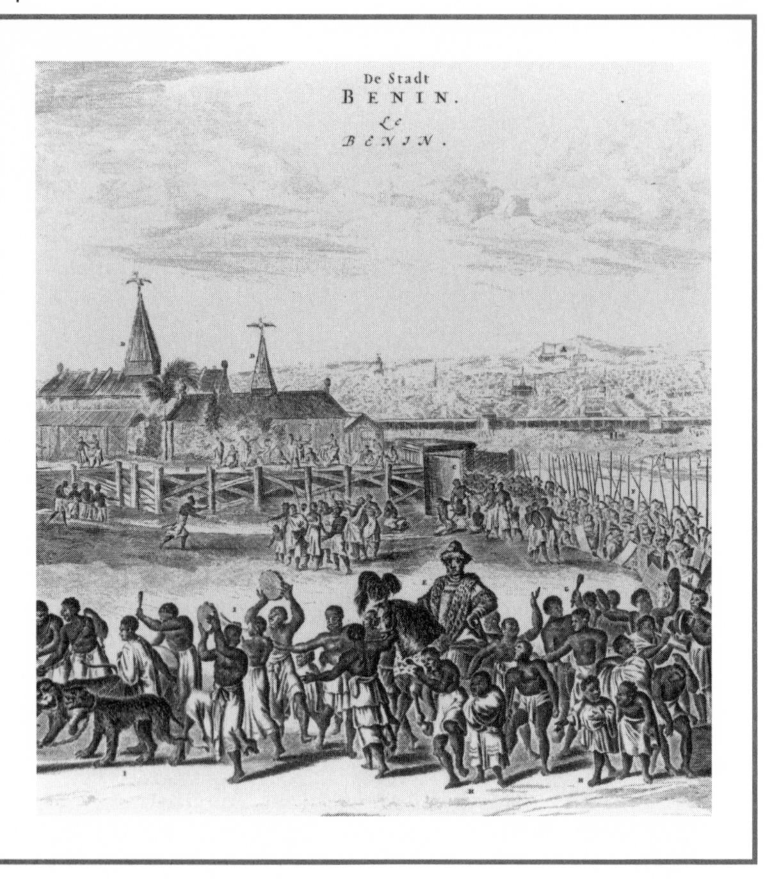

A PROCESSION IN THE CITY OF BENIN, 1668. *Benin, a West African city-state, reached the height of its prosperity between the sixteenth and seventeenth centuries and was known for its exceptional art and extensive commercial holdings. Here, Benin's vast capital stretches behind a procession of its king.*

JAMESTOWN LANDING. *Jamestown, the first permanent English settlement in North America, was a poor, rough encampment until settlers discovered that the land was perfectly suited to the cultivation of tobacco. The first landing at Jamestown is depicted here in an 1841 oil on panel by John Gadsby Chapman,* Good Times in the New World (The Hope of Jamestown).

INDENTURE CONTRACT, RICHMOND, VIRGINIA, 1698. *Indentured servants, gathered from the poor in London and other European cities, made up the majority of workers on Jamestown's tobacco farms in the early seventeenth century. They signed on for four to seven years' work in exchange for their passage to America and the promise of eventual freedom and land.*

THE LIBRARY OF VIRGINIA

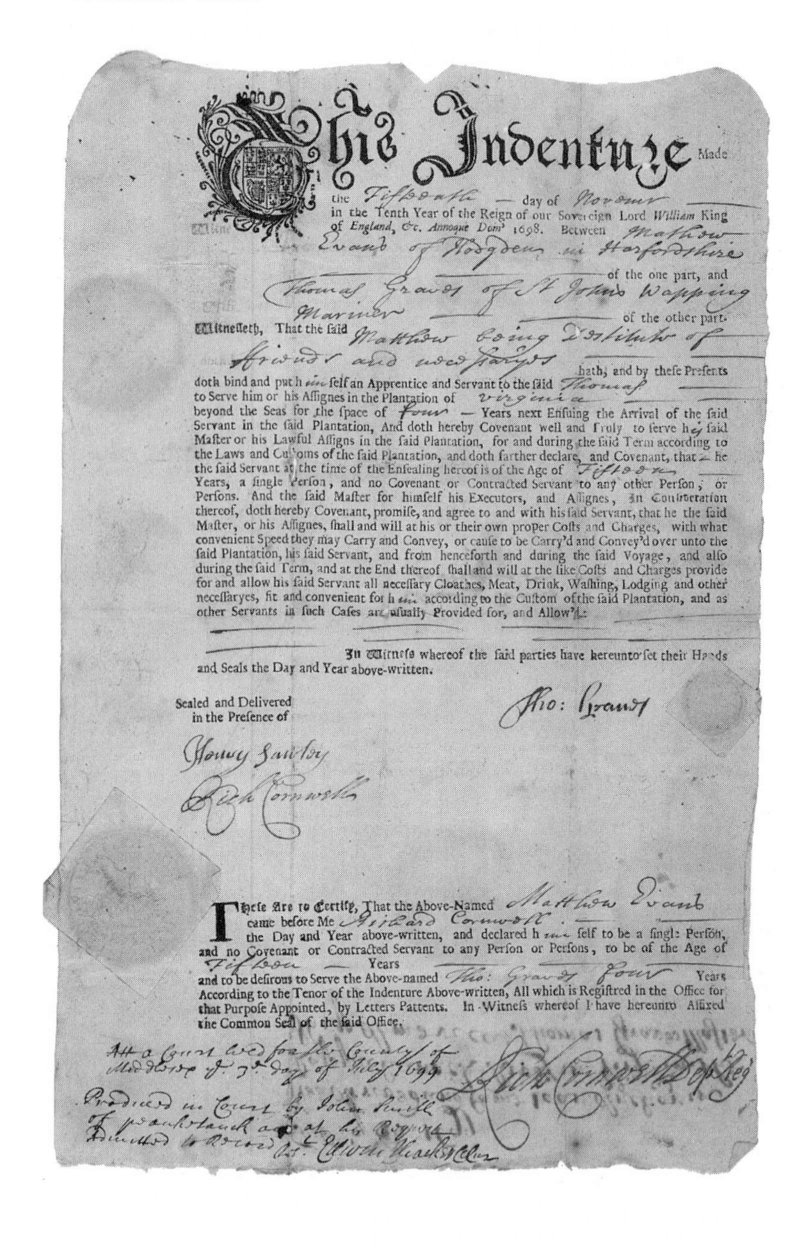

This Indenture Made the Fifteenth day of November in the Tenth Year of the Reign of our Sovereign Lord *William* King of *England*, &c. Annoque Dom' 1698. Between Mathew Evans of Hodgden in Herfordshire of the one part, and Thomas Graves of St John's Wapping Mariner of the other part.

Witneſſeth, That the ſaid Matthew being Destitute of friends and necessarys hath, and by theſe Preſents doth bind and put him ſelf an Apprentice and Servant to the ſaid Thomas to Serve him or his Aſſignes in the Plantation of Virginia beyond the Seas for the ſpace of four Years next Enſuing the Arrival of the ſaid Servant in the ſaid Plantation, And doth hereby Covenant well and Truly to ſerve his ſaid Maſter or his Lawful Aſſigns in the ſaid Plantation, for and during the ſaid Term according to the Laws and Cuſtoms of the ſaid Plantation, and doth farther declare, and Covenant, that he the ſaid Servant at the time of the Enſealing hereof is of the Age of Fifteen Years, a ſingle Perſon, and no Covenant or Contracted Servant to any other Perſon, or Perſons. And the ſaid Maſter for himſelf his Executors, and Aſſignes, In Conſideration thereof, doth hereby Covenant, promiſe, and agree to and with his ſaid Servant, that he the ſaid Maſter, or his Aſſignes, ſhall and will at his or their own proper Coſts and Charges, with what convenient Speed they may Carry and Convey, or cauſe to be Carry'd and Convey'd over unto the ſaid Plantation, his ſaid Servant, and from henceforth and during the ſaid Voyage, and alſo during the ſaid Term, and at the End thereof ſhall and will at the like Coſts and Charges provide for and allow his ſaid Servant all neceſſary Cloathes, Meat, Drink, Waſhing, Lodging and other neceſſaryes, fit and convenient for him according to the Cuſtom of the ſaid Plantation, and as other Servants in ſuch Caſes are uſually Provided for, and Allow'd.

In Witneſs whereof the ſaid parties have hereunto ſet their Hands and Seals the Day and Year above-written.

Sealed and Delivered in the Preſence of

Tho: Graves

Rich Cornwell

These Are to Certify, That the Above-Named Matthew Evans came before Me Richard Cornwell the Day and Year above-written, and declared himſelf to be a ſingle Perſon, and no Covenant or Contracted Servant to any Perſon or Perſons, to be of the Age of Fifteen Years and to be deſirous to Serve the Above-named Tho: Graves four Years According to the Tenor of the Indenture Above-written, All which is Regiſtred in the Office for that Purpoſe Appointed, by Letters Pattents. In Witneſs whereof I have hereunto Affixed the Common Seal of the ſaid Office.

Rich Cornwell Dep Reg

AD FOR JAMESTOWN SETTLERS, FROM *A PROSPECT OF THE MOST FAMOUS PARTS OF THE WORLD*, BY JOHN SPEED, 1631. *As Jamestown became more prosperous, it needed more than indentured workers. So it advertised for others to join the colony. By 1635 there were five thousand residents. Among them were a cargo of Africans who arrived in 1619.*

BY PERMISSION OF THE HARVARD MAP COLLECTION

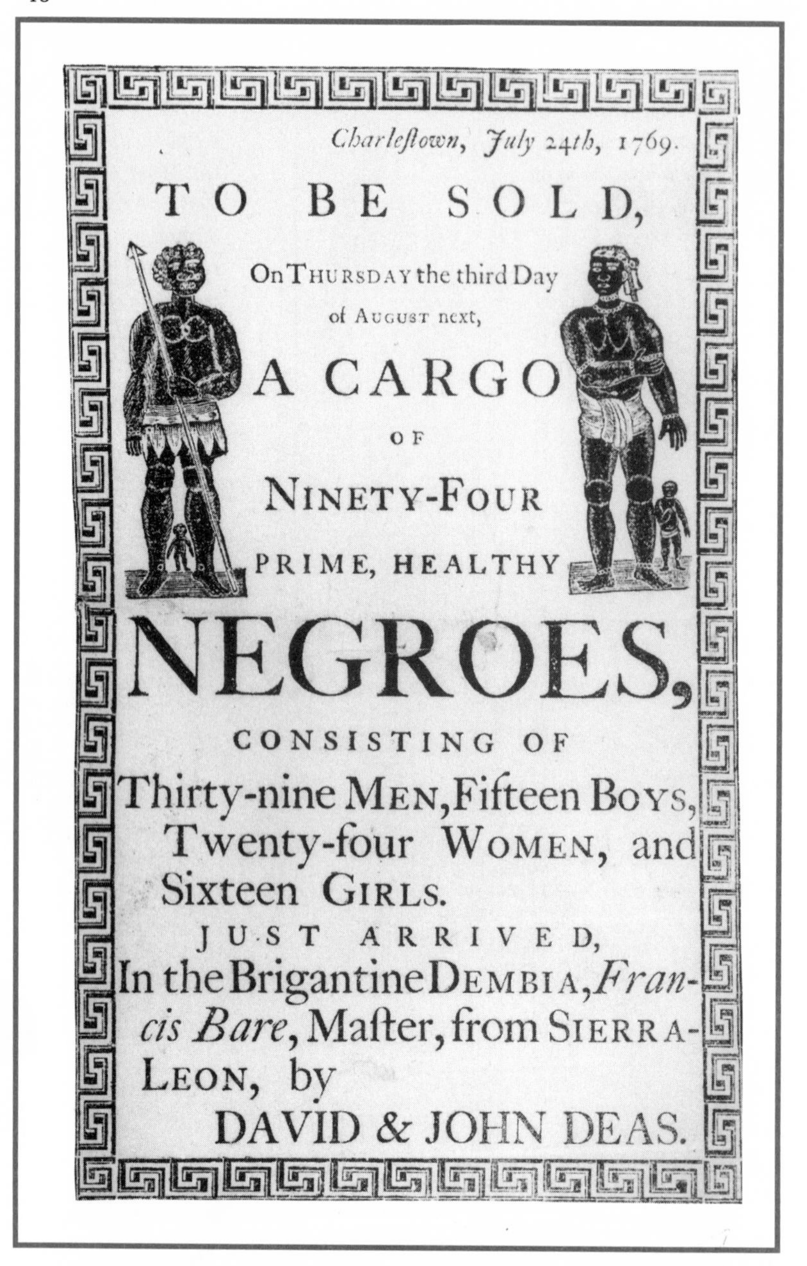

BROADSIDE ADVERTISING SLAVES FOR SALE, CHARLESTOWN, 1769. *In the eighteenth century, slavery replaced indentured labor as the backbone of the fledgling economies of Britain's colonies in the New World. By 1769, slaves accounted for over half of the population in Carolina alone.*

COURTESY, AMERICAN ANTIQUARIAN SOCIETY

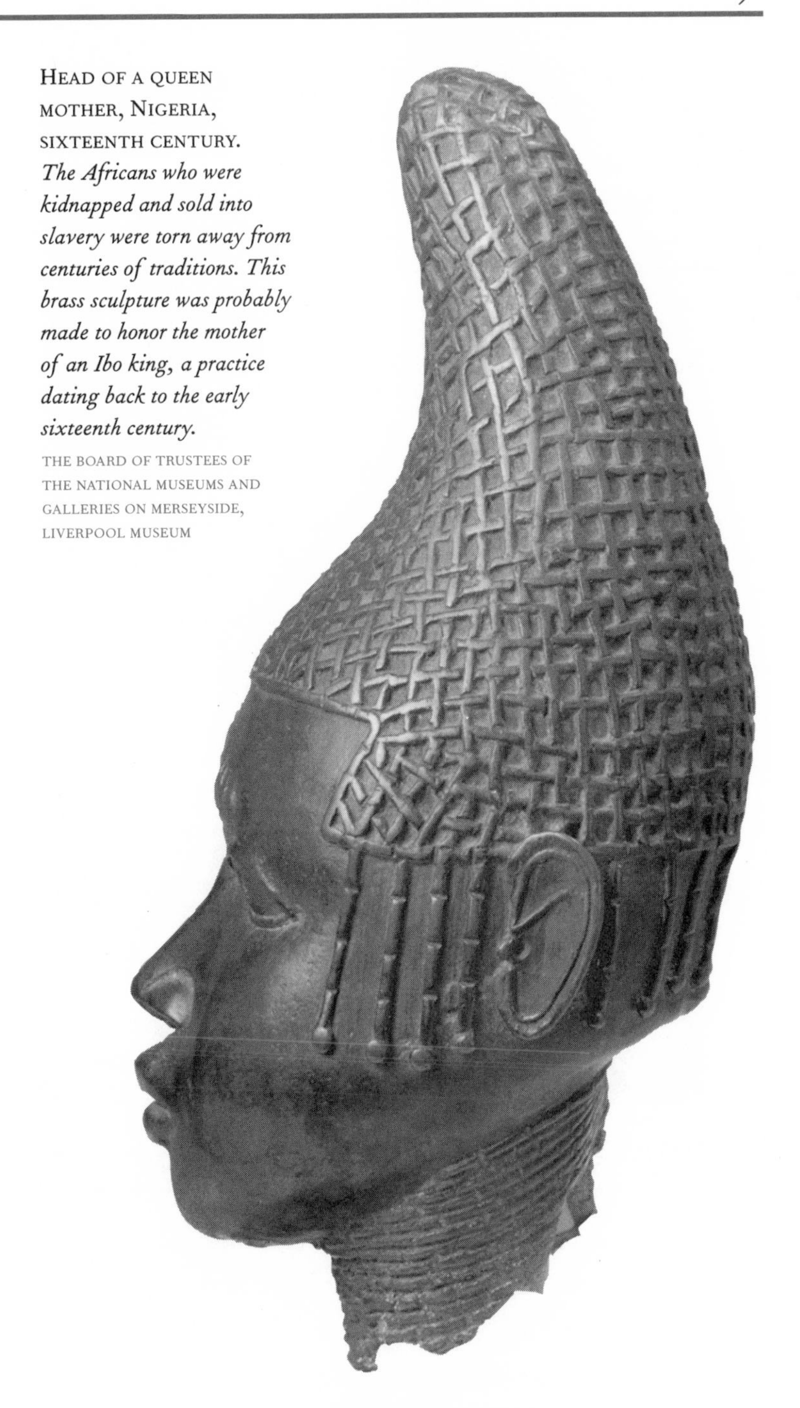

HEAD OF A QUEEN MOTHER, NIGERIA, SIXTEENTH CENTURY. *The Africans who were kidnapped and sold into slavery were torn away from centuries of traditions. This brass sculpture was probably made to honor the mother of an Ibo king, a practice dating back to the early sixteenth century.*

THE BOARD OF TRUSTEES OF THE NATIONAL MUSEUMS AND GALLERIES ON MERSEYSIDE, LIVERPOOL MUSEUM

THE CASTLE OF EL MINA, *LONDON ILLUSTRATED NEWS. El Mina, a Portuguese-built citadel on the coast of Ghana, was converted to a holding pen for recently captured Africans. By 1700, the Gold Coast had become known as the Slave Coast. Europeans controlled the trade, but many African kings and leaders were suppliers who profited from the traffic.*

COURTESY OF THE NEWSPAPER COLLECTION, THE BOSTON PUBLIC LIBRARY

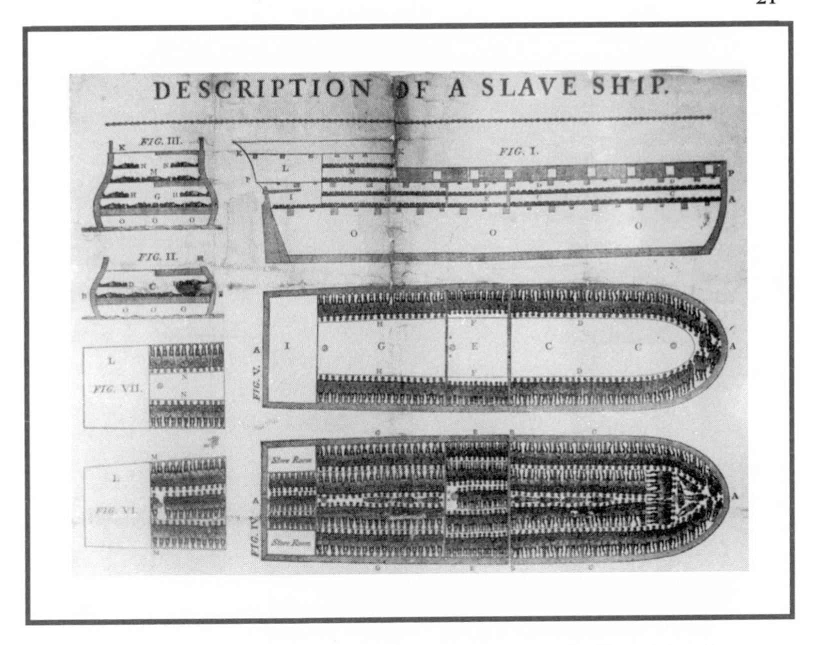

PLAN FOR THE TRANSPORTATION OF SLAVES, 1789. *To maximize profits, slaves transported across the Atlantic Ocean were often packed tightly in configurations like this one. Though many died on the voyage, those who survived would guarantee a healthy profit for the slave traders and shipping merchants who participated in the enterprise.*

WILBERFORCE HOUSE, KINGSTON UPON HULL CITY MUSEUMS AND ART GALLERY, UK

TOBACCO LABEL, SEVENTEENTH CENTURY. *By the eighteenth century, the majority of the world's tobacco came from the Chesapeake Bay colonies of British North America. Its leaves were accepted as currency in Maryland and Virginia. And wealth in tobacco became synonymous with wealth in slaves.*

COLONIAL WILLIAMSBURG FOUNDATION

FLORA, SOLD FOR TWENTY-FIVE POUNDS STERLING. *As abundant tobacco crops created affluence and ease, slaves became the most esteemed property in the colonies and a measure of a man's success. This pen-and-ink sketch was originally executed to accompany a 1796 bill of sale, transferring ownership of Flora from Margaret Dwight to Asa Benjamin.*

STRATFORD HISTORICAL SOCIETY

MIDDLETON PLANTATION, SOUTH CAROLINA. *A few families, like the Middletons of South Carolina, became extremely wealthy from the labor of hundreds of slaves. Countless other white families built prosperous lives through the work of ten to twenty enslaved Africans. The Middletons' crop was rice.*

MIDDLETON PLACE, CHARLESTON, SOUTH CAROLINA

AD FOR A RUNAWAY SLAVE, *CAROLINA GAZETTE. Cultivating rice was backbreaking work: slaves toiled ankle-deep in standing water, often under brutal sun. Many slaves resisted by running away, some within months of arrival.*

COURTESY CHARLESTON LIBRARY SOCIETY, CHARLESTON, SOUTH CAROLINA

weather, the reſpective ſale or ſales will begin the firſt fair day or days after.

RUN AWAY

on Saturday laſt, a middle-ſized yellowiſh Negro Fellow, named CYRUS, formerly belonged to Mr. *Williamſon* at *Stono*, and is well known in Town and moſt Parts of the Country. £. 20 reward for his Head, or £. 5 to any Perſon that ſecures him in the Work-Houſe, will be paid by *Thomas Tucker*, Pilot.

TO BE SOLD

AT the uſual place in *Charles Town* on tueſday

A TORTURE MASK, WOODCUT, 1807. *As African slaves began to outnumber whites in some areas of the South, the threat of resistance loomed large. So laws were passed to allow slave owners to practice severe punishments on slaves who ran away or attacked their masters. This is an example of a restraining mask, one means of punishment.*

LIBRARY OF CONGRESS

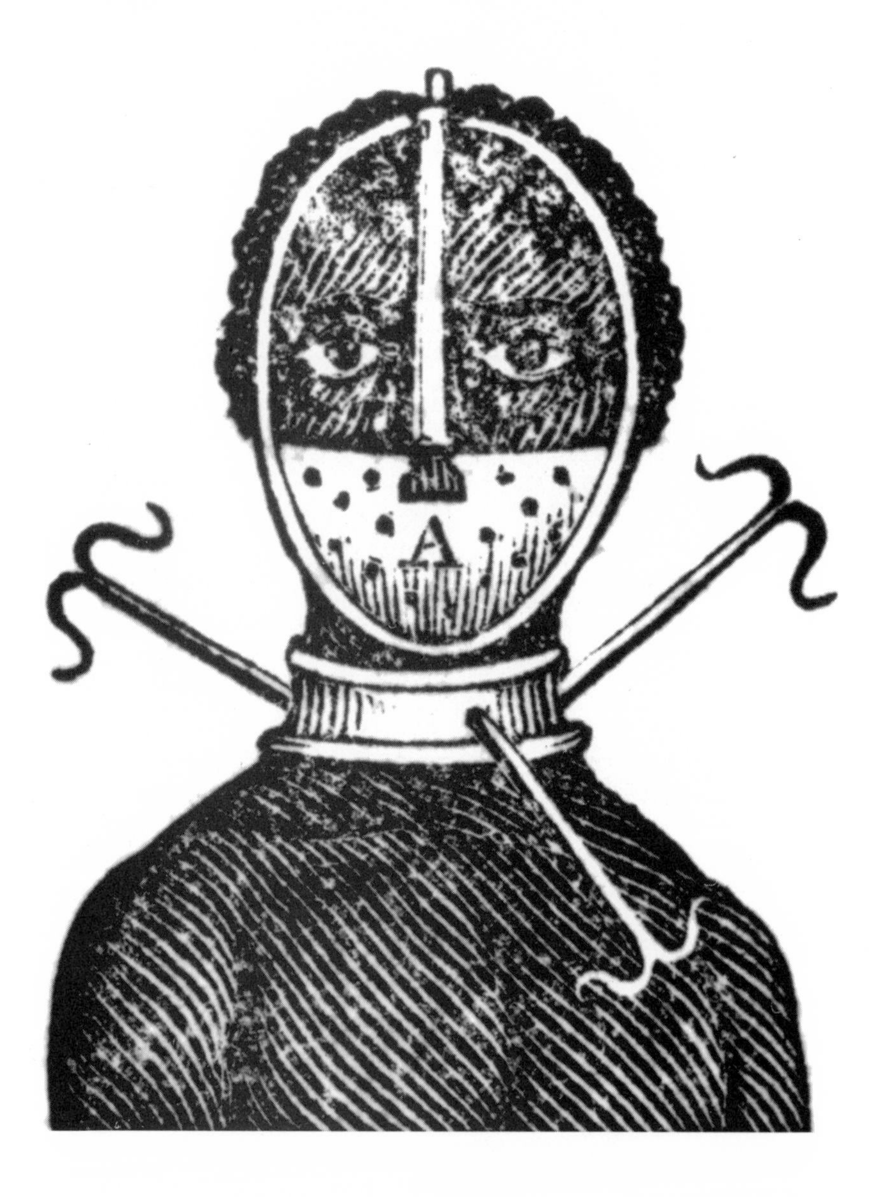

OLAUDAH EQUIANO, OIL, 1780S (PREVIOUSLY ATTRIBUTED TO JOSHUA REYNOLDS). *Son of an Ibo tribal elder, kidnapped at the age of eight and sold into slavery, Olaudah Equiano escaped and lived to record his story. "When you make men slaves," he wrote, "you compel them to live with you in a state of war."*

PORTRAIT OF A NEGRO MAN, OLAUDAH EQUIANO, BY ENGLISH SCHOOL (18TH CENTURY). ROYAL ALBERT MEMORIAL MUSEUM, EXETER/BRIDGEMAN ART LIBRARY INTERNATIONAL LTD., LONDON/NEW YORK.

CHAPTER ONE

It was at last concluded that three ships should be prepared and furnished out for the search and discovery of the Northern part of the world, to open a way and passage to our men for travel to new and unknown Kingdoms.

—CLEMENT ADAMS
from Richard Hakluyt's *Principal Navigations*, 1589

IN APRIL 1607, three such vessels manned by 120 colonists landed on the fringes of the Virginia wilderness at a place they named Jamestown. These men clung desperately to the hope of building the first permanent English settlement in the New World. Their mission, as outlined in the charter granted by King James, was "first to preach and baptize into the Christian religion . . . and recover out of the arms of the Devil a number of poor and miserable souls."

The colonists' picture of the New World was painted in warm, brilliant, eager colors. It was a place where men could grow rich, where the vanquished could be born again, where poisoned souls could be saved, and a heaven on earth built on the cornerstone of Christianity. It was expected that established Christians would work side by side with their eager new converts, and that their joint effort would cause the strange land to grow fruitful. It was an ambitious dream fueled by arrogance and imperialistic fervor. Englishmen believed that God had given them the right to the land and to impose whatever laws they needed to make it theirs.

Indeed, the English clung to a powerful vision. They had come to the New World to save it. Under the comforting cloak of Christianity, they would bond with converts, find an ally in the elements, and craft a utopia. Setting sail for Jamestown, the hopeful pioneers must have grasped a frightening but irresistible opportunity—broadening and expanding one's future, beginning life again, doing God's work. And perhaps growing wealthy in the process.

For the settling of Jamestown was not only a religious mission, it was a very important business venture. The Virginia Company of London, a group of English investors, recruited the first group of settlers. They paid them to find precious metals and minerals and useful plants for dyes and medicine, although they would settle for less-glamorous goods such as glass, tar, and iron.

The Virginia Company's plan was for settlers to combine their labors to produce whatever the land yielded. Once those products arrived in England, the company would pay out dividends to all members, determined by the number of shares they owned. Men could purchase shares, but could acquire them simply by paying for their passage to Virginia.

With the money obtained by selling shares, the company would ship unemployed laborers, and some skilled craftsmen, from England. These men would toil for the company for seven years in return for their transport. After that they would be free to engage in whatever work they wished, carving a niche for themselves in the New World.

Writing years before of his attempt to settle the first English colony in North America on Roanoke Island, Sir Walter Raleigh responded eloquently to his first glimpse of a world that must have resembled Jamestown:

> I never saw a more beautiful country, nor more lively prospects . . . the plains adjoining without bush or stubble, all fair green grass . . . the birds towards the evening singing on every tree . . . cranes and herons of white, crimson, and carnation perching on the river's side, the air fresh with a gentle easterly wind, and every stone that we stooped to take up, promised either gold or silver.

Not everyone was as giddily overwhelmed by the surroundings.

The colonists who ventured upon Jamestown's ragged shore were a varied lot. When King James granted the company charter in 1606, he called for "propagating the Christian religion to such people, as yet live in darkness and miserable ignorance of the true knowledge and worship of God." The all-male group, urged to make a success of the colony as soon as possible, perhaps viewed the settlement as a sort of military enterprise, despite their designated role as religious missionaries.

The land was a canny, time-tested adversary. Because the settlers were too lazy and arrogant to work the land, the land deprived them of food and gave them no clue as to where they were or how utterly they were surrounded by yet more land. Gentlemen and their servants felt overwhelmed. The Indians could have helped them, but the English considered them savages, then enemies. The idyllic picture described years before by Sir Walter soon proved no more than a mirage. The birds may have been singing on every tree—but that was because they knew the land intimately, understood its secrets.

Settler George Percy chronicled a snippet of time in 1607:

> The fourth day of September died Thomas Jacob Sergeant. The fift day, there died Benjamin Beast. Our men were destroyed with cruell diseases, as Swellings, Flixes, Burning Fevers, and by warres, and some departed suddenly, but for the most part they died of meere famine. There were never Englishmen left in a forreigne Countrey in such miserie as wee were in this new discovered Virginia.

The giddy ambition that had characterized the colonists' arrival soon became a clawing at the soil, a wail in their bellies. The cattle, hogs, and poultry had long ago been eaten. Then the settlers dined on the horses. There was even evidence of cannibalism—rather than die in their failed utopia, some colonists found sustenance in makeshift cemeteries by feeding on the bodies of those who had left this life before them.

In his *Generall Historie of Virginia*, written seventeen years after his arrival on the shores of Jamestown, Captain John Smith chronicled the gruesome fate of several hapless settlers:

> Nay, so great was our famine, that a salvage we slew and buried, the poorer sort tooke him up againe and eat him; and so did divers one another boyled and stewed with roots and herbs: And one amongst the rest did kill his wife, powdered her, and had eaten part of her before it was knowne; for which hee was executed, as hee well deserved: now whether shee was better roasted, boyled

> or carbonado'd, I know not; but of such a dish as powdered wife I never heard of. This was that time, which still to this day we called the starving time.

It was the colonists' third winter in the world they had hoped to make new.

In those first three years, nine hundred settlers arrived in Virginia. By the spring of 1610, only sixty were left alive. Many died still clutching their unattainable dream, the dream that Virginia, with all its lush promise, was supposed to be—a place where genteel Englishmen could come and, preferably overnight, find their fortunes.

The Virginia Company had paid money to establish the colony, and they wanted a quick return on their investment. The colonists felt pressured to discover and exploit commodities that would heap profits upon the motherland.

The commodities were not forthcoming. Explored rivers, expected to yield a route to China, led nowhere. After ten years, the dream had all but died. Desperate to revive it, the colonists experimented with tobacco seeds from Trinidad, hoping the fickle land would receive and nurture the crop. The land relented, and by 1617, the first shipment of tobacco to England suggested that the colony had found a key to survival. Three years later, nearly 55,000 pounds of tobacco were exported to England for sale. Plantations were everywhere, and tobacco was literally sprouting in the streets of Jamestown.

In London, King James cursed the "stinking suffumigation" and raised the import duty to stem the demand. But by then the English couldn't imagine life without tobacco. And in Jamestown, the fledgling settlement that had knocked at death's door, it was time for bigger dreams.

There was power to be had. Families who cultivated more acreage produced more tobacco. With cheap land available, there seemed to be no limit to how much one could make—if there were enough workers to handle the crop.

The colonists saw two very distinct choices. In what later became known as the Massachusetts model, they could call for whole families and communities to be brought over from England. Family units would work the farms, the businesses, the trade shops, with perhaps a hired hand or two to help out.

The second choice was for Virginia colonists to capitalize on the desperation of the lower classes in England, skilled and unskilled laborers who imagined that redemption awaited them in the New World. Promised access to an earthly paradise, those people became indentured servants, contracted to work an average of four to seven years. They were fed, sheltered, and clothed in exchange for their work. If they lived to complete their period of service, they could begin a free life with a bushel of corn, a new suit, and a parcel of land. The printed indenture forms were to be found everywhere in England, with blank spaces for names and periods of service.

The propaganda campaign of the Virginia Company of London succeeded. There were no moral or physical qualifications for the honor of being bound to servitude in Virginia. Criminals escaped the gallows by signing up. In some instances, innocent people were accused of crimes in order to force them into indentures. People were kidnapped, plied with alcohol. Children were offered sweets. And they were lured to a place where malaria and dysentery and starvation waited to kill them—that is, if they weren't worked to death by their owners.

In chaotic English ports, human beings were crammed into merchant ships for a long voyage on meager rations. On some Atlantic crossings, almost 20 percent of the recruited servants lost their lives. More died of scurvy upon arriving in Virginia.

But the rampant "sign-up" continued unabated, for Virginia's headright system gave landowners more property for each new arrival. Thousands of people—vagrants and ne'er-do-wells or honest farmers and craftsmen—were pulled from the villages and back roads of England, and later from the German Rhineland, by the promise of a new life. For the next hundred years, between half and two-thirds of all white immigrants to the American colonies came as indentured servants. Any dream in the New World was better than no dreams in the Old. Even if, for many, the dream turned out to be the worst kind of nightmare, each desperate individual willing to take the risk could still hope to overcome the odds.

The servant was concerned mostly with how long the indenture would be and the conditions under which work would be performed. At its best, the period of service was an amicable apprenticeship. At its very worst, it was a seemingly endless exploitation likely to end in death instead of freedom.

Loving Father and Mother,
This is to let you understand that I your child am in the most heavy case by reason of the nature of the country [which] is such that it causeth much sickness. . . . I have nothing at all—no, not a shirt to my back but two rags . . . nor but one pair of shoes, but one pair of stockings, but one cap, but two bands. . . . If you love me, you will redeem me. Good father, do not forget me, but have mercy and pity my miserable case. I know if you did but see me you would weep. . . .

Your loving son,
Richard Frethorne, March 20, 1623

Jamestown had survived due to the growth of the tobacco crop. But despite the convincing spiel served up by those hoping to recruit servants, the colony was far from ideal. As was fairly standard in Europe at the time, the settlers were driven by an almost mindless focus on profit and a chilling casualness about just how much suffering a human could endure. One man who stole two or three pints of oatmeal had a needle forced through his tongue; he was then chained to a tree and left to starve and die publicly. Servants were mutilated, maimed, and sold like cattle. They were put up as stakes in card games. They were murdered with impunity. The servants who didn't die of disease perished because they were abused by the people they worked for or killed by the Indians whose lands they threatened.

Of the fifteen thousand people transported to Virginia during the first fifteen years after 1607, only two thousand survived.

> About the last of August came in a Dutch man of warre that sold us twenty Negars.
>
> —John Rolfe, Jamestown, 1619

In the early seventeenth century, the Dutch sought to become major players in the Spanish and Portuguese maritime monopoly. They planned and executed well-timed raids on Portuguese ports in Brazil and West Africa and on colonial settlements in Central and South America. And in August 1619, a Dutch ship robbed a Spanish vessel of its cargo—Africans.

The ship emerged as if the violent storm had given it birth, drawing its shape from a clinging mist. Its shimmering edges hardened as it dropped anchor at Jamestown. Those aboard were ghosts before they became men. No one recorded the ship's name or investigated its origins.

The crew offered to trade the Africans for food, and twenty captives were released to their new owners. There had been Africans in North America before, but the first permanent African settlers in an English colony arrived that long-ago summer. It was a full year before the Pilgrims reached Massachusetts on the *Mayflower.*

The blacks who were put to work in Jamestown may have shared the same status as English indentured servants. On that day in 1619, there was probably no difference, no distinction made.

The conditions on early Virginia tobacco plantations were extremely harsh. Field workers were housed in overcrowded shacks and given barely enough food to fuel their work. They had little chance to provide for themselves, for nothing was as important as the efficient production of tobacco.

No one was a slave for life. All the indentured servants worked equally hard and were punished equally. And if they looked far enough into their futures, if the reality of their surroundings had not already destroyed their spirits, they could imagine freedom.

On a March morning in 1622, three years after the mysterious Dutch ship left its human offering at Jamestown, thirty nations of the Powhatan Confederacy sought to avenge the murder of a revered tribal head by waging a full-scale attack on the British. They wanted to push the settlers back into the sea. On the Bennett plantation along the James River, fifty-two colonists lost their lives in the massacre. Among the five survivors was a servant called Antonio.

Antonio may have arrived at the colony from Angola the year before aboard the *James.* Sold into bondage to toil in the tobacco fields, "Antonio, a Negro" is listed as a "servant" in the 1625 census. Virginia had no rules for slaves. So it was possible that Antonio knew hope. Perhaps he felt that redemption was possible, that opportunities existed for him even as a servant. Already, he had done what so many others had failed to do—stay alive.

"Mary a Negro woman" had sailed to the New World aboard the *Margrett and John*. Soon she became Antonio's wife.

"Antonio the Negro" became the landowner Anthony Johnson. His history, his motivations, the words he may have spoken, have the same ghostly edges as the mysterious ship that pierced the fog at Jamestown years before. Over the course of a lifetime, he and Mary bought their way out of servitude, raised four children, and struggled to claim a slice of the stubborn new world as their own. Determined to build an independent life, Anthony could not foresee the role his skin color would eventually play in his fate and the fate of his family.

Although it is not known exactly how or when the Johnsons became free, court records in 1641 indicate that Anthony was master to a black servant, John Casor. During that time, the couple lived on a comfortable but modest estate and Anthony began raising livestock. In 1645, a man identified as "Anthony the negro" stated in court records, "now I know myne owne ground and I will worke when I please and play when I please."

It cannot be proved that it was actually Anthony Johnson who spoke those words. But if he did not speak them, he felt them, felt them as surely as he felt land beneath his feet. The words didn't reflect his state of ownership as much as they reflected his state of mind. He owned land. He could till the soil whenever he wished and plant whatever he wished, sell the land to someone else, let it lie fallow, walk away from its troubles. He could sit in his house—*his* house—and ignore the land altogether. Anthony Johnson was a man in control of his own.

By 1650, the Johnsons owned 250 acres of land stretched along Pungoteague Creek on the eastern shore of Virginia, acquired through the headright system, which allowed planters to claim acreage for each servant brought to the colony. Anthony claimed five headrights, although there is no way to know if he was actually responsible for the servants' presence in Virginia or if he'd acquired their certificates some other way. Many landowners of the time purchased headrights to increase the size of their claims.

No matter how he amassed his acreage, Anthony's "owne ground" was now formidable.

The couple was living a seventeenth-century version of the American dream. Anthony and Mary had no reason not to believe in a system that certainly seemed to be working for them, a system that equated ownership with achievement. If not for the color of their skin, they could have been English.

Very few people who had inked their signatures on indenture forms received the promise of those contracts. At the end of their periods of servitude, many were denied the land they needed to begin their lives again. Anthony Johnson was one of a select few able to consider a piece of the world his own.

The first Virginia colonists thought of themselves as Christians or Englishmen, not white people. The word *white* was not yet used to refer to a type of person. There were owners and servants, and the only thing that made one servant different from another was the contracted length of servitude. If you were a servant, your color did not improve or exacerbate that situation. Black and white servants were oppressed equally. They performed the same tasks and were punished in the same way when they were perceived to have failed in some way. White women, later deemed fairest and most fragile, not only worked in the fields alongside black servants, but were also briskly reprimanded at the whipping posts.

Sometime in the mid–seventeenth century, that changed. Darker became wrong.

Europeans had long believed that they had the missionary right to enslave anyone who was not a Christian. But slaves could then convert to Christianity and gain their freedom. And since it was impossible to look at a person and determine his or her religious persuasion, physical difference was an easier, more permanent way to exploit the captives. Workers who had reached the end of their indentured period found contracts were not being honored, and the resulting unrest bordered on rebellion.

Treating black and white workers differently, making them suspect each other, may have been a swift and easy way to isolate the two factions, smash the budding alliances, and regain control over the workforce. Those in power lived in constant fear that beleaguered black and white laborers would realize strength in numbers and join to rise up against authority. As racial categories grew harsher, the English gradually chose to describe themselves not as Christians, but as white people.

In 1639, the colony of Maryland declared that a Christian baptism did not make a slave free. Religious salvation no longer spelled liberty. Soon the definition of who could be made a slave would change forever. No longer were non-Christians singled out. Now if you did not look European—if your skin was not white—you could be enslaved.

In 1640, three of farmer Hugh Gwyn's servants escaped to Maryland. The circumstances of their "crimes" were identical. When they were captured and carted back to Jamestown for trial, the disparities in their punishments mirrored the new chasm between black and white.

"The said three servants shall receive the punishment of whipping and to have thirty stripes apiece," the court record stated.

> One called Victor, a Dutchman, the other a Scotchman called James Gregory, shall first serve out their times according to their indentures, and one whole year apiece after . . . and after that . . . to serve the colony for three whole years apiece.
>
> The third being *a negro* named John Punch shall serve his said master or his assigns *for the time of his natural Life.*

It was John Punch's physical appearance that sparked the reprimand. In no surviving legal record has any white servant in America been sentenced to spend his life as a slave.

Over time, powerful Virginia landowners began to realize that enslaving Africans made good economic sense. England's economy had revived, and fewer indentured servants were signing up for the voyage to the colony. Colonists saw their life expectancy increase, and "slaves for life" became an attractive investment. No matter how difficult their lives might be, whites were assured that their degradation would never equal that of Africans.

In 1641, Massachusetts became the first English colony in North America to recognize slavery as a legal institution. Connecticut followed in 1650; Virginia in 1661. The impending tragedy now had a heartbeat. In 1663, a Virginia court decided that if a child was born to a slave, that child would also be enslaved.

An African woman could no longer rejoice in the fact that her child would be born free. Because she was black and the child came from her body, the child would serve a master.

There were other options. Blacks and whites could have both retained their indentured status, or both groups could have been doomed to eternal servitude. Standing at the first of many crossroads, the American colonies chose to focus on color difference. The foundation of the agrarian economic system would be the systematic oppression of black people. Once that decision was made, a huge door swung shut. Only the colonies' newest targets of discrimination felt the need to undo what had been done, to set matters back on even ground.

In the relentless march that is history, some changes are instantaneous, lightning swift, extreme enough to change a cultural or physical landscape almost overnight. But the colonies' gradual acceptance of slavery as a race-based economic solution spanned a generation, all the more chilling because there was no one moment to point to and say, "That is where it began." The individuals involved—blacks and whites, landowners and servants—were simply living their lives, day-to-day. And the misfortune of a group of people who were black at the wrong time and place certainly didn't seem to have consequences for the world.

Anthony Johnson symbolized that terrible transformation, that slow turn toward sanctioned oppression. Although he was still free, the proud landowner now wore the face of a slave. In his behavior, he was no different from his neighbors—he worked his land, raised his children, took pride in what he had built. His plantation was the nucleus for one of

America's first black communities. But there was nothing he could do about being black.

In 1653, a consuming blaze swept through the Johnson plantation. After the fire, court justices stated that the Johnsons "have bine inhabitants in Virginia above thirty yeares" and were respected for their "hard labor and known service." When the couple requested relief, the court agreed to exempt Mary and the couple's two daughters from county taxation for the rest of their lives. This not only helped Anthony save money to rebuild, it was in direct defiance of a statute that required *all* free Negro men and women to pay taxes.

The following year, white planter Robert Parker secured the freedom of Anthony Johnson's servant John Casor, who had convinced Parker and his brother George that he was an illegally detained indentured servant. Anthony later fought the decision. After lengthy court proceedings, Casor was returned to the Johnson family in 1655.

These two favorable and quite public decisions speak volumes about Anthony's standing in Northampton County. The very fact that Johnson, a Negro, was allowed to testify in court attests to his position in the community. In the case of the community benevolence following the fire, the fact that Anthony was a Negro never really seemed part of the picture. He was a capable planter, a good neighbor, and a dedicated family man who deserved a break after his fiery misfortune. In the case of his legal battle for Casor, Anthony's vision of property and the value accorded it mirrored that of his white neighbors and the gentlemen of the court. Anthony Johnson had learned to work the system. It was a system that seemed to work for him.

Two years after the Johnsons' servant Casor was returned, white planter Matthew Pippen claimed that one hundred acres of the family's land actually belonged to him. It is unclear why the Johnsons failed to contest the claim.

In search of more-yielding land, the Johnsons moved north to Maryland's Somerset County in 1665 after selling two hundred Virginia acres to planters Morris Mathews and John Rowles, on credit. Two years later, influential planter and officeholder Edmund Scarburgh delivered 1,344 pounds of tobacco to the Somerset County sheriff, payment due Anthony for the land he'd sold the two planters.

The next month, however, Scarburgh claimed the tobacco for himself and convinced the court to attach Anthony Johnson's estate for that amount. He'd forged a letter in which Johnson promised to repay money allegedly owed to Scarburgh. A Virginia county court ignored the fact that Anthony could not read or write and declared that the letter, "written under the said Anthony Johnson's hand," was legitimate. Anthony, perhaps sensing that it was useless to challenge the powerful, land-hungry Scarburgh, never contested the court's decision.

In Maryland, the Johnsons lived on a three-hundred-acre farm called Tonies Vineyard. And in the spring of 1670, Tonies Vineyard was where "Antonio, a Negro"—respected because he had managed to live so long on his own terms—met the end of his life. He was still a free man when the shackles binding him to this world were unlocked.

Upon her husband's death, Mary Johnson renegotiated the lease for ninety-nine years. In August of that year, however, an all-white jury ruled that Anthony's original land in Virginia could be seized by the state "because he was a Negroe and by consequence an alien." The disputed two-hundred-acre parcel was granted to sole occupant John Rowles. And fifty acres that Anthony had given to his son Richard wound up in the hands of wealthy white neighbor George Parker. It didn't matter that Richard, a free man, had lived on the land with his wife and children for five years.

The "hard labor and knowne service" that had served the family so well in the New World was now secondary to the color of their skin. The world that allowed captive slave "Antonio, a Negro," to grow confident as Anthony Johnson, landowner and freeman, ceased to exist. The Virginians no longer needed to lure workers to their plantations. Now they could buy them and chain them there.

Mary Johnson lived on Tonies Vineyard for another decade following her husband's death. In 1677, John Johnson or his son John Jr. purchased a forty-four-acre tract and called it Angola after Antonio's birthplace. Although they sought to live as well as their white neighbors, the world was changing around them, conspiring to remind them each moment of their lives that they were darker and therefore wrong. They were black, meant to be slaves even though they were free.

Perhaps Anthony Johnson's heirs were confused by the slow but relentless onset of the "terrible transformation." Although Richard and John Johnson fared fairly well after their father's death, the third generation of Johnsons faced conditions that even the perseverance and independent mind-set of their grandfather could not have overcome. They were forced to fight continually for their independence, since soon even free blacks could be captured and sold into a lifetime of slavery. No one would doubt a plantation owner's word if he claimed ownership of a black person, if he insisted that he had a perfect right to sell that person into servitude. Free Africans had no way of proving they were free.

The Johnsons may have turned inward, dependent upon the love and protection of family to keep their own dream from dying, as the institution of race slavery, long familiar in Spanish America and the Caribbean, began to flourish. Rules became more important. In 1669, Virginia declared it lawful to kill an unruly slave during punishment. In 1691, a white woman marrying a black man, whether or not he was free, would be banished. A year later, it became legal to kill runaway slaves. Owners would be paid two tons of tobacco for each life lost.

One hundred years after Anthony Johnson left his home in Africa, his grandson John died with no one left to carry his name. With his death, the family simply vanished. All further record of the Johnsons' achievements, their struggle—and the plantation named for a faraway birthplace—disappeared.

It had been a century since "Antonio, a Negro" had left his home in Angola. It was a hundred years and a million dashed dreams from the moment when Anthony Johnson saw a place for himself in the world and stood there, claiming his ground.

By the late seventeenth and early eighteenth century, the economic future of the new colonies would be tied to the buying, selling, and maintenance of black people, bred to be the lifelong slaves of whites. England became the dominant force in the slave trade.

Throughout the eighteenth century, England's triangular trade with Africa and the New World poured thousands of captives into the British colonies. Moreover, England became a major supplier of slaves for the Dutch, French, and Spanish. The slave merchants sometimes realized huge returns—in 1737, a voyage of the slave ship *Lively* netted a profit of 300 percent. Of course, that level of financial gain could not be guaranteed. A ship could sink or be captured. But the specter of misfortune didn't quell the enthusiasm of English merchants for that chance at a windfall.

The profits of the trade led to the miraculous economic and cultural transformation of cities in England. By 1800, Liverpool, a once-lackluster port, had absorbed enormous slave-trading profits that provided much of the foundation for the Industrial Revolution. One British economist wrote, "It is the first principle and foundation of all the rest, the mainspring of the machine which sets every wheel in motion."

Regarding the slave trade, the various factions of British society seemed to be of the same mind. It was an extremely positive undertaking. It provided steady employment for shipbuilders and seamen. It was a school for sailors. And it was legal, with the possibility of reaping enormous profit. Although the English had abandoned the practice of converting the Africans to Christianity, they felt that they were doing a good deed by liberating them from their homeland. Hearing of slavery in Africa, the English were convinced that the poor savages left behind would be condemned to a fate much worse than anything awaiting them on colonial shores.

With the English Parliament's 1698 abolishment of the African Company's monopoly on slaving, every freeborn British citizen had been granted the right to trade in slaves. The demand for slaves in the sugar colonies soared. For six years beginning in 1680, the Royal African Company had transported 5,000 slaves from their homeland; in the first nine years following the end of the company's monopoly, the port at Bristol shipped an average of 18,000 slaves a year. The total number of Africans transported annually on British ships increased swiftly from 8,000 to 45,000.

These captive people came directly from Africa, not from other colonies, so they lacked the English language and experience with the alien world they'd been thrust into. It became easier for whites to consider themselves superior—the language barrier made Africans seem so foreign, so unreachable. So unlike their English saviors.

The English took comfort in the fact that the Africans did not look like them, did not sound like them, and were thoroughly unfamiliar with English customs.

In 1705, the Virginia General Assembly declared:

> All servants imported and brought into this County . . . who were not Christians in their native Country . . . shall be accounted and be slaves. All Negro, mulatto and Indian slaves within this dominion . . . shall be held to be real estate. If any slave resist his master . . . correcting such slave, and shall happen to be killed in such correction . . . the master shall be free of all punishment . . . as if such accident never happened.

It was not uncommon to see a man's, woman's, or child's back crisscrossed with raw scars, not uncommon to see Africans hobble about with missing feet, to see a ragged stump where a hand should be. It was not uncommon to see their eyes swollen shut, their heads bound in rusty iron contraptions, their bones broken. It was not uncommon to hear that someone alive was now dead, someone who had dared to stand tall before his master and say, in his own language, *"No. No more."*

It was now legal to kill African slaves for the sake of discipline, and their deaths were not uncommon.

The Virginia colony designed laws to hold Africans in eternal slavery—not because they were poor, not because they were vagrant, not because they had been accused and found guilty of crimes, but simply because they were African. And although those first Africans may have come to Virginia as indentured servants, that semiprotected status was no longer available to them. While the indentured servant labored to fulfill a contract, the slave labored for his life, with no seven-, fourteen-, or twenty-one-year limit to his misery. A slave labored under the burden of knowing that his children, even those yet unborn, were destined to be slaves for the span of their natural lives.

THE TRANSMISSION

THEY WERE DEAD, and this was the boat to the Underworld.

In the darkness of its belly, the boy—his name was Malawi—lay pressed against its wet, wooden hull, naked and chained to a corpse that only hours before had been his older brother, Oboto. Down there, the air was curdled, thick with the stench of feces and decaying flesh. Already the ship's rats were nibbling at Oboto's cold, stiff fingers. Malawi screamed them away whenever they came scurrying through a half a foot of salt water toward his brother's body. He held Oboto as the boat thrashed, throwing them from side to side, and the rusty chains bit deeper into his wrists. But by now, after seven weeks at sea, the rats were used to screams, moaning, and cries in the lightless entrails of the ghost ship. All night, after the longhaired, lipless phantoms drove them below—the men into the hold, the females into the longboats and cabins, the children under a tarpaulin on deck—Malawi heard the wailing of the other one hundred captives, some as they clawed at him for more room. (Perhaps, he thought, this was why the phantoms clipped their nails every few days.) He couldn't always understand the words of the others, but Malawi gleaned enough to gather from his yokefellows that they were in the hands of white demons taking them to hell where they would be eaten. Many of the others were from different tribes and they spoke different tongues. Some, he remembered, had been enemies of his people, the Allmuseri. Others traded with the merchants of his village, men like his father Mbwela, who was a proud man, one wealthy enough to afford two wives. But that was before he and Oboto were captured. They were no longer Hausa, Tefik, Fulani, Ibo, Kru, or Fanti. Now they were dead, one and all, and destined for the Underworld.

Every day since this journey began, Malawi had lost something; now he wondered if there was anything left to lose.

They had been herded after their long trek from the lush interior to the bustling trading fort overlooking the sea. They came in chains, shackled in twos at their necks, in a coffle that contained forty prisoners, a flock of sheep, and an ostrich. When they arrived at twilight, their feet were crusted with mud and their backs stung from the sticks their captors—warriors from the nearby Asante tribe—used to force them up whenever they fell during the exhausting monthlong march. It was there, on that march, that the horrors began. Wearily, Malawi walked chained to Oboto. His father, Mbwela, and mother, Gwele (Mbwela's youngest wife), were shackled in front of him. His mother stumbled. One of the Asante struck her, and Gwele fought back, scratching at his eyes until he plunged a knife into her belly. In a rage such as Malawi had never seen, his father fell upon the Asante warrior, beating him to the ground, and would have killed him had not another of their captors swung his sword and unstrung Mbwela's head, but with a cut so poorly delivered his father did not die instantly but instead lay bleeding on the ground as the coffle moved on, with Mbwela cursing their captors, their incompetence, telling them how he *would have done the beheading right.*

How long it took to reach the fort, Malawi could not say. But he remembered their captors fired rifles to announce the coffle's arrival. Cannons at the fort thundered back a reply. Men fluent in several languages lifted their robes and ran to the fort's entrance to meet them. Their Asante captors chanted, Hodi, hodi, hodi, *asking permission to trade. The dragomen replied,* Karibu, *meaning they could, and then Malawi and the other prisoners were driven toward the receiving house as people inside the fort pointed and stared. Like slices of walking earth, they must have seemed, so chalky from their long trek, a few stumbling, some bleeding from their feet, mothers long since mad, their eyes streaming and unseeing, carrying dead children, the rest staring round the fort in shock and bewilderment.*

And Malawi was one of those. The bustling, slave market was like a dream—or, more exactly, like yet another nightmare from which he could not awaken, no matter how hard he rubbed his eyes. There were harem dancers in brightly colored costumes. Magnificent horses ridden by vast-bearded Arab traders who exchanged the cracking-fingers greeting of the coast. Bazaars. And musicians picking up the air and playing it on their koras, *as if everyone had come from all over the earth to an unholy festival. In this place human life was currency, like a cowrie shell. Starving families brought their children to sell. Slaves, stripped naked, were held down by other black men as the strangely dressed phantoms branded their shoulders with red-hot pieces of bent wire. They'd been shaved clean, soaked in palm oil. And when the wire touched their skin, burning flesh blended with rich food smells in the market and made Malawi cough until his eyes watered. Then, when his vision cleared, he saw along the beach, just below the warehouses, phantoms bartering for black flesh. They traded firelocks, liquor, glittering beads, and textiles for people from the Angola, Fula, Sesi, and Yoruba tribes. If they resisted or fought back, they were whipped until blood cascaded from their wounds. The phantoms forced open their mouths to examine their teeth and gums as if they were livestock and, laughing, fingered their genitals. They paid one hundred bars apiece for each man; seventy-five bars for each woman. Malawi, whose father had been a merchant, saw that what they called a "bar" was worth a pound of black gunpowder or a fathom of cloth, and he saw that they accepted no children under the height of four feet four inches.*

What, Malawi wondered, had he and the others done to deserve this? And, instantly, he knew: Those being sold were debtors. They were thieves. They were tribesmen who refused to convert to Islam. Were guilty of witchcraft. Or refused to honor the ruling tribe in their region. Or they'd been taken prisoner during tribal wars, just as he and Oboto had been captured.

He saw a bare-chested ghost, one with a goatish laugh and reddish whiskers, arguing with an Asante trader chewing on a khat leaf, yelling that the wrinkled old man he'd brought to sell, who was sweating and looked ill, had been drugged to conceal his sickness. No, that *one the ghost didn't want. Not the elderly. Only the healthy men who could work, the young women who could bear, and the children. He and his brother would surely be picked—Malawi was sure of that—or at least they would choose Oboto, who was strong, with tightly strung muscles and sharp features like the tribes of the far north. Yes, they would want a man as strikingly beautiful, as brave and wise, as his brother.*

Oboto touched Malawi's arm just before they were pushed into the warehouse, and Malawi saw—away in the distance beneath a day-old moon—a vessel a hundred times the size of the thatch-roofed homes in his village, with sails like white bird wings and great, skeletal trees springing from its deck and piercing the clouds. This he heard the phantoms call the Providence. *Then it was dark as they were shoved into the warehouses. Families in his coffle were separated—husbands from wives; children from their parents—so those in their cells, then later on the ship, could not* talk *to each other. By some miracle, one he thanked his ancestors for, they'd blundered and not separated him from his brother, who had seen twenty harvests, five more than Malawi himself.*

That night their jailers fed them a porridge made from roots and grainy honey beer. As they ate, Oboto told him, "Don't be afraid, little brother."

Malawi was indeed afraid but did not want to anger Oboto. "I'm not, as long as you are here—"

"No"—his brother cut him off— "listen *to me. Even if I am* not *here, you must not be afraid. Malawi, I have been watching these people who raided our village, and the ones from the ship . . . They are not strong."*

"But they have many guns," said Malawi, "and chains and great ships!"

"And they bleed when they are cut." Oboto moved closer to him as a guard passed their cell. He whispered, "I've seen them faint in the sun, and I watched one from that ship cry when he passed water, as if he was afflicted and doing so was painful. Did you see some of them up close? Their rotten teeth, I mean. A few are missing fingers. Or a hand. They touch others in places forbidden, and all the while they look afraid, fingering their rifles, looking over their shoulders. Their mothers have not yet finished with them. They are barbarians. Malawi, I don't *think the spirits respect them. How could they? They smell bad. They are unclean.*

They are dead here*"—he touched his chest above his heart—"not us. Some of the white men I saw, the ones with the whips, grovel before others in fear and have stripes on their backs as if* they *were slaves. The ones doing the hardest work, unloading crates from the ship for trade, don't understand as many tongues as you or I."*

"Yes . . ." Malawi nodded slowly, for his brother spoke well, as always. "I saw that." As a merchant's son, he'd picked up enough Ibo and Bantu to converse passably well when he accompanied Mbwela on trips to buy and sell goods. And he'd seen one of the phantoms, a young man close to his brother's age, fall down in the heat when unloading a crate of goods from the Providence, *and because he was slow in rising, one of the other ghosts beat him, bloodying his mouth. He'd seemed different from the other devils. His nose was hooked like that of a hornbill beneath blue eyes that could have been splinters from the sky. This was probably his first trip to Africa and it seemed no one had told him that it was a good idea to take fluids all day, even a little, because your body was constantly losing moisture, whether you were perspiring or not. "But," said Malawi, "I* am *afraid of them. I'm sorry . . ."*

"Don't be sorry." Oboto touched Malawi's arm gently. "I was afraid too when I saw them burning the village. When our parents died. And I prayed to our ancestors to let me *die—yes, I did that during the journey here—but they helped me understand."*

"What?" said Malawi. "Why they have taken so much from us?"

"No, they showed me what they cannot take. And I will show you."

Malawi knew—as their captors could not—that before the raid on their village Oboto was destined to be a griot, *a living book who carried within himself, like a treasure, his people's entire history from time immemorial. Its recitation took three full days. When he was a child all the adults agreed that Oboto's gift of recall distinguished him for this duty, and from his fifth harvest he could be seen trailing behind gruff, old Ndembe, who was* griot *then but getting a bit forgetful in his sixties, repeating after his teacher every chapter of their tribe's history. He learned their songs for war and weddings, the words they sang when someone died or was born. He learned the chronicle of their kings and commoners, the exploits of their heroes, folklore, and words for every beast, plant, and bird as well as the rhymes their women sang when they made* fufu, *taking into himself one piece of their culture at a time, then stitching it into an ever-expanding tapestry that covered centuries of his people's hopes and dreams, tragedies and victories. Now Malawi realized their village had not been wiped from the face of the world; its remains were kept inside Oboto. And during that night in the warehouse, while the other prisoners wailed or wept, Oboto began to teach his younger brother, transmitting all he knew, beginning with the story of how their gods created the world, and then the first man and woman.*

Oboto continued after he and Malawi were bathed, branded, and brought on board the Providence. *During the night they were kept below, tightly packed together, and forced to lie on their right sides to lessen the pressure on their hearts. Those on the ship's right side faced forward; those on the left faced the stern. Hatches and bulkheads had been grated and apertures cut around the deck to improve the circulation of air, though in those depths Malawi wheezed when he whispered back the ancient words his brother chanted.*

Come morning, they were forced topside. The phantoms covered their mouths with rags, went into the hold to drag from below those prisoners who'd died during the night, and then by 9 A.M.

cleaned this unholy space with chloride lime so it could be inspected by the ship's captain. Up above, more phantoms washed and scrubbed the decks and splashed buckets of salt water on Malawi and the others, then from buckets fed them a pasty gruel the color of river mud in messes of ten. And all the while, Oboto quietly sang to his brother—in a language their captors could not understand—how their people long ago had navigated these very waters to what the phantoms called the New World, leaving their hieroglyphics and a calendar among the Olmecs, and a thousand years earlier ventured east, sprinkling their seed among the Dravidians before their cities were destroyed by Aryans who brought the Vedas and caste system to enslave them. On and on, like a tapestry, Oboto unfurled their past, rituals, and laws in songs and riddles as they ate or when the phantoms shaved their hair and clipped their nails every few days.

Slowly, after weeks of suffering, it dawned on Malawi that this transmission from his brother, upon which he fastened his mind night and day like a prayer, was holding madness at bay. It left him no time to dwell on his despair. Each day the prisoners were brought together for exercise. To dance and sing African melodies beneath mist-blurred masts and rigging that favored the webwork of a spider. Week after week, Oboto used that precious time to teach, at pains to pass along as much of their people's experiences as his younger brother could absorb, though after six weeks Malawi saw he was weakening. His voice grew fainter, so frail that at night when they lay crushed together, Malawi had to place his ear close to Oboto's lips, catching the whispered words as his brother's chest rose and fell, each of his weak exhalations a gift from a world they would never see again.

When Oboto's wind was gone, Malawi held him close and chanted his brother's spirit safely on its journey to join their ancestors and he kept the rats away. The hatch creaked open. Sunlight spilled into the hold, stinging his eyes. The phantoms came below cursing—they were always cursing—and drove the prisoners onto the deck. One of them, the hook-nosed phantom, began unchaining Malawi from Oboto. "I guess he was some kind of kin to you, wasn't he? That's too bad. I've lost family too, so I guess I know how you feel." He removed the last of the shackles from Oboto, then stood back, waiting for Malawi to release his brother. "Go on now, you can turn him loose. He's dead."

Malawi did not let go. He tried to lift his brother, slipping his arms under Oboto's shoulders, but found him too heavy. The phantom watched him struggle for a moment, then took Oboto by his feet, and together they carried the body onto the deck, with Malawi still singing his people's funeral songs. They stepped to the rail, Malawi blinking back tears by then, the edges of his eyes feeling blurred. Then he and the phantom swung his brother overboard, dropping him into wind-churned waters. Instantly, Oboto disappeared beneath the roily waves. For a few seconds Malawi's heart felt so still he wondered if he might be dead, too, then involuntarily the words he'd learned came flooding back into his thoughts, and he knew there was much in him—beyond the reach of the ghosts—that was alive forever.

The phantom, his yellow hair flattened to his forehead by spray, was watching Malawi closely, listening to the lay on his lips. He was very quiet. Malawi stopped. The boy said, "Naw, go on. I don't understand what you're singing, but I like it. It's beautiful. I want to hear more . . . C'mon."

Malawi looked at him for a moment, unable to understand all his strange words. He glanced back down at the waters, thinking that Oboto's songs had only taken him so far. Just to before the time his village was raided. His people's chronicle was unfinished.

New songs were needed. And these he *must do. Hesitantly at first, and then with a little more confidence, he began weaving the events since his and Oboto's capture onto the last threads his brother had given him.*

Malawi sang and the phantom listened.

CHAPTER TWO

LISTEN TO THE VOICES, calling for the disappeared:

Who are we looking for, who are we looking for?
It's Equiano we're looking for.
Has he gone to the stream? Let him come back.
Has he gone to the market? Let him come back.
Has he gone to the farm? Let him return.
It's Equiano we're looking for.

Olaudah Equiano, son of an Ibo tribal elder, was one of 10 million to 12 million Africans sold to Europeans by men whose faces mirrored his own. But instead of succumbing to the terror of his circumstance, he survived to chronicle forty-six years of his life, beginning with his birth in 1745. Equiano died in London in 1797.

"I believe there are a few events in my life which have not happened to many," he wrote.

> It is true the incidents of it are numerous; and, did I consider myself a European, I might say my sufferings were

> great; but, when I compare my lot with that of most of my countrymen, I regard myself as a particular favourite of Heaven, and acknowledge the mercies of Providence in every occurrence of my life. . . .
>
> In one of the most remote and fertile [villages] . . . named Essaka . . . I was born. The distance of this province from the capital of Benin and the sea coast must be very considerable; for I had never heard of white men or Europeans, nor of the sea. . . .
>
> I was the youngest of the sons, I became, of course, the greatest favourite with my mother. . . . In this way I grew up till I was the age of eleven, when an end was put to my happiness.

Equiano penned the thoughts of every captive who believed that the sun was rising upon an ordinary day:

> When the grown people were gone far in the fields to labour, the children assembled together to play; and some of us used to get up a tree to look out for any assailant, or kidnapper, that might come upon us. . . .
>
> One day, when all our people were gone out to their works as usual, and only I and my dear sister were left to mind the house, two men and a woman got over our walls, and in a moment seized us both; and without giving us time to cry out, or make resistance, they stopped our mouths, tied our hands, and ran off with us into the nearest wood. . . .
>
> The next day proved a greater sorrow than I had yet experienced; for my sister and I were then separated, while we lay clasped in each other's arms. It was in vain that we besought them not to part us; she was torn from me and immediately carried away, while I was left in a state of distraction not to be described. I cried and

> grieved continually; and for several days I did not eat any thing but what they forced into my mouth.

On forest trails and rivers across West Africa, the captives were Ibo, believed by Europeans to be pliant, but prone to sickness and often suicidal when faced with the harsh realities of captivity; Angolans, rumored to be impossible to teach, and therefore perfect for repetitive physical work; Mandingo, with a reputation for cleanliness and courtesy; the Yoruba and Gold Coast natives, who were considered prime and well worth a hefty investment.

They disappeared. They were Fulani, Malinke, and Wolof, members of tribes with names like ringing bells. They were Whydahs, Asante, Fanti, Coromantees, pride filling their faces. They were broad noses, sun-kissed shoulders, tribal scars, hair kinked and beaded. They were Ga, Hausa. Their homes branched from the Senegal River, dotted south and east to just below the Congo River, half a continent away.

Landowners and tradespeople, servants and merchants, commoners and royalty disappeared from the broad and sweeping savannas, the parched plains, the rain forests. They were strong young men, frightened women clutching their children, children romping at play. The terrifying abductions could happen at any time, day or night. Hausa lay in ambush to capture Asante, Malinke to capture Coromantee.

On September 5, 1705, Willem De la Palma, director of the Dutch West India Company, wrote:

> Concerning the trade on this Coast, we notified Your Highness already that it has completely changed into a Slave Coast, and that nowadays the natives no longer occupy themselves with the search for gold, but rather make

> war on each other in order to furnish slaves. . . . The Gold Coast has changed into a complete Slave Coast.

The laughing children, craftsmen, farmers, wives, mothers, elders, commoners, kings—all sailing away from the place that birthed them and toward a nightmare that had not yet taken shape. Many of them were the seeds of many of us.

"There is great reason to believe that most of the negroes shipped off from the coast of Africa are kidnapped," wrote slave-ship surgeon Alexander Falconbridge in 1788. "I was told by a negroe woman that as she was on her return home one evening from some neighbours, to whom she had been making a visit by invitation, she was kidnapped and notwithstanding she was big with child, sold for a slave."

The African traders sacrificed much to maintain their unholy alliance with the Europeans. Some sold their own family members, friends, neighbors. Adulterers, those in debt, and those who challenged taboos could be put into slavery, which opened the way for false claims and personal vendettas. Sometimes entire families were required to follow a convicted relative into servitude.

According to historian David Northrup, a real or contrived transgression was only one route to bondage:

> The Igbo recognized a wider range of abominations (*nso*), such as a child whose upper teeth appeared before its lower, who walked or talked sooner than was usual, who had supernumerary fingers or toes, or who had any other deformity, or a woman who menstruated before attaining the "proper" age, gave birth to twins, or climbed trees. Depending on the circumstances, such a person might be killed outright, ritually cleansed, or sold into slavery.

Wars were waged to get prisoners of war to meet the demand for slaves. The African nations who engaged in this profitable treachery also grew more powerful politically and economically.

African suppliers of slaves had to pay "custom duties" to the coastal tribes before they were allowed to sell to the Europeans. They were quick to gauge the relative value of their goods, and they haggled relentlessly with European traders. If a supplier sensed that a trader desired slaves from a particular region, or only male adults, he would raise his prices accordingly. Or if he found himself with a surplus of women and children, he would package them with the most desirable males. However, the supplier always ran the risk that an impatient European would simply sail away to the next trading point, which was never too far away.

Between spurts of trade and profit, the Europeans were not necessarily having an easy time of it. The bargaining itself was often burdensome, the value of a slave constantly fluctuating. How many bolts of cloth or iron bars for a man or a woman? Guns. Brandy. Glass beads. Whiskey. How much to make a man?

Many Europeans had borrowed funds to finance their ventures and could not go home before recouping their investment. They waited to make money, in the form of African captives, and the money was not always there. So they waited for the Africans to wage war on one another; they waited for prisoners of war to be brought to them. From the diary of a Liverpool surgeon:

> DECEMBER 29, 1724. No trade today, though many traders came on board. They informed us, that the people are gone to war within land, and will bring prisoners enough in two or three days; in hopes of which we stay.

> DECEMBER 30, 1724. No trade yet, but our traders came on board today and informed us the people had burnt four towns of their enemies so that tomorrow we expect slaves.

The sweltering climate, unfamiliar food, and local maladies weakened the Europeans, and they died in great numbers. Yet many felt that the chance of speedy payoff well outweighed any risks involved.

Slave dealer Nicholas Owen put it this way in 1758:

> I have found no place where I can enlarge my fortune so soon as where I now live, wherefore I entend to stay in order to enlarge my fortune by honest mains. . . . I have sould three slaves, but have not receved all my goods yet upon account of the bad surf. . . . In this manner we spend the prime of youth among Negroes, scrapeing the world for money, the uneversal god of mankind, untill death overtakes us.

The sad irony of blacks selling blacks never slowed the African merchant's determination to do business with the Europeans, since tribal distinctions meant much more than racial ones. And he considered his involvement limited, failing to realize that he was an essential part of an enterprise that would make men wealthier than he could ever imagine.

The relationship with the Europeans damaged African life beyond the slave trade's siphoning of humans. With the introduction of firearms and ammunition into Africa, power struggles and acts of retaliation among Africans increased. The brutal roundup of captives forced others to arm themselves for protection. And to get that protection, they had to sell humans.

But the most frightening effect was the irreparable tear in the fabric of African custom and tradition. Men, women, and children were captured and pulled farther and farther away from the history and nurturing of each tribe. And they had, as far as they could see, no future.

In daring to give voice to the building nightmare, Olaudah Equiano wove the threads of that long-ago world into the one we live in today. He was the disappeared, found again.

Who are we looking for? It's Equiano we're looking for.
Has he gone to the stream? Let him come back.
Has he gone to the market? Let him come back.
Has he gone to the farm? Let him return.
It's Equiano we're looking for.

Let us grieve for the disappeared.

Olaudah Equiano was a child of noble parentage, someone for whom the circle of family meant everything. He often accompanied his mother to the markets, where his people traded with the Oye-Ibo, burnished men with stout, strong bodies. As he wrote:

> We call them Oye-Eboe, which term signifies "red men living at a distance." They generally bring us firearms, gunpowder, hats, beads and dried fish. Sometimes we sold slaves to them but they were only . . . prisoners of war, or such among us had been convicted of kidnapping, or adultery.

The fact that the child had never seen or heard of white people did not protect him from their hunger for Africans. So Olaudah Equiano became one of the disappeared.

> At last I came to the banks of a large river, covered with canoes. . . . I had never before seen any water larger

> than a pond or a rivulet, and my surprise was mingled with no small fear when I was put into one of those canoes, and we began to paddle and move along the river.

As he headed for the coast, Equiano was required to reinvent himself. No longer was he a son of noble parentage. Now he was considered property. Passed from master to master, he was once sold for 172 cowrie shells. He absorbed languages and met people who looked like him, but whose strange ways filled him with fear. For seven months, he traveled on foot and on small bodies of water until he reached the sea.

Passage to the coast was exceedingly difficult, and often deadly. The slaving routes were etched deeply inland, and the newly captured slaves, bound together, trudged along on foot. During this journey, which was often for hundreds of miles, they were denied adequate food, water, and rest. In 1738, English trader Francis Moore said, "Their way of bringing them is, tying them by the neck with leather thongs, at about a yard distance from each other, thirty or forty in a string, having generally a bundle of corn, or an elephants tooth upon each of their heads."

Like Equiano, some slaves were sold several times in the months before they reached the sea. Many died before they got there.

> The first object which saluted my eyes when I arrived on the coast was the sea, and a slave ship, which was then riding at anchor, and waiting for its cargo. These filled me with astonishment, which was soon converted into terror. When I was carried on board, I was immediately handled, and tossed up, to see if I were sound, by some of the crew; and I was now persuaded that I had gotten

> into a world of bad spirits and that they were going to kill me. Their complexions too differing so much from ours, their long hair and the language they spoke which was very different from any I had ever heard united to confirm me in this belief.

Other slaves encountered a "factory" or "slaving station"—a warehouse for European merchandise, and a processing center for the efficient and controlled management of newly acquired captives. El Mina, the fort built by the Portuguese in the late fifteenth century, had shifted its focus from gold to human beings. By the eighteenth century, El Mina was sending more than thirty thousand slaves a year to the Americas. Almost fifty forts and castles built along the shore of West Africa were also used as factories. Central to each structure was a slave house, a belowground network of vaulted cellars which, according to slave-trader Jean Barbot in 1732, "can easily hold a thousand slaves."

In a letter written in 1701 to a friend in Holland, Dutch trader Willem Bosman described the first stage of the selection process:

> *When these slaves come to Fida, they are put in prison alltogether, and when we treat concerning buying them, they are all brought out together in a large plain where, by our chirurgeons, whose province it is, they are thoroughly examined, even to the smallest member, and that naked too both men and women, without the least distinction or modesty. Those which are approved as good are set on one side; and the lame or faulty are set by as invalides. . . .*
>
> *The invalides and the maimed being thrown out, as I have told you, the remainder are numbered, and it is entred who delivered them. In the mean while a burning*

> *iron, with the arms or name of the companies, lyes in the fire; with which are marked on the breast. . . .*
>
> *I doubt not but this trade seems very barbarous to you, but since it is followed by meer necessity it must go on; but we yet take all possible care that they are not burned too hard, especially the women, who are more tender than the men.*

African traders were extremely cruel to their captives who had been rejected by the Europeans. According to ship's surgeon Alexander Falconbridge:

> It matters not whether they are refused on account of age, illness, deformity or for any other reason. At New Calabar, in particular, the traders have frequently been known to put them to death. Instances have happened at that place, that the traders, when any of their negroes have been objected to, have dropped their canoes under the stern of the vessel, and instantly beheaded them, in sight of the captain.

The brutish merchandising and unrelenting abduction of black bodies, the money that changed hands, the white skin of their captors, the eerie new language, the fact that none of the disappeared ever came home again—all these factors led frightened Africans to believe that the white men were not capitalists, but cannibals. Some thought blacks were eaten and their bones ground into gunpowder. No slave returned and said, "Here is what is happening." Africans simply dropped off the face of the earth.

"They cannot believe that they are only to be used for field labour," Dr. Paul Erdmann Isert said in 1787, "since from their experiences, field labour takes such little time and occupies so few hands."

The boy Olaudah Equiano also believed that the Europeans were feeding upon their African captives.

> When I looked round the ship too and saw a large furnace of copper boiling, and a multitude of black people of every description chained together, every one of their countenances expressing dejection and sorrow, I no longer doubted of my fate and quite overpowered with horror and anguish, I fell motionless on the deck and fainted. . . . I asked if we were not to be eaten by those white men with horrible looks, red faces and long hair?

As if two simple words could contain the horror, the journey was called the Middle Passage. It was the nightmarish middle leg of a triad that had its beginning and end in England. From English ports, ships loaded with manufactured goods set off for Africa where the goods were traded for humans. The human cargo was transported to the Americas and traded for raw materials to be sold in England. It was a terse, efficient triangle, unaffected by the mournful wails of those forever lost. Or by the moans of the dying.

Half of the more than 20 million Africans captured and sold into slavery never even made it to the ship. Most died on the march to the sea. It is impossible to determine how many more lost their lives during the crossing. Current estimates range from 1 million to 2.2 million.

"The men negroes, on being brought aboard the ship, are immediately fastened together, two by two, by handcuffs on their wrists, and by iron rivetted on their legs," wrote Alexander Falconbridge.

> They are then sent down between the decks, and placed in an apartment partitioned off for that purpose. The

> women likewise are placed in a separate apartment between decks, but without being ironed.
>
> Neither will the height between decks, unless directly under the grating, permit them the indulgence of an erect posture; especially where there are platforms, which is generally the case.

Traders argued over the most profitable ways to transport their human cargo. One captain might buy slaves rapidly, pack them closely, and feed them poorly, risking high mortality in search of extensive profits. Another might purchase captives more cautiously, allowing them more space, wider movement, and better food, in hopes that, with lower loss of life, he would have healthier slaves to sell in the Americas.

The Atlantic crossing could take as long as ten weeks, though the duration of voyages varied widely depending upon the wind, the weather, and the port of destination. Whatever its length in minutes and hours and days, it was a pilgrimage so hellish it battles description. No words can hold enough horror.

Infrequent exercise consisted of "dancing"—with none of the joy inherent in the word. Shackled, the slaves were physically punished to force the movement, which was nothing more than a frantic hopping. When they weren't dancing, the manacled slaves were packed together belowdecks like inanimate, unfeeling cargo, their limbs twisted and manipulated to conserve space. Slaves were positioned with their heads between the legs of other slaves, where they were forced to suffer through urine, feces, and a lack of breathable air.

Under those circumstances, madness was welcomed. Slaves shrieked and wailed, lost in the throes of fever, delirium, and terror. Imagine. The seemingly endless voyage, the damp stink in the bowels of the creaking ship, almost no food, a frightening numbness in the limbs—and the man chained to you is dead.

Disease was rampant. A sailor's common cold could be fatal to an African. In 1781 a ship captain, faced with an epidemic, dumped 132 living slaves into the water. His cargo was, after all, insured.

Africans from different areas had varying levels of immunity to diseases indigenous to the European continent. Alexander Falconbridge wrote:

> Some wet and blowing weather having occasioned the portholes to be shut and the grating to be covered, fluxes and fevers among the negroes ensued. . . . The deck was so covered with the blood and mucus which had proceeded from them in consequence of the flux, that it resembled a slaughterhouse. It is not in the power of the human imagination, to picture a situation more dreadful or disgusting.

The ship's surgeon—who was often medically ignorant, but one of few willing to undertake the expedition—made his rounds between the decks each morning to separate the dead from the living. When a dead slave was found manacled to one still living, the dead man was unshackled and thrown overboard. Free.

According to Falconbridge, slaves who were ill lay confined to bare plank under the ship's half deck. "By this means, those who are emaciated frequently have their skin, and even their flesh, entirely rubbed off, by the motion of the ship. . . . Few, indeed, are ever able to withstand the fatal effects of [the excruciating pain]."

Olaudah Equiano must have believed he had gone mad:

> I was soon put down under the decks, and there I received such a salutation in my nostrils as I had never experienced in my life; so that with the loathsomeness of the stench, and crying together, I became so sick and low that I was not able to eat, nor had the least desire to taste anything. I now wished for the last friend, Death, to relieve me. . . . I had never experienced anything of this kind before; and although, not being used to the water, I naturally feared that element the first time I saw it; yet, nevertheless, could I have got over the nettings, I would have jumped over the side.

It was no longer the fear of the unknown. It was the fear of what was known. And many slaves preferred death to the knowing.

Ship's captain Thomas Phillips wrote in 1693:

> We have likewise seen diverse numbers of them eaten by sharks, of which a prodigious number kept about the ships in this place, and I have been told will follow her hence to Barbadoes for the dead Negroes that are thrown overboard in the passage. . . . We had about twelve Negroes did wilfully drown themselves, and others starved themselves to death; for tis their belief that when they die they return home to their country and friends again.

Of course the ultimate control over his own life—whether to live or die—was denied the slave. If he chose to starve, he was simply forced to eat. His jaws were stretched open and food was crammed down his throat, or he was beaten or fitted with thumbscrews or tortured until he relented. Some slaves sliced their own throats and fought against forced feeding as best they could.

The slave was denied will and intention. He could not be allowed to die voluntarily. The only acceptable release from his state of perpetual misery was death at the hands of his captors.

"Often did I think many of the inhabitants of the deep much more happy than myself," wrote Equiano. "I envied them the freedom they enjoyed. Every circumstance I met with served only to render my state more painful, and heighten my apprehensions, and my opinion of the cruelty of the whites."

The captives must have sought to make sense of their situation: What taboo have I broken? Did I break a law? What could I possibly have done to find myself in this predicament, chained here, starving, beaten for asking?

As nightmarish as it was, the passage forced many of the Africans, who before their capture had been separated both physically and culturally, to find ways to communicate. In those watery, rocking tombs, a sense of unity began, as evidenced by this December 1752 chronicle by Captain John Newton:

> By the favour of Divine Providence made a timely discovery today that the slaves were forming a plot for an insurrection. Surprized two of them attempting to get off their irons, and upon farther search in their rooms, found some knives, stones, shot, etc. and a cold chissel. There appeared eight principally concerned in projecting the mischief and four boys in supplying them with the above instruments. Put the boys in irons and slightly in the thumbscrews to urge them to a full confession.

In 1700, sailor James Barbot and his fellow crewmen aboard the English slaver *Don Carlos* exacted a harsh punishment for rebellious slaves. "We stood in arms, firing on the revolted slaves, of whom we killed some and wounded many . . . and many of the most mutinous, leapt over board, and drowned themselves in the ocean with much resolution."

The sailors were victims of a different kind of enslavement. On an average voyage, approximately twenty-five or thirty seamen attempted to control three hundred or more bewildered, abused, and murderously rebellious slaves. Their control was built on fear. They, too, were subjected to harsh discipline. Captain John Newton had seen crew members "sick, beaten for being lazy till they had died under the blows." Moreover, European sailors faced a new environment rife with tropical diseases. At the end of the eighteenth century, the death rate for sailors was one in five.

Many of the sailors were impoverished, fleeing from criminal punishment, or coerced into serving on the ship. "We are for the most part supplied with the refuse and dregs of the nation," said Newton, "large quotas and boys impatient of their parents or masters, or already ruined by some untimely vice and for the most part devoid of all good principles . . ."

Newton was a slave-ship captain for ten years before becoming a clergyman and ardent abolitionist. His reminiscences and exhaustive daily chronicles of the trade give unprecedented insight into the mind of the English slave trader.

On January 26, 1753, in *Letters to a Wife,* he wrote:

> The three greatest blessings of which human nature is capable are undoubtedly religion, liberty and love. In each of these how highly has God distinguished me! But here in Africa are whole nations around me, whose languages are entirely different from each other, yet I believe they agree in this, that they have no words among

> them expressive of these engaging ideas. . . . These poor creatures are not only strangers to the advantages which I enjoy, but are plunged in all the contrary evils . . . they are deceived and harassed by necromancing, magic and all the train of superstitions that fear combined with ignorance can produce in the human mind.

In 1756, Newton described in his diary how ill health had forced him to abandon the slave trade. "Thus I was brought out of a way of life, disagreeable to my temper and inconvenient to my profession [of the Christian faith]."

Forty years later, in *Thoughts upon the African Slave Trade,* Newton wrote:

> I think I should have quitted [the slave trade] sooner had I considered it as I now do, to be unlawful and wrong. But I never had a scruple upon this head at the time; nor was such a thought ever suggested to me by any friend. What I did I did ignorantly; considering it as the line of life which Divine Providence had allotted me.

His colleagues at sea may have wrestled with the same ambivalence that led to Newton's change of heart. The slavers realized that the captives were made in their own image. But since they were to be treated as objects of profit, it was difficult for the slavers to reconcile the two concepts.

And so it seems that they managed to suppress any surges of compassion for the sake of gold.

CHAPTER THREE

FROM THE BEGINNING of the eighteenth century to the end of colonial times, the first glimpse of North America for almost half the arriving slaves was Sullivan's Island in the harbor of Charles Town (Charleston) in the Carolina colony.

After subjecting the captives to a mandatory ten-day quarantine, eager merchants would unload the human cargo, judge its worth, and advertise in newspapers and on handbills. Often an entire shipload of slaves would be sold on one day, and planters came from hundreds of miles away to get in on the bargaining. Although slaves were sometimes marketed singly or in pairs, many were sold in lots of ten or more.

The advertisements for newly arrived slaves reflected the prevailing belief that natives of particular regions were harder workers and better investments.

> A CHOICE CARGO OF ABOUT 250 FINE HEALTHY NEGROES JUST ARRIVED FROM THE WINDWARD AND RICE COAST. THE UTMOST CARE HAS ALREADY BEEN TAKEN AND SHALL BE CONTINUED TO . . .

SLAVES REMARKABLY HEALTHY, JUST ARRIVED IN THE SHIP *SALLY* . . . FROM CAPE MOUNT—A RICE COUNTRY—ON THE WINDWARD COAST, AFTER A SHORT PASSAGE OF FIVE WEEKS . . .

During the process of inspection and sale, both planters and traders were compelled to treat the Africans as cargo. Henry Laurens, Charleston's most prominent slave trader, imparted this bit of bad news to Gedney Clarke of Barbados in an impassive and businesslike missive dated January 31, 1756:

Permit us now to inform you what progress we have made in the Sale of your Slaves. . . . Our People thought them a very indifferent parcell, that they were much too small a People for the business of this Country & on this Account many went away empty handed that would otherways have purchas'd. . . . What we have sold at this day are 102. The Amount £ 21,291.10/ Currency. We have 14 more that are able to come abroad and 11 sick in the Hospital. Those which are well are a very diminutive parcell of Mortalls, Children in size but at their full growth, so that upon the whole we fear you must make a very indifferent Voyage & what will add to it is that the major part of those sold are on Credit to January next.

In South Carolina, the rice growers were treasured among the human cargo. Natives of Senegambia and the Windward Coast were skilled in the arduous cultivation of Carolina's cash crop. In the colony's low country, rice had begun to make Englishmen rich. Early African arrivals had shown English settlers how to grow this strange crop in freshwater swamps as early as the 1690s, and from then on, white Carolinians moved swiftly to import additional African labor.

By the 1750s, with a seemingly endless supply of black workers and a crop destined to plump their coffers, Carolina investors were deeply invested in a dream.

And there was no shortage of dreamers. Among them were the Middleton brothers, Edward and Arthur, two experienced Barbadian merchants who had arrived in Carolina in the late 1670s, capitalized on land options, and settled on 1,700 acres on Goose Creek, just north of Charleston, where they were immediately embraced as members of the colony's ruling elite.

They were eager to put into practice what they had learned in Barbados. For 400,000 Africans, the Middle Passage ended in the Caribbean on that tiny island crowded with sugarcane plantations, the most profitable plantations in the British empire. Olaudah Equiano spent two weeks in Barbados before he was brought to the mainland.

> At last we came in sight of the island of Barbadoes, at which the whites on board gave a great shout, and made many signs of joy. . . . [T]here was much dread and trembling among us . . . insomuch that at last the white people got some old slaves from the land to pacify us. They told us we were not to be eaten but to work, and were soon to see many of our country people. Sure enough, soon after we landed there came to us Africans of all languages. . . .
>
> We were not many days in the merchant's custody before we were sold. . . . In this manner, without scruple, are relations and friends separated, most of them never to see each other again. . . . [T]here were several brothers who were sold in different lots; and it was very moving to see and hear their cries at parting.

The settlers who received Equiano harbored no illusions regarding the slave's humanity. As far as they were concerned, he had none.

Throughout the West Indies, slavery's brutal signature was stamped on the very structure of society. A person's community standing was determined by his relationship to the slave trade, and that social niche was secured by rapidly deepening racial divisions. Barbados was one of the worst places in the world to be a slave.

The Dutch had taught the island's English settlers to produce sugar, and it was sugar that consumed the island and swelled the ratio of slaves to freemen. In a short period of time, hundreds of sugar producers purchased plantations averaging two hundred acres each. Proprietors of smaller plots turned their land over to the cane crop. Barbados housed the first sugar factory in the English New World, equipped on credit by Dutch investors. Because so much land on the tiny island was devoted to sugar, the settlers depended on England and England's North American colonies for their food supply. There was simply no room to grow anything but sugar.

Although indentured servants continued to arrive from England, the supply couldn't keep up with the demands of Barbados's sugar industry. Once again, the Dutch saved the day, whispering in the island's ear about the effectiveness of black slave labor and even offering to provide the slaves. The black population skyrocketed; in 1660, the ratio was roughly 20,000 slaves to 22,000 whites. By 1713, it was about 45,000 to 16,000.

Barbados led the way in the creation and enactment of slave codes to manage the burgeoning population of enslaved Africans. Soon planters had the right to exert excessive force to keep their slaves in line. If an owner insisted the punishment was warranted, courts could order a slave's death or the removal of a finger, arm, or leg. If a slave was killed in the course of "correction," his master was protected from prosecution. The planters had reckoned that it was cheaper to lose and replace slaves than it was to feed them, treat their illnesses, punish them humanely, and keep them alive.

The Middletons' experiences there had prepared them well for their Carolina adventure. They knew that a series of small, well-thought-out investments could spark substantial wealth. They were well acquainted with the use of chattel slavery as a labor source. They'd learned the efficient rhythm of plantation economics, and their merchant's sagacity qualified them to master and exploit that rhythm. They were poised to conquer the New World.

Within two years of his arrival in Carolina, Edward Middleton had commanded 4,130 acres in land grants and a choice parcel of real estate. He had cemented his niche in the local aristocracy with a powerful position in the colony's only governing body. In 1680, he and his wife, Sara, established the family plantation, The Oaks, where they experimented with different plantings, searching for that one cash crop. But they never found it. When Edward died five years later, rice cultivation in South Carolina had not yet taken firm hold.

It was Edward's son Arthur, a determined man in his early twenties, who finally realized his father's dream. By the beginning of the eighteenth century, he had built The Oaks into a sprawling five-thousand-acre plantation. The impressive spread instantly made him one of the most influential men in British North America. He also continued the family political ambitions by representing Berkeley County in the Commons House of Assembly.

Although no records remain to document the number of slaves Arthur Middleton owned, it was certain that he had to rely on slave labor to clear his lowlands for the cultivation of rice. By 1730, the entire plantation was devoted to its production. And the production of Carolina's favorite crop required many men, many hours of backbreaking labor designed to reap profits even as it shattered the spirit.

On the Windward Coast of Africa, rice planting had been a celebration, a time of rebirth and promise. In the New World, beneath the biting sun and the lash of the whip, it meant only misery, rampant disease, and a courtship with death.

Preparing a rice field for cultivation, first in inland swamps and later in extensive coastal fields, was an almost superhuman task. Strict requirements had to be met to guarantee a successful harvest.

The crop required extremely moist soil, which had to be nourished by rain or flooded artificially. First, a sizable dike was built around the field to stem the water flow so that stubborn stumps, large rocks, and other obstacles could be removed. Smaller dikes separated the land into smaller, twenty-acre parcels. Then a sluice gate was constructed so the field could be drained or flooded as needed, using the freshwater that washed up in coastal estuaries at high tide.

The cycle of three plantings began in March and continued through April; each planting was usually aligned with the full and new moons when tides were high. At a space every twelve inches, seed rice was sown in shallow trenches. At high tide the field was flooded for four or five days, then drained, then flooded again until the plants were approximately three inches high. Again drained for three weeks. Then came the "long water," a flooding of two to three weeks. Drained again.

Finally, the field was underwater for six to eight weeks during the "harvest flow."

The harvesting and threshing began in late August, at the height of the summer heat. The work in the rice fields had to be done mostly by hand—by hoe, rice hooks, wooden flail, mortar and pestle—without the assistance of animals or machines. Each day, a slave was allotted to a task—usually the hoeing, plowing, or harvesting of half an acre. An industrious prime hand completed a task in nine or ten hours.

The cycle of harvesting, separating seed from grain, and pounding and polishing the finished product was finally completed in November. Then the land was turned, given a new face. The water was let in. And the nightmare began anew.

Observed Captain Basil Hall:

> [Rice] is the most unhealthy work in which the slaves were employed, and they sank under it in great numbers. The causes of this dreadful mortality are the constant moisture and heat of the atmosphere, together with the alternate floodings and dryings of the fields, on which the negroes are perpetually at work, often ankle deep in mud, with their bare heads exposed to the fierce rays of the sun.

The sun parched bare skin. Snakes and alligators sliced through the murky water. Men dropped from exhaustion and illness under the staccato crack of the whip. And, miraculously, there was singing. As they worked, the slaves raised their voices to the sky, lending a melody to the madness.

Some sang to welcome death, their one chance at release. Ironically, life in a climate that contained malaria had given many West Africans (through the sickle-cell trait) a partial resistance to the disease, and this fact was not lost on opportunistic planters even if they were ignorant of what caused the disease or what helped contain it. Nevertheless, the slaves lost their lives in huge numbers. South Carolina planters, like their counterparts in Barbados, believed it cheaper to lose a slave than to treat one humanely. So the captives were destined to labor in the steamy, sodden fields, sacrificing their souls for the crop.

For many slaves, that sacrifice was too great. It was usually during the summer, the season of malarial fevers, that they set out for freedom. Some believed that if they ran far enough through the lush, unfamiliar territory, they would find their own country. Many took flight in search of their families. Some lived simply to escape. Burdened by the weight of their shackles, they fled, were captured, took flight again.

Detailed notices advertised runaways:

> RUNAWAY . . . TWO NEGRO MEN . . . ONE THIS COUNTRY BORN, NAMED GEORGE, HE SPEAKS GOOD ENGLISH, A SHORT, THICK, WELL-SET SENSIBLE FELLOW . . . THE OTHER NAMED DERRY, A TALL LIKELY YOUNG IBO NEGRO BRANDED ON THE BREAST . . .

> HERCULES . . . HAD ON WHEN HE WENT AWAY TWO LEG IRONS ON HIS FEET . . .

> TOM . . . ONE LEG GALDED BY WEARING A SPURR . . .

Running away was often a painfully lonely, silent, solitary enterprise. There were no well-trod routes to follow. Untried trails through water and over mountain spelled death for many. Moonlight was both friend and enemy: while it could light the way, it could also make the runaway visible to would-be captors—volunteer vigilantes; organized local patrols; the chance white man; or the professional slave hunter, whose hound was rumored to be versed in "nigger-smell."

Man was not the only worry. Snakes slithered through swamps. Woods twisted and led nowhere. The cry or bark of an animal could pinpoint a person's location. And a slave's fear was an almost visible thing.

Sometimes it was just a second of freedom the slave coveted, a chance to pull in a breath that wasn't supervised by someone else. The runaways searched for friends and family and other escaped slaves in the swamps and forests, hoping to establish a community of renegades. Perhaps they tasted freedom for no longer than a week, a month, an hour. But that hour belonged to them. It was an hour when freedom washed over them like clear water flowing down.

While isolated runaway slaves posed no major threat, slave owners knew that bands of runaways could lead to orchestrated insurrection. So they took increasingly brutal measures to prevent escape. They rationalized the threat of violence to prevent violence.

Carolina had enacted its first comprehensive slave law on March 1, 1696. Designed to bring the restless captives under control, the law relied on the brutish Barbados slave code for its preface and most of the components relating to police control. Slaves were defined as "All Negroes, Mollatoes and Indians which at any time heretofore have been bought and Sold or now are and taken to be or hereafter Shall be Bought and Sold . . . and their Children."

The preamble called for special legislation to subdue the slaves' "barbarous, wild, savage Natures" because they were "naturally prone and inclined" to "disorders, Rapines and Inhumanity." Masters regularly searched slave quarters for weapons. They were allowed to exact painful, maiming retribution on any slave who ran away or attacked his owner. Slaves needed written permission to leave the plantation for any reason. And to keep the captives from organizing escape or rebellion, planters could disrupt slave gatherings on the Sabbath.

To conquer their fear and assert their dominance, planters granted themselves the power of life and death over the black men, women, and children shackled to their land.

The young slave Equiano, laboring in British America, struggled to understand the matter-of-fact cruelty that surrounded him.

> I had seen a black woman slave as I came through the house, who was cooking the dinner, and the poor creature was cruelly loaded with various kinds of iron machines; she had one particularly on her head, which locked her mouth so fast that she could scarcely speak; and could not eat or drink. I was much astonished and shocked at this contrivance, which I afterwards learned was called the iron muzzle.

In 1721, the year South Carolina became a crown colony, the population of 18,000 included almost 12,000 blacks, with 1,000 Africans arriving each year. The Europeans contended with an ever-growing and increasingly hostile slave majority obsessed with escape or revenge.

In a system based on fear, physical punishment was the only reliable answer the slave owners had to prevent rebellion. And since even a minor infraction, real or imagined, called for correction, masters were constantly called upon to determine how harsh the treatment should be. A whipping? The amputation of a hand or foot? Should the slave be shackled for the rest of his life? The punishments sent a message to all the others: *This—or worse—will happen to you.*

Slave owners wove brutal acts into the fabric of their daily lives. The 1709 diary of Virginia planter William Byrd illustrates:

> 8 FEBRUARY 1709. I rose at 5 o'clock this morning and read a chapter in Hebrew and 200 verses in Homer's *Odyssey.* I ate milk for breakfast. I said my prayers. Jenny and Eugene were whipped. I danced my dance. I read law in the morning and Italian in the afternoon. . . .
>
> 17 APRIL 1709. Anaka was whipped yesterday for stealing the rum and filling the bottle up with water. . . .
>
> 10 JUNE 1709. I rose at 5 o'clock this morning but could not read anything because of Captain Keeling, but I played at billiards with him and won half a crown of him and the Doctor. . . . In the evening I took a walk about the plantation. Eugene was whipped for running away and had the bit put on him. I said my prayers and had good health, good thoughts, and good humor, thanks be to God Almighty. . . .
>
> 3 SEPTEMBER 1709. I read some geometry. We had no court this day. My wife was indisposed again but not to much purpose. I ate roast chicken for dinner. In the afternoon I beat Jenny for throwing water on the couch. . . .
>
> 1 DECEMBER 1709. I rose at 4 o'clock and read two chapters in Hebrew and some Greek in Cassius. I said my prayers and ate milk for breakfast. I danced my dance. Eugene was whipped again for pissing in bed and Jenny for concealing it. . . .

> 3 DECEMBER 1709. I rose at 5 o'clock and read two chapters in Hebrew and some Greek in Cassius. I said my prayers and ate milk for breakfast. I danced my dance. Eugene pissed abed again for which I made him drink a pint of piss. . . .

> 27 FEBRUARY 1711. In the evening my wife and little Jenny had a great quarrel in which my wife got the worst but at last by the help of the family Jenny was overcome and soundly whipped. At night I ate some bread and cheese. I said my prayers and had good health, good thoughts, and good humor, thank God Almighty.

Even as he whipped his slaves and danced his dance, William Byrd worried that someday the battered captives might seek revenge:

> Their numbers increase every day as well by birth as importation. And in case there should arise a Man of desperate courage, exasperated by a desperate fortune, he might kindle a Servile War. Such a man might be dreadfully mischievous before any opposition could be formed against him, and tinge our rivers as wide as they are with blood.

Slavery thus affected the enslaver as well as the enslaved. Planters were keenly aware of the mental and moral price exacted for being a part of the system. Most decided the price was worth paying. The moral manipulations made to justify such an inhumane institution trapped owner and captive in their opposite roles. The slave wanted to be free, and the slave owner wanted to prevent his freedom.

Slave and master circled each other warily, waiting.

On some large plantations across the colonies, the living quarters for the slaves were miles from the main house. Quartered by themselves, the slaves were trapped in lives that were neither African nor American, a community Anglican missionaries described as a nation within a nation. Disparate African peoples forced together under desperate, demeaning circumstances developed their own language and created new cultures. Although many of them had been in America for most of their lives, the slaves lived among a growing population of people from all parts of Africa and were isolated socially and culturally from their masters.

As the slaves communicated and sometimes married across tribal and regional lines, their culture became an intriguing mixture of African traditions and those developed in the Americas as a means for survival. Blacks from different parts of Africa combined their beliefs, their music, and their languages while borrowing from the European culture to create a commonality. Africa still existed as an ideal. Many slave colonies attempted to replicate African villages, but the slaves knew that there was very little chance they would see their homes again. Instead, they developed their own way of comprehending and negotiating the world.

Amid the madness of the plantation system, the African captives forged communities and worked so those communities would operate as normally as possible. They negotiated for the right to control their own movements, visit members of their family on other plantations, and sell the goods they managed to produce on their own tiny parcels of land, set aside by planters who saved on supplies when slaves raised their own food.

In October 1706, one year after Arthur Middleton and his wife, Sara, settled in at The Oaks, Francis Le Jau, a missionary for the Society for the Propagation of the Gospel, arrived as Goose Creek's first full-time vicar. The staunch Anglican convert was sent from England to steer both slave and slave owner toward the colony's official faith. To that end, he kept a daily chronicle of events in the region of St. Paul's Parish, where whites, Indians, and slaves lived in a potentially volatile climate.

Le Jau's observations mirrored the troubles of the times:

> A poor slavewoman was barbarously burnt alive near my door without any positive proof of the Crime she was accused of, which was, the burning of her Master's House and protested her innocence even to myself to the last. Many Masters can't be persuaded that Negroes and Indians are otherwise than beasts, and use them like such. . . . I dayly perceive that many things are done here out of a Worldly and Interested principle, little for God's sake.

Le Jau was shocked by the cruelties he witnessed. However, he never questioned what we would perceive today as a glaring inconsistency between Christianity and the institution of slavery, or the fact that one Christian was holding another Christian captive. Instead, slave owners were frequently assured that owning humans was a perfectly Christian thing to do, as long as the slaves were well taken care of and instructed in religious matters.

Throughout the colonies, planters had no problem balancing sin and salvation. "Mr. D. told me he once cut off a negro-man's leg for running away," wrote Olaudah Equiano.

> I asked him, if the man had died in the operation? How he, as a Christian, could answer for the horrid act before God? And he told me, answering was a thing of another

> world; what he thought and did were policy. . . . He then said his scheme had the desired effect—it cured that man and some others of running away.

Some planters were indifferent to the religious upbringing of their slaves, rejecting the notion that their property was entitled to seek religious salvation. They reasoned that slaves lacked the common sense and reasoning abilities needed to grasp the tenets of Christianity. Secretly, they feared that an unwavering focus on the rewards of religious belief was the first step on the road to freedom.

During a time when both Barbados and the Deep South still relied upon the transatlantic slave trade, African natives clung tenaciously to their ethnic roots and surveyed their current realities through a lens tinged with tradition. Since their basic beliefs had some very similar foundations, Africans from different regions were able to agree on basic religious rites, including marriage and interment of the dead.

All slaves did not subscribe to the docile, whitewashed version of Christianity preached by their masters. Instead they reached deep into themselves, reestablished a dim and distant link with a long-ago homeland many of them had never seen. The spirit with which they worshiped was vitally expressive, physically unleashed, musical, and mystical. It was an earthy combination of what they had been told and what they inherently knew.

They had no doubt that their masters had misrepresented Christian principles—slavery was not "God's plan," but a glaring sin that only emancipation could correct. Even as they accepted Christianity, slaves shaped it to fit the particulars of their oppression, drawing the strength and perseverance needed to believe in something beyond a bleak and dismal reality. And they identified with the Supreme Being in a deeply personal way; the Father and his children were linked in suffering. Although he had given them an extraordinary burden to bear, God was on their side.

And he tested them in extraordinary ways.

"I have had of late an opportunity to oppose with all my might the putting of a very unhumane Law and in my Judgmt very unjust it is in Execution, in Relation to run away Negroes," wrote Francis Le Jau.

> [S]uch an Negroe must be mutilated by amputation of Testicles if it be a man, and of Ears if a Woman. . . . I must Informe you of a most Cruel Contrivance a man has Invented to punish small faults in slaves. He puts them in a Coffin where they are crushed almost to death, and he keeps them in that hellish Machine for 24 hours commonly with their feet Chained out, and a Lid pressing upon their stomack.

The savage daily dramas that troubled Le Jau were common occurrences throughout the American colonies. Violence against slaves escalated in response to a growing concern among colonists that the enslaved population would soon grow too large to control. But the plantations were ever greedy for labor.

So the planters hid their own fear and anxiety, suppressed their slaves even more harshly, and looked for ways to further restrict the movements of their burgeoning captive population.

The resultant laws were specifically designed to humiliate and control. In Charleston, a black found without a pass after 9 P.M. could be imprisoned or shot if he refused to answer questions satisfactorily. A slave who ran away or physically struck a white person was whipped, branded, or castrated.

Insurrections plotted by South Carolina blacks were regularly uncovered. An Anglican minister in Goose Creek wrote of "secret poisonings and bloody insurrection by certain Christian slaves." The slave owner's fear was so consuming and pervasive that he killed without conscience.

The Spanish, still bitter rivals of the English, took advantage of the climate of suspicion by offering to shelter runaway slaves. And blacks and Indians were rumored to be traveling from Spanish Florida to attack planters.

In 1728, Arthur Middleton, now acting governor of South Carolina and one of British North America's wealthiest men, complained of Spain's intervention:

> The Spanish are receiving and harboring all our runaway negroes. They have found a new way of sending our own slaves against us, to rob and plunder us. They are continually fitting out partys of Indians from St. Augustine to murder our white people, rob our plantations and carry off our slaves so that we are not only at a vast expense in guarding our southern frontiers, but the inhabitants are continually alarmed and have no leizure to look after their crops.

This was particularly troublesome for Middleton, who held slaves close to Florida, and who—with properties in Charleston, London, and Barbados—had become a true American success story. He was the type of man other planters held in high esteem, an example of what could be done with a savvy business sense and a bounty of slaves.

The following year, Middleton doubled his landholdings by acquiring more than 4,700 acres along the Savannah River. In 1733, the founding of Georgia to the south of the river encouraged settlement to create a buffer zone between British America and Spanish Florida. Although slavery was legal in the other twelve colonies, the trustees of the colony decided that Georgia would be Europeans only.

> It is shocking to human nature that any race of Mankind and their Posterity, should be sentenced to perpetual Slavery . . . and as freedome to them must be as dear as to us, what a Scene of horrour must it bring about!
>
> —Petition by the Settlers and Freeholders at Darien, Georgia, 1739

Although some Georgia settlers had taken an admirable stance, trustees of the colony also banned slavery to avoid the constant threat of rebellions and to encourage poor white workers from Europe to settle there. They knew that Georgia's proximity to Florida would be an open invitation for slaves to flee their captivity.

Meanwhile, a South Carolina yellow-fever epidemic may have been the cause of Arthur Middleton's death in the fall of 1737. The formidable task of maintaining the eight-thousand-acre estate and more than a hundred slaves fell to his son William. But a year later, William lost his wife to yet another plague. The trouble was just beginning.

During the four-year period from 1735 to 1739, eleven thousand Africans passed through Sullivan's Island. More than eight thousand were from the Angola region. These slaves were rumored to be prone to rebellion. Living in squalor on Carolina's rice plantations, whole communities of Angolans cohabited, communicated, suffered together under European rule.

In 1739, Jemmy decided it was time for the suffering to stop.

A recent arrival from Angola, Jemmy built important alliances with his fellow Angolans, Africans from other countries, and those who had been born in America. He found the deeper language they all shared, the language of the oppressed when speaking of the oppressor. He had a plan, and they began to listen.

The year 1739 seemed intent on turmoil. Slaves were fleeing to St. Augustine, lured by the Spanish offer of liberty. In February, rumors of a Negro uprising were heard throughout the colony. In April, four slaves joined with an Irish indentured servant and reached St. Augustine on stolen horses—but not before killing one white man and wounding another. In July, Spanish soldiers were reported just off the Carolina coast. In September, the official word arrived: England and Spain were at war.

In the dawning hours of September 9, 1739, Jemmy led approximately twenty slaves, most of them Angolan, toward Stono Bridge, south of Charleston. The band of renegades hungered for the freedom the Spanish would grant them if they toppled the English and fled to Florida.

At Stono, they overwhelmed the proprietors of the general store and obtained firearms and gunpowder. The storekeepers, Robert Bathurst and Mr. Gibbs, died first. The runaways left their heads on the doorstep before setting southward toward St. Augustine. Retribution was a key element of this rebellion, and a clear message was being sent to whites who had grown fat on the system of servitude and suppression.

The Godfrey family died, as did the Lemys. But Jemmy and his followers spared the lives of those who treated their slaves well. By the end of the day, they had killed more than twenty people.

This description, excerpted from a "Letter from South Carolina Dated October 2," appeared in the London publication *Gentleman's Magazine*:

> They increased every Minute by new Negroes coming to them; so that there were above Sixty, some say a Hundred; on which they halted in a field, and set to Dancing, Singing, and beating Drums, to draw more Negroes to them, thinking they were now victorious over the whole Province, having marched ten Miles, and burnt all before them without Opposition.

The rebels may have expected Spanish support; they may have hoped eventually to disappear in the wilderness. But it wouldn't be long before the mighty fist of the colonial forces came down upon them. A rapid and decisive quashing of the violent uprising would speak volumes, not only to enslaved South Carolinians, but to every colonist who had long feared this moment. It would send a message to other slaves: *You can't win. You will die if you try.* There would be reprisals. But for the time that Jemmy and his men rested beneath their own flag, they were an army.

What might success have meant to those with no chance of succeeding? It may have meant a moment to stand and say, "If I live, I live free. If I die, I die free."

The white man called them slaves. But they shrugged off the white man's rules to wage war against their captors. They stood strong, and still. They waited. And when the Carolina militia surrounded and attacked their camp, some refused to run from their moment of liberty. Standing their ground, they died free.

At least fourteen of Jemmy's men lost their lives in the attack; others were shot after being questioned.

CONFESSION

Y'ALL WANT ME TO sit there?" he said, nodding toward the barrel amiddlemost the old barn because his hands were tied behind his back. Tiberius was wearing a linen frock and red velvet waistcoat. He was thin, clubfooted, and not too happy that the militiamen had brought him back to Colonel Hext's place after what he and the others had done to the old man's wife. But they hadn't killed him, as they'd done with fourteen of his co-conspirators—laying waste to them in a one-sided battle—and maybe, Tiberius thought, they'd let him live if he just did what they asked. He sat down heavily on the barrel, taking just a moment to glance round at the bins of grain, the lofts of hay and straw overhead, and the frail light shafting down from cracks in the roof to the spot where they'd placed him. "All right now, I'm sittin' down, just like you asked, but you don't have to push. *What's that? You want to know* why *I joined up with Jemmy?"*

Tiberius looked down at his bare feet, took a long breath, then his eyes fluttered up at the three white men surrounding him. They were passing a flask of home brew between them. Of the trio he recognized two. Mr. Hutchenson, owner of the general store in Stono. Tiberius placed his age at forty. Forty-five. He wore a pair of riding boots and a tattered balandranas. His eyes were a bit red-webbed from the whiskey, his chestnut hair was thinning, and Hutchenson looked at him with a profound sadness, or so Tiberius thought. He'd ran errands for his Bathurst family since he was a boy, and prayed that Hutchenson, if no one else, would understand how his life had been turned upside down in the last twenty-four hours—or, more precisely, since the king of Spain promised to shelter and protect runaway Negroes if they made it to Augustine. The other man he knew was Ethan Whittaker, an overseer with a gray Cathedral beard, who worked on the farm of Tiberius's master, William Boswell, and Tiberius was more than a little afraid of him, seeing how ruthlessly the heavyset Whittaker drove blacks at planting time; he was drumming a short-handled whip over and over against his palm. The last man—Ethan called him Colonel Bull—was dressed in a travel-stained coat and had a double-barreled gun loaded with buckshot hitched under his arm. He had the air of a parson or maybe a politician, somebody important at least, but Tiberius'd never seen him before—or had he?—so when he spoke, staring up at the three men standing over him, he directed his words at Hutchenson.

"Sir, you know *me. I ain't never been one for trouble, or for fightin', or steppin' out of line in any way. Ain't that so? I was born right here, not like Jemmy and them others who come from Africa. I played with your children when we was growin' up. You remember that? I don't know nothin'* but *here. And I always been thankful Mastah Boswell let me work in the house, seeing how I can't get around too well. You ask him, he'll tell you what a good worker I am. I'm always hup before* anybody *at the house, even before the daylight horn is blown to wake hup the field hands. It takes me time to walk from the quarters, but I'm there before Mastah*

Boswell, wearin' his Beard box, gets outta that big bed with its pewterized nickel headboard. See, I'm the one lays out every day his razors imported from England—he likes a different one every morning, you know? I lays out his linen shirt with lawn ruffles on the sleeves, his cravat, and breeches. If it's cold, I'm the one lights the fireplace downstairs, and I carries coal in a pan to all the other fireplaces upstairs and down—it stays colder in them second-floor rooms than downstairs, you know. And it's me makes sure Mastah Boswell's breakfast is just like he wants it. Toast with a li'l flavor of woodsmoke in it. And he likes his coffee roasted and ground no more'n two hours before I serves it to him. His wife, well, she favors egg bread, grilled fowl, bricks of cheese, and fish from New Orleans, along with ice water and mint tea in the morning. You ask them if I don't make that old cook Emma have everything just so *on the table, with the pewter bowls and plates set out right pretty, before the mastah and missus come downstairs."*

He saw Hutchenson nodding. He'd eaten more than once at Boswell's home, knew how much effort went into preparing those elaborate meals, and Tiberius felt consoled by the slight upturn at the corner of his lips. "I've always done my best by 'em, and read my Bible like they wanted. You know, just between you'n me, some folks in the quarters didn't like me much 'cause I worked in the house. I told *'em it was on account of my affliction that Mastah Boswell didn't send me to the fields. But that didn't change their minds. They still thought I had it easier than they did. I swear, sometimes I felt like I was livin' in two worlds, just 'cause I worked in the house. On Sunday, the day y'all give us to ourselves, I'd bring food the mastah and missus didn't eat over to that spot near the general store where coloreds get together to talk and dance and such. If Mastah Boswell complained to his wife 'bout one of the field hands, I'd take that fellah aside and tell him what I heard so Mistah Whittaker there wouldn't wind up havin' to whip him. What's that? How'd I meet Jemmy? Yessir, all right. I'll talk about that. Just let me collect my thoughts a li'l . . .*"

The white men waited. Tiberius, facing the open barn door, could see other Carolina militiamen bringing their bound captives to Hext's farm. The sky above Colleton County was fast losing light. He found it hard to swallow, but cleared his throat, licked his dry lips, and went on:

"*I reckon Jemmy come to St. Paul's Parish 'bout a year ago, him and a wagonload of other saltwater Negroes. That's what we call them come straight from Africa. I don't know who his mastah is. At first I didn't pay them no mind when I seen them on Sundays at the gatherin' place. I couldn't* talk *to most of them, they bein' from Angola and all. They couldn't read or figure. Jemmy, he spoke better English than them others. I guess what they talked was Portuguese. It sounds a li'l bit like Spanish, don't it? Thing is, there was somethin' 'bout Jemmy that was . . . different. Oh no, I'm not just talkin' 'bout the way Jemmy looked. They was all big, strappin' boys. Jemmy stood six feet five. You got to figure they* had *to be strong 'cause workin' rice broke so many people down. Visit any of the quarters, and you'll find somebody got malaria. Cholera. Whooping cough. The children* keep *intestinal worms. So, yessir, Jemmy, he was fit. But more'n that, he had somethin' . . .* inside. *You could see it in his eyes. The way he looked right through you. If I recollect rightly, them Angolans was workin' on a road crew round the time we heard about the Spanish king's proclamation. That was* last *Sunday. Della, she took a newspaper from Mastah Boswell's study, and Jemmy asked me to read it, which I did, tellin' 'em 'bout how slaves who fled to the Presidio at St. Augustine, Florida, was free. Jemmy listened real close when I read that newspaper. His eyes got real quiet. Then he told the others what I said in Portuguese. Just 'bout that* time, Mistah Whittaker, you come out of Mistah Hutchenson's store, seen what we was doin', and ripped that paper right outta my hands. Jemmy snatched it back. And him doin' that liked to make you so mad"—Tiberius laughed, then caught himself—"you commenced to beatin' on him with a harness strap. I ain't never seen you so wild. But Jemmy took it straight up without makin' a sound. Didn't take his eyes off you either or move until finally you was all sweaty and breathin' hard and tuckered out, and just threw down that strap and rode off. You remember that last Sunday?"

The other white men looked quizzically at Whittaker, whose cheeks flushed bright red. The muscles around his eyes tightened. He spat a foot from where Tiberius sat, then turned away.

"Yeah," he nodded, "Jemmy had that effect on lots of people. It was like there was somethin' inside him too heavy to move. Excuse me? Come again, Mistah Hutchenson? Was I afraid of Jemmy? Well, yessir, I suppose I was. And . . . What? . . . If I was scared, why'd I join up with him? Oh sure, I was just getting to that . . ." Tiberius leaned forward, stretching out his arms behind him to take the pressure of the ropes off his wrists, then sat back, both feet planted on either side of the crate. "The way it come 'bout was when I went to the meetin' place this mornin'. When I got there I was surprised. Wasn't nobody playin' music. Or dancin'. Or carousin'. They was all sittin' together under a tree, and Jemmy was right in the middle. I smelled liquor. I turned round to leave, but Jemmy told me to sit down. They was all starin' at me. 'Bout eighteen field hands. Fellahs you didn't fool with. I'm talkin' 'bout men so tired from that awful work in the rice fields that in the morning some of 'em was so stiff and sore they couldn't bend over to put on their shoes. Men that'd cut you just as soon as look at you. And at one time or another, Jemmy'd either gone heads up with every one of

’em, or backed ’em down, or done somethin’ to make them respect him. I figured, yeah, maybe I better sit down. Once I found a place, Jemmy went back to talkin’. He talked a long *time. Listenin’ to him, I felt maybe like I was in church or somethin’. He was citin’ all the things—horrible things—white people had done. Like cripplin’ runaways. Castratin’ ’em. Pesterin’ the women. Workin’ the field hands ’til they dropped in the water, and all that evil, says Jemmy, was done just so people like Mastah Boswell could have his fresh coffee and grilled fowl every morning. But it didn’t* have *to be that way, Jemmy says. Back in Africa, he knew somethin’ different and he never let it go. And* we *didn’t have to either. I heard him say somethin’ like ‘The enemy of my enemy is my friend.’ He was talkin’ ’bout the Spanish down in Florida. Jemmy said if we struck out together, we could make it to St. Augustine.”*

Tiberius stared past his captors, his eyes narrowing a little, watching something only he could see. “I never thought *about bein’ free ’til then. Never* saw *how things could be different than they was until I listened to Jemmy. Everythin’ looked* changed *after he spoke. Like I’d lived alla my life in a cave, believin’ the shadows I seen were real until Jemmy held up a light and they all melted away. For the first time I could see what things would be like if the best food we had wasn’t leftovers from the mastah’s plate, how I wouldn’t need to tip around all the time, peepin’ and hidin’ and worryin’ ’bout what white folks might be up to. What I’m sayin’ is that if you listened to Jemmy—*really *listened—you come to see that slavery was mad.* Just mad. *We was all like folks in one of them madhouses, black and white, thinkin’ the way we lived and died was the nat’ral ways of things when, from top to bottom, it was crazy as can be.* We *were crazy. I felt like a sleeper. A man who’d been dreamin’ his whole life. But Jemmy woke me hup. And when I looked at the men Jemmy’d brought together, some of ’em wearin’ old shoes fixed up with wire or no shoes at all, I seen they’d follow him anywhere.”*

From outside two rifle shots exploded, shattering the air. Tiberius stopped. Through the barn door he saw two militiamen dragging a black body across the yard. He stood up, taking a hesitant step toward the door. Ethan Whittaker shoved Tiberius back onto the barrel.

"Like I said, Jemmy swore he'd kill me if I told on 'em. I knew they was gonna break into the general store to steal arms and gunpowder, but I swear I didn't know they planned to kill Mr. Bathurst and Mr. Gibbs. Nossir. I let on like I was with 'em, but as soon as I could, I slipped away and come back to the house. I wanted freedom, you know, but I wasn't ready to kill nobody, 'least not on the Sabbath."

Tiberius began coughing from the smell of gunpowder drifting into the barn. Outside, every few moments another Negro was executed by the Carolina militia. He looked at the nearly empty bottle in Colonel Bull's hand and, panting a little, said, "You think I could whet my throat with some of that?" Bull stepped forward, grabbed Tiberius's hair in his left hand, and held the flask to the prisoner's lips with his right. Liquor ran down the sides of Tiberius's mouth. After his last swallow, he clamped shut his eyes as the home brew burned its way down. Then Tiberius sighed, and went on:

"So I knew what they was hup to, yessir. But I wasn't part of it, not at first. When I got to Mastah Boswell's house, it wasn't cold enough to start a fire, so I went right to the smokehouse and got some ham hanging from the rafters, then to the dairyhouse. I took all the fixin's for breakfast back to the kitchen. I didn't see Della. So I started makin' Mastah Boswell's breakfast myself. That took, oh, maybe two hours. Then, just as I was settin' the food on the table, I heard singin' outside. Thought I heard a drum too. Then the back door burst open. All of a sudden, I seen Jemmy and another fellah named Hannibal come flying barefoot through

the dining room, so fast if I'd blinked I woulda missed 'em. Me, I stopped breathin'. I froze right where I was, butterin' a slice a toast, starin' at the ceilin' overhead. It was quiet, quiet, quiet. My head felt light. Didn't a sound breathe through that house until from hupstairs I heard a thump. *Godamercy, they musta cut Mastah Boswell's throat straightaway. Next come his wife screaming. They took their time with her, playin' with her, I reckon. And since I didn't know what else to do—I mean, I was part of this thing now, whether I was ready or not—I sat down at the table, stuck a napkin under my collar, and commenced to eatin' that nice breakfast I put out before it got cold. I figure there wasn't no sense in it goin' to waste, right? 'Bout time I was finishin' my second cup of mint tea, Jemmy and Hannibal come downstairs, blood splattered over 'em like they been to a butcherin'. Hannibal was carryin' Mastah Boswell's head. He put it on the front porch like a Halloween pumpkin . . ."*

Colonel Bull muttered something, then swung the butt of his gun against Tiberius's head, knocking him off the barrel. Hutchenson and Whittaker pulled him off the prisoner, who was bleeding now from a gash on his forehead. Hutchenson helped him back onto the barrel.

"Why'd you'd do that?" Tiberius's head was tucked like a turtle's. He asked Hutchenson, "Why'd he do *that? I been tellin' the truth!" He watched them talking among themselves, whispering, and angrily brought out, "No, I'm* not *lyin'! What's that? What'd he say? Colonel Bull sayin' I tried to drag him off his horse? Oh,* that's *where I remember you from! Well sir, I . . . I ain't callin' you no liar, I wouldn't do* that. *I guess maybe me'n some of the others* did *pull a white man off his horse when he come ridin' down Pon Pon Road . . . but I just got swept hup in the rebellion, that's all."*

They were quiet for a few moments. Hutchenson had that sad look on his face again. Colonel Bull began loading his rifle. Whit-

taker took a step toward Tiberius, who flinched, waiting to be hit again, but all the overseer did was ask a simple question.

"Nossir, Mistah Whittaker, I did not *kill anybody. You know me better'n that. I wouldn't hurt a fly, sir. It's just that, like I was tryin' to tell you, I felt like I'd been sleepin'* all *my life and just woke hup. You a Christian man, right? You understand how it feels when the spirit hits you at meetin' time, like you was blind but suddenly you can see. That's how it was for me. I* was *with them when they left the farm, that's right, and marched over to the Godfrey place, then to the Lemy farm, pickin' up as they went more field hands ready to risk everythin' for just one day of freedom and folks like me, who wanted it too but was used to the old ways and had to be swept along. I reckon Jemmy had an army of over a hundred by the time y'all found our camp. We'd covered ten miles and Jemmy thought maybe he'd brought the whole Province to its knees. Guess that was a mistake, eh?" He tilted his head left to keep the blood trickling from his forehead out of his eyes. "I just want you to know the reason they let so many good white people live—the ones what treated colored folks right—is 'cause I took hup for 'em. That's right."*

"That's enough," said Hutchenson. "You don't have to tell us any more. I understand. I believe in freedom, too." He lifted Tiberius to his feet, gripping his left arm. Whittaker took hold of his right. They began walking him toward the barn door.

"Thank you, Mr. Hutchenson," he said. "I knew *you'd understand. I guess y'all fixin' to let me go now, huh?"*

From the *Gentleman's Magazine* letter:

> The Negroes were soon routed, though they behaved boldly; several being killed on the Spot, many ran back to their Plantations, thinking they had not been missed; but they were then taken and shot; such as were taken in the Field also were, after being examined, shot on the Spot; and this is to be said to the Honour of the Carolina Planters that, notwithstanding the Provocation they had received from so many Murders, they did not torture one Negro, but only put them to an easy Death.

As an enraged militia headed for Charleston, they left the heads of the dead rebels on mileposts along the way.

Although Jemmy's passionate revolt had been quashed, with more time the ragtag army could have doubled or tripled, and the rebellion might have been impossible to control. If that had happened, the white community would have been forced to confront both the moral price of the system and its inherent dangers. And the slaves would have had evidence that slave revolts could succeed.

For whites the lesson of the Stono Rebellion was that the slave population would have to be unconditionally controlled. Freedom of movement, communal gatherings, and learning to write were outlawed by a 1740 slave code.

Some efforts at restriction resulted in moves that seemed compassionate. Attempting to buy slave loyalty, the Assembly guaranteed Sunday as a day off and reduced workdays to fourteen hours during the fall and winter, fifteen hours during growing season. These actions were also designed to make slaves think their situation was improving.

When colonists in New York City heard of the massacre at Stono, their hearts pounded. They knew that it was only a matter of time until their own city erupted. New York City at that time housed the second-largest urban population of Africans in the English colonies. The southern tip of Manhattan Island was home to eleven thousand people, and one in five was enslaved. Only Charleston had a denser slave population.

This was a consequence of the city's direct, almost casual, trade with the West Indies; New Yorkers provided foodstuffs in exchange for slaves from the Caribbean. These slaves were a convenience, not a necessity, and were used primarily for domestic service. Packed into New York City's three square miles, enslaved women, consistently the largest segment of the city's black population, were employed as household servants; African men worked as manservants, stable hands, or drivers, or sometimes as assistants to craftsmen or merchants.

There had been trouble before. In April 1712 in the colony of New York, rebellious slaves torched a building. As the fire raged and spread, enslaved Africans and Indians lay in wait for the whites who came out to extinguish the flames. Before the melee subsided, at least nine white men lost their lives—shot, stabbed, or beaten to death. It was the slaveholder's nightmare, painted in too-vivid colors on the streets of a colonial town.

So white New Yorkers had reason to fear the slaves; they slept warily because of their presence. They imagined the streets running scarlet with the blood of the privileged. Now they believed a larger, more violent uprising was imminent.

The whites in New York were troubled by the strength of young black men, their numbers, their shared language. They were intimidated by the men's tiny rebellions, how they somehow avoided many of the laws meant to control them.

Although the law dictated that slaves were not supposed to be on the streets after sunset, possess money, or gather in numbers greater than three, every night those laws were broken publicly. Control was lax and loosely enforced, granting the slaves a treasured degree of independence.

Many other factors fueled the fear in New York. With England at war with Spain, it would take a fleet of Spanish warships approximately ten days to reach the city from Florida. To the north of New York, the French could cross the Canadian border and invade at any time. In the winter of 1740, New York City was an absolutely miserable place.

The cold siphoned the spirit. Food and firewood were running out. Grain prices had spiraled out of control. A special fund designated for the poor was exhausted. And rumor had it that discontented slaves planned to poison the water. New Yorkers didn't wonder *if* disaster would come. They just wondered when.

It came on the eighteenth of March 1741.

The first building to burn was the governor's residence in Fort George, on the southernmost tip of Manhattan Island. It was also the main military barracks. By the middle of the afternoon, it was nothing more than ash and rubble. The following week, another fire broke out, followed by more than a dozen in the next three weeks. This was no small concern, since New York City, like all colonial towns, was a settlement of wooden structures.

Townspeople suspected arson. They believed that perhaps slaves were setting the fires as an act of revenge or as preface to a larger rebellion. Van Sant's warehouse burned. Gergereau's cow stable. The home of Agnes Hilton. A haystack on Joseph Murray's property.

One particular fire adjoined a residence where a slave lived who belonged to a group known as the Spanish Negroes, sailors who'd been captured aboard a Spanish sloop and sold into slavery while their white shipmates were jailed as prisoners of war. In a petition, the black sailors had threatened to burn the place down if they weren't set free. So after a fire began next door to one of them, all were rounded up and imprisoned.

Soon after, a black man named Cuff Philipse was seen running from another fire, a sure sign for many that the long-feared Negro uprising had begun. In response, almost every African American male over sixteen was hunted down and locked in the city jail. It was time to find out who was at the heart of this wretched insurrection. Punishment had to be swift and sure.

The official investigation was headed by Daniel Horsmanden, a chief court justice in colonial New York. The main witness, sixteen-year-old white indentured servant Mary Burton, worked for tavern and brothel proprietor John Hughson. Hughson's business regularly catered to black customers, in direct violation of the law.

Mary Burton, inspired by a promise of freedom and a payoff of one hundred English pounds, talked. By the time she finished, thirteen blacks had been burned at the stake, eighteen had been hanged, and more than seventy had been banished to the West Indies, Newfoundland, Suriname, and Spain. Mary Burton implicated every black brought into Horsmanden's courtroom, as well as four whites who were also sent to the gallows.

She testified against the slaves Caesar and Prince, who were hanged for the crime of burglary. Cuff and Roosevelt's Quack, convicted of arson and conspiracy, were granted a stay of execution, but a rabid, vengeful mob forced the authorities to kill them anyway. Then Mary Burton testified that her employer, John Hughson, and a prostitute named Peggy Carey were in alliance with the Negroes in their plot to kill every white inhabitant of the city. Hughson; his wife, Sarah; and Peggy Carey were hanged. Hughson's daughter Sarah escaped the same fate by joining Mary Burton to spew allegations.

On July 1, 1741, convinced solely by the highly questionable testimony of Mary Burton, Judge Horsmanden convicted five of the Spanish Negroes. All five were hanged. Other dead and banished included Antonio. Cuba. Cuffee. Africa. Diego. London. Sussex. Jamaica. Quamino. Othello.

Burton then accused English schoolteacher John Ury of being a Jesuit priest in disguise and urging the slaves to violence. On the twenty-ninth of August, Ury was hanged.

The travesty came to an end only when Mary Burton began accusing influential, moneyed New Yorkers. She was then hurriedly paid a hundred pounds, freed from her indenture, and, probably, urged to relocate immediately.

An unknown writer beseeched Dr. Cadwallader Colden of New York's Governor's Council in a letter dated June 23, 1741:

> *[Sir] . . . the horrible executions among you . . . puts me in mind of our New England witchcraft in the year 1692. . . . I am humbly of the opinion that such confessions . . . are not worth a straw; for many times they are obtained by foul means, by force or torment . . . or in hopes of a longer time to live. . . . I entreat you not to go on . . . making bonfires of the negros and . . . loading yourselves with greater guilt than theirs. For we have too much reason to fear that the Divine vengeance does and will pursue us for our ill treatment to the bodies and souls of our poor slaves.*

During 1741 and 1742, some 160 slaves were accused of conspiring against the city of New York. Only seventeen were acquitted.

The message was that colonial Manhattan's blacks had to be brought under stricter control. In his written report on the conspiracy, Judge Horsmanden felt that, given their track record, slaves were likely to revolt again. His vision was of a New York without slaves or slavery, a city that was the exclusive province of white men. He saw ending slavery in the city as the only way to put an end to the shocking interracial carousing that came to light during the trial. It was the only way to stop the development of a society that was strange and frightening.

The "conspiracy" uncovered during the showcase trial was more than likely a tactic to mask growing political unrest in the city. Lieutenant Governor Clarke's administration, between 1736 and 1743, was beset with problems, including a spate of unsolved local crimes and the threat of a Spanish invasion. The "plot of 1741," discovered and punished on a very public stage, convinced residents that a devious Spanish plot, not political ineptness, was to blame for all their woes. Conflicts between political factions were forgotten as the community unified against non-English, non-Protestant "outsiders."

Us. Them. The mind-set was prevalent, pervasive. Nothing could stop the expansion of slavery. By the 1740s, there were over 150,000 slaves in the British North American colonies, approximately one-fifth of the total population. In the years leading up to the Revolution, there was a higher proportion of blacks in the population than at any other time in American history. By the 1750s, an average of five thousand Africans a year were being sold into slavery on American docks.

In 1750, Georgia, the last holdout colony, legalized human bondage. Now there was no place in British America where there were no slaves. The free and captive continued to clash, fighting for the right to America's heartbeat.

> Is not the slave trade entirely at war with the heart of man? And surely that which is begun by breaking down the barriers of virtue, involves in its continuance destruction to every principle, and buries all sentiments in ruin! When you make men slaves, you . . . compel them to live with you in a state of war.
>
> —Olaudah Equiano

PART TWO

Revolution

AMERICA'S DECLARATION OF INDEPENDENCE. *In this draft of the Declaration of Independence, Thomas Jefferson attacked the British involvement in the slave trade, charging that it violated the "most sacred rights of life & liberty." This passage was struck from the final version.*

LIBRARY OF CONGRESS

+ Dr. Franklin

+ abolishing our most valuable ~~important~~ Laws

for taking away our charters ^ & altering fundamentally the forms of our governments;

for suspending our own legislatures & declaring themselves invested with power to legislate for us in all cases whatsoever:

he has abdicated government here, [withdrawing his governors, & declaring us out of his allegiance & protection:] (by declaring us out of his protection & waging war against us.)

he has plundered our seas, ravaged our coasts, burnt our towns & destroyed the lives of our people:

he is at this time transporting large armies of Scotch and other foreign mercenaries to compleat the works of death, desolation & tyranny, already begun with circumstances of cruelty & perfidy scarcely paralleled in the most barbarous ages, and totally unworthy the head of a civilized nation:

he has excited domestic insurrections amongst us, and has endeavored to bring on the inhabitants of our frontiers the merciless Indian savages, whose known rule of warfare is an undistinguished destruction of all ages, sexes, & conditions [of existence:]

[he has incited treasonable insurrections of our fellow-citizens, with the allurements of forfeiture & confiscation of our property.

he has constrained [illegible] to become the executioners of their friends & brethren [illegible]

he has waged cruel war against human nature itself, violating it's most sacred rights of life & liberty in the persons of a distant people who never offended him, captivating & carrying them into slavery in another hemisphere, or to incur miserable death in their transportation thither. this piratical warfare, the opprobrium of *infidel* powers, is the warfare of the Christian king of Great Britain. determined to keep open a market where MEN should be bought & sold, he has prostituted his negative for suppressing every legislative attempt to prohibit or to restrain this ~~determining to keep open a market where MEN should be bought & sold:~~ execrable commerce: and that this assemblage of horrors might want no fact of distinguished die, he is now exciting those very people to rise in arms among us, and to purchase that liberty of which *he* has deprived them, by murdering the people upon whom *he* also obtruded them: thus paying off former crimes committed against the *liberties* of one people, with crimes which he urges them to commit against the *lives* of another.]

+ Dr. Franklin

in every stage of these oppressions we have petitioned for redress in the most humble terms; our repeated petitions have been answered ^only by repeated injuries. a prince whose character is thus marked by every act which may define a tyrant, is unfit to be the ruler of a free people [who mean to be free. future ages will scarce believe that the hardiness of one man, adventured within the short compass of twelve years only, to build a foundation so broad & undisguised, for tyranny over a people fostered & fixed in principles of ~~liberty~~ freedom.]

James Armistead Lafayette, oil, c. 1824. *Many Africans held in bondage in the United States seized eagerly on the Declaration's language of freedom and equality. When war broke out, hundreds of African Americans, like James Armistead, showed up at patriot camps to join the fight for liberty. James enlisted under General Lafayette and won the French general's praise for his work as a master spy. As a result, James was granted his freedom by the Virginia Assembly, and he adopted Lafayette's name for his own.*

THE GRANGER COLLECTION, NEW YORK

George Washington at Princeton, Charles Willson Peale, 1779. *Distinguished veteran of the French and Indian War, George Washington was chosen to lead the campaign for American independence in 1775. Washington was a southerner and a slave owner, and it was hoped his presence would ensure southern support for what had started out as a New England war.*

132

To the Honorable Council & House of Representatives for the State of Massachusetts-Bay, in General Court assembled January 13th 1777 —

The Petition of a great number of Negroes who are detained in a State of Slavery, in the Bowels of a free & Christian Country — Humbly shewing —

That your Petitioners apprehend that they have, in common with all other Men, a natural & unalienable right to that freedom, which the great Parent of the Universe hath bestowed equally on all Mankind & which they have never forfeited by any compact or agreement whatever — But they were unjustly dragged, by the cruel hand of Power, from their dearest friends & some of them even torn from the Embraces of their tender Parents — From a populous, pleasant & plentiful Country — & in Violation of the Laws of Nature & of Nations & in defiance of all the tender feelings of humanity, brought hither to be sold like Beasts of Burthen, & like them condemned to slavery for Life — Among a People professing the mild Religion of Jesus — A People not insensible of the sweets of rational freedom — Nor without spirit to resent the unjust endeavours of others to reduce them to a State of Bondage & Subjection — Your Honors need not to be informed that a Life of Slavery, like that of your petitioners, deprived of every social privilege, of every thing requisite to render Life even tolerable, is far worse than Non-Existence — In imitation of the laudable example of the good People of these States, your Petitioners have long & patiently waited the event of Petition after Petition by them presented to the Legislative Body of this State, & can not but with grief reflect that their success has been but too similar — They can not but express their astonishment, that it has never been considered, that every principle from which America has acted in the course of their unhappy difficulties with Great-Britain, pleads stronger than a thousand arguments in favor of your Petitioners — They therefore humbly beseech your Honors, to give this Petition its due weight & consideration & cause an Act of the Legislature to be passed whereby they may be restored to the enjoyment of that freedom which is the natural right of all Men — & their Children (who were born in this Land of Liberty) may not be held as Slaves after they arrive at the age of twenty one Years — So may the Inhabitants of this State (no longer chargeable with the inconsistency of acting, themselves, the part which they condemn & oppose in others) be prospered in their present glorious struggles for Liberty; & have those blessings secured to them by Heaven, of which benevolent minds can not wish to deprive their fellow Men. —

And your Petitioners, as in duty bound shall ever pray —

PETITION OF A GREAT NUMBER OF NEGROES, 1777. *This slave petition appeared just months after the Declaration of Independence was published. It called on the American patriots to live up to their proclamation and ensure "life, liberty and the pursuit of happiness" to all Americans.*

By His Excellency the Right Honorable JOHN Earl of DUNMORE, His MAJESTY's Lieutenant and Governor General of the Colony and Dominion of VIRGINIA, and Vice Admiral of the ſame.

A PROCLAMATION.

AS I have ever entertained Hopes that an Accommodation might have taken Place between GREAT-BRITAIN and this Colony, without being compelled by my Duty to this moſt diſagreeable but now abſolutely neceſſary Step, rendered ſo by a Body of armed Men unlawfully aſſembled, firing on His MAJESTY's Tenders, and the formation of an Army, and that Army now on their March to attack His MAJESTY's Troops and deſtroy the well diſpoſed Subjects of this Colony. To defeat ſuch treaſonable Purpoſes, and that all ſuch Traitors, and their Abetters, may be brought to Juſtice, and that the Peace, and good Order of this Colony may be again reſtored, which the ordinary Courſe of the Civil Law is unable to effect; I have thought fit to iſſue this my Proclamation, hereby declaring, that until the aforeſaid good Purpoſes can be obtained, I do in Virtue of the Power and Authority to ME given, by His MAJESTY, determine to execute Martial Law, and cauſe the ſame to be executed throughout this Colony: and to the end that Peace and good Order may the ſooner be effected, I do require every Perſon capable of bearing Arms, to reſort to His MAJESTY's STANDARD, or be looked upon as Traitors to His MAJESTY's Crown and Government, and thereby become liable to the Penalty the Law inflicts upon ſuch Offences; ſuch as forfeiture of Life, confiſcation of Lands, &c. &c. And I do hereby further declare all indented Servants, Negroes, or others, (appertaining to Rebels,) free that are able and willing to bear Arms, they joining His MAJESTY's Troops as ſoon as may be, for the more ſpeedily reducing this Colony to a proper Senſe of their Duty, to His MAJESTY's Crown and Dignity. I do further order, and require, all His MAJESTY's Leige Subjects, to retain their Quitrents, or any other Taxes due or that may become due, in their own Cuſtody, till ſuch Time as Peace may be again reſtored to this at preſent moſt unhappy Country, or demanded of them for their former ſalutary Purpoſes, by Officers properly authoriſed to receive the ſame.

GIVEN under my Hand on board the Ship WILLIAM, off NORFOLK, the 7th Day of NOVEMBER, in the SIXTEENTH Year of His MAJESTY's Reign.

DUNMORE.

(GOD ſave the KING.)

LORD DUNMORE'S PROCLAMATION. *At the same time that General Washington was officially barring further enlistment by black men in the American army, John Murray, Earl of Dunmore and Royal Governor of Virginia, issued a proclamation promising freedom to all Indians, rebel-owned Negroes, and indentured servants willing to fight for the British.*

THE LIBRARY OF VIRGINIA

PASS GIVEN TO A BLACK LOYALIST, 1783. *Some slaves were given their freedom and passage to Nova Scotia or Sierra Leone in exchange for their military service to the British crown during the Revolution. Many more, however, were returned to their owners after the war.*

NOVA SCOTIA ARCHIVES & RECORDS MANAGEMENT

NEW-YORK, 21st April 1783.

THIS is to certify to whomſoever it may concern, that the Bearer hereof Cato Ramsay a Negro, reſorted to the Britiſh Lines, in conſequence of the Proclamations of Sir William Howe, and Sir Henry Clinton, late Commanders in Chief in America; and that the ſaid Negro has hereby his Excellency Sir Guy Carleton's Permiſſion to go to Nova-Scotia, or wherever elſe He may think proper.

By Order of Brigadier General Birch,

(73)

Negroes Names	Age	Description	Remarks
Sally York	18 Months	Likely [illegible]	Daughter to Betsey York and born within the British lines
Richard Swan	22	Stout fellow	Formerly the Property of John Willoughby of Norfolk Virginia, left him seven years ago G. B.
Sally Dennis	20	Stout Wench	Formerly the Property of Lucas Burrell of Williamsburgh Virginia, left him two years ago Ditto
Wm. Dennis	19 months	Likely Child	Son to Sally Dennis and born within the British lines
Peter Plestrin	22	Stout fellow	Formerly the Property of William Wilder of Summerset County Maryland, left him three years ago Ditto
Henry Herrington	40	Ditto	Formerly the Property of Joseph Blake of Charlestown South Carolina, left him five years ago Ditto
Sally Herrington	35	Stout Wench	Formerly the Property of Smith McKenzie of Savannah Georgia, left him five years ago Ditto
George Talbot	36	Stout fellow	Formerly the Property of Solomon Talbot of Norfolk Virginia, left him five years ago Ditto
Susannah Talbot	37	Stout Wench	Formerly the Property of Bayley Guy of Norfolk Virginia, left him four years ago Ditto
Amos Talbot	13	Fine Boy	Formerly the Property of Thomas Bate of Norfolk Virginia, left him four years ago Ditto
James Hallstead	63	Feeble fellow	Formerly the Property of Samuel Hallstead of Norfolk County Virginia, left him seven years ago Ditto
Sally Hallstead	60	Feeble Wench	Formerly the Property of Edward Mosely of Princess Ann County Virginia, left him seven years ago Ditto
George Small	10	Fine Boy	Ditto Ditto Ditto
Jane Milligan	20	Stout Wench	Formerly the Property of James Johnson of Savannah Georgia, left him two years ago Ditto
Maria Milligan	9 months	Healthy Child	Daughter to Jane Milligan and born within the British lines
Abby Brown	30	Stout Wench	Formerly the Property of John Willoughby of Norfolk County Virginia, left him seven years ago Ditto
William Patrick	12	Fine Boy	Ditto Ditto Ditto
Dinah Brown	3	Likely Child	Daughter to Abby Brown and born within the British lines
Venus Miller	24	Stout Wench	Formerly the Property of John Whitten of Norfolk County Virginia, left him four years ago
Betsey Herbert	26	Ditto	Formerly the Property Robert Brown of Norfolk County Virginia, left him three years ago
Jenny Herbert	6	Fine Child	Ditto Ditto Ditto
Lancaster Herbert	10	Fine Boy	Ditto Ditto Ditto
Peter Herbert	28	Stout Fellow	Formerly the Property of John Whitten of Norfolk Virginia, left him three years ago
Rose Stewart	25	Stout Wench	Formerly the Property of Thomas Brown of Portsmouth Virginia, left him four years ago
Mary White	21	Ditto	She says she was born free and produces General Birch's Certificate, she came from Virginia three years ago
Jane Parks	65	Feeble Wench	Formerly the Property of Jonathan Parks of Norfolk Virginia, left him seven years ago
Francis Jones	42	Stout fellow	Formerly the Property of Thomas Moody of Charles City Virginia, left him three years ago
Philip Gordon	23	Ditto	Formerly the Property of George Gordon of Nancy [illegible] Virginia, left him three years ago
Priscilla Gordon	20	Stout Wench	Formerly the Property of Willis Wilkinson of Charlestown South Carolina, left him five years ago
Stephen Bluckie	31	Stout fellow	Says he was born free in the Island of Barbadoes and produces General Birch's Certificate
Margaret Bluckie	40	Stout Wench	Says she was born free in Mr. Courtney's Family of N. York & bought her freedom fourteen years ago
Isabel Gibbins	20	Likely Girl	Margaret Bluckie purchased her of Mr. Courtney's Daughter & gave her freedom
Benjn. Heolin	50	Stout fellow	Formerly the Property of John Heolin of Elizabeth Town New Jersey, left him seven years ago
Nancy Brown	13	Stout Girl	Formerly the Property of Mathew Phelps of Norfolk Virginia, left him six years ago
Peter Johnson	30	Stout fellow	Formerly the Property of Robert Moore of Philadelphia, left him six years ago
Betsey Johnson	32	Stout Wench	She produces a certificate of freedom from Margaret Gilroie her former Mistress
Peter Johnson	4	Fine Child	Ditto Ditto Ditto Ditto
Betsey Johnson	2	Ditto	Ditto Ditto Ditto Ditto
York Lawrence	30	Stout fellow	Formerly the Property of Katharine Lawrence of Albany Beaver of N. York, left her six years ago
Dinah Lawrence	26	Likely Wench	Formerly the Property of Peter Stanethorn of New York, left him six years ago
Betsey Lawrence	3	Fine Child	Daughter to Dinah Lawrence and born within the British lines
Gabriel Lawrence	8 Months	Ditto	Son Ditto Ditto Ditto
Martha Johns	32	Stout fellow	Formerly the Property of John Taliaferro of Philadelphia, left him five years ago

BOOK OF NEGROES. A register, known as the Book of Negroes, *listed three thousand black Americans who evacuated with the British from New York at the end of the war—1,336 men, 914 women, and 750 children. Some would finally return to African shores.*

MUM BETT, PICTURED IN 1811. *Elizabeth Freeman, known as Mum Bett, was one of nearly 700,000 enslaved Americans during the Revolution. In 1781, she petitioned the state of Massachusetts and won her freedom. Her case was based on Massachusetts's Declaration of Rights, which pronounced that "all people were born free and equal."*

COURTESY, MASSACHUSETTS HISTORICAL SOCIETY

List of Negro Men & Boys, also their ages & Value

Names	Ages	Full Hands	Half Hands	Value		Remarks
Perry-Driver	40 Years	1"	"	900	00	disposed to meddle with women
Old Daniel	70 "		1/2	100	00	old and decriped
John Miller	28 "	Full Hand		600	00	a Runaway
Jim Bassy	25 "	"		600	00	Sickly
Claiborn West	28 "	"		800	00	good Negro
Jack Page	35 "	"		700	00	has Runaway
Claiborn Anderson	35 "	dead "		400	00	has Runaway
Orange	38 "	"		800	00	good Hand
Anderson. M	25 "	"		800	00	good Negro
Bob. Scooner	28 "	"		700	00	well disposed but Slow
Izor M	45 "	"		500	00	African, good but Slow
George. M.	25 "	"		600	00	a Cooper, Sickly but good
Jim Wilbot	45 "	dead "		400	00	a Runaway no account
Carter Allen	23 "	"		400	00	a Runaway, very Slow
Charles. Mena	45 "	"		500	00	African, verry good
Randle	45 "	"		800	00	Sugar Maker, good hand
Edmond	40 "	"		600	00	A great drunkard
Sam Williams	25 "	"		600	00	A good hand
Gallant	45 "	"		500	00	Rather trifling, but will do
Old Mat. M.	35 "		1/2	300	00	Sickly Consumptive
Bill Kenty	45 "	"		700	00	good hand
Fleming	45 "	"		400	00	a Runaway
Jefferson	38 "	"		800	00	Superior Hand
Simond carpenter	45 "	"		800	00	the greatest rascal on Plantation
				14300	00	

INVENTORY OF NEGROES ON A VIRGINIA PLANTATION. *For many of those who remained enslaved in the United States, the end of the war meant returning to work. Large plantation owners often kept detailed inventories of their human property, listing their slaves' ages, values, and brief descriptions.*

BRUCE FAMILY PAPERS (#2692), SPECIAL COLLECTIONS DEPARTMENT, UNIVERSITY OF VIRGINIA LIBRARY

LIFE IN THE SLAVE QUARTERS, 1800. *Large plantations offered the slave the best opportunity at community life and the most freedom from the oversight of masters. Since the average week's work lasted six days, most social activities, like weddings or dances, took place in the quarters on Saturday nights and Sundays.*

ABBY ALDRICH ROCKEFELLER FOLK ART CENTER, WILLIAMSBURG, VIRGINIA

POEMS ON VARIOUS SUBJECTS, PUBLISHED IN 1773. *As the slave of a Boston merchant, Phillis Wheatley lived a relatively isolated life. Wheatley was, however, encouraged by her mistress to pursue her talents as a writer and published her first poem when she was about sixteen years old.*
LIBRARY OF CONGRESS

ATLEY, NEGRO SERVANT to M^r. JOHN WHEATLEY, of BOSTON.

blished according to Act of Parliament, Sept. 1. 1773 by Arch.d Bell, Bookseller N.o 8 near the Saracens Head Aldgate.

P O E M S
ON
VARIOUS SUBJECTS,
RELIGIOUS AND MORAL.
BY
PHILLIS WHEATLEY,
NEGRO SERVANT to Mr. JOHN WHEATLEY, of BOSTON, in NEW ENGLAND.

LONDON:
Printed for A. BELL, Bookseller, Aldgate; and fold by Messrs. COX and BERRY, King-Street, BOSTON.
MDCCLXXIII.

ABIGAIL ADAMS. *Abigail Adams, wife of John Adams, the second president of the United States, was an outspoken advocate for women's rights and the abolition of slavery. The slaves, she once wrote, "have as good a right to freedom as we have."*

GILBERT STUART, *ABIGAIL SMITH ADAMS (MRS. JOHN ADAMS)*, GIFT OF MRS. ROBERT HOMANS, NATIONAL GALLERY OF ART, WASHINGTON, D.C.

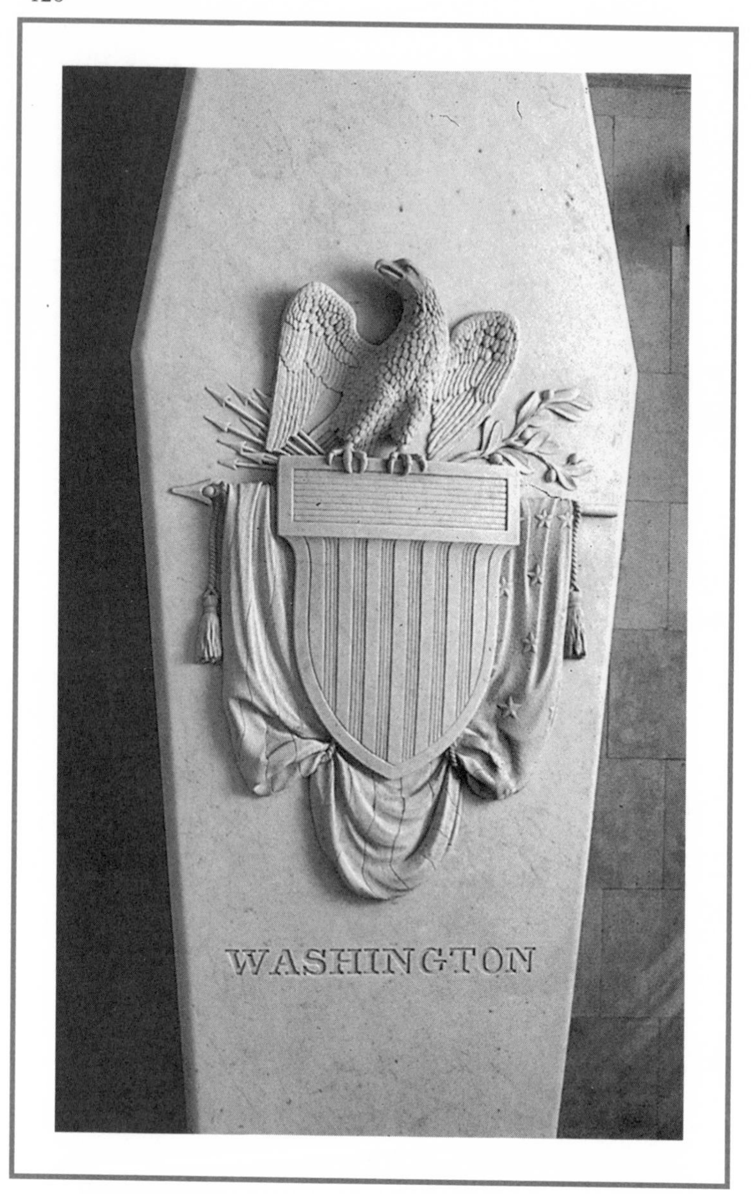

George Washington's tomb. *Late in his life, George Washington expressed strong misgivings about the institution of slavery. When he died on December 14, 1799, his final will stipulated that upon his wife's death the slaves that he owned outright would be free.*

COURTESY OF THE MOUNT VERNON LADIES' ASSOCIATION

VENTURE SMITH'S FINAL RESTING PLACE. *Venture Smith was one of a growing number of slaves freed by their own labor in the North. By the early nineteenth century, in fact, the number of free people of color in the northern states was slowly overtaking the number of slaves.*

PHOTO BY KEVIN TULIMIERI, COURTESY OF *HOMETOWN NEWS* PUBLICATIONS, © 1998

CHAPTER FOUR

I remember this place. . . . I was born at Dukandarra, in Guinea, about the year 1729. . . . [A] large river runs through this country . . . and great dews fall in the night.
—VENTURE SMITH

IN THE MID–EIGHTEENTH century, America was home to a new generation of the privileged and the captive. Now homes dotting the landscape and crowding the cities were permanent fixtures. Families touted their bloodlines. For some, the nation was still a land of opportunity. For the enslaved still arriving from Africa, it was a land of questions.

The child Broteer was only eight years old. In Guinea, West Africa, the comfortable place where he was celebrated and treasured, those who loved him believed he would grow to be a prince like his father. But Broteer's future was shaped by other hands.

> The army of the enemy was large, I should suppose consisting of about six thousand men. . . . [T]hey were instigated by some white nation who equipped and sent them to subdue and possess the country. . . . I then had a rope put about my neck. . . . [A]fter destroying the old prince, they decamped and immediately they marched [us] toward the sea.

One of thousands of slaves brought to North America in the 1730s, the child was kidnapped and thrust into a world of violence he had not lived long enough to understand. He had been part of a place of perfect colors, a world that fit him, a place that seemed crafted for his comfort. The soft cocoon of family seemed forever. Then there was war, and that world was ripped open. The gaping maw revealed itself. And the child was swallowed.

Broteer, a human child with limitless potential, was sold for four gallons of rum and a snippet of calico cloth. His new owner, Robertson Mumford, called him Venture "on account of him having purchased me with his own private venture." So the child Broteer was lost and the man Venture began. He lived to dictate *A Narrative of the Life and Adventures of Venture, a Native of Africa,* which allows us to live most of his story.

Broteer arrived on these shores in 1737. The colonies were a fresh and unsullied canvas, a chance for Europeans to wipe out personal history and start anew. While less than a quarter of the white population owned slaves, the African trade created a bustling economy directly linked to iron production, shipbuilding, sawmills, and distilleries.

What mattered was becoming an American.

A man could start over, become whatever he yearned to be. Even if he had crossed the sea belowdecks as an indentured servant, already bound to the New World for five to seven years, he could hope that there were other things waiting there for him to believe in.

George Haworth touted his new home. "It is a great deal better living here than in England. . . . So if any of my relations have a mind to come to this country, I think it is a very good country and that they may do well, but be sure to come free."

During the 1730s, 45,000 European colonists came to North America. Venture Smith, who began his American adventure in Rhode Island, was one of almost 41,000 Africans transported to the colonies during the same decade.

As a youth Venture "was pretty much employed in the house carding wool and other household business. . . . My behavior had as yet been submissive and obedient. I then began to have hard tasks imposed on me . . . or be rigorously punished. . . . These tasks I had to perform when only about nine years old." In his teens, Venture grew stronger in both mind and body. He began to resent those who sought control over him, particularly his master's son James who "came up to me . . . big with authority," and "would order me to do *this* business and *that* business different from what my master had directed me."

Tension between the two young men escalated until one day young Mumford attacked Venture with a pitchfork. The slave clearly dominated the ensuing battle, sending the boy home in tears. James Mumford never raised his hand to Venture again.

Victories of that kind were small and infrequent. For Venture Smith and his fellow Africans, the American promise was bleak and foreboding—it meant a lifetime of labor.

In New England, money from the slave trade fed several thriving industries, such as the building of seaworthy vessels. Although most New Englanders did not own slaves, the region was heavily involved in the system. Their molasses profit came from slave labor in the West Indies, and the fish they caught went south to feed the slaves working the plantations.

In the South, the wretched institution was woven into the very fabric of life. In Virginia, men who were not yet men could become slave owners. It was not uncommon for children to own other children. From the time he was eleven years old, George Washington owned human beings, left to him by his father.

> I, Augustine Washington . . . being sick and weak but of perfect . . . sense and memory, do make my last Will and Testament in the manner following . . .
>
> I give unto my son Lawrence Washington and his heirs forever, all that Plantation and Tract of Land at Hunting Creek . . . all the slaves, Cattle and Stocke of all kinds whatsoever.
>
> I give unto my daughter Betty a Negro child named Mary Daughter of Sue and another named Betty Daughter of Judy.
>
> I give unto my son George Washington and his heirs the Land I now Live on, which I purchased . . . and ten Negro slaves.

Young George Washington was perfectly comfortable with the idea of Negroes as property. For as long as he'd been aware of their presence, there was absolutely no reason to consider slaves any further than the purpose they served—tending the tobacco crop, feeding his family, making sure his genteel southern life ran like clockwork. They were simply an inescapable part of his surroundings. His parents, grandparents, and older brothers were slave owners.

The shy, awkward teenager had less than a year of formal schooling. In order to become a proper Virginia gentleman, he took fencing and dancing lessons, but throughout his long and accomplished life, he would be embarrassed by what he called his "defective education." His model was his brother Lawrence, fourteen years older, dashing, sophisticated, and educated in England.

George Washington's family was not entrenched in the upper echelons of Virginia society. Educated as a land surveyor, George knew early in life that a comfortable, well-to-do lifestyle was not inherent in his birthright. When his father died, George was left with property—but not too much property; slaves—but only a few.

When his brother Lawrence died prematurely, George came to own their father's estate, Mount Vernon. He set about transforming the home into a genteel country dwelling, and he dressed as English aristocracy would. Although he seemed to be destined for political power and comfortable social standing, Washington knew hard work was ahead if he wanted to make a name for himself and build a life that mattered.

Washington set out to build that life. And in the South, accumulating wealth meant accumulating slaves.

> *Dear Sir:*
> *. . . I will take six or more negroes . . . if you can spare such, upon the terms offered in your letter. . . . If you agree to it, and will appoint a time, I would send for them, relying on your word that the whole are healthy and none of them addicted to running away. The latter I abominate; and unhealthy negroes, women or children, would not suit my purpose on any terms.*

Venture Smith would have suited Washington's purpose. He was a broad, hulking, charismatic young man with a reputation as an indefatigable worker. At twenty-two, six feet one inch and tipping the scales at 250 pounds plus, he was both a formidable presence and nearly a foot taller than most men of this time. He was a prime hand, broad and muscled, with a back strong enough to carry the weight of the world. A farmhand and carpenter by day, Venture toiled for himself once the sun went down, selling whatever fish and game he caught. During those times when his work and his time were his own, Venture Smith began to craft a dream of freedom. And he set out to build that life.

Before he reached twenty-three, Venture stole a boat and fled with an Irishman named Heddy and two other white indentured servants. He left his wife, Meg, and their unborn child behind. The ragtag group, fueled by provisions stolen from their master's home, "promised not to betray or desert one another on pain of death." They steered across the sound toward Montauk Point, on the east end of New York's Long Island.

On the shores of Long Island, Heddy deceived the fugitives, pilfering their meager supplies and stealing away on his own. Venture, who had trusted and believed, was heartsick. Before he could be hunted down and punished, he returned voluntarily to his owner, Robertson Mumford. Freedom had been sweet, but fleeting. Perhaps he believed that there was a way to work through the system, become a free man by standing strong instead of continuing to live as a fugitive. The following year Venture was sold to Thomas Stanton.

In 1752, Venture's daughter Hannah was born, the property of Thomas Stanton. She and other children born in America would not know an Africa. They would not be wrapped in the comforting cloth of family and tradition. They would not feel a link to a faraway home or long for a freedom that they could remember. None of these children had ever been free.

In the eighteenth-century American colonies, married women spent most of their lives with child, impregnated every eighteen months to two years. Slave women, in addition to the mental and physical toil required of their station, had to carry and bear children in order to replenish and strengthen the supply of plantation labor.

There was a bittersweet irony in giving birth to a child you could never really call your own. While an enslaved mother could gaze lovingly upon her child and see a wriggling bundle, ten toes and ten fingers and a wild halo of shiny black hair, the slave owner would look at the same child and envision another body bent double in the fields, another pair of hands in the kitchen—in time, another pathway to profit.

In many plantation households, mistress and slave were often pregnant at the same time. If the white woman was unable or unwilling to nurse, the slave woman nursed the child of her owner. And as the white child suckled at her breast and drew life from it, the slave was tortured by the knowledge that the child she nurtured owned both her and her newborn utterly and completely. The white child could grow to separate the slave mother and her child, sell one from the other, demean and humiliate them, dispense lashes from the whip. He was born with that power. And by offering him her milk, the slave woman helped him become more powerful.

If the slave woman had given birth to a girl, it pained her to know that the child would grow to be pursued, possibly sexually exploited. There were no laws to protect the children, and plantation life revolved around the wants and needs of the male slave owner.

Harriet Jacobs, in her nineteenth-century slave narrative, peeled back the layers of a mother's heart to show the peculiar torment of knowing that her infant son had been born a slave.

> When I was most sorely oppressed I found solace in his smiles. I loved to watch his infant slumbers; but . . . I could never forget that he was a slave. Sometimes I wished that he might die in infancy. God tried me. My darling became very ill.
>
> I had prayed for his death, but never so earnestly as now I prayed for his life; and my prayer was heard. Alas, what mockery it is for a slave mother to try to pray back her dying child to life! Death is better than slavery.

The relationship between mistress and female slave was by nature potentially volatile, often teetering on the brink of eruption. Many people on both sides of the racial divide were questioning the boundaries of authority, the boundaries of servitude. A household that utilized slave labor was the perfect battleground for a test of wills.

Venture Smith's real journey to freedom began with a heated exchange between his wife, Meg, and her mistress while the master of the house was away from the farm. "When I entered the house," said Venture, "I found my mistress in a violent passion with my wife."

Meg Smith spoke her mind. The mistress didn't like what she heard. The women went toe-to-toe.

Venture begged his wife to retreat—but in the midst of his peacemaking efforts, his mistress turned her blows on him. He grabbed the whip from her hand and tossed it into the nearby fire.

> When my master returned . . . he seemed to take no notice of it, and mentioned not a word of it to me. Some days after . . . in the morning as I was putting on a log in the fireplace, not suspecting harm from anyone, I re-

> ceived a most violent stroke on the crown of my head with a club two feet long and as large around as a chair post.

Although he was surprised by the attack, Venture soon got the upper hand. He threw Stanton to the ground and gave him a beating.

Then Venture Smith did the unthinkable. He contacted a Connecticut justice of the peace and accused his holder of abusing him. Although the justice expressed regret at the news of the slave's treatment, he told Venture that there was nothing he could do because Venture was not considered a man. He had no rights. He was property.

After coming to collect Venture, the Stanton brothers began to beat the slave. Venture fought back, and eventually overwhelmed the men. The town constable was summoned, and a blacksmith fitted Venture with a pair of iron shackles as if Venture were an animal who simply needed to learn reason.

> I continued to wear the chain peaceably for two or three days. . . . [N]ot anyone said much to me, until one Hempstead Miner of Stonington asked me if I would live with him. . . . and that in return he would give me a good chance to gain my freedom.
>
> I answered that I would.

But soon after, Hempstead Miner sold Venture to a Colonel Smith of Hartford, Connecticut. Smith, too, promised that Venture could earn his freedom. For five years, Venture slaved for the colonel and hired himself out on his own time, managing to save small amounts of money.

At age thirty-six, Venture Smith paid the good colonel seventy-one pounds and two shillings—roughly the cost of four thousand acres of land—and twenty-eight years after being kidnapped from his African home, he was a free man.

> I left Colonel Smith once more for all. I had already been sold three different times . . . had been cheated out of a large sum of money, lost much by misfortunes, and paid an enormous sum for my freedom.

Venture Smith finally owned what mattered most—the right to his own life. He was free. Free was a skip in the heartbeat, a lightness to the bones, a giddy scream into a vast, welcoming sky. Gaining freedom was like having a new body built over the old. What mattered was this first, not second, chance. It was not uncommon for the newly freed slaves to give all thanks to God and devote themselves to living a Christian life. There had to be someone to thank continually for the miracle of Free.

Venture Smith, free man, bought a boat and worked hauling goods along the waterways. There was work to be done. His wife, daughter, and two sons were still in slavery and he wouldn't rest until he obtained their freedom. He wanted to build a life with all of his family at his side. He'd seen the American promise. He wanted that, and more.

By the middle of the eighteenth century, *more* was the operative word. Expectations in the colonies were high. Slavery had granted some financial rewards, and colonists began to search for a deeper meaning in that prosperity.

They began to reconsider their relationship with God.

Slave owners had turned a suspicious eye toward Anglican instruction of their slaves. Missionaries taught writing and reading and spoke freely of an equality in spiritual terms. Not only did this eagerly absorbed education detract from the constant, unquestioning labor the slave owner demanded, it also contributed to the development of literate black leaders. Some were religious leaders.

Fiery evangelical ministers traveled the colonies, preaching a gospel that shattered the crusty tenets of Anglicanism and rattled the haughty stability of the upper class. They taught that God was nearby, involved daily in the lives of those who toiled in his name. He controlled thought, he controlled action.

Slaves and poor whites gathered around the idea of spiritual parity, and the movement toward this new gospel became known as the Great Awakening. They rallied around the concept of a God who saw and listened to their suffering, one who might reach out any minute to release them. This God had their interests at heart when it seemed no one else did. And an evangelical message didn't need time to sink in—if it was powerful enough, it could instantly change anyone who heard it.

Thousands, black and white together, would gather and listen to preachers map a new road to deliverance. David George was among the believers who followed that road to a prayer service in the woods of Georgia:

> I lived a bad life and had no ferious thoughts about my foul; . . . I could not read, and had no fcriptures. Soon after, I heard brother George Liele preach. . . . His fermon was very fuitable on "Come unto me all ye that labor and are heavy laden and I will give you reft."
>
> Indeed, his whole discourfe feemed for me.

George was born on a Virginia plantation in 1742. As he came of age, he was repelled by the way a particularly brutish master treated his family:

> Our master's name was Chapel—a very bad man to the Negroes. My older sister was called Patty; I have seen her several times so whipped that her back has been all corruption, as though it would rot. . . . [T]he greatest grief I then had was to see them whip my mother, and to hear her, on her knees, begging for mercy.

George escaped at nineteen and settled along the Savannah River, where he was captured by the Creek Indians and again placed in servitude. His former master's son tracked him there and bought him for "rum, linnen and a gun." But before he could be returned to the cruelty that sparked his escape, George fled to the Natchez Indians, whose chief soon sold him to a white trader named George Galphin. While in Galphin's employ, at Silver Bluff near the Savannah River, David George stumbled upon the prayer meeting and found God.

> [A] man of my own color, named Cyrus, who came from Charlefton, South Carolina, to Silver Bluff, told me one day in the woods, That if I lived so, I should never see the face of God in glory. . . . I did not think of Adam and Eve's fin, but *I* was fin. I felt my *own* plague; . . . I felt myfelf at the difpofal of Sovereign mercy. At laft in prayer to God I began to think that he would deliver me.

The occasion so moved him that he taught himself to read and eventually became a preacher himself.

> I went to a fwamp and poured out my heart before the Lord. I then came back to Brother George Liele, and

> told him my cafe. . . . It gave me great relief, and I went home with a defire for nothing elfe but to talk to the brothers and fifters about the Lord.

Christianity reminded slaves of their humanity. But slaveholders didn't want the missionaries circulating among the slaves, changing their outlooks on their situation. Baptism was a step up, a step away from. It taught the slave more about himself and his place in this world, and that was a knowledge the white man could not afford.

By the mid-1750s, one in every five Americans was a slave—nearly 300,000 out of a total population of a million and a half. And five thousand new captives arrived from Africa or the Caribbean each year. "The custom of the country is such," a Baptist minister wrote, "that without slaves, a man's children stand but a poor chance to marry in reputation."

On the frigid January day in 1759 when Martha Dandridge Custis, probably the wealthiest widow in the colony of Virginia, married for the second time, she married "in reputation." As custom and law dictated, she surrendered control of all property she owned to her new husband—military standout, French and Indian War veteran, budding politico, promising planter on the verge of aristocracy—George Washington.

Like Venture Smith, Washington was powerfully built, and a foot taller than the average man. He was also one of the most graceful horsemen in Virginia. His marriage catapulted the ambitious Washington into the upper tier of Virginia society.

That fall, Washington pinned his hopes on his tobacco

crop, transporting it to England to be appraised and sold. Tobacco was still the crop that built men's fortunes. But the harvest, judged inferior, did not command a good price—and in two years' time, Washington was 1,900 pounds in debt. And since riches defined the man, Washington was losing sight of the man he wanted to be.

And the liberated Venture Smith was almost the man he'd dreamed of being. But he was not complete. Although he was free, his wife and children were still enslaved, and beginning in 1765, the former captive worked feverishly to free his family: "In four years, I cut several thousand cords of wood. . . . I raised watermelons, and performed many other singular labors."

Venture "shunned all kind of luxuries" and "bought nothing that I absolutely did not want" until he and his wife accumulated both coin and paper money. In 1768, he bought his two sons, Solomon and Cuff, perhaps believing that profits from their labor as free men would more quickly help secure the purchase of his wife and daughter.

But Venture's dream of liberating his family took a tragic turn in 1773 when his eldest son, Solomon, hired out to a Rhode Island ship's captain for one year, died of scurvy during a whaling voyage. That same year Venture paid forty pounds for Meg's freedom. He worked feverishly for the money, since Meg was pregnant at the time. And he could only afford to buy one life.

The Smiths named their new son Solomon, in honor of the child they had lost.

For some blacks, the quest for freedom was urgent and lyrical, a song constantly sung.

Should you, my lord, while you peruse my song,
Wonder from whence my love of freedom *sprung,*
Whence flowe these wishes for the common good,
By feeling hearts alone best understood.
I, young in life, by seeming cruel fate
Was snatch'd from Afric's *fancy'd happy seat:*
What pangs excruciating must molest,
What sorrows labour in my parent's breast?
Steel'd was that soul and by no misery mov'd,
That from a father seiz'd his babe belov'd,
Such such my case. And can I then but pray
Others may never feel tyrannic sway?

—Phillis Wheatley,
"Verse to the Earl of Dartmouth," 1773

Phillis Wheatley was seven years old, a year younger than Broteer, when she was taken from her home in Africa. Although it remains unclear exactly what day and on what vessel she arrived in Boston, one man remembered:

> Aunt Wheatley was in want of a domestic. She went aboard to purchase. In looking through the ship's company of living freight, her attention was drawn to that of a slender, frail female child, which at once enlisted her sympathies. Owing to the frailty of the child, she procured her for a trifle, as the captain had fears of her dropping off his hands, without emolument, by death.

That child would become Phillis Wheatley. The year was 1761.

From the time she joined the Wheatley household, the young girl displayed a curiosity and intelligence far beyond her years. Embraced and tutored by the family, she quickly mastered geography, history, astronomy, and English and Latin literature. She began to write classically influenced poetry, rich with rhythm and detail and informed by a wisdom she was too young to possess.

Inevitably, Phillis became a curiosity outside the circle of home—clergymen, literati, and members of the socially elite visited to marvel at her myriad talents. Prominent physician Dr. Benjamin Rush insisted that her "singular genius and accomplishments are such as not only do honour to her sex, but to human nature." The pampered young slave girl was a miracle, a voracious learner with poetry as her pulse.

However, she remained frail and prone to ill health. To bolster her strength, doctors prescribed a London sojourn, which coincidentally would also promote the publication of the young woman's first book of poetry. The book was published in London because American publishers did not believe that a black person could have written it.

Once she arrived in London in 1773, Phillis was the object of intense and mostly favorable scrutiny. Her *Poems on Various Subjects, Religious and Moral* was the first book of poetry by a black American writer. But upon hearing that her mistress was critically ill, concern brought her back to Boston.

When Mrs. Wheatley died, Phillis wrote in a letter to her friend Obour Tanner:

> *I have lately met with a great trial in the death of my mistress; let us imagine the loss of a parent, sister, or brother, the tenderness of all these were united in her. I was a poor little outcast and a stranger when she took me in.*

Hardly the words of a slave.

POETRY AND POLITICS

"PHILLIS, HAVE YOU a moment to talk?"

"Of course, ma'am, but should you be up at this hour? The doctor said—"

"I know *what he said. Pooh! You've been reminding me of it every day since you returned from England, which I wish you'd* not *done for my sake. I'm an old woman, and far poorer company, I would guess, than the Countess of Huntingdon and Benjamin Franklin. He isn't* really *a nudist, is he?"*

"To hear others tell it, yes! I swear I heard them say it! And you're not *poor company. I'd rather be here, helping you and Master John, than riding in carriages from one court to another in London and being called the 'Sable Muse.' Isn't that* silly*? I've never seen so many people astonished—there and here—that an Ethiop could write verse!"*

"No, not an Ethiop. They're dazzled, and well should they be, at a girl barely thirteen translating Ovid from the Latin and publishing her first book at twenty. I daresay you are a prodigy, probably the most gifted poet in New England."

"Oh my . . . Better than Michael Wigglesworth?"

"Leagues beyond him, *my dear."*

"Perhaps you are . . . biased. Is that possible?"

"Not a'tall . . ."

"But Mr. Jefferson, his opinion of my work is less than laudatory."

"As is my opinion of him. Come now, show me what you're working on. That is a new poem, isn't it? Is that why you're up before cock's crow?"

"Oh, I couldn't sleep! But, no! Don't look! Give it back, please. *I know it's not good. At least not yet. It could be years before it's ready—"*

"I just want to see. May I? Well . . . this is *a departure for you. 'On the Necessity of Negro Manumussion.' What prompted you to begin this?"*

"You . . . and Master John."

"How so?"

"Just prior to sending me to London for medical treatment you granted me manumission—"

"We were worried. Your health has always been frail."

"—and when I was there I discovered that everyone of my color was free. Just a few months before I arrived, Chief Justice Mansfield passed a ruling that freed all the slaves in England. I was thinking, would that we had such a ruling here!"

"But there are *free black men and women in Boston."*

"Yes, and they live miserably, ma'am! My contact with them is slight, but I've seen them languishing in poverty and ostracized by white Christians. I wonder sometimes what they think of me. *I imagine some mock the models I've chosen—Alexander Pope—and my piety and the patriotism of my verse, such as the poem to General Washington, which you know I labored long and hard upon, though he is a slaveholder (and who replied not at all to my*

gift), so that, the hardest work sometimes, at least for me, has been to honor in my verse the principles of the faith that brought me freedom, yet—and yet—I have not spoken of its failures, here in New England or in the slaveholding states that justify my people's oppression by twisting scripture."

"Must you speak of these things?"

"Yes, I think so . . ."

"Is this why you could not sleep last night?"

"Yes, ma'am."

"Phillis . . . are you . . . unhappy here?"

"No, no! That's not what I'm saying. I'm thankful for the blessing that brought me from Senegal to America. Thankful that you took on the sickly child that I was, carried me here to be a companion for you, taught me to write and read, and introduced me to Horace and Virgil, associates with whom I can spend hours, and ne'er once have they rebuked me for my complexion—"

"The finest thoughts have no complexion."

"So I have believed, ma'am. I believe that still. But while the greatest thoughts and works of literature and the gatekeepers of heaven vouchsafe no distinctions based on color, the worst prejudices and passions of man reign throughout the colonies. Will it not be odd, a hundred years hence, when readers open Poems on Various Subjects, Religious and Moral by Phillis Wheatley, and discover that in not a single poem do I address the anguish of bondage, the daily horror that is happening around us, the evil of men bleeding their sable brethren for profit? Will I not be suspect? Or censured? For it is our hope—isn't it?—that freedom will come to all? If it does, ma'am, what will free Negroes think of me? That I wrote nothing to further our cause?"

"Would you become a pamphleteer then? A writer of newspaper articles?"

"Well, no, but—"

"And why *not a pamphleteer?"*

"It's obvious why, isn't it? At the end of the day one wraps garbage in newspapers. And while a pamphlet can be valuable and stir people to action, a hundred years hence it may be forgotten—as the injustice it assails is forgotten—or it will be preserved only as a historical document, interesting for what it reveals about a moment long past, but never *appreciated as art. I'm speaking of writing* poems *about oppression."*

"Is poetry the right means for that?"

"How do you mean?"

"Tell me, Phillis, what is it about Virgil, Pope, and Horace that you love? Come now, don't be shy."

"The beauty, which age does not wear—"

"And?"

"The truth . . ."

"Which is timeless, no?"

"Yes, that's right."

"May I suggest something?"

"Please."

"I cannot read tea leaves so I have no idea what the future will bring or how your poetry will be received in the colonies a century from now. But of one thing I can assure you: You can never be censured. You are the first internationally celebrated woman poet in the colonies. The first American poet of your people. I'm sure they will take pride in your achievement, as John and I do. And you, my dear, are*—by nature and temperament—a poet, regardless of what Jefferson says. You are not a pamphleteer. Your job is simple. I did not say* easy, *for no one knows better than you how difficult it is to create even* one *line of verse worth passing along to the next generation, or a poem that speaks to the heart of Christendom—white and colored—on both sides of the Atlantic.*

It is a noble calling, Phillis, this creating of beauty, and it is sufficient unto itself."

"Is it? Sometimes I wonder if my people see me—my work—as useless."

"Useless?"

"It doesn't serve *their liberation, does it?"*

"Why? Because you do not catalog horrors? Only praise what on these shores is praiseworthy?"

"Yes, exactly."

"Dear, dear Phillis . . ."

"Why are you laughing? What did I say? Am I amusing?"

"Oh no, of course not! But would you call Benjamin Banneker's work useless?"

"Hardly! While still a boy, he built from wood the first clock made wholly in America. From what I hear, it keeps perfect time to this very day."

"What, then, of Santomee?"

"Who?"

"He was a slave in New York, one trained in Holland, who practiced medicine among the Dutch and English, probably saving many lives. And there is Onesimus, who in 1721 came up with an antidote for the smallpox. All of them proved the genius of your people. All of them enriched others through their deeds, thereby providing in the example of their persons, and the universal value of their products, the most devastating broadside against the evils of Negro bondage imaginable. And you have done no less."

"You think so?"

"I know *so."*

"Thank you, ma'am. You are most kind."

"Will you continue, then, with this bristling, new poem?"

"Perhaps, if I can find my way into it. The problem *is not that I don't feel outrage whenever I read or see or hear of injustice, it's rather that I fear I have no real talent for that sort of writing and rhetoric. For things I hate. I think I can compose passably well a hymn to morning, but as soon as I turn my pen to painting a portrait of a slave suffering beneath the lash, I cut myself off from what flows most easily from me—the things I love—and the words fall woodenly, unconvincingly, onto the page."*

"No, it's not your best work."

"You're not supposed to say *that!"*

"Sorry! I was just agreeing with you, that's all. You needn't bite my head off!"

"You're supposed to tell me it's good."

"Fine, it's good."

"You don't mean *that."*

"You're right, I don't, but I'm in no mood for an argument before breakfast. And it's not why I wanted to talk to you."

"Why did you?"

"You know how yesterday I felt poorly and stayed in bed?"

"Yes?"

"Well, I didn't bother with the post. All the mail, scented and sealed with candle wax, sat on a wig stand until I awoke this morning. I began looking through it, and I found a letter addressed to you. Perhaps I shouldn't give it to you if you're planning now on starting a new life as a composer of pamphlets."

"Oh, please! Who is it from?"

"Phillis, I think you should sit down."

"Who?"

"May I read it to you?"

"I *can read!"*

"But I would enjoy it so!"

"All right, then! Read!"
"Ahem . . .

"Miss Phillis,
Your favor of the 26th of October did not reach my hands till the middle of December. Time enough, you will say, to have given an answer ere this. Granted. But a variety of important occurances, continually interposing to distract the mind and withdraw the attention, I hope will apologize for the delay, and plead my excuse for the seeming but not real neglect. I thank you most sincerely for your polite notice of me, in the elegant lines you enclosed; and however undeserving I may be of such encomium and panegyric, the style and manner exhibit a striking proof of your poetical talents; in honor of which, and as a tribute justly due to you, I would have published the poem, had I not been apprehensive that, while I only meant to give the world this new instance of your genius, I might have incurred the imputation of vanity. This, and nothing else, determined me not to give it place in the public prints. . . . If you should ever come to Cambridge, or near headquarters, I shall be happy to see a person so favored by the Muses, and to whom nature has been so liberal and beneficent in her dispensations. I am, with great respect . . .

Your obedient, humble servant,
George Washington"

"He said . . . servant*?"*
"Here, see for yourself."
"This a complicated time, isn't it?"
"Yes, dear, I think it is."

In many ways Phillis Wheatley was white America's experiment, a slave afforded a nurturing and supportive environment unknown to most other captives. She was loved and admired. And, in return, she loved the country that gave her the opportunity to thrive. Although her work exhibited a growing racial awareness, piety and patriotism were more common themes. Phillis Wheatley was enamored of young America.

But, as expected, a refined, educated, and culturally popular slave was threatening to some Americans. Richard Nisbet, author of a tract titled *Slavery Not Forbidden by Scripture*, chastised abolitionist Dr. Benjamin Rush for holding up Phillis as "a single example of a negro girl writing a few silly poems to prove that the blacks are not deficient to us in understanding." And philosopher Bernard Romans wrote that "against the Phillis of Boston (who is the Phaenix of her race)" he could "bring at least twenty well-known instances of the contrary effect of education on this sable generation."

Thomas Jefferson was also less than enamored: "Religion, indeed, has produced a Phillis Wheatley; but it could not produce a poet. The compositions published under her name are below the dignity of criticism."

Despite her critics, Phillis became a spokeswoman for the cause of the country. She was an American, and in her heartfelt, socially righteous verse, she identified wholly and unapologetically with America. While she condemned slavery, the popular poet also believed that she had been taken from a non-Christian land and brought to a place where salvation was possible.

And Boston had come to terms with the trade; slavery was an undeniable beat in the city's rhythm. It was generally acknowledged that blacks were socially and educationally inferior. Phillis, for all her advantages, for all the trappings of freedom and independence, was writing from a captive place. She had found a voice that was content, often questioning, but never angry at her plight as a slave.

The most important thing, however, was that it was *her* voice. Phillis's writings reflected original thought, creative spark, the musings of a complex mind. As her elegant poems cemented her place in colonial history, more adamant and insistent voices rose to speak out for the cause of liberty. Petitions were sent to the Massachusetts Colonial Assembly in 1773:

> The humble PETITION of many SLAVES, living in the town of Boston . . . is this, namely That . . . the Honorable Representatives would be pleased to take their unhappy State and Condition under your wise and just Consideration. . . .
>
> We expect great things from men who have made such a noble stand against the designs of their *fellow men* to enslave them. We cannot but wish and hope, Sir . . .
>
> We have no Property! . . . We have no City! No Country! But we have a Father in Heaven, and we are determined as far as his Grace shall enable us . . .
>
> Although some of the negroes are vicious . . . there are many others of quite a different Character, and who, if made free, would soon be . . .
>
> We cannot but expect that your house will again take our deplorable case into consideration and give us that ample relief which, *as men*, we have a natural . . .

> The divine spirit of *freedom,* seems to fire every humane breast on this continent. . . .

The pleadings and entreaties, rising from the depths of the spirit, were pure poetry. They came not from the pen of a pampered, learned young slave, but from captives and former slaves who led lives where absolutely nothing rhymed.

CHAPTER FIVE

GENTLEMAN FARMER George Washington was not the only colonist suffering at the whim of a finicky British market. The British colonies were a captive market; increasingly independent Americans didn't like being told where and when to sell and where and when to buy. An electric undercurrent of resentment began to alter the formerly bustling commercial relationship between colonists and the British government.

Great Britain, meanwhile, had troubles of its own. The country was sorely in need of revenue, its coffers practically depleted from the expense of battling in the French and Indian War and maintaining occupying forces in Ireland, Scotland, the Caribbean, and India. In March of 1765, reluctant to raise taxes at home, Parliament slapped a direct tax on the American colonies. It was called the Stamp Act.

Protest was widespread and immediate. An enraged mob in New York City stormed the British fort. Boston protesters pillaged the residences of tax collectors and torched the stamp distributor in effigy. Although many transplanted Europeans still considered themselves subjects of the crown, they had enjoyed a tremendous amount of freedom and independence in the governance of local affairs and saw British meddling as a deliberate move to restrict their relative autonomy.

In Parliament, Charles Townshend captured the mood of the English when he asked, "[N]ow will these Americans, Children planted by our Care, nourished by our Indulgence . . . grudge to contribute their mite to relieve us from the heavy weight of that burden which we lie under?"

As a collective howl went up in Boston, in Philadelphia, in Charleston, enslaved blacks watched the colonists march for their freedom from the English. Black residents in Charleston watched the Sons of Liberty march down Broad Street with flags that proclaimed LIBERTY, LIBERTY and felt perhaps this was their chance to champion their quest for liberty as well.

Black slaves acknowledged that colonists had a right to protest, march, hoist placards, and wax poetic about their suppression under English rule. But they struggled to remind the protesters that there was another fight for liberty being waged. The very presence of the slaves during the revolt against the Stamp Act unnerved the colonists. When a group of black residents in Charleston began to shout, "Liberty, Liberty," armed patrols were quickly called out to quash the disturbance. There would be none of their brand of liberty.

When the Stamp Act was repealed in 1766, white Americans rejoiced in the streets, reveling in their continued financial independence. The young man Equiano, an enslaved sailor at the time, recalled seeing the bonfires of celebration in Charleston.

However, the crown's effort to enforce its faraway authority left a bitter taste. In the late 1760s, the city of Boston seethed with anti-British sentiment. Customs officials could not go about their duties without being harassed. Smuggling was rampant, as local leaders defied the constraints of empire. The Massachusetts General Assembly defiantly went about its business "in the stile of a ruling and Sovereign nation."

The cry was for liberty—but for Africans in America, the question was, *Whose* liberty? Was everyone, including those held in bondage, entitled to yearn for freedom?

"I speak it with grief—I speak it with anguish," said Boston's Josiah Quincy in 1774. "Britons are our oppressors: I speak it with shame—I speak it with indignation—*we are slaves.*"

John Adams echoed the sentiment: "[We are] the most abject sort of slaves."

The colonists had become so incensed that they clearly saw themselves as slaves to the British.

In 1775, Connecticut preacher Levi Hart railed against the obvious contradiction:

> What have the unhappy Africans committed against the inhabitants of the British colonies . . . to authorize *us* to seize them, or bribe them to seize one another, and transport them a thousand leagues into a strange land, and enslave them for life?

Baptist preacher and pamphleteer John Allen also pointed out the ironies of the fight for freedom:

> "[Y]e trifling patriots, who are making a vain parade of being advocates for the liberties of mankind . . . by trampling on the sacred natural rights and privileges of

> Africans; for while you are fasting, praying, nonimporting, nonexporting, remonstrating, resolving, and pleading . . . you at the same time are continuing this lawless, cruel, inhuman, and abominable practice of enslaving your fellow creatures.

In 1772, a London judge ruled that it was illegal to hold a human being in bondage in the free air of England. In England's American colonies, however, the decision meant nothing. Bondage would continue as a legal fact, even as blows for independence were being struck.

In fall of 1768, after bitter reactions to new constraints imposed by Britain prompted the fearful Massachusetts governor to beg for troops, a fleet of British ships dropped anchor in Boston Harbor. Four thousand soldiers flooded the shore, intent on enforcing British law. Boston's citizens were forced to house, feed, and entertain the interlopers. They were even required to supply each soldier with five pints of beer or a quarter pint of rum every day. Resentment bordered on the feverish, and some citizens began to call for a military response to England's show of force.

The inevitable unrest following the British "invasion" led to spates of street fighting and barroom brawls throughout the following year. Puritan rebels thumbed their noses at the established government, and haughty Boston loyalists, who supported the goals of Great Britain, squared off against incensed patriots. During the brutal winter of 1769, the colonial masses joined the fray, rioting and openly advocating a revolution that would create a new political and social landscape. Black people and poor white Bostonians were at the forefront of the struggle.

The mob that gathered on March 5, 1770, was described by John Adams as "a motley rabble of saucy boys, negroes and mulattoes, Irish teagues and outlandish jack tarrs." Leading the angry group up what is now Boston's State Street was Crispus Attucks, a forty-seven-year-old fugitive slave and free-spirited sailor rumored never to have backed away from a battle.

Some say Attucks was in Boston on that crisp March evening awaiting sea transport to North Carolina. No one knows for sure what circumstances catapulted the man into history, but the six-foot two-inch, quick-tempered Attucks was a picture-book leader. Half African, half Wampanoag, he had spent his life in pursuit of that fleeting thing, freedom.

That evening, confusion sparked chaos. Shortly after 8 P.M., anxious and weary British soldiers decided to put up a brave front by leaving their barracks for an evening stroll. Upon spying the sauntering soldiers, someone rang the fire bell in the Old Brick Meeting House, and agitated people spilled into the street. Angry voices mixed with drums and clanging bells, rising in a symphony of rebellion.

When a young barber's apprentice burst upon the scene screaming that he'd been attacked by a British sentry, the mob eagerly refocused its energy. The story grew more volatile with each repetition; some in the crowd believed that the sentry had murdered the young man in cold blood. When reports of the incident reached Crispus Attucks, he armed himself with a hefty cordwood stick and headed to the lair of the British main guard. A large group of citizens followed him, yelping and waving homemade weapons.

When they reached the square that housed the Customs House, the barber's apprentice, very much alive, pointed out his attacker. As the crowd called for the sentry's death, the marked man readied his musket and backed away from the rebels just as British reinforcements broke through. Attucks watched events unfold from the rear of the crowd and was among those who yelled, "They dare not fire, we are not afraid of them."

The sailor and his followers pushed to the front, coming face-to-face with British soldiers and their bayonets. It was almost 9:30. The moon lent an eerie quality to the standoff, glimmering upon the weapons and illuminating the moment.

Someone punctured the tension by tossing a stick that hit Private Hugh Montgomery. As the soldier lost his footing, he raised his musket and fired. Crispus Attucks fell forward, blood pouring from his chest wounds. A ruckus ensued and British troops opened fire. According to eyewitness accounts, Attucks was the first of five men to die—"killed on the spot, two [musket] balls entering his breast."

Almost immediately, the battle came to be known as the Boston Massacre—and the men who died were eulogized, romanticized, practically canonized. Years later, President John Adams said, "On that night, the foundation of American independence was laid."

Wendell Phillips would later write in March of 1858:

> Who set the example of guns? Who taught the British soldier that he might be defeated? Who first dared look into his eyes? Those five men! The fifth of March was the baptism of blood. . . . I place therefore, this Crispus Attucks in the foremost rank of the men that dared.

Three days after the massacre, Boston shut down for a public funeral honoring the fallen heroes. Bells rang tribute on the air.

Even though the events of that day have often been embellished, in 1770 the colonies were aware that they now possessed bona fide heroes who had given their lives for the cause. Now there was passion and fire and resolve. Now there were the rumblings of war.

"The die is cast," said Abigail Adams in 1775, reflecting on England's attempts to regain control of its colonies in America. "It seems to me the Sword is now our only, yet dreadful, alternative."

In the dawning hours of April 19, 1775, seven hundred British soldiers forged a path toward Concord, Massachusetts, to confiscate a cache of weapons. As they reached the town of Lexington, they were confronted by seventy colonial militiamen. As the British moved in to disarm the colonists, a gun discharged and soldiers panicked and began to fire. The British got their bearings and descended upon the colonists with a barrage of gunfire, killing eight of them.

The news traveled quickly. In Concord, hiding behind stone walls and trees, the Americans fired upon the British troops, effectively halting their advance. It was "the shot heard round the world." As the British started back, they were met by thousands of colonists who had left their homes and lined the road to Boston. By the time they reached Boston, British forces had lost several hundred men: 73 killed, 174 wounded, 26 missing.

The American Revolution had begun.

Slaves would fight for a freedom that actually had very little to do with Britain's hold on the Americas. They were considered important beyond their ability to work in the fields. Some found a purpose in fighting alongside men who had long considered them nothing more than property to be battered and bartered.

"[I]n every human Breast, God has implanted a Principle, which we call Love of Freedom," wrote Phillis Wheatley. "[I]t is impatient of Oppression and pants for Deliverance. I will assert, that same Principle lives in us. God grant Deliverance."

A determined army of roughly twenty thousand colonists surrounded Boston, trapping the British forces inside. This colonial force proved savvy and tenacious. Attempting to escape their trap, the British garrison mounted a full frontal assault on Breed's Hill in Charlestown on June 17, 1775. The desperate, bloody advance cost them 1,054 troops, but they finally won the day by driving the Americans from high ground. This Battle of Bunker Hill, as it came to be known, was the first toe-to-toe battle between the colonials and the Brits.

The best-known black hero of the battle was Peter Salem, who hailed from Framingham, the town Crispus Attucks had fled. Samuel Swett, a chronicler of the battle, described the slave's heroics: "Among the foremost of the leaders was the gallant Maj. Pitcairn, who exultingly cried 'the day is ours,' when Salem, a black soldier, and a number of others, shot him through and he fell." Salem was credited with slaying Pitcairn.

While the war scarred the American landscape, the Second Continental Congress met to raise an army and find a general who could turn a New England conflict into one for all the colonies. The overwhelming choice was George Washington. He was a formidable presence, knowledgeable in strategic matters, and already a war hero.

Washington vigorously opposed the inclusion of black soldiers in the ranks. African Americans had battled at Concord and Lexington, had participated in the siege around Boston, and were still ready to serve when Washington arrived. But Washington was convinced that slaves and free blacks would be more albatross than aid. He believed they would be difficult or impossible to train, have trouble understanding what was required of them, and prove to be disciplinary nightmares. He also wondered how southerners would react to the sight of slaves and former slaves bearing arms.

Once a black man was given a uniform and a weapon and asked to risk his life alongside other men on the field of battle, how could you deny him his freedom?

African Americans already in the ranks could serve out their tour of duty, but no new blacks would be accepted into the army. Lord Dunmore, the royal governor of Virginia, felt no such reservations about blacks joining the fray. Leaking a rumor that he would consider freeing rebel-owned slaves who fought for the British, he waited for a reaction—and got it. African Americans showed up, ready to fight for nothing more than their freedom. In the fall of 1775, as Washington was moving to bar officially further black enlistment in the Continental Army, Dunmore issued a formal proclamation:

> And I do hereby further declare all indented Servants, Negroes, or others, (appertaining to Rebels,) free that are able and willing to bear Arms, they joining HIS MAJESTY'S TROOPS, as foon as may be, for the more fpeedily reducing this Colony to a proper Senfe of their Duty, to HIS MAJESTY'S Crown and Dignity.

It was clearly a stroke of genius, a savvy tactic designed to make a shambles of the economy and fill out the British ranks with men who were fighting for their lives. And without slaves to guard their homes, rebel planters would be forced to desert the battle and return to safeguard their property and protect their families. "Negroes are double the number of white people in this colony," said Lord Dunmore. "An enemy would find facility in procuring Such a body of men, attached by no tye to their Masters or to the Country."

He called his recruits the Ethiopian Regiment. Before long, three hundred black men had donned British uniforms.

George Washington carefully assessed Dunmore's challenge:

> If that man is not crushed before spring, he will become the most formidable enemy America has; his strength will increase as a snow ball by rolling; and faster, if some expedient cannot be hit upon to convince the slaves and servants of the impotency of his designs.

Many white Americans feared that Dunmore's proclamation would spark a full-scale insurrection among the slaves. For many free blacks who considered themselves patriots, and for some whites as well, Dunmore's clever chess move underscored the contradiction of racial enslavement within the patriot cause and made them seek to broaden the bounds of the budding revolution.

But for many others, including the army's new Virginia-born commander, the specter of a slave with a gun in his hand was beyond terrifying.

Southern planters who had been uncommitted to either side suddenly began to switch to the patriot cause. Up North, irate patriot farmers in New York burned Dunmore in effigy. Slave owners attempted to control by terror—in August, Charleston residents had publicly hanged and burned Thomas Jeremiah, a black boat pilot found guilty of inciting insurrection. Jeremiah's smoldering body was meant to serve as a warning.

"Hell itself could not have vomitted any thing more black than this design of emancipating our slaves . . . ," declared a letter from Philadelphia printed in the *Morning Chronicle and London Advertiser* in January 1776:

> We know not how far the contagion may spread. The flame runs like wild fire through the slaves. . . . The subject of their nocturnal revels, instead of music and dancing, is now turned upon their liberty. I know not whence these troubles may lead us.

Harsh restrictions were imposed to prevent slaves and free blacks from holding meetings. But determined slaves realized that the colonies were in turmoil and the state of enslavement in chaos. Some chose to gather provisions and take off on their masters' horses to work their way toward the British, whom they hoped to be saviors.

The word of Dunmore's proclamation spread quickly up and down the Atlantic coast, and blacks, tasting freedom, grew bolder. A Philadelphia newspaper told of a Negro man who had refused to step into the muddy street when a gentlewoman walked past. "Stay you d——d white bitch," he reportedly said, "till Lord Dunmore and his black regiment come, and then we shall see who is to take the wall."

Britain's offer of freedom for slaves threatened the foundation of the entire plantation system. Many of the slaves answering Dunmore's call were skilled in the jobs that made a plantation run smoothly and efficiently. With a mass exodus of slaves, the system would crumble.

In 1775, John Adams offered this "melancholy account of the State of Georgia and South Carolina":

> They say that if one thousand regular troops should land in Georgia, and their commander be provided with arms and clothes enough, and proclaim freedom to all the negroes who would join his camp, twenty thousand negroes would join it from the two Provinces in a fortnight. The negroes have a wonderful art of communicating

> intelligence among themselves; it will run several hundreds of miles in a week or fortnight.

When news of black liberation spread to South Carolina, fugitive slaves began to gather on Sullivan's Island in Charleston Harbor, plotting ways to free their comrades in bondage. But South Carolina's Revolutionary Council of Safety intervened, sending a force to attack the encampment of refugees at night. Fifty slaves lost their lives, but not before the fever for freedom spread to Georgia.

Charleston slave trader Henry Laurens, president of the Council of Safety, learned that two hundred slaves had taken refuge on Tybee Island off the Georgia coast and suggested immediate action before they were rescued by British vessels:

> It is an awful business notwithstanding it has the sanction of the Law, to put even fugitives and Rebellious Slaves to death—the prospect is horrible. . . . We think the Council of Safety in Georgia ought to . . . seize and if nothing else will do to destroy all those Rebellious Negroes upon Tybee Island or wherever they may be found.

The colonists were both militarily and psychologically prepared to undermine the British offer of sanctuary. Increased local patrols guarded the streets and waterfronts, and highways were heavily monitored. The *Virginia Gazette* published a letter pointing out that Dunmore was not to be trusted, since he was a slave owner himself. The letter writer also insisted that English failure to halt the slave trade had persecuted Negroes much more than any action by their benevolent colonial masters, and that slaves should continue to serve those masters and count on salvation in the next world.

In its official response to Dunmore's proclamation, the Virginia Convention issued a declaration that was a textbook example of punishment and persuasion. With a reminder that the reward for insurrection was death, the document stated runaways who laid down their weapons would be pardoned. Later the Convention decreed that the captured slaves of patriots would be returned to their masters.

Slaves were risking everything to join the British; yet, members of the Ethiopian Regiment were finding death instead of deliverance. Dunmore wrote an English superior, insisting that his regiment would have been successful "had not a fever crept in amongst them, which carried off a great many very fine fellows." By summer, a raging smallpox epidemic reduced Dunmore's force by eight hundred men and discouraged any further black reinforcements.

The persistent epidemic, periodic defeats, and constant harassment by colonial forces drove Dunmore's sickly corps and British regulars to refuge on Gwynn's Island in the Chesapeake. In July, survivors moved to St. George Island in the Potomac. But with no imminent reinforcements, a dwindling freshwater supply and no reason for optimism, they destroyed more than half their vessels and set sail on August 6, 1776. Three hundred Negroes were aboard the ships, headed for Sandy Hook, New Jersey, and the Bermudas. Lord Dunmore's grandiose plan had come to a rather disappointing conclusion.

But his brash invitation lit a fire within those who remained in captivity in America. For many, it was as close as they'd ever been to the prospect of real freedom. Whatever his actual sincerity, Dunmore had offered the slaves membership in a very exclusive fraternity—men who were free. And the very offer, tainted as it was by the man's rampant self-interest, was enough for dreamers to dream on.

While Dunmore's drama played out in the harbors and on the seas, the revolutionary struggle flared in deadly campaigns and heated battles from Canada to the Carolinas. In Boston, on the morning of March 5, a British sentry at Dorchester Heights awoke to find American artillery surrounding the British troops and the fleet in the harbor. The artillery had been hauled overland hundreds of miles from Fort Ticonderoga, New York, on Lake Champlain. With those big guns, Washington's troops forced the British to evacuate the city. The redcoats sailed north to the more amiable colony of Nova Scotia, taking many loyalist families with them.

The British were not taking these defeats lightly. This was no longer an irritated crown out to spank its obstinate colonial child—it was a powerful empire about to wage a full-scale war. And the American forces weren't prepared.

Congress appealed to France and Spain, Britain's sworn enemies, for financial and military backing. But before those countries would commit to aiding the colonists' cause, they needed assurance that the American upstarts visualized their own nation. A committee of five drafted the Declaration of Independence.

> We hold these truths to be self-evident that all men are created equal. . . .

The document railed against the English monarchy with language that was determined and elegant. And at its heart was a belief in the equality of man.

It didn't matter that the man who penned those words owned more than two hundred slaves at the time. It couldn't matter. In laying down a foundation for the ideals of American liberty, Thomas Jefferson ignored the fact that, as a slaveholder, he violated those ideals.

In his first draft, Jefferson laid the blame for slavery squarely at the feet of George III.

> He has waged cruel war against human nature itself, violating its most sacred rights of life and liberty in the persons of a distant people who never offended him, captivating and carrying them into a slavery in another hemisphere, or to incur miserable death in their transportation thither.

The antislavery paragraph was stricken from the document.

White people were not the only ones envisioning a just and democratic America. Even before Thomas Jefferson wrote the Declaration, Lemuel Haynes, a New England minister, wrote his own. Included were these words:

> As all are of one species . . . Liberty is Equally as pre-[c]ious to *a Black man* as it is to a *white one* . . . a Jewel which was handed Down to man from the cabinet of heaven. . . . [A]n affrican, has Equally as good a right to his Liberty in common with Englishmen.

Haynes, a riveting sermonizer, was born in West Hartford, Connecticut, in 1753 to a black father and white mother who abandoned him when he was five months old. Later, legally an indentured servant, he was taken in and raised by a God-fearing white family. Turning to the ministry after gaining his freedom, he became widely known as the black pastor to an all-white, conservative congregation in Rutland, Vermont, where he preached for thirty years. The passionate, outspoken clergyman was lauded for overcoming obstacles of race and family.

Before the Declaration of Independence's plea for equality, Lemuel Haynes created a less hypocritical forty-six-page treatise that embraced all men. Unfortunately, "Liberty Further Extended" was never published.

After the Declaration, France put up one million livres'

worth of munitions, and Spain matched that sum in support of the Revolution. But it was a revolution not all Americans believed in. According to John Adams, only a third of the population actively supported the war.

It was difficult to inspire or motivate the Continental Army, which by 1777 was populated primarily by those without property seeking bounties of cash or land. Key battles were lost. The soldiers were underfed, ill-housed, and paid next to nothing. Infectious disease was rampant. Poor whites still did not consider the battle *their* revolution. At the end of the year, George Washington and 23,000 men settled into their winter camp at Valley Forge. Five thousand were gone by spring.

It was obvious that it would take more than foreign finance to fuel the Continental Army's flagging ambition. It would take manpower. And in its desperate state, the Continental Army's hunger for more men would overwhelm its initial reservations about the danger and futility of recruiting blacks. Black men had once been soldiers. If it meant securing victory for those who had enslaved them, they could be soldiers once again.

In early 1778, a reluctant Washington endorsed a plan to form a Rhode Island regiment consisting of free blacks and slaves. Congress quickly approved.

Many of the slaves changed their names to mirror their goals. Pomp Liberty. Dick Freedom. Jupiter Free. Jeffrey Liberty. They came ready to bear arms, ready to fight for their freedom. Free black men in New Hampshire were promised the same pay as their white counterparts. Slaves in Massachusetts and Connecticut, often serving in place of their owners, were promised freedom if they survived the rigors of battle.

A SOLDIER FOR THE CROWN

*Y*OU *ALWAYS were a gambler.*

*Before the war broke out, when you were still a servant in Master William Selby's house, you'd bet on anything—how early spring thaw might come, or if your older brother Titus would beat your cousin Caesar in a wrestling match—and most of the time you won. There was something about gambling that you could not resist. There was suspense, the feeling that the future was not already written by white hands. Or finished. There was chance, the luck of the draw. In the roll of dice or a card game, there was always—what to call it?—*an openness, *a chance that the outcome would go this way or that. For or against you. Of course, in bondage to Master Selby there were no odds. Whichever way the dice fell or the cards came up, you began and ended your day a slave.*

But did you win this *time?*

Standing by the wooden rail on a ship bound for Nova Scotia, crammed with strangers fleeing the collapse of their colonial world—women and children, whites and blacks, whose names appear in Brigadier General Samuel Birch's Book of Negroes*— you pull a long-shanked pipe from your red-tinted coat, pack the bowl with tobacco, and strike a friction match against a nail in your bootheel. You know you are fortunate to be on board. Now that the Continental Army is victorious, blacks who fought for the crown are struggling desperately to leave on His Majesty's ships departing from New York harbor. Even as your boat eased away from the harbor, some leaped from the docks into the water, swimming toward the ship for this last chance to escape slavery. Seeing them, you'd thought,* That might have been me. *But it wasn't; you've always been lucky that way, at taking risks. Running away from bondage. Taking on new identities. Yet you wonder what to call yourself now. A loyalist? A traitor? A man without a country? As the harbor shrinks, growing fainter in the distance, severing you forever from this strange, newly formed nation called the United States, you haven't the slightest idea after years of war which of these names fits, or what the future holds, though on one matter you* are *clear:*

From the start, you were fighting for no one but yourself.

The day after Lieutenant General Sir Henry Clinton promised liberty to all blacks deserting the rebel standard and willing to fight on the side of the British, you learned that Titus and Caesar were planning to flee. In the evening, on your way to the quarters after finishing your duties in the house, Titus stopped you outside the barn, and asked, "Can you go back to the kitchen and sneak out some provisions for us?" Naturally, you'd asked him what for, and he put his fingers to his lips, shushing you. They planned to steal two horses, he said. Then ride to safety behind British lines. "You're leaving?" You were almost speechless with anger. "And you're not taking me*?"*

"How can I?" he asked. "You're only fifteen."

"What's that got to do with anything? I can fight!"

"You ever fired a gun?"

"No, but I can learn!"

"Once I'm free, and got the papers to prove it, I'll come back."

"Titus, if you don't take me, I'll tell."

For a heartbeat or two, Titus looked as if he might hit you. Grudgingly, he agreed to bring you along, despite your age and his declaration after your parents' deaths that he'd keep you from harm. You did as he requested, returning to the house and filling a sack with food, Master Selby's clothing, even some of the mistress's jewelry that the three of you might barter, then delivered all this to your brother and Caesar in the barn. The three of you left that night on two of the master's best horses, you riding behind Titus, your arms tightly circling his waist until you stopped to make camp in the woods. There, Caesar suggested that it would help if you all changed your names and appearances as much as possible since Master Selby was sure to post your descriptions. Titus said fine, he'd grow a beard and call himself John Free. Caesar liked that, said, "Then I'll be George Liberty." They waited for you to pick a name, poking sticks at the campfire, sending up sparks into the starless sky. "Give me time," you'd said, changing into buckskin breeches, blue stockings, and a checkered, woolen shirt. "I'll shave my hair off, and I'll think of some*thing before we get there. I don't want to rush." What you didn't tell them that night was how thrilling, how sweet this business of renaming oneself felt, and that you wanted to toy with a thousand possibilities—each name promising a new nature—turning them over on your tongue, and creating whole histories for each before settling, as you finally did, on "Alexander Freeman" as your new identity.*

Thus, it was Alexander Freeman, George Liberty, and John Free who rode a few days later, bone weary from travel, into the British camp. You will never forget this sight: scores of black men in British uniforms, with the inscription LIBERTY TO SLAVES *on their breasts, bearing arms so naturally one would have thought they were born with a rifle in their hands. Some were cleaning their weapons. Others marched. Still others were relaxing or stabbing their bayonets at sacks suspended from trees or performing any of the thousand chores that kept a regiment well-oiled and ready. When you signed on, the black soldier who wrote down your names didn't question you, though he remarked he thought you didn't look very strong. The three of you were put immediately to work. Harder work, you recall, than anything you'd known working in Master Selby's house, but for the first time in fifteen years you fell to each task eagerly, gambling that the labor purchased a new lease on life.*

Over the first months, then years of the seesawing war, you, Titus, and Caesar served His Majesty's army in more capacities than you had fingers on the hand: as orderlies to the white officers, laborers, cooks, foragers, and as foot soldiers who descended upon farms abandoned by their white owners, burning the enemy's fortifications and plundering plantations for much-needed provisions; as spies slipping in and out of southern towns to gather information; and as caretakers to the dying when smallpox swept through your regiment, weakening and killing hundreds of men. Your brother among them. And it was then you nearly gave up the gamble. You wondered if it might not be best to take your chips off the table. And pray the promise of the Virginia Convention that black runaways to the British side would be pardoned was genuine. And slink back home, your hat in your hand, to Master Selby's farm—if it was still there. Or perhaps you and Caesar might switch sides, deserting to the ranks of General Washington who, pressured for manpower, belatedly reversed his opposition to Negroes fighting in the Continental Army. And then there was that magnificent Declaration penned by Jefferson, pro-

claiming that "We hold these truths to be self-evident, that all men are created equal, that they are endowed by their Creator with certain unalienable Rights, that among these are Life, Liberty and the pursuit of Happiness," words you'd memorized after hearing them. If the Continentals won, would this brave, new republic be so bad?

"Alex, those are just words," said Caesar. "White folks' words for other white folks."

"But without us, the rebels would lose—"

"So would the redcoats. Both sides need us, but I don't trust neither one to play fair when this thing is over. They can do that Declaration over. Naw, the words I want to see are on a British pass with my name on it. I'm stayin' put 'til I see that."

Caesar never did. A month later your regiment was routed by the Continental Army. The rebels fired cannons for six hours, shelling the village your side occupied two days before. You found pieces of your cousin strewn everywhere. And you ran. Ran. You lived by your wits in the countryside, stealing what you needed to survive until you reached territory still in British hands, and again found yourself a pawn in the middle of other men's battles—Camden, where your side scattered poorly trained regulars led by General Gates, then liberated slaves who donned their masters' fancy clothing and powdered wigs and followed along behind Gates as his men pressed on; and the disastrous encounter at Guilford Court House, where six hundred redcoats died and Cornwallis was forced to fall back to Wilmington for supplies, then later abandon North Carolina altogether, moving on to Virginia. During your time as a soldier, you saw thousands sacrifice their lives, and no, it wasn't as if you came through with only a scratch. At Camden you took a ball in your right shoulder. Fragments remain there still, making it a little hard for you to sleep on that side or withstand the dull ache in your shoulder on days when the weather *is damp. But, miraculously, as the war began to wind down, you were given the elusive, long-coveted British pass.*

On the ship, now traveling north past Augusta, you knock your cold pipe against the railing, shaking dottle from its bowl, then reach into your coat for the scrap of paper that was so difficult to earn. Behind you, other refugees are bedding down for the night, covering themselves and their children with blankets. You wait until one of the hands on deck passes a few feet beyond where you stand, then you unfold the paper with fingers stiffened by the cold. In the yellowish glow of the ship's lantern, tracing the words with your forefinger, shaping your lips silently to form each syllable, you read:

> This is to certify to whomfoever it may concern, that the Bearer hereof . . . Alexander Freeman . . . a Negro, reforted to the Britifh Lines, in confequence of the Proclamations of Sir William Howe, and Sir Henry Clinton, late Commanders in Chief in America; and that the faid Negro has hereby his Excellency Sir Benjamin Hampton's Permiffion to go to Nova-Scotia, or wherever elfe he may think proper . . . By Order of Brigadier General Ruttledge

The document, dated April 1783, brings a broad smile to your lips. Once your ship lands, and you find a home, you will frame this precious deed of manumission. At least in this sense, your gamble paid off. And for now you still prefer the adopted name Alexander Freeman to the one given you at birth—Dorothy.

Maybe you'll be Dorothy again, later in Nova Scotia. Of course, you'll keep the surname Freeman. And, Lord willing, when it's safe you will let your hair grow out again to its full length, wear dresses, and perhaps start a new family to replace the loved ones you lost during the war.

Before the end of the war, approximately five thousand black soldiers would fight for the Continental Army. Many thousands more would flee to the British.

In New York in April of 1776, British commander Sir Henry Clinton commissioned the Black Pioneer company, patterned after similar regiments in Pennsylvania, Virginia, and the Carolinas. Sixty to seventy black recruits were under the command of a white lieutenant and ensign. Surprisingly, pay was equal to that of white soldiers. The recruits were employed as pilots, executioners, hunters, drummers, and horsemen. Blacks with specialized knowledge of certain areas were often used as spies.

In choosing to battle for either side, blacks realized that there was a strong possibility they would be betrayed. But the pull of freedom was strong.

On April 6, 1776, the Continental Congress called for a wartime halt to the slave trade. Their motives were primarily economic, but there was a secondary message: A war for the "Rights of Man" could not come to terms with the contradictions of the trade. "I wish most sincerely there was not a slave in the province," said Abigail Adams. "It always appeared a most iniquitous scheme to fight ourselves for what we are daily robbing and plundering from those who have as good a right to freedom as we have."

In 1777 and 1778, while British and American troops fought fiercely in Pennsylvania, New Jersey, and upstate New York, a large segment of the British forces maintained their tenacious grip on New York City. They seemed formidable enough to go unchallenged. From their perch in New York, they were within striking distance of New England, the Jerseys, and territories up the Hudson. And since the Royal

Navy controlled the Atlantic Ocean, troops could ship out of New York City to any point on the coast.

Clinton had a solution to the lack of a decisive victory in the North—invade the South. By now, white planters, fearful that zeal for armed revolution might spread to their slaves, were perhaps likely, he hoped, to give the British a warm—or at least a neutral—reception.

By the end of 1778, the British had captured Savannah; in 1779 they took Augusta and then Norfolk. By the spring of 1780, Clinton and his troops had stormed Charleston and given the Americans their worst pummeling of the war. As the British advanced, whites began to flee their plantations. Some attempted to take their slaves along, but fear of the encroaching battle overwhelmed concern for property and many slaves were left behind. The abandoned blacks raided the plantation homes, looted them of goods, and pilfered clothing, food, cattle, and horses for transportation.

Clinton then issued a proclamation promising "every NEGROE who shall desert the Rebel Standard . . . full security to follow within these lines, any occupation which [they] shall think proper." Although Lord Dunmore's similar promise and subsequent defeat were fresh in many minds, slaves ran for the British lines.

They ran away from bondage to some barely glittering specter of independence. Some lived for years on the run. It didn't matter that slavery still thrived in the remaining British colonies or that the very country that tempted the captives with freedom had also prospered mightily from the slave trade. The slaves ran toward the British lines, hoping that the opposing army held the key to their liberation. Some, like Boston King, ran because there was no other choice.

After losing a horse that he had borrowed from "a very bad man," King fled to the British to escape the harrowing punishment that was forthcoming. In his memoirs, the hard-working, religious King chronicled a pattern of brutal treatment he'd received at the hands of his owners and others who failed to value his humanity. After losing the horse, he prayed to God to deliver him—and was able to get past the guards who stood watch for slaves running for safe haven promised by the Brits. "They received me readily," he wrote.

Boston King reached that "safe" haven—and found a hellish camp ravaged by disease and disorganization. He was soon infected with smallpox as an epidemic raged through the ranks. Blacks who suffered were removed from the camp to a site at least a mile away, where they were left to die or to somehow recover without medical aid. King persevered and rejoined the army as they moved to the headquarters of General Cornwallis near Camden, South Carolina. There he served as a military messenger and an orderly for Captain Grey, becoming one of the runaway slaves who would fight and toil for the British.

King was present at the battle at Camden in August of 1780. Congress sent a contingent of almost 3,500 men to stop Cornwallis's northward advance. They failed miserably. Eight hundred American men died.

Left behind by the British troops, King was taken into custody by southern loyalists, who although on the British side, wanted to return him to slavery. Upon escaping, he returned to the British regulars as a servant to the commanding officer at Nelson Ferry, South Carolina. Since the 250 British soldiers at Nelson Ferry were surrounded by an American force of 1,600, it was a less than desirable assignment. King "expected every moment to fall in with the enemy, whom I well knew would shew me no mercy."

However, in siding with the British, he felt he had made the right choice. It was his only chance to experience what he described as "the happiness of liberty, of which I knew nothing before."

CHAPTER SIX

Three pounds reward. Runaway from the fubfcriber . . . a NEGROE man, named TITUS but may probably change his name; he is about twenty one years of age, not very black, near six feet high.

—*PENNSYLVANIA GAZETTE,*
Runaway Notice, November 12, 1775

HE WAS A SLAVE who fled bondage in New Jersey. Titus was the name he'd been given. But as a militarist, a savvy strategist, an indefatigable fighter, he would become Colonel Tye, an emboldened twenty-one-year-old from Monmouth who commanded both blacks and whites in the British forces. Tye's lofty title wasn't as surprising as it sounds—the British often bestowed rank, or the appearance of rank, upon black recruits as a sign of respect.

The colonel was part of a loose assemblage of blacks known as "followers of the Army and Flag," a faction of the

British army less noted than Sir Henry Clinton's Black Pioneers. Once their importance was recognized, they were organized into the Black Brigade, a spirited unit manned mostly by fugitive slaves lured by the British promise of freedom.

Joining the call to battle after Lord Dunmore's 1775 declaration, Tye fought with his sights set on that promised freedom. As a member of the Brigade, one of two black Royal units in New York, he hunted down and executed patriots, terrorized slave owners, and liberated other captives. Under the cloak of darkness, the Brigade amassed supplies and food for the British.

Tye was a spirited and driven soldier whose legend grew quickly. At one point, he was the leader of approximately eight hundred men. Many blacks rallied behind him. And those blacks who didn't join him were thrilled to see one of their own disrupting the patriots' agenda, setting slaves free.

Since Tye knew the region so intimately, the raids he led were stealthy, and meticulously planned. He and his men—black recruits and white refugees—would invade the homes of patriots, kidnap the inhabitants, and steal away with valuables and livestock. Of course, the raids gave the British a psychological and military advantage. But for Tye's fiery army, they were also retaliatory strikes at former slave masters and their colleagues.

In 1779, during a steamy summer where racial tension in New Jersey ran high, Tye led a series of raids against the patriots of Monmouth. According to the July 15 issue of the *New Jersey Journal*, "about fifty negroes and [white] refugees landed at Shrewsbury and plundered the inhabitants of near 80 head of horned cattle, about 20 horses and a quantity of wearing apparel and household furniture. They also took off William Brindley and Elisha Cook, two of the inhabitants."

And that was just the beginning.

In the spring of 1780, Colonel Tye and his men terrorized and captured several ranking Monmouth militiamen and ardent patriots. On June 9, they murdered Private Joseph Murray, who had called for the execution of several people who opposed the patriot cause. Three days later, Tye led a large army of white refugees and slaves into the home of patriot resistance leader Barnes Smock while the main faction of the British army challenged Washington's troops. They captured Smock and a dozen other patriots, crushing the Monmouth militia leadership so they were unable to come to Washington's aid.

In one week, Colonel Tye had spirited away most of the ranking members of the Monmouth militia, destroyed their cannon, and flaunted his ability to succeed in the most daring and blatant attacks. He may have begun as a pesty renegade, but he was now a force to be reckoned with. And he was not yet finished with the patriots of New Jersey. At the end of the month, Tye slipped past patriot scouts at Conascung, New Jersey, and captured James Mott, the militia's second major of the Second Regiment, as well as eight other patriots. It was a devastating, decisive blow.

Colonel Tye seemed a miracle, but he was not immortal. On the first day of September 1780, he captured Captain Josiah Huddy, a patriot infamous for his heartless executions of captured loyalists. During the battle, Tye was shot in the wrist, and he later succumbed to a fatal infection. He was free, but it was not the freedom he envisioned.

In an ironic twist, Huddy—who had escaped his captors during transport—was captured again after two years and hanged on the fringes of Monmouth County. A black man was his executioner.

Patriots respected Tye's military savvy and remembered him as a worthy adversary. Many in the vicinity believed that the war would have ended sooner if he had fought with the Americans instead of against them. With his death, the British lost a vital communication and supply link to their forces in New York, and by 1780 the importance of that link was glaringly apparent.

The British army held on to New York, Charleston, and several port cities. Pressure to shatter the American resistance was growing in London, where the seemingly endless war was seen as a financial drain. In the summer of 1780, when Cornwallis defeated American forces in South Carolina, he rode the momentum into North Carolina, then pushed north toward Virginia, which had seemed unreachable a few months before.

In the spring of 1781, the British sloop *Savage* had anchored in the Potomac River outside the estate of George Washington and made off with rations, supplies, and seventeen slaves. The affront was painfully embarrassing for the Continental Army and its commander, whose own house had fallen to the enemy.

Virginia governor Thomas Jefferson pleaded with Washington to move his troops south to rescue the state, but it was too late. The government was in a shambles, and Jefferson fled. As he wrote:

> Cornwallis destroyed all my growing crops . . . he burned all my barns . . . he used all my stocks of cattle, sheep and hogs for the sustenance of the army, and carried off all the horses capable of service; of those too young for service he cut the throats, and he burned all the fences on the plantations, so as to leave it an absolute waste.

Thirty slaves deserted Jefferson's plantation. On other plantations, every single slave took flight. Some sought to form their own military units. Others worked for the British as foragers and orderlies, laborers, cooks, and craftsmen.

In Cornwallis's wake trailed approximately five thousand black men and women, fugitive slaves flaunting the fancy clothes, elaborate hats, and powdered wigs of their former owners. It was an odd, strangely jolting sight—a black wave of humanity heading for Yorktown.

While many blacks in the South followed the British general for protection, Venture Smith's son Cuff made another decision. At twenty-three, he joined the Connecticut militia. For the Smiths, who had so long lived on the fringes of the war, Cuff's departure was a reminder that the battle for true liberty never really stopped. Their son was going off to war. And that strange conflicted mixture of pride and fear they felt was an experience being shared by parents all over the seaboard states, parents in the North and in the South, parents both black and white.

Venture and Meg Smith had settled in Connecticut in a stretch of forest near Haddam's Neck. There they built a home—a home that was truly theirs, crafted and constructed by Venture and his sons. But the family not only owned a house, a physical structure. They owned land, which meant that they had carved a niche for themselves in a society where acquisition of land was the measure of a man.

Their son Cuff fought three years for his country. And, at least on paper, he had all the rights and freedoms afforded every other soldier.

In 1780, Massachusetts had adopted a state constitution that began with a bill of rights stating that all men were born free and equal. With so much of the colonies' prosperity built on the backs of black men, women, and children, the declaration was contradictory. But other states began to pass constitutions with versions of the same claim.

A slave woman, Mum Bett, took "free and equal" seriously, and forced Massachusetts to include *her* in its declaration of equality.

Mum Bett—a children's lisping and adoring abbreviation of Mother Betty—was Elizabeth Freeman, a formidable, compassionate woman who belonged to Colonel Ashley of Sheffield, Massachusetts. While the colonel was considered a reasonable master, his wife ran a household that was regimented to the point of cruelty.

Mum Bett was in servitude along with her timid and sickly sister Lizzy. One day, incensed that the young girl had scraped enough dough from a bowl to make a wheaten cake for herself, Mrs. Ashley grabbed an iron shovel directly from the fire and threatened to strike Lizzy with it. Mum Bett raised her arm and took the full force of the blow, which slashed through to bone. She was forever marked with a soul-deep scar.

"But Madam never again laid her hand on Lizzy," she said in later recollections of the incident. " I had a bad arm all winter, but Madam had the worst of it. I never covered the wound, and when people said to me, before Madam, 'Why, Betty! What ails your arm?' I only answered—'Ask missis!' "

Mum Bett's staunch, righteous character did not allow her to succumb to servitude. She ached for her liberty—and she had no reason to assume that she was excluded from the protection afforded by the Declaration of Independence and the bill of rights prefacing Massachusetts's constitution. Those words made her free and equal to Colonel Ashley, as well as free and equal to Mrs. Ashley, the woman who had picked up a red-hot shovel and scarred her for life.

So she and another slave, Brom, talked Sheffield's leading lawyer into taking her case. *Brom & Bett* v. *Ashley* questioned the very institution of slavery—its fundamental hypocrisy, its immoral underpinnings.

The lawyer, Theodore Sedgwick, was an outspoken advocate for the patriot position and a dear friend of Colonel John Ashley. The friendship was outweighed, however, by Sedgwick's pessimistic view of slavery. He considered the institution wildly illogical at a time when Massachusetts was fighting to free itself from British control.

To prepare for the landmark trial, Sedgwick reviewed the history of slavery in the state. The slave population in Massachusetts had never been high, and public sentiment seemed to favor slavery's gradual and complete abolishment. Legislative moves in that direction, however, were sluggish. Slavery's opponents had pinned their hopes on the first article in the new constitution's Declaration of Rights: "all men are born free and equal." Although the statement may have simply been designed as a sweeping moral pronouncement, Sedgwick was about to put it to an extraordinary test.

In August, the case came before the Court of Common Pleas. Sedgwick wasted no time, declaring that no one in Massachusetts had the right to own a slave. He argued that since slavery had never truly been legally sanctioned, any laws that supported it were nonbinding. Mum Bett and Brom were given the gift of freedom. A slave woman had forced a powerful state to face its contradictions and answer for them.

She was the woman who said:

> Anytime while I was a slave, if one minute's freedom had been offered to me, and I had been told I must die at the end of that minute, I would have taken it—just to stand one minute . . . on God's airth a free woman. I would.

Colonel John Ashley was offered no compensation for his loss.

A few months after being freed, Mum Bett became a trusted and integral part of Theodore Sedgwick's household as cook, nurturer, and confidante. The family's children regarded her as a second mother, which was especially poignant since Mrs. Sedgwick was struck by several bouts of debilitating mental depression.

Mum Bett's road to freedom made her a loyal member of an elite household, and that loyalty was tested dramatically years later during Shays's Rebellion, a loosely organized resistance of debtors to Massachusetts's newly organized state government. In 1786, a group of irate farmers faced with farm foreclosures took up arms. Led by revolutionary veteran Daniel Shays, the rebels forced the county courthouse to close for three months.

The occasionally violent uprising raged in central Massachusetts and ended in the Berkshires. At one point the dissidents threatened the Sedgwicks' property in Stockbridge, and there is some irony in the fact that Mum Bett, having struggled for her own betterment, now sided with the local gentry in resisting these impoverished farmers. Local historian Electa F. Jones described Mum Bett's courage in single-handedly defending the Sedgwicks' property from a band of marauders who sought to loot the family home in Stockbridge:

> [Mum Bett] was prepared for them. . . . She allowed them to search the drawers, knowing that the valuable papers were on the hill, and the silver all in her own chest, and to run their bayonets under the beds and into the darkest corners. . . . But she forbade all wanton destruction, of property; and arming herself with the kitchen shovel, no light weapon in those days, she escorted them to the cellar, jeering them at her pleasure, and assuring them that they dare not strike a woman.

Mum Bett shamed the rebels when they moved to search her chest, thus saving the Sedgwicks' valuables.

The woman who broke her chains and fled into history lived sixteen years longer than her friend and liberator Theodore Sedgwick.

> I Elizabeth Freeman of Stockbridge Massachusetts do make & publish this my last will & testament as follows:
>
> 1st After the payment of my just debts I hereby give bequeath to Charles Sedgwick Esq. Of Lenox all my real Estate (excepting that conveyed to my Great Grandson Amos Josiah Van Schaac). . . .

She succumbed in the winter of 1829, believing that she had lived more than a hundred years. The stone that marks her grave, however, states that "Her supposed age was 85 years."

> To my daughter Elizabeth I give the following articles viz—three gowns—1 black silk—1 do got from Philadelphia—1 do rec'd of my father—my largest silk shawl—a large home made birds eye petticoat—a short gown that was my mothers a white shawl with flowers. . . .

She abandoned a life that was richly textured, impassioned—and most importantly, her own.

> To my great grand daughter Wealthy Anne Dean a yellow shawl—Brown chintz & muslin apron—1 pr. Cotton hose—a small blue broad cloth cloak white—bonnet-hair trunk—white woolen shawl—small gold ear rings.

Mum Bett was buried in the Stockbridge cemetery in the Sedgwick family plot. Her simple headstone told the story of a woman who not only dreamed freedom, but pursued it:

> She was born a slave and remained a slave for nearly thirty years. She could neither read nor write yet in her own sphere she had no superior or equal. She neither wasted time nor property. She never violated a trust nor failed to perform a duty. In every situation of domestic trial, she was the most efficient helper, and the tenderest friend. Good mother, farewell.

By 1781, the year after Mum Bett petitioned for her freedom, Cornwallis had conquered Virginia. For two months, he stockpiled victories. For most of the war, George Washington and his generals waited for the moment when a major offensive might cripple the British army and change the direction of America's fortune.

When Washington learned that Cornwallis had set up a base of operations in Yorktown, a small tobacco port on the York River, he marched his army from New York to Virginia. There he was joined by a French naval fleet from the West Indies, and the British were suddenly confronted by a show of superior force.

> OCTOBER 16, 1781: Today there was stupendous cannonading on both sides. During these twenty-four hours,

> 3600 shots were counted from the enemy, which they fired at the town, our line, and at the ships in the harbour. The bombs . . . hit many inhabitants and negroes of the city. . . . One saw men lying nearly everywhere . . . whose heads, arms and legs had been shot off.
>
> —Johann Conrad Doehla,
> with British forces at Yorktown

> I have more than once witnessed fragments of mangled bodies and limbs of British soldiers thrown into the air by the bursting of our shells.
>
> —James Thacher, surgeon, Continental Army

The British suffered numbing casualties. Their food and medical supplies ran perilously low. To remedy the drain on their rations, the British turned out the black refugees who had fought alongside them. The desperate, famished men and women fled to the woods and hid there, halfway between the Continental Army and the British "liberators," who had so thoroughly deceived them.

"We drove back to the enemy all our black friends . . . ," said Johan Ewald. "We had used them to good advantage and set them free, and now, with fear and trembling, they had to face the reward of their cruel masters."

American officer Joseph Plumb Martin told of Negroes hiding in the woods who were "turned adrift, with no other recompense . . . than the small pox for their bounty and starvation and death for their wages." Some evidence suggests Cornwallis hoped these suffering blacks might infect the American forces with smallpox.

Cornwallis surrendered on October 19, 1781, three weeks after the siege at Yorktown had begun. American forces found the town littered with black bodies. The thousands of blacks who had taken refuge in the woods could hear the dim strains of music from the ceremony of surrender—while the American forces played "Yankee Doodle," the British played the dirgelike "The World Turned Upside Down." Britain's spirit had been broken by the devastating defeat at Yorktown.

George Washington captured two of his escaped slaves after the battle. And the Americans posted guards along the beach to keep fugitive slaves from escaping with the British. "Many Negroes and mulattos have concealed themselves on board the ships in the harbor. Others have attempted to impose themselves as freemen to make their escape," said Washington. "In order to prevent their succeeding . . . such Negroes are to be delivered to the guards which will be established for their reception."

The British had lost a southern stronghold, but the war continued. Additional British forces and their loyal supporters rapidly retreated toward the coast.

As the battlers for the crown moved across the South to the seaports, thousands of escaped slaves clung to them. They fought to gain passage on ships headed for New York City, where there was still forlorn hope that the British might somehow emerge victorious. Hoping to recover their property, many southern slaveholders traveled north and waited to lay claim to slaves who had fled to fight for the crown and their freedom.

On November 30, 1782, diplomats from Britain and America signed a provisional treaty granting full independence to the former colonies. A petulant British delegation refused to sit for the official portrait. The strict, overbearing parents were finally letting the child go. But they weren't happy about it.

Henry Laurens, a retired South Carolina slave trader turned diplomat, was the American negotiator. His friend and former partner Robert Oswald negotiated for the British. Although Laurens was no longer in the business of trading slaves, and in fact had expressed reservations about it, he was first and foremost a businessman. He believed that landowners would "need" slaves to rebuild regions torn apart by the war, and he insisted that the British could not leave the United States with property that had not been properly purchased. That included cattle, ammunition, and Negroes.

> His Britannic Majesty shall with all convenient speed and without Causing any destruction or carrying away any Negroes or other property from the American inhabitants, withdraw all his Armies.
>
> —Provisional Peace Treaty, Article Seven

All former slaves, even those who had spent three or four years living among the English, were to be returned to their masters.

"Peace was restored between America and Great Britain, which diffused universal joy among all parties except us," said Boston King.

> [A] report prevailed that all the slaves were to be delivered up to their masters. This dreadful rumour filled us all with inexpressible anguish and terror especially when we saw our old masters coming from Virginia, North Carolina and other parts and seizing upon their slaves in the streets of New York, or even dragging them out of their beds.

Thousands of African Americans had chosen to fight with the British. The most desperate elements of the vanquished forces crowded Manhattan, realizing that only a chosen few would actually make the trip to Britain. There was no way to know who was going to go and who would remain behind to face the wrath of their former owners.

It was George Washington's job to obtain the delivery of all escaped slaves and other property in British possession. But Sir Guy Carleton, the acting British commander, refused to cooperate. In a May 6 meeting with Washington, he declared that his government couldn't possibly ignore the debt owed to Negroes who had fought for the crown. To deliver them into American hands, where they would be punished or returned to slavery, would be "a dishonorable Violation of the public Faith." Carleton declared that refugees who had joined the British before the November 30 peace treaty would be free, and those arriving after that date would be returned to their owners.

However, Carleton added, if the continued evacuation of the blacks was indeed a break with the treaty, the British would see that owners were compensated for their slaves.

Washington was deeply disturbed by Carleton's proposal. But despite his reservations, the discussion ended with Carleton unflinching in his determination. Washington concluded that the slaves who had escaped from their masters would never be recovered.

Brigadier General Samuel Birch, the commandant of the city of New York under British occupation, was charged with creating a process to ascertain which blacks had fought for the crown prior to the treaty and were therefore free to depart with the fleet.

He decided to issue formal certificates to prove length of service with British forces. The treasured certificates would serve as passage aboard a British ship. But, of course, the pieces of paper meant much, much more to those who bargained their lives for a chance at freedom. Thousands lined up to plead their cases to a few British officers. They simply had to get themselves, their families, on board.

To quiet former colonists' resistance to the process, Birch also created a commission and devised a list of everyone to whom he issued a certificate. The list, which could also be used to aid in any further arbitration over lost property, became known as *The Book of Negroes.* It was a list of every man, woman, and child who could prove their length of time with the British. Every Wednesday afternoon between May and November 1783, the book was opened in a tavern packed with slaves wishing to prove their qualifications for freedom and owners petitioning for the return of their human property.

> Fine boy, stout wench, blind and lame, nearly worn out, ordinary wench, stout woman, ordinary child, stout man . . .
>
> —Descriptions from *The Book of Negroes*

Among the three thousand names listed in the book is that of twenty-three-year-old Boston King, "stout fellow" and former property of Richard Waring of Charleston, South Carolina. King had been a part of the British forces for four years and had invaded North Carolina with Cornwallis.

After the campaigns in South Carolina, Boston King went to Charleston; when the British surrendered that city, he was then taken to New York on one of their warships. Since he was too poor to buy tools, he was unable to practice carpentry. With thousands of other black refugees, he lived in crammed barracks and did odd jobs to support himself. While in New York, he married Violet, a woman of African and Native American descent. In *The Book of Negroes,* she is Violet King, thirty-five, "stout wench" of Wilmington, North Carolina.

To earn extra money, King worked on a pilot boat. On

one excursion, he was abducted by an American rebel and sold back into slavery in New Jersey. His new master treated him well, but King burned for freedom:

> [I]ndeed the slaves about Baltimore, Philadelphia and New York have as good victuals as many of the English; for they have meat once a day, and milk for breakfast and supper; and what is better than all, many of the masters send their slaves to school at night, that they may learn to read the scriptures. This is a privilege indeed. But alas, all these enjoyments could not satisfy me without liberty.

King later managed to escape and return to New York and Violet.

Now the couple faced a freedom they had never known. Their futures were tumultuous, uncertain. Climbing aboard *L'Abondance* in New York harbor, there was no way of knowing what fortune awaited on the other end of the voyage. On board was the Black Brigade—escaped slaves and free blacks who had fought for the British during the Revolutionary War—the last of an estimated four thousand black refugees fleeing servitude.

With 408 other passengers, Boston and Violet King sailed from New York to Port Roseway in Nova Scotia. Those aboard *L'Abondance* formed the community of Birchtown, named in honor of the man who had graced them with the coveted certificates to freedom.

In his new home, Boston King began to focus on his relationship with the Lord. He attended prayer meetings and mused over the salvation of his soul:

> I thought I was not worthy to be among the people of GOD, nor even to dwell in my own houses, but was fit

> only to reside among the beasts of the forest. This drove me out into the woods, when the snow lay upon the ground three or four feet deep, with a blanket, and a fire-brand in my hand. I cut the boughs of the spruce tree and kindled a fire. In this lonely situation I frequently entreated the Lord for mercy—but in vain.

One Sunday in March, on his way to service, King "thought I heard a voice saying to me, 'Peace be unto thee!' . . . All my doubts and fears vanished away: I saw, by faith, heaven opened to my view, and Christ and his holy angels rejoicing over me."

Following his religious transformation, King became obsessed with helping others achieve the same state of spiritual well-being. He visited his neighbors and preached during prayer meetings. Then, in 1787, "I found my mind drawn out to commiserate my poor brethren in Africa, and especially when I considered that we have the happiness of being brought up in a christian land . . ."

King got his wish. Eventually he boarded a ship to Sierra Leone in a journey arranged by the Sierra Leone Company, which was incorporated to barter on the African continent. The company also sought to reestablish former slaves in Africa to show that they could govern and support themselves. Boston King was going to introduce his God to brothers and sisters he'd never seen.

He had fought for the British and finally achieved what he'd been promised so long ago. His body was free. Now so was his soul.

By the end of the American Revolution, 100,000 slaves had escaped bondage. Close to twenty thousand left with the British military while others fled in private vessels. Some returned to

Africa. Thousands who begged their way aboard the ships lost their freedom anyway. Some wound up as slaves in the Caribbean, trading one misery for another.

The future of those still on American soil was as uncertain as the future of those whose precious certificates had granted them new lives. Their scarred, broken new country failed to embrace them.

> All . . . was desolation . . . every field, every plantation showed marks of ruin and devastation. It is impossible to describe in words how altered these once beautiful fields are.
>
> —The Reverend Archibald Simpson,
> Stoney Creek, South Carolina

> This cursed war has ruined us all.
>
> —Robert Baillie, Georgia planter

> Not the vestiges of horses, cattle, hogs or deer was to be found. The squirrels and birds of every kind were totally destroyed. . . . No living creature was to be seen, except now and then a few camp scavengers.
>
> —General William Moultrie, on the Ashley River

The war nearly destroyed the burgeoning rebellious colonies. The economy was flattened. Although 100 million pounds of tobacco were produced in the year preceding the Revolution, 1782 production was a mere 1 million pounds.

The six-year halt on slave importation left its mark in several devastating ways. At war's end, fewer than one hundred slaves were available for sale in the entire state of Georgia.

The shortage resulted in skyrocketing prices for slave labor—a field hand who cost 40 pounds in 1776 cost 210 pounds in 1782.

As the colonies sought to rebuild, one thing was clear, particularly in the South: Plantations had to become productive again. The lifeblood of the economy was land that grew rice, tobacco, indigo, and other products that could be sold. And the land could not produce unless there was adequate labor to tend it.

At times it felt the tide was turning against slavery. In 1780, Pennsylvania lawmakers, mindful of Revolution principles, declared that all black children born after that time would be freed at age twenty-eight. Three years later, Massachusetts outlawed slavery entirely. Rhode Island and Connecticut voted for gradual emancipation in 1784. New York banned slavery in 1785. The following year, New Jersey forbade the importation of slaves.

War had stopped the slave trade. But with the arrival of peace, landowners were anxious to get back to the business at hand. That business, in their eyes, demanded the trade be restored.

Peace did not bring an end to the chaos wrought by war. America's fledgling government lacked the power to remove a string of frontier forts still occupied by the British, and Native American tribes struggled to stem the tide of white settlement in the Ohio Valley.

In the fall of 1786, an unsuccessful, poorly attended conference of state representatives was held in Annapolis, Maryland. There was so little interest that everyone was sent home. A second convention was planned for the spring of 1787 in Philadelphia. This Constitutional Convention succeeded when

Virginia delegate James Madison guaranteed that George Washington would be present—and would preside over the convention.

The genteel Virginia gentleman and soldier realized that the true revolution was far from over. He knew that building a new, independent nation would take organization, commitment, and unflinching leadership.

It was James Madison who set the tone for a discussion of the framework needed for a strong federal union. The delegates analyzed, argued, and tweaked Madison's original plan throughout the summer of 1787. There were several pressing questions: How would parity in representation between large and small states be ensured? Could one government foresee and ensure the needs of both? How would taxes be levied?

Delegates voiced great concern over the protection of individual liberties and personal property. For southern delegates, one of the most important liberties was the right to own slaves. While they wanted a federal government that would protect their rights, they did not want a governing body that would free their slaves.

Which raised another question: Should slaves be counted as persons? Those who owned slaves said yes. Those who did not own slaves said no. They didn't want slave holders to have greater representation by counting their property. One question was never answered: How could a country built on freedom justify slavery?

It took six months for the fifty-five delegates to draft the foundation of law and government. For black Americans of that generation and those to come, the new Constitution was a tragedy.

After more than ten years of the war and its ravages, the

Founding Fathers wanted to establish an orderly, prosperous society that valued property. Slaves were property. The Constitution held the respect for property at its center, and for southerners in particular, human property was most important. The document indirectly endorsed the continued bondage of people of African descent.

"Domestic tranquillity" depended upon the forced enslavement of those who ensured profitable enterprise. The general welfare was not as general as the Constitution hinted. And the blessings of liberty were bestowed only on the privileged, those whose skin color automatically made them free.

"The constitution that is submitted is not free from imperfection," said George Washington. "Yet, in the aggregate, it is the best constitution that can be obtained."

America's young government decided that slavery was necessary. Free blacks and slaves were openly discussed during the constitutional debate, along with other property such as livestock. However, neither the word *slave* nor *slavery* appears anywhere in the Constitution. The Founding Fathers wanted their actions and consciences scrubbed clean in the history books.

According to Benjamin Rush, prominent Philadelphia physician and signer of the Declaration of Independence:

> No mention was made of negroes or slaves in this constitution, only because it was thought the very words would contaminate the glorious fabric of American liberty and government. Thus you see the cloud, which a few years ago was no larger than a man's hand, had descended in plentiful dews and at last covered every part of our land.

The new Constitution prohibited Congress from banning the slave trade for twenty years. Fugitives in free states were to be returned to slave states.

And each slave—man, woman, or child—was three-fifths of a human being when it came to determining representation in Congress.

The Constitution was ratified in 1788, the year before George Washington was sworn in as the first elected president. The country's new leader immediately made himself accessible, visiting each state in the union and providing the citizens with a visible figurehead. Here was their war hero, shaking hands and carving a concept for the country. But he was not being totally forthright with the public. He didn't share with them his doubts about the institution of slavery. The president of the United States privately told a visitor that "Nothing but the rooting out of slavery can perpetuate the existence of our union."

Washington had begun to question the economic benefits of a slave system, as well as the immorality of one human being "owning" another. However, he was officially silent on the matter. As word of his doubts spread, Washington's endorsement was sought by abolitionists.

But he hesitated to make a definitive statement explaining his apparent change of heart. His first priority was a strong and viable union, and to voice his objections to the slave system would certainly upset many whose support he would undoubtedly need in the building of that union. Privately he spoke of a gradual emancipation, an imperceptible change that would just "happen" without much prodding from him or his fledging government.

"I can only say that there is not a man living who wishes

more sincerely than I do to see a plan adopted for the abolition of [slavery]," he said. "An evil exists which requires a remedy."

Through it all, George Washington still owned slaves.

There was a very practical reason why. The new president had decided to live comfortably, and he could not continue to live that way without his slaves. During the war he placed himself in the path of danger. He risked his life and lived under conditions that had killed many of his colleagues. Now, in his later years, slaves provided the comfort he felt he had earned.

The morally bereft stance tortured him: "I wish I could liberate a certain species of property which I possess, very repugnantly to my own feelings."

Washington was not the only leader who maintained a public silence on the topic. Add to that list the Jeffersons, the Madisons. James Madison could not even bring himself to free Billy, a slave who had been his friend throughout childhood. Jefferson despaired of achieving racial harmony and was convinced that if all of America's slaves were freed, they would have to be shipped out of the country. He rationalized:

> It will probably be asked, "Why not retain and incorporate blacks into the state, and thus save the expense of supplying, by importation of white settlers, the vacancies they will leave?" Deep-rooted prejudices entertained by the whites; the thousand recollections, by the blacks, of the injuries they have sustained; new provocations, the real distinctions which nature had made; and many other circumstances, will divide us into parties, and produce convulsions which will probably never end but in the extermination of one or the other race.

Many people had grown comfortable and accustomed to slaves providing a carefree way of life. Inside glorious mansions and plantation homes, the inherent grandeur was dependent upon the enslavement of humans who worked without even a flickering dream of freedom. There was no upward movement for most, no way of working themselves or their children out of that dire predicament.

On a chilly night in December of 1799, George Washington, the country's first president, breathed his last. The resplendent funeral ceremony at Mount Vernon was re-created in Philadelphia. Six thousand mourned his passing at the Old South Church in Boston. Memorial services took place in virtually every city in the United States. John Marshall solemnly addressed the Congress: "Our Washington is no more."

What the Virginian couldn't do in life, he did after his death. Washington's will stated: "Upon the decease of my wife, it is my will and desire that all the slaves which I hold in my own right shall receive their freedom."

Martha Washington lived in fear. She was despondent, melancholy, and worried about the conditions of the will, which were common knowledge in the slave quarters. There were 125 slaves on her property who would be free upon her death, and she was afraid they might be plotting to kill her.

Instead of living immobilized by fright, she went to a Fairfax County court and freed the slaves a year after her husband's death. Perhaps George Washington had foreseen the dilemma she would face, but at the end of his life he had sought only to unburden his stormy conscience.

Martha Washington lived for another year after granting freedom to her husband's slaves.

MARTHA'S DILEMMA

*N*OTHING HAS BEEN *quite the same since George's funeral, including his Negroes. I've been managing the affairs at Mount Vernon, as I always did when he was away, first during the Revolution, then when they kept calling him back to a government service he never truly felt equal to, nurturing the fledging nation that is, I suppose, the child we never had. But even as I devote my days to managing this sprawling estate, particularly instructing the servants to maintain the arcade connecting the house to our workshops and greenhouses, of which he was so proud, I cannot help but think about how little time we had together after the Old Man turned in his resignation at the Philadelphia State House. Two years! They passed so quickly, and much of it was consumed by his entertaining visitors from all over the world when he wasn't laboring—with those nice, two young men he hired—to keep up with voluminous correspondence. And even then that owlish old curmudgeon John Adams had the nerve to ask him out of retirement to help refine the military when Talleyrand tried to blackmail* *us for the right of Yankee ships to have free passage on the seas, knowing—as Adams always knew—that George could never say no, that he'd struggle into his old uniform and leave for Philadelphia to once again transform pitifully unprepared farmer-soldiers into fighting men for a new republic. If he'd only known how sick the Old Man was sometimes; I doubt Adams realized, despite his being right there, that on Inauguration Day, by the time George reached the balcony of the Federal Building, where he would place his hand on the Bible and become president, he was so ill he collapsed onto the first chair he found.*

Yes, they were careless with him, his admirers—I always *told him that. But he was careless with himself, too, believing perhaps in his own indestructibility after his surveying work on the Virginia frontier, that dreadful winter at Valley Forge, the illnesses he'd overcome during the Revolution before he was even aware that he was ill, and having two horses shot out from under him in the midst of terrible gunfire during the French and Indian War. On December 13 I gave him a good piece of my mind about that, when he returned from riding on a day as dreary and damp as any I've seen. Naturally, he waved off my objections, "Oh, it's not all that bad outside, Martha," but he was shivering and sneezing when the servants took his wraps. At dinner, he barely touched his food. When he spoke I could tell his voice was getting stuffy. That he had the beginnings of a bad cold, and here we were so close to the holidays—and just after George's nephew Lawrence married Nellie Custis—with so many people on our social calendar to see! Oh, I scolded him severely, the big oaf, and sent him off to bed, to which he shyly retreated with a rum and toddy.*

I should have known *something was wrong.*

Two hours later when I climbed under the covers, kissing him on his cheek, I discovered he had no voice at all. He couldn't talk.

I rang the bell for Billy Lee, one of our most trustworthy servants, and when he arrived, breathless after running from the kitchen, I told him to saddle a horse immediately and ride to Dr. James Craik's home nearby, and to fetch him, regardless if he'd turned in for the night or not. Poor George could only communicate with me in writing. He took a quill, paper, and ink from his study, smiled at me, and scrawled, Not to worry, James will fix me up. If he forces me to stay in bed, do remember to have someone see to the lame horse I told you about, and take care of the washout in the fields.

Dr. Craik, an old friend, arrived just before midnight. He examined the Old Man, and then looked very grave. Turning to me, he said, "Lady Washington, your husband has a severe case of quinsy. That's an inflammation of the tonsils," he explained, though I knew perfectly well what quinsy was and felt a little miffed by his condescension, but this is a cross women have had to bear from time immemorial, that and living in the shadow of their spouses, of course. He recommended, as was right, that Billy ride all night to Alexandria (By Billy's crabbed expression at this chore I should have seen a portent of things to come) to bring two physicians of his acquaintance to help with cupping the Old Man, which our servant did. The next day Dr. Craik and those two men he'd summoned bled George. I was by his bedside all the while, holding his piebald hand firmly, and I must say that it is to Billy's credit that he never left my side except to jump to any task or errand that Dr. Craik asked of him. Our house servants waited solemnly outside the door, whispering among themselves, in part because I believe they loved the Old Man, and in greater part because all had heard that upon his (and my) death their manumission was promised in our will. They too were godsent that day. They saw to the chores I was too distracted to discharge, some prayed for my husband's swift recovery, and others wept. Nevertheless, all our ministrations came to nought. At ten o'clock on December 14, 1799, the man with whom I'd shared life for forty years—since our wedding when we both were twenty-seven—went on to his reward.

What, I have been wondering, is my *reward, now that he's gone?*

All over this new country he served indefatigably, flags were lowered when word of his death went abroad. In America's churches, state assemblies, and the government he'd created, there were eulogies, the finest of them coming from Harry Lee—known as "Light Horse Harry" when he served under George during the Revolution—who said my husband was "First in war, first in peace, and first in the hearts of his countrymen." These were beautiful tributes, for which I am thankful. I can even turn an appreciative, albeit amused, smile toward the well-meaning mythmakers who began enlarging his legend before we could properly bury him in Mount Vernon's family tomb, spinning outrageous tales of his throwing a silver dollar across the Rappahannock River (What balderdash!), and that when his father, Augustine, discovered one of his cherry trees cut down, young George confessed to the deed, saying, "I cannot tell a lie." Well, I can tell you this: No one knew the Old Man as well as I did. He could lie, oh yes. He was, after all, a politician. *Oh, and if one could see his temper when he was angry! Like Vesuvius, that was. Nor did he have the Olympian self-confidence so many attributed to him, what with the paucity of his education. He was painfully shy with every girl before he met me, possibly because his face bore scars from the smallpox he endured while journeying as a boy with his half-brother Lawrence to the West Indies. He was a slow reader. A poor speller. He was a man of deeds, not ideas. He knew no French at all and thus signed a miserable terms of surrender when he was captured during the battle of Great Meadows. Those are matters I assisted him with—matters of culture—as well as adding five thousand acres to his estate when we wed—indeed, you could say it was seventeen thousand acres, if you count the land now owned by my son. No, he was not perfect, but what woman could have asked for a better companion for these last forty years?*

When I was a very young girl, studying the classics, I read that the ancient Greeks honored their Olympic game heroes by knocking out a portion of the wall that protected their city—the heroes stood in that spot for the rest of the day, the idea being that with champions such as them a wall was not needed. On December 14 it felt across this country, and especially at Mount Vernon, that we had lost not only a hero but one of the very foundations of our house. For days after his passing I spoke to no one about the depth of this absence save to my dearest and closest friends. Nor did I speak of how subtly I began to see a change in our servants. At first, I thought the smiles with which they greeted me were simply intended to cheer me a little. Then, ever so slowly, I realized they were smiling too much. And too often. Sometimes when I started to enter the kitchen, I'd stop outside the door, listening to the blacks laughing whilst they prepared my meals, and once our cook told the chambermaid how pleased she was that now she'd never again have to slave all day to prepare the elaborate desserts the Old Man was so fond of. At that point, I strode inside. Seeing me, both women went fussily back to work, ducking their heads, but I saw one of them, I swear, wink at the other.

Strangely enough, the worst among them was Billy Lee. With my husband dead and buried, he started behaving as if he *was now the master of Mount Vernon, or at least over the other servants. This would have been impossible, I realized, had George and I not* become so dependent upon the blacks. We'd delegated so many household responsibilities to them, and not just in the manor but in the tobacco fields as well, that I would be at pains to tell you the inventory of our kitchen, or how well the Old Man's latest agricultural experiments were proceeding. Ironically, we were enslaved to them, shackled to their industry, the knowledge they'd acquired because we were too busy running the country to develop it ourselves!

One afternoon last week Billy brought me my tea as I was writing thank-you notes to those many people who'd sent me condolences. He actually pointed his dark finger at me, wagged it, and said, "Lady Washington, you should let them scribes the master hired do that." I mean, he was telling me what I should do. More than once I sniffed our best brandy on his breath. I heard him swearing at a stable hand, and do you think he was at all ashamed when I chastised him? Hardly!

It was, then, perhaps a month after the Old Man's death, that I began to fear the Negroes who resided in every nook and cranny of my life. At night, from their quarters, I began to hear drums, which George had expressly forbidden them to play. Food began to disappear from our pantries. Many of our plants died in the greenhouse from neglect. And there I was, an old woman still grieving over the love of her youth, surrounded on all sides by George's slaves who knew that when I expired they were free. (My own servants we had not yet decided about.) Privately, with me and friends, my husband declared his repugnance for slavery. He knew it was wrong. And hoping to right that wrong—one he'd known as a slave master since his eleventh year—he built liberation for his Negroes after my death into his last will and testament. (No, I was not thoroughly consulted on this matter.) And by doing so, he created the most frightening prison for me.

I am afraid to be alone in any room in my house with Billy Lee, given the way I sometimes catch him looking at me out of the *corner of his eye. My Lord, I am afraid to* eat, *for anything they serve me might be poisoned. It chills me to hear the footsteps of any of our servants behind me when I am on the stairs, or outside my bedroom door at night. Oh, George, you were* not *a thinker. Had you been, you would not out of Christian kindness to the blacks unwittingly consigned me to a hellish house, where in the face of each of our formerly loving attendants I now see my possible executioner.*

How many days, or weeks, I have lived in this agony, I do not know. How long I have to live after my dear husband's departure is also a mystery. But I awoke this morning with a clear resolve. I bade one of the black children to have our coachman ready the carriage to take me in a few moments to Fairfax County court. There, I will sign the papers necessary to release from servitude all of George's Negroes. They must be manumitted now. This very afternoon.

Then, and only then, will they and I be free of the errors of George Washington.

In East Haddam, Connecticut, Venture Smith had become a local legend, using the courts, language, and lifestyle of the white man who had kidnapped Broteer from Guinea. He was a free black man who had made his own way, a man who had been able to buy himself, his wife, and his children out of bondage. He was an African who became an African American without surrendering his heritage. When his path home was forever closed to him, he forged a new path.

Smith never accepted his lot as a "slave for life" or counted on an eventual spiritual freedom instead of one he could taste in this world.

In 1793, the former slave sat down and told his amazing tale to a Connecticut schoolteacher, who recorded it for the ages.

> I am now sixty-nine years old. Though once straight and tall measuring without shoes six feet, one inch and an half, and every way well proportioned, I am now bowed down with age and hardship. . . . I have many consolations; Meg, the wife of my youth, whom I married for love . . . is still alive . . . my freedom is a privilege which nothing else can equal . . . I am now possessed of more than one hundred acres of land and three houses.

Weary and infirm, Venture Smith died in 1805 at the age of seventy-seven. His body was ferried across the cove in a boat and carried three miles to the cemetery. Four pallbearers—two black men in the rear, two white men in front—carried him to his resting place alongside the First Congregational Church in East Haddam.

It was a church Venture helped build.

PART THREE

Brotherly Love

JEFFERSON'S *NOTES ON THE STATE OF VIRGINIA. In 1781, Thomas Jefferson wrote what was to be his only book,* Notes on the State of Virginia. *Though his main focus in the book was the state's natural landscape, he also set forth controversial assertions that black people were biologically and morally inferior to whites.*

THE LIBRARY OF VIRGINIA

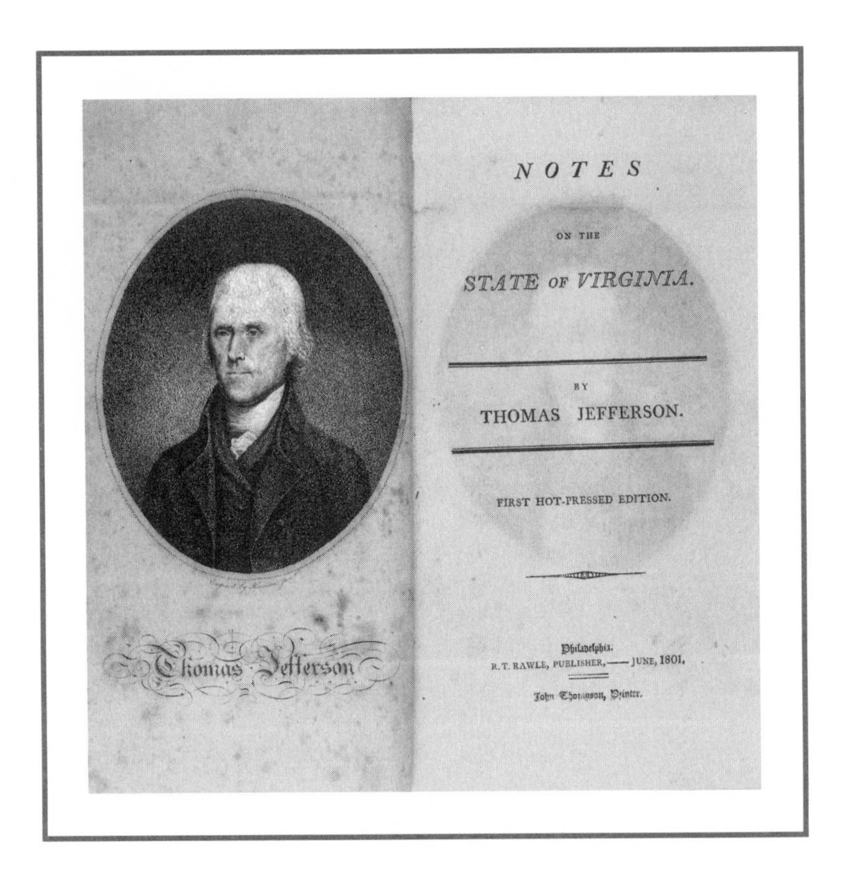

Thomas Jefferson

NOTES

ON THE

STATE OF VIRGINIA.

BY

THOMAS JEFFERSON.

FIRST HOT-PRESSED EDITION.

Philadelphia.

R. T. RAWLE, PUBLISHER,—— JUNE, 1801.

John Thompson, Printer.

MEASUREMENT OF FACIAL ANGLES. *Following the publication of* Notes on the State of Virginia, *many scholars used Jefferson's suspicions as the basis for a new science that put forth a racially based biological hierarchy. This copper engraving accompanied a treatise on black inferiority published in 1791.*

"VERHANDELING VAN PETRUS CAMPER . . ." 1791, BY PERMISSION OF THE BRITISH LIBRARY (TAB1)

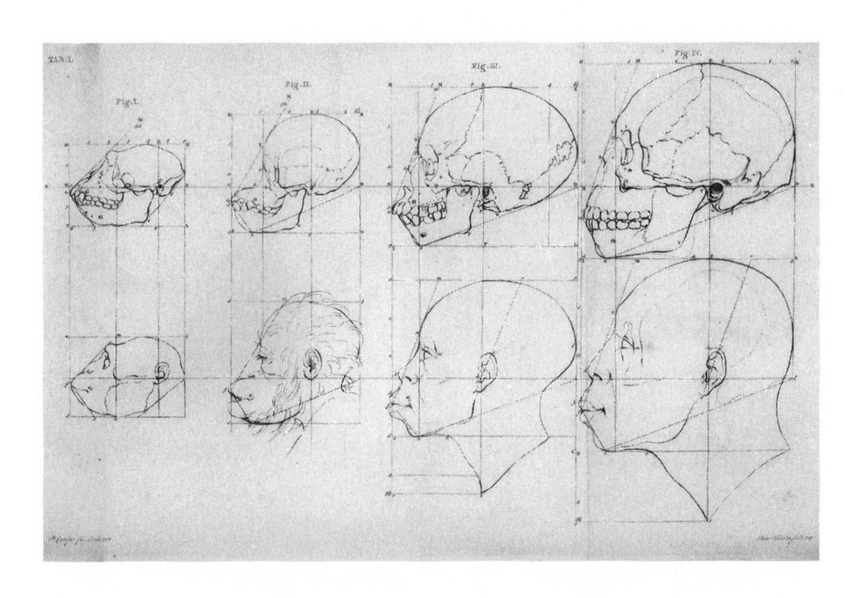

ELI WHITNEY'S COTTON ENGINE. *The first cotton gin, patented by Eli Whitney, went into operation in 1795, revolutionizing both agriculture and slavery in America. Due to the escalating need for laborers to plant and pick cotton for the gin, the value of a "prime negro field hand" skyrocketed to over $1,800 by 1861.*

ELI WHITNEY PAPERS, MANUSCRIPT AND ARCHIVES, YALE UNIVERSITY LIBRARY

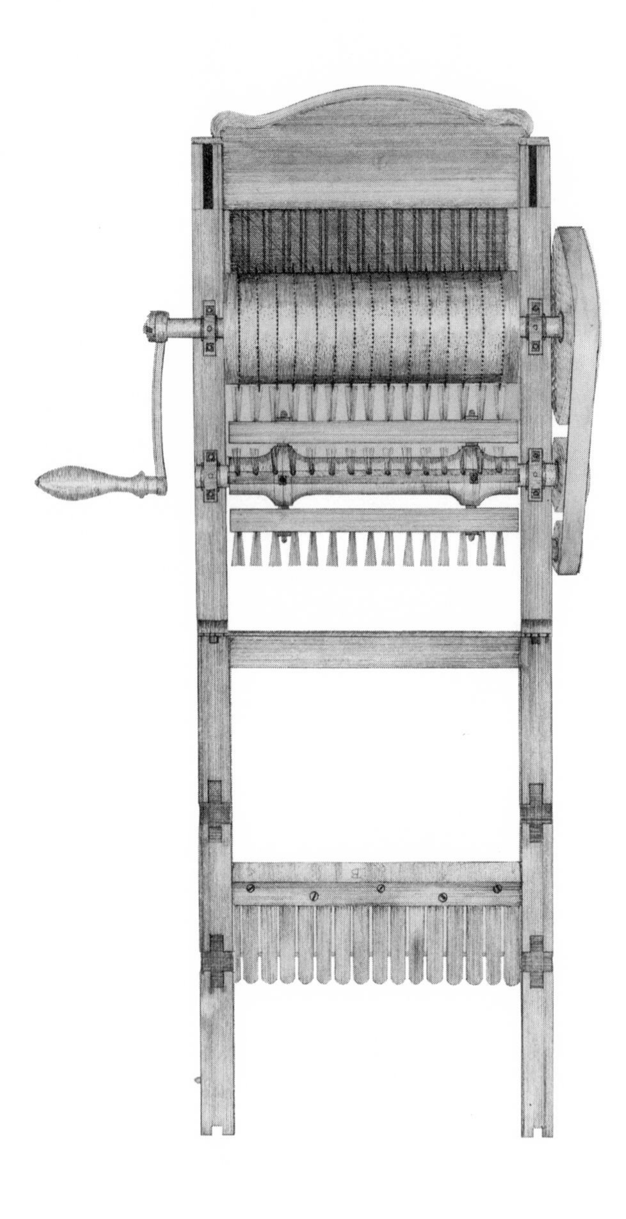

SLAVE AUCTION HOUSE, ALEXANDRIA, VIRGINIA. *As U.S. cotton production soared in the nineteenth century, over 200,000 African American slaves were sold from their homes in Virginia to the Deep South. As a result, slave auction houses, like this one, were erected to handle the large volume of sales.*

LIBRARY OF CONGRESS

METHODS OF SLAVE TORTURE IN THE FRENCH ISLANDS. *In the French colony of St. Domingue, the enslaved Africans who comprised the majority of the population were subjected to severe means of torture. But by 1801, St. Domingue's plantation economy had been overturned by a bloody civil war involving hundreds of thousands of slaves.*

BY PERMISSION OF THE HOUGHTON LIBRARY, HARVARD UNIVERSITY

TOUSSAINT L'OUVERTURE, C. 1795. *Toussaint L'Ouverture was instrumental in bringing about revolution in St. Domingue. A former slave, he became governor of the colony in 1801 but was captured by the French and died before he could see St. Domingue, renamed Haiti, become the second free republic in the Western Hemisphere.*

CLICHÉ BIBLIOTHÈQUE NATIONALE DE FRANCE, PARIS

BENJAMIN RUSH (1745?–1813). *Benjamin Rush was a pioneer in the field of American medicine, a signer of the Declaration of Independence, and an advocate for the abolition of slavery. Rush assisted black leaders in Philadelphia in raising money for what would become Philadelphia's first African American church.*

THE PRINT AND PICTURE COLLECTION, THE FREE LIBRARY OF PHILADELPHIA

REVENGE TAKEN BY THE HAITIAN ARMY AFTER THE REVOLUTION, 1805. *Unlike Rush, who opposed slavery on moral grounds, some white Americans argued for the abolition of slavery out of fear. The violent revenge taken by the black rebels in Haiti was held up as an example of the desire for retribution that many believed all slaves harbored.*

THE LIBRARY COMPANY OF PHILADELPHIA

Revenge taken by the Black Army for the Cruelties practised
on them by the French.

Rev. Richard Allen.
FOUNDER of the AFRICAN METHODIST EPISCOPAL CHURCH,
in the UNITED STATES of AMERICA, 1779.
Phila: Pub. by J. Dainty 1813.

RICHARD ALLEN (1760?–1832). *Richard Allen was one of the most outspoken advocates for the rights of African Americans in the early nineteenth century. In 1817, he founded the African Methodist Episcopal (AME) denomination, the first national African American institution of its kind.*

THE LIBRARY COMPANY OF PHILADELPHIA

An Account of the Late Intended Insurrection, Charleston, South Carolina. *In 1822, thirty-five black men were executed in Charleston for their part in a conspiracy, led by Denmark Vesey, to free the city's slaves. After the testimony of many of those involved revealed that Charleston's AME church had been a primary meeting place for the conspirators, the church was torn down.*

RARE BOOK, MANUSCRIPT, & SPECIAL COLLECTIONS LIBRARY, DUKE UNIVERSITY

CLASS No. 1.

Comprises those prisoners who were found guilty and executed.

Prisoners Names.	*Owners' Names.*	*Time of Commit.*	*How Disposed of.*
Peter	James Poyas	June 18	Hanged on Tuesday the 2d July, 1822, on Blake's lands, near Charleston.
Ned	Gov. T. Bennett,	do.	
Rolla	do.	do	
Batteau	do.	do.	
Denmark Vesey	A free black man	22	
Jessy	Thos. Blackwood	23	
John	Elias Horry	July 5	Do. on the Lines near Ch.; Friday July 12.
Gullah Jack	Paul Pritchard	do.	
Mingo	Wm. Harth	June 21	Hanged on the Lines near Charleston, on Friday, 26th July.
Lot	Forrester	27	
Joe	P. L. Jore	July 6	
Julius	Thos. Forrest	8	
Tom	Mrs. Russell	10	
Smart	Robt. Anderson	do.	
John	John Robertson	11	
Robert	do.	do.	
Adam	do.	do.	
Polydore	Mrs. Faber	do.	
Bacchus	Benj. Hammet	do.	
Dick	Wm. Sims	13	
Pharaoh	— Thompson	do.	
Jemmy	Mrs. Clement	18	
Mauidore	Mordecai Cohen	19	
Dean	— Mitchell	do.	
Jack	Mrs. Purcell	12	
Bellisle	Est. of Jos. Yates	18	
Naphur	do.	do.	
Adam	do.	do.	
Jacob	John S. Glen	16	
Charles	John Billings	18	
Jack	N. McNeill	22	Do. Tues. July 30.
Cæsar	Miss Smith	do.	
Jacob Stagg	Jacob Lankester	23	
Tom	Wm. M. Scott	24	
William	Mrs. Garner	Aug. 2	Do. Friday, Aug. 9.

MOTHER BETHEL AME CHURCH, PHILADELPHIA. *Bethel AME Church stands today on the site purchased by Richard Allen in 1792 and remains the mother church of the AME denomination. Bethel Church was a center of community life as African Americans were increasingly shut out of other public places.*

SCHOMBURG CENTER FOR RESEARCH IN BLACK CULTURE, NEW YORK PUBLIC LIBRARY

THE FOURTH OF JULY IN PHILADELPHIA, C. 1811. *Though the Fourth of July became a popular holiday for white Americans in the early nineteenth century, James Forten, a black businessman in Philadelphia, once remarked that it was a "well-known fact that black people . . . dare not be seen after twelve o'clock in the day" on the anniversary of American Independence.*

COURTESY OF THE PENNSYLVANIA ACADEMY OF THE FINE ARTS, PHILADELPHIA. PENNSYLVANIA ACADEMY PURCHASE (FROM THE ESTATE OF PAUL BECK, JR.).

MR. T. RICE AS JIM CROW. *In the 1830s, blackface minstrelsy became both a popular art form and a means of dehumanizing African Americans. Jim Crow, a favorite character on the minstrel stage, seemed the personification of Jefferson's observations that blacks could not "utter a thought above the level of plain narration."*

BEQUEST OF EVERT JANSEN WENDELL, THE HARVARD THEATRE COLLECTION, THE HOUGHTON LIBRARY

FREE BLACK COUPLE IN VIRGINIA. *As demeaning caricatures of African Americans gained popularity, free black people began to organize as never before. In 1830, the American Society of Free Persons of Colour held its first national convention at Bethel Church in Philadelphia to strategize against segregation, disenfranchisement, and slavery.*

COLLECTION OF GREG FRENCH

CHAPTER SEVEN

The first command to man to "subdue the earth," like every other divine command must be fulfilled.

—Benjamin Rush

In January 1793, the sky above America's capital was filled with a miracle. A huge gas balloon drifted on the Philadelphia breeze, its basket carrying French aeronaut Jean-Pierre Blanchard. He stayed aloft for forty-six minutes, landed near Woodbury, New Jersey, and returned in time to meet with President Washington, who had witnessed his pioneering feat. It was Blanchard's first ascent in the United States, and everyone who watched was dizzied by the possibilities.

This was the Age of Enlightenment, and there seemed to be no limits to what man could accomplish. The human mind could decipher and conquer natural forces and encompass a world of curiosities and apparent miracles. Many in a country touting a bevy of inspired minds were not yet comfortable justifying the enslavement of a people.

The American Revolution was over. One of five Americans was being held in bondage. And the majority of the 700,000 slaves who tended and nurtured the fields, cleaned the homes, and fed the occupants, who pounded the nails and sawed the wood, had been born in North America. Opportunities for peace eluded them; by the time the war was over, it was becoming clear that the country's sweeping declarations of equality and liberty did not include them. America prided itself on lofty documents that outlined a vision for the country. But neither the Declaration of Independence nor the Constitution recognized slaves as human beings.

The Revolution had promised the country a progressive destiny—but that fact ignored the contradiction that built America. The nation wanted so much to be that glittering new republic where each and every person is endowed with certain natural rights. But an asterisk would accompany that claim. The Founding Fathers espoused a doctrine they could never live up to.

Slaveholder Thomas Jefferson was a craftsman of the American viewpoint and one of the most vocal proponents of liberty. His stirring and determined writings sparked resistance and gave democracy a guiding line. In the early years of the new country, his words prodded America's budding conscience. "Can the liberties of a nation be thought secure," he asked, "when we have removed their only firm basis, a conviction in the minds of the people that these liberties are the gift of God?"

Although it is impossible to say what he actually believed, Jefferson often stated publicly that the very idea of slavery was wrong. However, his doubts about slavery didn't change the fact that he owned more than 130 slaves himself or that he found it impossible to live comfortably without the labor of captives. His writings indicated that he knew a day of reckoning would come: "I tremble for my country when I reflect that God is just: that his justice cannot sleep forever."

While Jefferson wrestled with slavery's contradictions, former slaves in Philadelphia had, by 1793, formed the largest community of free blacks in America. Many had been freed during the Revolution by patriots who believed that the declarations of equality applied to all men; others were granted liberty by members of religions that opposed slavery; still others were slaves brought into the state and freed by Pennsylvania's unique Gradual Abolition Act of 1780. Some had run away to freedom. Some were born free.

As they sampled the trappings of freedom, these black Philadelphians were plagued by troubling questions about their place in American society.

Although Philadelphia seemed a haven for free blacks, they were often denied the vote. And a strong, poisonous undercurrent of racism—embedded in continuing beliefs of black inferiority—ran through the city. In confronting these obstacles, a sense of community grew. African Americans began to develop their own institutions, stamped with their undeniable signature.

It was the perfect time for a man like Richard Allen.

Allen was a free man when he arrived in Philadelphia in early 1786. In February of that year, he was preaching the gospel to a small, racially mixed congregation in Radnor, twelve miles west of Philadelphia. A Methodist elder called him to preach to blacks attending services at St. George's Methodist Church in Philadelphia's German section. He preached before dawn to avoid a conflict with later white services. Although he had planned to stay for only a short time, his message was so well received that he decided to settle down in the bustling city. Soon after his arrival, Allen joined Absalom Jones and other recently liberated slaves to discuss forming a separate black religious society.

In many ways, Richard Allen was born dreaming that dream.

Born into slavery in Philadelphia in 1760, Allen surrendered to the sweet inner rumblings of religious conversion sometime around his seventeenth birthday:

> I was awakened and brought to see myself, poor, wretched and undone, and without the mercy of God. . . . I cried to the Lord both night and day. . . . [A]ll of a sudden my dungeon shook, my chains flew off, and glory to God I cried. My soul was filled. I cried, enough for me—the Saviour died.

After his transformation, Allen went from house to house, spreading his newfound gospel of joy. He also began to participate in Methodist class meetings. The showcase preaching and simple, forthright tenets of Methodism, along with the religion's traditional antislavery stance, appealed to many blacks. One preacher's fiery sermon on "Thou art weighed in the balance and art found wanting," a message that targeted the wavering conscience of slave owners, convinced Allen's owner, Stokely Sturgis, that owning human beings was wrong. In January of 1780, he signed a document allowing Allen free time to raise money to buy himself out of slavery.

In the five years before the final payment was made, Allen preached whenever and to whomever he could. After the Revolutionary War, he became a traveling sermonizer, pulling both black and white believers into his circle. Now, years later, he and his colleagues envisioned a church that would meet the spiritual needs of former slaves. Allen remarked:

> I preached in the commons, in Southwark, Northern Liberties, and wherever I could find an opening. I frequently preached twice a day, at 5 o'clock in the morning and in the evening, and it was not uncommon for me to preach from four to five times a day. . . . And I saw the necessity of erecting a place of worship for the colored people.

But a church was not the immediate result of Allen's dream. Although Philadelphia's white ministry ridiculed the idea, Allen and Jones nurtured it until April 1787, when they organized the Free African Society (FAS), a compassionate mutual-aid organization which stressed ideas of self-worth and charity—the very ideas it took to forge a strong, viable black community.

Allen, objecting to the society's gradual drift toward Quaker practices, broke with the FAS after two years. Following his departure, Absalom Jones stepped up to lead the organization. And it was Jones who was a crucial element in the discovery and nurturing of connections in the white community—connections that eventually led to the building of a black church.

Under Jones's guidance, the FAS garnered support from dedicated and concerned whites. The Pennsylvania Abolition Society had rededicated itself to the cause, becoming the Pennsylvania Society for Promoting the Abolition of Slavery and for the Relief of Free Negroes Unlawfully Held in Bondage and for Improving the Condition of the African Race. One of the organization's most fervent members was Dr. Benjamin Rush, a signer of the Declaration of Independence and Philadelphia's leading physician.

When Jones and his allies resurrected their quest for a black church, they sought Rush's advice. Not only did the doctor support their bold move toward religious independence, he helped draft a general plan for the church's organization, which the members voted to embrace. To be called the African Church of Philadelphia, the tenets of the church were "so general as to embrace all, and yet so orthodox in cardinal points as to offend none." The ambitious planning also caused Richard Allen to rejoin the group.

The determined group, still enthusiastically aided by Rush, went about the business of funding the construction of the African Church of Philadelphia. Small donations came in from George Washington and Thomas Jefferson. The planners had to face a grim reality—many whites who vocally supported the church were timid when it came to actually financing the venture. White church leaders wondered how the plan would affect their own places of worship. They realized that the church would help blacks move away from white control—and not everyone was sure that was such a good idea.

Initial subscriptions allowed the group to purchase two adjacent lots, but money barely trickled in after that. It was getting difficult to keep the dream alive.

But in the fall of 1792, a chilling incident at St. George's reminded blacks that they were still discriminated against and illuminated the need for them to build their own separate church.

Some black leaders still attended St. George's; they were among those who contributed money to expand the church, which was too small for its growing congregation. On the first Sunday after the new construction was finished, the church elders informed black worshipers that they were to sit upstairs in the church's recently added rear gallery. It didn't matter that the blacks had contributed physically and financially to the remodeling of the church.

"We expected to take the seats over the ones we formerly occupied below, not knowing any better," said Richard Allen.

> We took those seats; Meeting had begun, and they were nearly done singing, and just as we got to the seats, the elder said, "Let us pray." We had not been long upon our knees before I heard considerable scuffling and low talking. I raised my head up and saw one of the trustees, H—— M——, having hold of the Rev. Absalom Jones, pulling him up off of his knees, and saying, "You must get up—you must not kneel here." Mr. Jones replied, "Wait until prayer is over, and I will get up and trouble you no more." With that he beckoned to one of the other trustees, Mr. L—— S——, to come to his assistance. He came and went to William White to pull him up. By this time prayer was over, and we all went out of the church in a body, and they were no more plagued by us in the church.

It was time to build a church of their own.

But by late 1792, the dream was all but dead. Money for the construction of the church was still slow in coming, and it seemed the lots would remain empty. But the planners attracted an unlikely ally in Welsh immigrant John Nicholson, a former land speculator and state comptroller, who provided a loan large enough to begin building.

In March of the following year, Philadelphia's free blacks and their white supporters turned out to see ground broken for the church. Twenty-five years later, Richard Allen said, "As I was the first proposer of the African Church, I put the first spade in the ground to dig the cellar for the same. This was the first African Church or meeting house that was erected in the United States of America."

In August, in a wide-open field at Philadelphia's edge, a sumptuous banquet was held to celebrate the raising of the church roof. First, approximately one hundred white construction workers were served by a group of free blacks; then, in an encouraging about-face, fifty blacks sat down to dine, served by six of the most prominent whites. Benjamin Rush said it would be "a day to be remembered with pleasure as long as I live."

But in the sweltering summer of 1793, a raging outbreak of yellow fever, the worst in the country's history, delayed the completion of the church and gave the burgeoning black community a chance to exhibit its newfound strength.

The poisonous fever was a swift and ruthless killer, often taking a life in less than a day. Victims were often shut out, ostracized, summarily deposited in the street to avoid the spreading of infection. It didn't matter if the afflicted was a child, a strapping adult, an elderly person, a young pregnant woman.

The horror of the rampaging disease can be sensed in the matter-of-fact snippets from the journal of Philadelphian Elizabeth Drinker.

> SEPTEMBER 2, 1793. We have heard this day of the death of a poor, intemperate woman of the name of Clarey, who sold oysters last winter in a Cellar in Front St. She was taken out of her senses, and went out of town; was found dead on the road. . . .
>
> SEPTEMBER 3, 1793. We have heard this day of five persons who died in one house in Chestnut Street. . . .

> SEPTEMBER 6, 1793. Caleb Hopkinson, T. Scattergood's brother in law, died this morning of this raging fever. Doct. Hutchinson is also gone. 'Tis said he got ye disorder by putting a young woman in her Coffin, who died at his house, not being able readily to procure anyone to do that office. The ringing of Bells for the dead is forbidden for several days past.

Rumor was that the fever had been imported by people escaping a violent rebellion in Haiti. Fear and confusion about the disease's progression and strength turned Philadelphia into a nightmare. Those entrusted with the city's safety threw up their hands in the face of a fever that killed indiscriminately.

Secretary of State Thomas Jefferson said, "The week before last the deaths were about 40. The last week about 80. And this week I think they will be about 200. All persons who can find asylum elsewhere are flying from this city."

Dr. Benjamin Rush refused to leave the city. He continued to treat those stricken with the fever until he, too, felt his temperature soar and his body weaken. Although he eventually recovered, he knew help would be needed to bring the outbreak under control.

Rush heard reports that Africans were immune to yellow fever, and he formulated an idea: If the most resented, despised, and misunderstood segment of the population were immune and could be of service to the majority community, whites would certainly be overwhelmingly grateful. The doctor, well-respected among the blacks of Philadelphia, saw his plan as a move toward equality in the city. He urged Richard Allen to convince black citizens to serve as medical aides, gravediggers, and drivers of the carts carrying the dead.

Despite the obstacles recently thrown in their path—the staunch opposition to the building of a black church, the demoralizing incident at St. George's—the blacks organized under the leadership of Allen and Jones and began to assist with the massive medical effort of struggling to curb the disease. And although the rumor that they were immune persisted, many died. In a pamphlet written by the two men, it was evident that they thought God had given them a chance to prove their worthiness: "[T]he meek and humble Jesus, the great pattern of humanity, and every other virtue that can adorn and dignify men, hath commanded to love our enemies, to do good to them that hate and despitefully use us."

People who were repulsed at the thought of black people entering their homes were now dependent on them to stay alive. Jones and Allen wrote, "[We] think, that when a physician was not attainable, we have been the instruments, in the hand of God, for saving the lives of some hundreds of our suffering fellow mortals."

Isaac Heston, a twenty-three-year-old law clerk, wrote this letter to his brother on September 19, 1793:

> *You can not immagin the situation of this City. . . . they are aDieing on our right hand & on our left. . . . great are the number that are called to the grave, and numbered with the silent Dead. last third Day there were buried in Potters field 26. in the Dutch Calvinist ground 22 & in Friends 7. . . . there is now scarsely any body to be seen in many parts of the town. . . . indeed, I don't know what the people would do if it was not for the Negroes, as they are the Principal nurses.*

Ten days later, Isaac Heston was dead.

THE PLAGUE

July 5, 1793
Friday, 8:30 p.m.

I have kept this journal for a few months now, initially to document for posterity the early work I am doing to open—soon, I hope—the doors of a church I will call Bethel, but as we now enter the second (or perhaps it is the third) month of deaths due to the yellow fever, I wonder if it might be more appropriate to title these pages The Plague Journal.

Death is all around us, like a biblical parable on (white) vanity. Should I make that the subject of my five o'clock sermon tomorrow morning? I wonder how it might be received? Perhaps well, insofar as my congregation is entirely Cainite—so white men call us—the colored outcasts violently driven from St. George's, one of Philadelphia's largest Methodist churches just last year. I know in the eyes of God, the behavior of this city's Abelites was scandalous. We, free men and women, came humbly to their church to pray to the Creator. Rev. Absalom Jones and I were a little late. Without causing any noise or commotion whatsoever, we quickly went up the stairs of St. George to the newly built gallery, which was just above the seats we'd occupied the week before. The strains of the first hymn were ending as we sat down, then the church elder told all those present to pray. Obediently, we got down on our knees. But hardly was I a minute into silent meditation when at my right I heard Absalom make a sound. Opening my eyes, I saw one of St. George's trustees hauling my companion to his feet, telling him Negroes were never, never, never to sit in this section of the gallery. Naturally, my friends and I left, turning our backs on all of Philadelphia's white churches. One Sabbath after the next we were subjected to humiliations it pains me to remember. Good Christians, for example, who refused to take the sacrament if it meant sipping from the same chalice that had touched the lips of their darker brethren. Oh yes, Absalom was compelled to organize St. Thomas Episcopal Church after that sad incident, and I dream of a ground-breaking ceremony someday at Bethel, that we might better separate ourselves from those who reject us, and all of this simply that we can worship our common Father in the spirit He intended.

Yet now, ironically, He has visited upon this city's whites a plague of medieval proportions. It is a swift disease. It can kill in a single day. Week by week, the death toll mounts. Frightened whites flee this capital city of Philadelphia by the thousands, abandoning their families and friends. Those who remain are helpless in the grip of this growing malignancy, for the country's government is paralyzed. The crisis is unparalleled in this country's history. But word has spread that Negroes are immune to the disease, which is not true, of course. Nonetheless, the Abelites believe we are protected, and so Dr. Benjamin Rush, knowing of the leadership position I occupy through God's grace among my own people, has appealed to me to plead with them to assist the city's remaining civic leaders in combating the curse that is laying them low.

I prayed—and prayed—on his proposal. And in the midst of my appeal to the Most High for guidance, I remembered the injunction, "Bear ye one another's burdens, and so fulfill the law of Christ" (Galatians 6:2). This crisis, the Lord let me see, is possibly our invitation as a people back from our exile east of Eden. If we help the Abelites in their hour of need, mightn't they be thankful to the Negroes of Philadelphia? Wouldn't their hatred be replaced by gratitude? Such has been my hope since I enlisted my people in the dangerous work of saving others who have long despised them.

JULY 21, 1793
SUNDAY, 6 P.M.

Preached four sermons today in the Commons, in Southwark, and Northern Liberties, and as always after such a day I feel a bit emotionally drained, yet also exhilarated, so I know it will be difficult to fall asleep at my usual hour of 9 P.M. But do I *preach? It seems more fitting to say that when I stand before my people, the Book in my left hand, the words come flooding out of me, as if I were merely a conduit, an anonymous instrument through which the music of our Lord and Savior bursts forth. Afterwards, it's true, I cannot recall everything I said, though the laity always seem pleased and tell me that I am good. No, I've told them time again, not I but the Father within me doeth the works, and I ask them to read Matthew 19:17.*

However, that glow that comes after a day of sermonizing lasted no longer than it took for me to step back onto the streets of Philadelphia and begin my walk home. The dead lie in ditches alongside the roads. I saw a white child who was crying, wandering about like a phantom because she has the plague and her parents turned her out into the street. They did not want her to infect the rest of their family. Yellow fever is no respecter of age, color, sex, caste, or social position—the doctors are dying just as swiftly as their patients, which reminds me that I must look in on Dr. Benjamin Rush, a good and decent white man, and a true Abolitionist.

Note: My businesses need attention.

One other thing about this plague troubles me. God does nothing, we know, without having a purpose in mind. We cannot, of course, fathom His will entirely, though my hope, as I've written, is that this affliction will soften the hearts of whites to the Negroes laboring to help them. But is there a deeper message in this sickness that has befallen Philadelphia like the Flood, or locusts darkening the sky? I have taken this question each day into my mid-afternoon meditation, but as of yet I have no answer.

AUGUST 6, 1793
TUESDAY, 5:20 P.M.

Spent this morning digging a common grave outside the city for burying the dead, which we loaded onto wagons at 6 A.M. *Three of my congregation and I rode slowly up one street, down another, shouting, "Bring out your dead." Which six people did, dragging the corpses from their homes, then pitching them onto our wagon. As we bore them out of town, I looked back at their bodies. They were heaped together like broken dolls. Their flesh was yellow. Already two of them had gone ripe. The other three were more recently dead, their limbs stiff as boards. In that pile of putrefying flesh I saw—or thought I saw—the trustee from St. George's, the one who'd expelled Absalom and myself. I believe it was him, but the decomposition of his face made a definite identification difficult.*

He had not wanted me in his church, or touching him. As things turned out, once we had dug a hole six feet deep and wrapped the fetid corpses in sackcloth, my black hands were the last ones in this world to touch him. We shoveled dirt onto the bodies, and when I could no longer see the trustee's face—which, God forgive me, I hated—I said a brief prayer that all their souls might wing heavenward, though should that doubtful event happen, I'm sure the trustee would be standing at the gate when I arrived, telling Jesus that my black brethren and I should not be admitted.

But I prayed for him, yes. And for myself (II Timothy 2:1–3), for the removal of my anger. For does not the Light of the World tell us that we must forgive seven times seventy, if need be?

AUGUST 12, 1793
MONDAY, 8:45 P.M.

Just returned from making my rounds to the sick. Walked this morning at approximately 7 A.M. into the palatial home of a woman well known in Philadelphia for the lavish parties she holds in her ballroom. Everywhere my gaze fell I saw wealth. A chandelier, for example, that would pay for the building of ten Bethels. Furniture imported from France. I am certain this woman does not dwell often on Matthew 6:27, where it is written, "Which of you by taking thought can add one cubit unto his stature?" Her servant, a colored girl in my congregation, led me up the quarter-turn stairs to the woman's bedroom, where she lay semiconscious, emaciated as a skeleton. I could tell the disease was far along with her. Most likely, she was bleeding internally. Most of her golden hair—now stiff as straw—had fallen out onto her pillow. I began unpacking the apothecary case Dr. Rush had given me, laying out glass vials of various medicines, the little weighing scale, and instruments necessary for cupping. The old woman began to rouse. Seeing me, that I was a Negro—and one in her bedroom no less—she began to scream, shouting, "Get out! Get out!"

I repacked my case and promptly left. I did not plead with her or beg for the opportunity to save her life so that she could begin plans for her next party. Later in the day, through her servant girl, I was informed of her passing at 4 P.M. Perhaps God has sent this plague for the same reason His wrath destroyed Sodom. To cleanse our city of human corruption . . .

SEPTEMBER 1, 1793
SUNDAY, 7:00 P.M.

I have been ill, feverish for the last few weeks. Unable to write in addition to my other duties. It is not true that the plague bypasses people of color. For our numbers in Philadelphia, as many Negroes have perished as whites. What, then, heavenly Father, do you want us to learn from this unending devastation?

SEPTEMBER 12, 1793
THURSDAY, 4:18 P.M.

As I promised him, I again visited earlier this afternoon with Dr. Benjamin Rush, and as always our time together was uplifting. I cannot condemn white people precisely because I know someone like the good doctor. From the beginning he supported our black agents of mercy during this epidemic, and he could have fled Philadelphia along with the reportedly twenty thousand others who have abandoned the city, but being a true physician, and man of God, he remained during these months when his services were most needed.

I was discouraged to see, however, that the yellow pallor was upon his face this afternoon. He looked feverish, weakened by his own bout with the disease, and so I begged him not to stand, as he was struggling to do, when I entered his parlor. Slowly, he settled back against the cushions, perspiration beading along his brow, and tried to smile. He gave me the intelligence—blessed to hear—that across Philadelphia there were signs that the fever was beginning to abate. Fewer cases had been reported this week than the week previous. "Then we are winning?" I asked, too soon. "And when this is over, the citizens of this city will acknowledge the role played in its restoration by Negroes?" Dr. Rush looked down. His eyes narrowed. He gave a great, sad sigh, and said, "Would that were so, Richard, but already I am hearing the opposite of what we'd hoped. Rather than singing your people's praises, white men and women are saying blacks used the plague for their own profit. They tell me reports that Negroes stole when, in the guise of nurses, they entered white homes—and like vultures pilfered the bodies of the dead. Some have been accused of murdering, not saving, others. And even you, my friend, are being accused." I asked him of what, and he replied that many believed I was pocketing money because in the past week or two I was obliged to charge for some of the labors my people performed. I explained that it was true. We were *asking for some remuneration, but only because we had exhausted all the volunteers who stepped forward to give freely of their time, and so I was forced to hire five men to assist me. The doctor nodded, "Oh,* I *believe you, and I will tell* everyone *what you have told me. But I doubt it will change many of their hearts. In that case of medicines I gave you, there are many potions and elixirs for curing the ailments of the flesh. I wish to God we could invent something for curing the sickness in the white soul."*

So he spoke. I thanked him, then took my leave.

OCTOBER 16, 1793
WEDNESDAY, 9:50 P.M.

Unable to sleep, I walked the streets for long hours after dark this evening, and at every alleyway, park, and corner I came to, where the sick huddled round a fire, or wild dogs nibbled the flesh off a dead man's fingers, I saw a memento mori. *A reminder that Dr. Rush and I had been foolish to believe the hearts of (white) men might ever change in the Earthly City. No, our salvation awaits only in that house not made by hands, eternal in the heavens. Wandering tonight after another day of delivering five sermons, I did see signs that the yellow fever was lessening its grip upon the city. I mused that perhaps soon that plague would be gone. Things would be as they were before. I stepped through now-healing white neighborhoods, ones I'd delivered medicines to only a month ago; I saw lily-white faces glaring at me through the windows, twisted lips drawn down in disgust at my very presence, and I knew at last, and with the certainty of revelation, that the exoteric lesson the good Lord wanted me to see was that, despite the best efforts by men of goodwill, some plagues never end.*

By October, out of a population of 50,000, some 20,000 whites had run from Philadelphia and its contagion, and 4,000 were dead or dying, including a tenth of the city's 2,500 blacks. The fever continued to rage—it spared few in its path, black or white.

With November's first chill, the outbreak ended as suddenly as it began—and long before anyone would know that it had been transmitted by mosquitoes.

Once the epidemic waned, the blacks who had banded together to help were immediately accused of profiting financially from the epidemic. Publisher Mathew Carey typified the attitude with this terse accusation: "The great demand for nurses afforded an opportunity for imposition, which was eagerly seized by some of the vilest of blacks." Carey was also sure he had identified the source of the fever. "[F]rom the resemblance of its leading symptoms to those of the yellow fever of the West Indies, there can be no doubt that the contagion, which gave rise to the disease here, was imported."

Carey's *A Short Account of the Malignant Fever* went through four printings and was read with great interest in all corners of the country. (It was, at best, a secondhand account, since Carey was one of those who fled the city during the outbreak.) But with each edition of his reports, the accusations by white Philadelphians grew more pointed. The perilous veneer of cooperation and friendship cracked.

Blacks were accused of profiteering in the epidemic, even though they had worked so hard to pull the city from its grip.

Construction of the African Church had been delayed for nearly three months due to the yellow-fever epidemic. As the building neared completion, the city's blacks turned their attention to the choice of a denomination, which they now considered necessary. Jones and Allen favored Methodism, although St. George's had so thoroughly insulted black worshipers two years before.

The majority of the blacks favored uniting with the Episcopal Church. Not only was their most dedicated supporter, Dr. Benjamin Rush, of that faith, but blacks had been allowed to participate in the services of the city's three Episcopalian churches since the 1740s. Allen, steadfast in his belief that the Methodist faith was the best choice for blacks, withdrew from the proceedings. Absalom Jones stayed with the Episcopalians and founded St. Thomas's Church.

Although he had broken ties with the Episcopalian group, Richard Allen never stopped dreaming of a separate church. On May 5, 1794, he called together a small group of men to plan a Methodist place of worship "separate from our white brethren." Using his own money, Allen bought a blacksmith's shop and had it hauled to Sixth and Lombard, a short distance away from St. Thomas's. Seven weeks later, and eight years after Richard Allen set out to realize a singular goal, his own Methodist church stood in the shadow of Independence Hall. The church was called Bethel—*Bethel*, in Hebrew, means "the House of God." It was a name that sounded like singing. Later, it would become Mother Bethel, the center of a new African Methodist Episcopal denomination.

In its first year, St. Thomas welcomed 246 members, Bethel 108. The following year, membership had increased to 427 and 121. The movement for independent black churches reflected a determination and dignity that defined Philadelphia's black community in the early 1790s.

But by the end of the eighteenth century, 900,000 human beings—Africans and their descendants—were slaves in the United States.

Ethan Andrews, a white Philadelphia professor who traveled extensively in the South, sensed an impending danger in a rapidly growing slave population.

> To keep millions in ignorance, while knowledge, like the light of day is beaming all around them, and to continue them in unconditional slavery, among a people who glory in being as free as the air of heaven, will be alike impracticable.
>
> . . . [T]he brutes whom he will most resemble are not the ox and the ass, those patient and harmless drudges who quietly toil for the benefit of their masters, but beasts of prey, who want only the power to destroy those by whom they are held in chains.

In 1791, on a Caribbean island, the beasts of prey had bared their teeth. And their masters fell before them.

Slaves, rebelling against years of inhumane treatment, set ablaze the plantations in the small colony of Haiti, then called St. Domingue. Conditions in the colony were so brutal that one out of every ten Africans who arrived there died within four years. And they died in the most horrible ways—of sickness and abuse. They were tortured, starved to death, maimed, mutilated, raped.

Before the revolt, St. Domingue had been France's pride and joy as well as its cash cow—the colony led the world in the exportation of sugar and coffee.

The revolt was fueled by a heady mixture of anger, desperation, and voodoo mysticism. Despite regulations meant to limit their movements and communication, slaves traveled freely, practiced voodoo rites, exchanged news, and celebrated their imminent victory. By the end of July, in and around Le Cap, an intricately planned mass rebellion was set to go into motion. The spiritual and strategic leader of Le Cap's twelve thousand slaves was Boukman, a voodoo priest and headman of a local plantation.

In late August, while traveling to a Colonial Assembly, French colonial deputies encountered a group of slaves who were openly defiant and abusive. Some were taken as prisoners and questioned; they hinted vaguely that an uprising was forthcoming. But the whites had a hard time believing that the slaves had the savvy and foresight to organize a rebellion of any consequence.

On the thunderous, rain-swept night of August 22, 1791, rebellion leaders met in a forest clearing. There Boukman outlined last-minute instructions and prayed the prayer that damned the whites to their destiny:

> The god who created the sun which gives us light, who rouses the waves and rules the storm, though hidden in the clouds, he watches us. He sees all that the white man does. The god of the white man inspires him with crime, but our god calls upon us to do good works. Our god who is good to us orders us to revenge our wrongs. He will direct our arms and aid us. Throw away the symbol of the god of the whites who has so often caused us to weep, and listen to the voice of liberty, which speaks in the hearts of us all.

The symbol of the white god? The cross.

Shortly after 10 P.M., the drums rose from a deeper throat. And slaves all over plantations surrounding Le Cap, from Acul to Flaville to Gallifet, armed themselves with blades and torches and invaded the homes of their masters. They raped. They murdered. They set fire to the houses they had helped to build, the fields they had tended.

One witness remembered:

> a wall of fire from which continually arose thick vortices of smoke whose huge black volumes could be likened only to those frightful storm clouds which roll onwards charged with thunder and lightning. The rifts in those clouds revealed flames equally great which rose darting and flashing to the very sky. . . . The most striking feature of this terrible spectacle was a rain of fire composed of burning cane-straw which whirled thick before the blast like snow and which the wind whipped, now toward the harbor and ships, now over the houses of the town.

Whites were dismembered, sawed in half, nailed to posts and fencing. Women were raped as they lay on the bodies of their dead spouses. In a ghoulish show of determination, rebels impaled the head of a white baby on a sword and paraded through the capital. Surprisingly, in the midst of the carnage, slaves took care to safeguard the lives and properties of former masters who had exhibited compassion.

But it wasn't long before the whites got over their shock and began to fight back. When slaves tried to destroy Le Cap, their unfamiliarity with firepower worked against them. Believing that they were rendered invincible by Ogun, an African god of war, they ran toward musket fire and tried to stop cannonballs by jamming their path with their hands. With the slaves' initiative weakening, whites established cordons designed to contain the revolt, and they began to invade slave strongholds.

A soldier named du Rouvray, in charge of the defense at Le Cap, built a determined force consisting of planters and militia. After a tense confrontation near the Gallifet plantation, he and his men killed 600 slaves. At Limonade, he killed 150 slaves in one afternoon.

During the 1791 rebellion, a British army officer reflected on the chaos that was once Le Cap:

> The City presents a terrible spectacle; surrounded by ditches and palisades, the streets blocked by barricades, and the squares occupied by scaffolds on which captured negroes are tortured—the whole forming a depressing picture of devastation and carnage.

Many blacks paid dearly for their brutal lurch toward freedom. British historian Bryan Edwards was an eyewitness to two executions at the gallows of Place de Clugny:

> One of them expired on receiving the third stroke on his stomach, each of his legs and arms having been first broken in two places. . . . The other had a harder fate. When the executioner lifted up the instrument to give the finishing stroke on the breast . . . the mob, with the ferociousness of cannibals, called out *arretez!* and compelled him to leave his work unfinished. In that condition the miserable wretch, with his broken limbs doubled up, was put on a cart-wheel, which was placed horizontally, one end of the axle-tree being driven into the earth. At the end of some forty minutes, some English seamen, who were spectators of the tragedy, strangled him in mercy.

The fighting continued off and on for thirteen years.

A French officer in Le Cap described a horrific scene in 1793:

> From the summit of the mountains down the roads to the plain, came immense hoards of Africans. They arrived with torches and knives and plunged into the city. From all sides flames were lifted as in a whirlwind and spread everywhere. What a spectacle of cruelty. I can still hear the whistling of bullets, the explosions of powder, the crumbling of houses. . . .
>
> I still see the feeble inhabitants in flight, half-naked, dragging in the streets . . . the mutilated corpses of their families or their friends.

St. Domingue was approximately a week's sail from the shores of America. The murderous unrest so close to home was an uncomfortable reminder for white Americans. Slaves always had their minds set on freedom, and they could use violence to attain it. Whites feared that the bloody revolt in Haiti had set a dangerous precedent that would turn all blacks into unquestioning enemies. If an economic and productive paradise could be brought to its knees, the fever for revolution could easily spread to Virginia, to South Carolina, to Georgia, to New York.

In 1793, at least three slaves set fire to Albany, New York. Three years later, when a series of fires broke out along the eastern seaboard, rumor had it that there was an organized effort to torch the urban haunts of slaveholders.

But many slaves chose silent, more insidious forms of rebellion—they would fabricate sicknesses, distort the truth, or just stop laboring. Then there were those who would steal that which they were denied.

In 1799, caught stealing a pig, a slave named Gabriel was brought into a Richmond, Virginia, courthouse to answer for his crime. But that crime went far beyond the theft of the animal. Gabriel was an imposing man, over six feet tall, a bit of a legend for his reluctance to forgo fisticuffs. Caught in the act, Gabriel refused to sit still for the physical punishment he knew was coming. Instead, he wrestled the pig's owner to the ground, clamped his teeth onto the man's ear, and bit down, tearing off a portion of the lobe.

Gabriel could have gotten off with a simple beating for the common crime of pilfering livestock. But black assault of a white person was a capital crime. Gabriel escaped execution only through a loophole in the law—but he was branded with a hot iron in open court as a public lesson to discourage others from following his example.

Inspired by the rebellion in Haiti, Gabriel began to formulate a dangerous strategy. It was time, he reasoned, for Richmond's slaves to fight back. Collectively.

The skilled blacksmith was allowed to occasionally hire himself out on his own time. He began to use that time to forge weapons and ammunition while he began to enlist men for the upcoming battle. As the plan began to take shape, one of Gabriel's lieutenants told a potential recruit, "The negroes are about to rise and fight the white people for our freedom." And the recruit answered matter-of-factly, "I was never so glad to hear anything in my life. . . . I could slay the white people like sheep."

Conspirator Ben Woolfolk said, "All the whites were to be massacred, except the Quakers, the Methodists, and the Frenchmen and they were to be spared on account . . . of their being friendly to liberty. . . . They intended also to spare all the poor white women who had no slaves."

Gabriel was not plotting another American Revolution, although he had been inspired by that conflict as well as the revolt in Haiti. He kept his plans on a manageable scale, intending to wreak just enough havoc to scare whites to the bargaining table. He wanted to see the whites of Richmond recognize that freedom for slaves was a viable issue, one worthy of discussion and debate. He believed they wouldn't listen unless they were made to fear for their own lives.

Solomon, Gabriel's brother and co-conspirator, later outlined the plan:

> 1,000 men was to be raised from Richmond, 600 from Ground Squirrel Bridge and 400 from Goochland. . . . Swords . . . were to be used by Horsemen, two hundred of whom were appointed, but it was expected there would be 400. . . . The business of the insurrection had so far advanced that [we] were compelled, even if discovered, to go forward.

Gabriel decided on a time for his well-planned revolt—at midnight, August 30, 1800, his "soldiers" would march on the town, hefting flags that sported the St. Domingue call to battle—"Death or Liberty."

On that day the sky opened and a drenching rain, unprecedented in memory, pelted that region of Virginia. The rain flooded the very rivers and creeks Gabriel and his men needed to ford to reach their goal. There was no ferry available for crossing and no bridges spanning the deep, rushing rivers. With all of Virginia in flood, there was no way to swim or float an army of rebels across. So they stood, weapons in hand, and watched as their rebellion died under the weight of the water.

After the plot was betrayed by two slaves and the rebels were captured, the leader of the failed insurrection went to trial on October 6, 1800. He maintained his silence throughout. However, one rebel offered this statement:

> I have nothing more to offer than what General Washington would have had to offer, had he been taken by the British and put to trial by them. I have adventured my life in endeavoring to obtain the liberty of my countrymen, and am a willing sacrifice in their cause: and I beg, as a favour, that I may be immediately led to execution. I know that you have pre-determined to shed my blood, why then all this mockery of a trial?

When the sentences came down, twenty-seven black men, including Gabriel, were executed. The owners of the dead men were fully reimbursed for their loss of property. Thomas Prosser, Gabriel's owner, lost his slaves and gained $1,954.99.

Thomas Jefferson, running for the presidency, wanted to avoid the bad publicity in his home state. In a letter to Virginia governor James Monroe about Gabriel's rebellion and subsequent punishments, he wrote:

> *There is a strong sentiment that there has been hanging enough. The other states and the world at large will forever condemn us if we indulge in a principle of revenge or go one step beyond absolute necessity. . . . Our situation is indeed a difficult one: for I doubt whether these people can ever be permitted to go at large among us with safety.*

Monroe suggested to Jefferson that the rebels be deported. Jefferson petitioned the Sierra Leone Company, a British colonizing society, but the rebels were refused admittance. The surviving rebels were sold to a slave dealer and ultimately brought to Spanish-held New Orleans.

While whites looked for meaning in the frightening revolt and its aftermath, the free black population steadily increased. By 1810, more than thirty thousand freedmen lived in Virginia; fifty years later, Virginia had the second largest number of free blacks of any state in the nation.

Though the Richmond revolt failed to happen, it didn't fail to attract attention all over the South. A northern traveler, Jesse Torrey, saw and felt the fear as he moved through the country.

> [O]ne cannot go to bed in the evening without the apprehension of being massacred before morning! . . . [M]asters and overseers are obliged to retreat to some secure place during the night or employ armed sentinels. . . . A gentleman of high respectability lately informed me, that he personally knew a master of slaves, who retreated every night into an upper room, the entrance into which was by a trap door, and kept an axe by his side for defence.

The fear was tangible—the violent example set by the rebels in St. Domingue chilled slaveholders. Not only did the rebels in Haiti shed the blood of white men, but they made great strides toward a future without slavery. And in 1801, they took a bold and important step, crafting a constitution built around the abolishment of slavery. Former slave Toussaint L'Ouverture, now St. Domingue's governor, was the father of that constitution.

That same year, Thomas Jefferson became the third president of the United States. He had been the principal writer of the Declaration of Independence, a former president of the Continental Congress, and a former governor of Virginia. At the time of his inauguration, the population of the United States was 5,308,000; of those, 900,000 were slaves.

Fearing Haiti's influence, Jefferson had, as vice president, urged the United States to cease trade with Toussaint. But Congress, addicted to the profits, had ignored the danger. Now Jefferson branded Toussaint and his army as cannibals. He feared their successful rebellion would be imitated in America, where resentment and unrest presented the perfect climate. So he spent an inordinate amount of time and energy attempting to stop any flow of information between the island and mainland America.

In one of his first official acts as president, Jefferson appointed Tobias Lear as his consul to St. Domingue. Lear, a fledging politico, had been George Washington's personal secretary—but that was the extent of his experience in government. After arriving in St. Domingue on the fourth of July 1801, Lear presented his credentials, such as they were, to Toussaint L'Ouverture.

The governor was not impressed. Furthermore, he was insulted that the papers did not include a personal greeting from Jefferson. He insisted that Lear must have misplaced the greeting.

"I told him I had not," Lear said. "He immediately returned my Commission without opening it, expressing his disappointment and disgust in strong terms, saying that his Colour was the cause of his being neglected, and not thought worthy of the Usual attentions."

The following day Toussaint reluctantly accepted Lear's appointment as consul.

A REPORT FROM ST. DOMINGUE

Sir,

I beg that you will forgive me for the inordinate lapse between this letter and my last. As I mentioned in that hasty missive of 4 July 1801, my initial meeting with Governor-General François-Dominique Toussaint went poorly. No, I mustn't lie. It was, Mr. President, a disaster of diplomacy, with Toussaint being haughtily unimpressed by my credentials, despite my previous work in President Washington's administration. He strutted about his chamber with the air of a Coriolanus, and all but looked down his nose at me (You know this expression of disdain—it is thoroughly French), asking why I had not brought from Monticello a personal greeting from you, for he fancies himself to be a freedom fighter like yourself; he insisted repeatedly that I must have misplaced such an important item of protocol; then he summarily postponed

---

In this letter our consul is fictitious (Thomas Jefferson, in fact, sent Tobias Lear to represent him), but his fears are real.

any further meetings with me until I found it. I daresay, it would have helped matters considerably if you had, in fact, written such a letter, though I understand your refusal to acknowledge in any way whatsoever (or treat as an equal head of state) St. Domingue's governor-general and the bloody Revolution he and his cohorts Jacques Dessalines and Henri Christophe have created on what was once the richest European colonial possession.

But, as I say, it was my intention to write you much earlier concerning your plan to help Bonaparte re-establish Gallic rule and Negro slavery on this sea-girt island. And I would have done so, I assure you, had not your consul gotten off to such a bad start, and then found such difficulty acclimating himself and his family to the extremes of this savage post to which you have assigned him. My health has been exceedingly tender. During the day the temperature here is well nigh 95 degrees. My French, as you know, is flawless, but most of the people I meet speak Creole *French: a blend of Indian, French, and Spanish that I must at times strain my ears to decipher. In addition to this taxing problem of translating their native tongue, the food is unfamiliar; the favorite dish is a rice-and-bean concoction called* pois ac duriz colles, *which the natives wash down with rum and* tafia, *a head-ruining spirit made from sugarcane. Gastronomically, this diet of Negro dishes for the past several weeks has wreaked havoc with my digestion, that of my wife, and especially my eight-year-old son, Cornelius, who suffers from borborygm and stomach cramps, as do I, though if the truth be known, I suspect our physical distress has a darker cause, which I will try to summon the courage to speak of shortly.*

Yet all that, Mr. President, is nothing compared to the fear.

To a man, the natives of St. Domingue believe in voodoo. During the nights of sweltering heat, when one's bedsheets are soaked through before dawn, we can hear from our lodgings in the capital the endless pounding of drums—the same tom-toms that one heard on August 22, 1791, when the voodoo priest Boukman, his leaders (among them Toussaint), and the blacks they incited swept from one village to another, torching buildings and killing every white man, woman, and child they saw. (Yes, it is true that the insurrectionists hoisted on high dead white babies impaled on their swords, but as to the report of cannibalism, which you inquired about, I have yet to receive confirmation.) The smell of that white massacre lingers on the air. I have been informed that for weeks the sky glowed with sheets of fire, and that more than 6,000 coffee plantations and 200 sugar refineries were destroyed. It is a chilling sound, these drums. Three are employed: the natives call them the Mama Drum, Papa Drum, and Baby Drum, and as they are played, the blacks perform a wild dance called the Méringue. *I have personally witnessed them crooning a half-spoken, half-sung chant at their voodoo rites, where witch doctors transmogrify the dead—and sometimes living men—into zombies (The Enlightenment, I assure you, has yet to reach the outlying villages here), which are mindless slaves who do the bidding of their masters. (I've been told the witch doctors who conspired with Boukman and Toussaint took a special pleasure in turning their former owners into such spectral creatures.) For a white man, there* is *the fear here of being murdered in one's sleep. Since hearing of these unholy practices, my poor Cornelius has not slept well in days, and he screams at every sound in the night. I must assure him each evening that I keep a firearm by my bed in the room next to his own where my wife, Emma, and I sleep, and that we have trustworthy sentries—the more-Europeanized mulattoes—stationed with rifles just outside our doors.*

Lately, I have been rereading your splendid Notes on the State of Virginia, *partly because some nights sleep and I are strangers, and partly because my position as consul in the first all-black nation in the Western Hemisphere has whetted my curiosity to better understand what transpires beneath the ulotrichous skull of the Negro. You are right, I believe, when in your* Notes *you observe the inferiority of pure-bred blacks at Monticello, their childlike nature, their physical proximity to the apes, and their inability to grasp the arts and sciences as, for example, you have so wondrously done in your writings and studies on architecture, geology, natural history, and scientific farming. Clearly, as you state, the white race is blessed with greater beauty and in America is destined—as if by divine decree—to be the black man's master, to guide him as the parent does the child, and surely this is for the Negro's own good, lest he, in our state of freedom, fall deeper into savagery. No, none of these matters do I question as I revisit your* Notes. *But I have begun to wonder since our arrival at Le Cap, and after such close contact with Negroes like Jacques Dessalines (during their Revolution he cried to the other slaves, "Those who wish to die free, rally round me now," which is hardly different than our own Patrick Henry's "Give me Liberty or give me death"), if perhaps the lower standards and performance you so precisely observed in the Virginia slaves are not innate, after all, but rather the product of the severity of American slavery itself.*

I venture this hypothesis, sir, only because in the blacks of St. Domingue, living now free of whites—Spaniards and Frenchmen—for the first time since 1512, I have seen a pride, independence, and ambition (as well as arrogance) that favors the confidence of our own patriots after they defeated King George. Nowhere is this pride more evident, or infectious, than in Le Cap, and in the person of the island's beloved leader, Toussaint L'Ouverture. As General Washington is to us, he is to them: a warrior legendary for his courage; the framer of their Constitution; and a statesman capable of forgiving his defeated enemies, for Toussaint has approved trade with France, and it is well known that he has sent both his sons to study at world-acclaimed institutions in Paris.

You will be interested to learn that after his cold rejection of my Commission, and of me as your consul, the governor-general relented and has now allowed me to visit with him on five occa-

sions, the most recent being yesternight. Due to illness, my wife and son could not accompany me to dinner with Toussaint and other officials of this new republic. I must say I felt a bit lightheaded during the aperitif, and a little off-balance in that dining room of stunningly beautiful mulatto ladies and darker-skinned heads of state, but I smiled until the muscles round my mouth began to ache, and drank as lustily as my hosts, who seemed—I was sure of this—amused by my discomfiture. Perhaps it was the wine, or my generally fatigued condition in this horseshoe-shaped country's merciless heat, but when I looked at the head of the table, where Toussaint sat, he presented a magnific figure of manhood, one far better-looking and more dashing in his French uniform and black knee-boots than that runt Bonaparte. Gradually, I began to see why his people called him L' Ouverture ("the Opener"), and then later added "Deliverer" to his many honorific titles. He chatted now with Jacques Dessalines, who sat at his right side, and with Henri Christophe, at his left, ignoring me deliberately for as much as fifteen minutes at a time, so that all I could do was stare down at my dinner plate, shoveling down the entrée, then dessert, in humiliating silence until he deigned to politely ask me a question about you, our system of government, or our relations with the French. I believe he deliberately seated me on a chair shorter than the others at the table, so that even the women looked down at me all during the meal. Try as I might, I could not intimidate him or the others with my superior breeding, credentials as a representative of the United States government, or the color of my skin, which before their Revolution would have been enough to make most slaves treat me with deference. No, none of that worked on them. All during that evening, after we'd eaten, I felt a sharp pain slice through my abdomen, but you will be relieved to know, sir, that despite my weakening condition I was alert and overheard Christophe discussing with Toussaint his idea for constructing a mountaintop fortress to protect this fledging nation from attack. He wants to call it the Citadelle. His plan is to equip it with 365 heavy bronze cannons.

I must confess, sadly, that as your consul it seems to me that Toussaint knows that, despite the decision of Congress to continue trade with St. Domingue, you—as our president—have no plans to support his Revolution, indeed, that you consider its leaders to be property that has illegally seized a freedom it does not deserve, and that their successful example of insurrection sends a dangerous message to Negroes on our shores. It is this suspicion of you that led to the poor treatment I received last night, and to Toussaint's remark to Christophe that his color alone was the reason you failed to send him a greeting.

These, as I say, are the tribulations I have endured in your service since my arrival, troubles I gladly endure for my country. I list them here only for one reason. As I was leaving the governor-general's mansion, almost doubled over by the recurrent complaint in my lower regions, but smiling nevertheless, shaking the hand of my host, then Christophe's, I came to Jacques Dessalines, and swung out my palm. He took it in a firm grasp, but then I saw *it. Just for a moment. There, in his left hand, which he kept behind his back, Dessalines held a clay homunculus—a white doll—of* me, *one with a pin stuck in its belly.*

Sir, I have barely started my tenure as consul in St. Domingue. However, I pray you will consider the problems, political and personal, that my family and I have encountered and repeal my appointment. If you do not, I fear this may well be the last communication from

Your most obedient, and most obliged,
And most dutiful humble Servant,
Theobald Wedgwood

Indeed, Jefferson believed that only whites of European descent were entitled to advancement through revolution. He dismissed the Haitian rebellion as an illegal attempt by property to obtain freedom where none was deserved. In an August 1797 letter to St. George Tucker, Jefferson's fear of a similar rebellion had been evident: "[W]e shall be the murderers of our own children. . . . [T]he revolutionary storm, now sweeping the globe, will be upon us. . . . [O]nly a single spark is wanting."

As Lear courted Toussaint's favor, Jefferson entertained a representative of Napoleon Bonaparte, who had named himself France's first consul in 1799. Napoleon desperately wanted to reestablish slavery in St. Domingue.

In 1802, his troops breached St. Domingue's harbors. Suddenly, four years of peace meant nothing. Negotiation was out of the question. War broke out immediately.

"Remember that this soil, nourished on our blood and sweat, must not yield a crumb of food to our enemies," said Toussaint.

> Keep all roads under constant fire, throw the bodies of men and horses into all wells and springs, destroy everything and burn everything so that those who have come to make slaves of us again will find before their eyes, wherever they turn, the image of that Hell they so richly deserve.

Although he died a prisoner of the French, Toussaint's vengeful strategy worked. The French were soundly defeated; Napoleon lost 35,000 troops, many to yellow fever. On January 1, 1804, the rebels established a country that was free and independent.

Though it had no official recognition, the new country of Haiti would never again be a haven for slavery. The revolt took thirteen years and cost more than 100,000 black lives.

Despite his openly hostile view of the St. Domingue revolution, Jefferson profited mightily from the success of that rebellion. Since Napoleon could no longer use Haiti as a military buffer to shield French interests in North America, he abandoned his stake in the New World to concentrate on his wars on the European continent. His sale of the 830,000-square-mile Louisiana Territory to the United States for $15 million is considered the greatest bargain in American history. The Louisiana Purchase doubled the size of America and paved the way for the creation of thirteen new states.

And, of course, more slaves.

CHAPTER EIGHT

In June 1793, Secretary of State and inspector of patents Thomas Jefferson received an intriguing request for a patent from Eli Whitney, a twenty-nine-year-old schoolteacher. Jefferson was keenly interested in the device, which was designed to remove the seeds from cotton while leaving the fiber intact. It was called an engine—"gin" for short.

Jefferson's official reply to Whitney's request took on a personal tone:

> As the state of Virginia, of which I am, carries on household manufactures of cotton to a great extent, as I also do myself . . . I feel a considerable interest in the success of your invention for family use.

His interest also stemmed from the fact that he was an inventor who wanted to see if the machinery would work in an efficient and practical way; a patriotic individual who hoped that inventions like the cotton gin would help assure the success of the new nation; and a planter, who hoped that the intense of the new nation; and a planter, who hoped that the intense labor involved in cotton production could be cut significantly.

Jefferson asked Whitney a series of practical questions:

> Has the machine been thoroughly tried in the ginning of cotton, or is it as yet but a machine in theory? What quantity of cotton has it cleaned on a average of several days, worked by hand, & by how many hands? . . . Favorable answers to these questions would induce me to engage one of them to be forwarded to Richmond for me.

Whitney had written:

> That with this Ginn, if turned with horses or by water, two persons will clean as much cotton in one Day, as a Hundred persons could cleane in the same time with the ginns now in common use.

If its inventor's claims were correct, the cotton gin was to be the most important invention in the country's short history. And it was.

In 1795, the first year of the cotton gin's operation, American planters produced 8 million pounds of cotton. By 1800, production increased more than 400 percent, fueling the demand for additional labor. The price of field hands, which had skyrocketed after the Revolutionary War, continued to rise. As the demand went up, African slaves were rounded up and forced to march into the Deep South and West into territories acquired after the Louisiana Purchase. They were forced to work under a gang system, supervised by overseers and drivers.

Before Whitney's invention, short-staple cotton could not

be grown for profit because of the labor needed to filter out the seeds. Now the cotton could be successfully cultivated in a long belt from South Carolina through the Mexican territory of Texas. Climate was the primary factor in determining the boundaries of the region. To thrive, the crop required abundant rainfall and not less than two hundred days free of frost. The northern boundary of the belt was determined by temperature. The western boundary, by rainfall.

On January 1, 1808, fifteen years after the patent of the cotton gin, Thomas Jefferson signed the bill that officially ended America's international slave trade, blindly believing that it would lead to the gradual abolition of the institution itself. "The spirit of the master is abating," he had written, "that of the slave rising from the dust, his condition mollifying, the way I hope preparing, under the auspices of heaven, for a total emancipation, and that this is disposed, in the order of events, to be with the consent of the masters."

The law reduced but did not eliminate totally the Atlantic slave trade, as some slaveholding states looked the other way. And although it did help thousands of Africans avoid forced servitude in the United States, the law did nothing to stem the increase in domestic trade.

And the prohibition actually strengthened the domestic slave trade in a place where it had been on the wane. By artificially creating a shortage of black laborers, it sparked trade between the upper southern states with a surplus of slaves, such as Maryland and Virginia, and those in the lower South.

Despite the fact that people would try to circumvent the law, there was still cause to celebrate. In Philadelphia, Absalom Jones joined black ministers all over the country in celebration of the historic day:

> Let the first of January . . . be set apart in every year, as a day of publick thanksgiving. Let the history of the sufferings of our brethren, and of their deliverance, descend by this means to our children, to the remotest generations; and when they shall ask, in time to come, saying, What mean the lessons, the psalms, the prayers and the praises in the worship of this day? Let us answer them by saying, the Lord, on the day of which this is the anniversary, abolished the trade which dragged your fathers from their native country, and sold them as bond men in the United States of America.

The Constitution had set 1808 as the first year that an end to the trade could be considered—but the lessons of St. Domingue had been well learned and the debate was greatly influenced by the specter of revolt. Congress hastened to seal the borders to prevent further importation of slaves from the Caribbean or Africa. The ban on the transatlantic slave trade was seen by many Americans as a simple measure of protection—for African Americans it was yet another moment to pray on, yet another hope that slavery might soon be abolished completely.

But cotton continued to grow, a bright beacon on the other side of the destruction wrought by the Revolution. The crop ruled with a blatant disregard for existing statutes.

More labor was always needed.

Charles Ball was a slave sold into the cotton kingdom from the border state of Maryland. His purchaser

> ordered me to cross my hands behind, which were quickly bound with a strong cord; and then he told me that we must set out that very day for the South. . . . I joined fifty-one other slaves . . . thirty-two of these

> men and nineteen women. . . . A strong iron collar was closely fitted by means of a padlock around each of our necks. . . . [W]e were handcuffed in pairs, with iron staples and bolts.

It was the nightmare of their forebears, all over again.

As late as 1809, cotton was a secondary crop in the South. Its production was centered mostly in South Carolina and eastern sections of Georgia, with just 7 percent of the crop raised west of that region. But as cotton moved west, so did slavery. Thomas Jefferson supported the sojourn, believing it best to spread blacks out across the country, hoping that slavery would eventually "disappear" altogether.

Tobacco plantations had exhausted the land. As Virginia's agricultural economy declined, it no long needed the vast labor force the crop demanded. Without the economy to support the burgeoning slave population, the state became a key supplier of human labor. Ambitious traders siphoned the surplus and then plumped their coffers by transporting blacks south and west.

From the time of the cotton gin's invention to 1860, more than 835,000 slaves were moved into the western cotton states. "To sell cotton in order to buy negroes—to make more cotton to buy more negroes 'ad infinitum' is the aim and direct tendency of all the operations of the thorough-going cotton planter," said Joseph Ingraham. "His whole soul is wrapped up in the pursuit. It is, apparently, the principle by which he lives, moves, and has his being."

Virginia and Maryland were the main exportation states—shipping slaves mostly to Alabama, Mississippi, Louisiana, and Texas. The painful western migration tore apart the fabric of families and broke the spirits of slaves who didn't believe matters could get any worse.

Charles Ball's chilling chronicle, written with abolitionist Isaac Fisher, mirrors the experience of hundreds of thousands torn from their birthplaces and families by the wretched internal slave trade.

Ball wrote that after the sale of his mother, his father's master

> resolved to sell my father to a southern slave dealer. About midnight, my grandfather silently repaired to the cabin of my father, gave him a bottle of cider and a small bag of parched corn, and then praying to the God of his native country to protect his son, enjoined him to fly from the destruction which awaited him. In the morning, the Georgian could not find his newly purchased slave, who was never seen or heard of in Maryland from that day.

Later, Ball told of the anguish he felt at the prospect of being taken away from his wife and children:

> We all lay down on the naked floor to sleep in our handcuffs and chains. The women, my fellow slaves, lay on one side of the room; and the men who were chained with me, occupied the other. . . . I at length fell asleep, but was distressed by painful dreams. My wife and children appeared to be weeping and lamenting my calamity; and beseeching and imploring my master on their knees not to carry me away from them. My little boy came and begged me not to go and leave him, and endeavored . . . with his little hands to break the fetters that bound me.

When he was sold, Charles Ball simply asked to see his family. He was told he would be able to "get another wife in Georgia."

In her memoirs, Harriet Jacobs, a slave who managed to escape from North Carolina, wrote of a mother leading her seven children to the auction block:

> She knew that *some* of them would be taken from her; but they took *all*. The children were sold to a slave-trader, and their mother was bought by a man in her own town. Before night her children were all far away. She begged the trader to tell her where he intended to take them; this he refused to do. How *could* he, when he knew he would sell them, one by one, wherever he could command the highest price? I met that mother in the street, and her wild, haggard face lives to-day in my mind. She wrung her hands in anguish, and exclaimed, "Gone! All gone! Why *don't* God kill me?"

The selling of slaves still stands today as a symbol of the evil men are capable of. The intimate ties of man to wife, mother to child, brother to sister, meant nothing as each human head was slapped with a price. If a master encountered some physical or financial disaster, if the crops failed to thrive, the slaves would be herded toward the block.

Imagine a mother being forced to stand apart from her children, her heart straining forward, the child's cries withering in the hot air. Imagine grown men struggling to stand motionless as they are matter-of-factly inspected—their teeth checked, their genitals poked and prodded, their bodies moving automatically as they are commanded to "turn," "bend," "come closer," "move back." Imagine, if you can, a young black woman who falls under the lustful eyes of a white man who sees in her not a worker, but a perverse and twisted entertainment.

Some "benevolent" masters attempted to keep mothers and children together. But slave men were often regarded as having no connection whatsoever to family. Potential buyers didn't need pesky emotional attachments getting in the way of a prime acquisition, such as a stout, strapping fellow with a broad back and an even temperament.

Flowery official documents touted the natural God-given rights of every man. There was the appearance of stature attained by free blacks throughout the country. But the slave's lot during cotton's reign was wretched, at times unspeakable. Masters struggling with economic necessity, a smidgen of compassion, and a hefty dose of guilt still chose abuse as the most effective method of control. Runaways could be shot. A slave's day-to-day existence depended on the whim of his owner or any other white person he encountered. In a court of law, his word meant nothing.

In Georgia and Alabama, it was legal to work a slave for nineteen hours out of twenty-four. Some slaves died in the process.

Many slaves came to rely on small nuances in servitude that could make the situation bearable. Working on a small farm or as a personal servant provided the slave opportunities to prove his worth as he shared experiences that could draw him and his owner closer together. House slaves or body servants were often afforded privileges envied by other servants. They prepared the food, drew the baths, set the tables, laid out clothes, and were trusted with personal errands. Privy to their owners' unguarded moments, these slaves often looked down on their field-hand counterparts.

And some slave owners were truly benevolent. Although, as far as the slave was concerned, benevolence was often a simple matter of *not* being beaten, degraded, or torn away from family members. With little hope of ever being considered an equal, he or she was thankful for little things—a private moment, a discarded dressing gown, an extra bit of supper, a snippet of music.

There was nothing benevolent or nurturing about the system of slavery itself. The South, in particular, was a virtual police state designed to keep blacks in their place. An intricate network of overseers, state militia, federal troops, local patrols, privately hired guards, and ever-present vigilantes assured that slaves would think twice about fleeing and that freedmen would never consider themselves entirely free.

Blacks sensed that they would never be considered full-fledged members of society. In Philadelphia former overseer Thomas Branagan circulated a pamphlet suggesting that free blacks—the "poison fruit" of slavery—be shipped to the Louisiana Territory. A bill banning black migration into Pennsylvania was introduced in 1806. It failed to pass. On July 4 of 1805, black citizens of Philadelphia had been set upon by white mobs and chased away from Independence Hall. They would not be allowed to return until after the Civil War.

To combat those who sought to defer their dream of true liberty, free African Americans closed ranks to protect themselves from economic and physical attack. They began to stress the importance of their own, singular experience.

As a vital part of that pulling away, free blacks built churches that became the cornerstones and support systems in their communities. On April 9, 1816—after a Pennsylvania Supreme Court decision that removed Bethel Church from white Methodist authority and recognized it as legally independent—the African Methodist Episcopal (AME) denomination united congregations from Maryland, Delaware, Pennsylvania, and New Jersey to become the most visible African American institution. Richard Allen was its first bishop. The alliance inspired community leadership, economic independence, and political discourse. It was what many black communities needed—a center, a focal point, a heart.

Soon, Bethel Church would be the meeting place for a community-wide decision on leaving America. The trouble began on New Year's Day 1817 with the founding of the American Colonization Society (ACS), an organization that sought to resettle free blacks outside of the United States. The group, of course, included many prominent southern slaveholders—Henry Clay, John C. Calhoun, Bushrod Washington. Francis Scott Key, the man who had penned the "Star Spangled Banner," America's official anthem, was a member of the organization's constitution committee. Although black Massachusetts shipping merchant Paul Cuffe had touted the same plan for almost ten years, membership in the ACS was restricted to whites.

Cuffe, a Quaker convert and native of New Bedford, Massachusetts, had a grand vision of introducing Christianity to West Africa and providing America's free blacks with a place where they could live lives that were truly free. With the support of Quaker merchants, he sailed to Sierra Leone in late 1810; upon his return, he attempted to organize a Philadelphia branch of the Friendly Society of Sierra Leone, a group interested in promoting trade between blacks in America and black colonists in that African country. Cuffe's plans were thwarted by the War of 1812.

But he didn't give up. A second voyage carried thirty-eight black settlers to Sierra Leone in 1815. Now he saw yet another chance to reenergize his efforts at colonization.

The American Colonization Society held its first organizational meeting in Washington, D.C.; Richard Rush, the son of Benjamin Rush, was a vice president. The ACS felt that the free black segment of the population walked a tightrope. They were no longer subjected to all of the indignities suffered by their enslaved counterparts, but they didn't share the social status of free white men. So the organization advocated returning them to their homeland. The organization would purchase a substantial tract of property in Sierra Leone and hoped to entice free blacks to relocate to Africa.

Elias B. Caldwell, clerk of the Supreme Court, addressed the meeting to outline the ACS's straightforward and chilling agenda:

> It has been a subject of unceasing regret, and anxious solicitude, among many of our best patriots, and wisest statesmen, from the first establishment of our independence, that this class of people should remain a monument of reproach to those sacred principles of civil liberty which constitute the foundations of all our constitutions. We say in the Declaration of Independence "that all men are created equal, and have certain unalienable rights." Yet it is considered impossible, consistently with the safety of the State, and it is certainly impossible with the present feelings towards these people, that they can ever be placed upon this equality, or admitted to the enjoyment of these "unalienable rights" while they remain mixed with us. Some persons may declaim and call it prejudice. No matter! Prejudice is as powerful a motive, and will as certainly exclude them, as the soundest reason.

Once the idea of colonization took root, ACS chapters sprang to life in the Carolinas, Virginia, Maryland, and Georgia. The society, working for the ultimate goal of the removal of "free people of color," never openly challenged slavery's legal and moral status and vowed not to interfere with the rights of slaveholders.

Supporters of colonization feared a "blackening" of America. Their racism, as was not unusual, also had an economic base. White workers were growing more hostile to the idea of competing with blacks, slave or free.

Days after its creation, the ACS contacted James Forten in Philadelphia, a well-to-do sailmaker and veteran of the Revolutionary War. The organization hoped that the outspoken leader could convince others in the free black community that their future was in Africa, especially since it was clear that the American dream did not include them. A large number of fairly prosperous blacks were intrigued by the idea. In a letter to Forten, Paul Cuffe reported that black citizens in Africa enjoyed every freedom, including the right to vote.

On January 15, 1817, a meeting was called at Bethel Church in Philadelphia to discuss the proposal presented by the ACS. Three thousand men packed the pews. The meeting was led by Ministers Richard Allen, Absalom Jones, John Gloucester, and Forten—black men who had asserted their strength and thrived in oppressive times.

And they would advocate leaving Philadelphia to return to Africa, realizing that even their most targeted efforts to end slavery had failed, and that settlement of territory acquired in the Louisiana Purchase was continuing to spark slavery's westward expansion. A halt to the slave trade with Africa had done nothing to siphon the wretched institution's strength in the States. And with blacks denied many of the rights afforded whites, North America certainly didn't feel like home. Perhaps Africa would.

But it was ordinary members of the community, not its leaders, who would set a definitive course of action. "[A]nd there was not one sole that was in favor of going to Africa," Forten later reported.

The men at the meeting—no women were present—suspected that the American Colonization Society, despite its platform of voluntary emigration, would eventually seek to relocate all free blacks, by force if necessary. And since the voices of freedmen were most persistent in speaking out against slavery, a forced emigration would effectively silence a most visible segment of protest.

The thousands of free blacks who gathered in the country's birthplace rejected the government's plan to "disappear" them. The black community's voice was unwavering in its strength:

> Whereas our ancestors (not of choice) were the first cultivators of the wilds of America, we their descendants feel ourselves entitled to participate in the blessings of her luxuriant soil, which their blood and sweat manured; and that any measure, or system of measures, having a tendency to banish us from her bosom, would not only be cruel, but in direct violation of those principles, which have been the boast of the republick.
>
> [It is resolved] That we never will separate ourselves voluntarily from the slave population in this country; they are our brethren by the ties of consanguinity, of suffering, and of wrongs; and we feel that there is more virtue in suffering privations with them, than fancied advantages for a season.

THE PEOPLE SPEAK

A News Item from the Philadelphia Liberator
(Philadelphia, Pennsylvania, January 16, 1817)

A Vote on Colonization

Yesterday a reported three thousand black people packed into Bethel Church to vote on a proposal by the newly created American Colonization Society that free blacks in the United States should be resettled in Africa. The tempestuous meeting, which lasted most of the day, and was peppered throughout by passionate speeches for and against the proposal, ended with a historic vote that will no doubt be decisive—if not fateful—for the future of all people of African descent in this nation.

Fiction often changes the facts for dramatic effect. Paul Cuffe did not attend the meeting described here, and he learned of the vote by letter. There were no women present, and the actual vote was by voice, not paper ballot. The author hopes readers of this tale can forgive the liberties taken with facts in order to conjure a moment in time with feeling.

It was, some observers remarked, a debate on two equally powerful yet antithetical dreams within the black American soul.

The meeting came but fifteen days after the founding of the American Colonization Society, a creation of Robert Finley that has been endorsed with enthusiasm by President James Madison and former president Jefferson. Its mission, according to its founder, is to redress the evils of exploitation visited upon Negroes in Africa, and to establish on that continent a homeland for American people of color, a place to which they can emigrate, live free from white persecution, and pursue their interests without interference. The idea has great popularity these days, among both blacks and whites, who question whether the Negro, once released from bondage, will ever be accepted in or assimilated by American society.

In attendance at Wednesday's gathering were some of the most prominent leaders and luminaries from Philadelphia's growing black community. On hand was the ubiquitous Rev. Absalom Jones; maritime entrepreneur Paul Cuffe and his Indian wife, Alice; businessman James Forten; and Rev. Richard Allen, who, as on many occasions previously, provided his church as the site for this great Negro debate and introduced Mr. Forten as the day's first speaker.

Taking the stage, Mr. Forten, fifty-one, explained how he was contacted by a representative of the American Colonization Society who sought his support in swaying Philadelphia's Negroes to the idea of leaving America. "You all know me and what I stand for," said Mr. Forten, his voice breaking with emotion. He reminded the gathering of his humble beginnings as a powder boy in the American Navy when he was fifteen, how at twenty he was foreman in a sail loft, and by age forty owned it and now employed more than forty men. "My life has been nurtured in the ground of this fledging nation," he said. "I have been an American patriot *through and through, but I have also been one of this country's greatest critics as well."*

He cited his "A Series of Letters by a Man of Color," composed four years ago, which opposed the legislature's attempt to force all blacks in the city to register, and his lifelong work as an abolitionist. Mr. Forten then reminded the audience of how central Negroes have been to every dimension of life in the colonies, and how Crispus Attucks was the first to die opposing British tyranny.

"But despite our contributions to this country," Mr. Forten said, "we have not been—and perhaps will never be—accepted by its white citizens. And so, although it makes my heart heavy to do so, I intend to vote—as I hope you will—for taking my chances in the land of our forebears."

The audience was greatly moved by Mr. Forten's address. The applause lasted for several minutes.

He was followed by Paul Cuffe, fifty-eight, a Quaker who for over a decade, and long before the formation of the American Colonization Society, has urged free blacks toward expatriation. As reported earlier in this newspaper (September 8, 1815), Mr. Cuffe, owner of the 268-ton Alpha, *is a man whose wisdom is seasoned by his world travels. Among his many vessels are sloops, schooners, and two brigs. He has sailed to Sweden and, on his ship the* Traveller, *visited Sierra Leone in 1811. There, he set up the Friendly Society, an organization dedicated to helping American blacks migrate to Africa. In fact, three years later Mr. Cuffe transported thirty-eight colored men and women to Sierra Leone and paid for their $4,000 voyage himself. A philanthropist, he created a school for Negro children on his farm and acquired a teacher for them.*

As he walked slowly to the stage, still weak from a recent illness, a cheer rose from the gathering. Mr. Cuffe, smiling gently, waited patiently at the podium for the audience to settle down.

"Thank you," he said. "We are all old friends here and have suffered much together over the years. We struggled together

thirty-seven years ago to protest taxation of our people when we have no representation. I led that fight, you'll recall. And twenty years ago, my friend there, Absalom Jones, spearheaded our effort to repeal the Fugitive Slave Act. We have all shed our blood for freedom, and of our triumphs I think we should be proud. But as an old *fighter, one who has seen many campaigns to achieve justice for the colored people of America, I sometimes wonder how much farther we can go. I won't lie to you. I never have, and I can't start now. My doctor tells me I'll be lucky if I see Thanksgiving this year. With so little time, I think I should tell you the truth, at least as I've been privileged to perceive it.*

"Here, in America, we face an uphill struggle. Our victories can be taken away with a single stroke of the pen by men like former president Jefferson. He and others like him have always envisioned the United States as a white man's nation, irrespective of our deep and enduring contributions to its economy, its culture, and its precious Revolution. I've never avoided a good fight in my life. You know that. But now, after much reflection, I believe it is time to withdraw from white men. Our great energies, talents, and love would be better applied, I think, to the nurturing of a democracy on the continent of our origin. Visit Sierra Leone, if you dare. I have. And it gladdened my heart to see Negroes who possessed every freedom this republic withholds from us. I say, my friends, that it is doubtful the black man and the white can ever live in harmony. Can he *ever relinquish his desire to be dominant? Can* you *ever forget the horrors of our history in this country at the hands of white men? No, methinks it is asking too much for both sides, theirs and ours, to live peacefully as one people. Does that sound defeatist? If so, you hear me wrong. In the impossibility of the Madisons and Jeffersons ever treating us like equals there lies the great opportunity for you and I, as freemen, to return to our mother country with skills and knowledge that will raise*

that continent, benighted by centuries of slavery and oppression, to its rightful place as a powerful black presence in the world. Leave America to the white man. A far greater and nobler civilization beckons, if we but have the courage to answer its call."

When Mr. Cuffe was done, the church was silent for a moment. Then, spontaneously, those in attendance responded with thunderous applause.

Other leaders of the colored community took the podium for the next few hours, all passionately arguing to their unlettered brethren the position of emigration. At various times the assembly became raucous, with members of the audience shouting their positions from the floor, so that Rev. Allen found it necessary to bang his gavel over and over, calling for order. "Please settle down," he said. "Everyone will have a chance to speak. Gentlemen, remember what we are deciding here. It has taken the American Colonial Society to bring this crisis to the surface. We are at, I daresay, a crossroads. Future generations will judge us by our sobriety. Our wisdom—or our lack of it! We are voting—be advised—not merely on the future position of the Philadelphia Negro vis-a-vis America, but on which direction all *our people will take in the future. Now, if you'll look to the rear of the room, you'll see ushers are moving down the aisles, each carrying a basket filled with ballots. I ask you to take one. Take a prayerful moment to review the discussion you've heard, then vote knowing your decision carries as much weight for the direction of this nation as that of the white men who assembled at the Constitutional Convention."*

Concluding his instructions, Rev. Allen went back to his seat to vote. Ten minutes later, the votes were collected. The ushers took them into the back of the church to tally "yeas" and "nays" for the Society's proposal. As they worked, Bethel's choir sang two beautiful hymns. Before they could begin a third, one of the ushers, a young man, brought a slip of paper to Rev. Allen, who again stepped up to the podium. Those gathered grew quiet. Rev. Allen cleared his throat.

"You, the people, have voted unanimously against the position of your leaders," he said. "You have rejected returning to Africa. Whatever our future is to be, you have decided that it will be here, *on these shores. God help us all . . ."*

The signs of a growing black independence were everywhere.

Following the lead of Philadelphia's black Methodists, the Charleston worshipers moved toward independence from white authority—they held separate conferences and managed their own collections. The idea that the church would unify blacks and guide them toward control of their own destinies was frightening in the only state in America with a black majority. This autonomy angered the city's white Methodist hierarchy, and in 1815, they moved to take away the black church's freedom.

Instead of weakening the church, however, the acts sparked a secession movement based on the unwavering ideal of independence: 4,376 black Methodists resigned from the regular church in 1817.

Dissident black Methodists formed a new AME church that in just one year would be second only to Bethel as the largest black church in America. The congregation included both slaves and free blacks. The church was opening psychological doors long closed—suddenly blacks were part of a larger world, cared for by a benevolent God. Everyone's God. That was an idea that could not be tolerated. White ministers in Charleston preached a gospel that was unabashedly proslavery: Jesus, after all, had failed to condemn the institution.

When, in 1818, the city closed the Hamstead church—a focal point of the movement—Denmark Vesey and other parishioners started thinking about out-and-out rebellion.

Vesey had been paying close attention to the treatment of the black community. He was a polygamist, an enterprising mulatto, and a former slave who had purchased his freedom with lottery money. Those who knew him characterized him as ornery, quick-tempered, and lacking in compassion. But he was also a voracious reader and an outspoken critic of blacks who kowtowed to whites. When Vesey considered the Old Testament, the God who resided there was not a God of love, but a vengeful, wrathful deity who hefted a sword for justice.

The former property of slave-ship captain Joseph Vesey, Denmark had experienced the most brutal aspects of servitude. He was in St. Domingue briefly before the revolution, and later, in South Carolina, he was forced to bring ashore slaves and transport them to the Charleston slave pens. And even though he was able to purchase his freedom, at least one of his wives and all of his children remained captive. They were still captive when their father died.

A leader in Charleston's strong African church, Vesey decided it was high time to free the city's blacks from their shackles. He formulated the rebellion for at least four years. In his task of rousing the beleaguered populace, Vesey was aided by Gullah Jack, a huge and imposing native of Angola who practiced the conjure and tribal rituals of his homeland. In their call to action, the two employed a persuasive combination of traditional African beliefs and Christian ideals.

A black witness to the rebellion said:

> Jack Pritchard called on me, he is sometimes called Gullah Jack, sometimes Couter Jack, he gave me some dry food, consisting of parched corn and ground nuts, and said, "eat that and nothing else, on the morning when it breaks out, and when you join us as we pass, put into your mouth this crab claw, and you can't be wounded." He said all his country born promised him to join, because he was a Doctor (that is, a Conjurer). . . . He said,

> his charms would not protect him from the treachery of his own colour.

And this passage from Exodus, chapter 21, verse 16, was an example of the Christian ideals Vesey and his followers had in mind: "[H]e that stealeth a man, and selleth him, or if he be found in his hand, he shall surely be put to death."

Frank, a black citizen of Charleston, told of a meeting with the rebel leader:

> I one night met at Vesey's a great number of men. . . . Vesey said, the negroes were living such an abominable life, they ought to rise. I said, I was living well. He said, though I was, others was not, and that it was such fools as I, that were in their way.

Vesey's plan excluded slaves who had received presents from their masters, as well as AME pastor Morris Brown. Brown and Vesey failed to see eye to eye on many things. Brown was concerned with the spiritual well-being of his congregation and sought to keep the church a focus in the community. Vesey suspected Brown's motives and felt he had entered into an alliance with Charleston's white citizens. The pastor spoke often about an all-encompassing brotherhood. The seething Vesey saw no reason to consort with white folks.

Although indications are that it was probably the most well-thought-out of all American slave rebellions, Denmark Vesey's uprising was over before it began. In May of 1822, a Charleston slave revealed the plot. The following month, another confirmed it. Soon the conspirators were rounded up, and the trials began. They lasted nearly two months.

South Carolina's white citizenry was shocked to learn the scope of the rebellion and that trusted servants of high standing were essential to the conspiracy.

More than one hundred men and women were jailed, questioned, and released. Forty-two were deported. And thirty-five black men were executed. On one steamy July day, the state executed twenty-two of Vesey's men, all slaves, in one horrible moment. All were sentenced to hang, but because the platform they stood on was so low, their necks didn't break when they fell. Instead they slowly and agonizingly began to strangle. To resolve the unfortunate mess, finally the captain of the guard rode past each man and shot him in the head.

Lionel Kennedy, the presiding magistrate at Vesey's trial, couldn't understand the frustration and pain that had fueled the rebel's plan:

> Denmark Vesey . . . It is difficult to imagine what *infatuation* could have prompted you to attempt an enterprise so wild and visionary. You were a free man; were comparatively wealthy; and enjoyed every comfort. . . . you *ought* to have known, that success was impracticable. A moment's reflection must have convinced you, that the ruin of *your race,* would have been the probable result.

Vesey, a free man, died for his beliefs. In doing so, he proved that the fates of free and enslaved blacks were inextricably linked. Both groups had set their sights on the same goal and would risk their lives to attain it.

In determining the fate of Gullah Jack, the court was particularly angry at the Angolan's frequent boasts of invincibility:

> In the prosecution of your wicked designs, you were not satisfied with resorting to natural and ordinary means, but endeavored to enlist on your behalf, all the powers of darkness, and employed for that purpose the most disgusting mummery and superstition. . . . Your days are literally numbered. You will shortly be consigned to

> the cold and silent grave, and all the powers of darkness cannot rescue you from your approaching fate!

Once the trials were over, the white citizens of South Carolina established public policy designed to restrict communication among blacks. Church assemblage was monitored, reading was forbidden, and mail was inspected. And once again they set upon the focal point, the AME church. This time they tore it down completely. For blacks, the church represented a crucial sense of autonomy. And among Charleston whites, that autonomy was deemed dangerous.

Secret meetings and prayer services continued until the church was rebuilt in 1865 by Denmark Vesey's youngest son. But the physical destruction of the Charleston church weakened the bond between the AME's strongest congregation in Philadelphia and the branches of the church in slave states.

In 1817, Jarena Lee reestablished that bond. She became the church's first female preacher, as much a rebel as Gabriel or Denmark Vesey. She asserted her independence as a woman and as a free black woman, forming practical and spiritual bonds with slaves in a society that limited what blacks, free or captive, could do.

Jarena had been born in 1783 in Cape May, New Jersey. She was a black child born free but living in a slave state where gradual emancipation did not begin until 1804, well after the Revolution.

At the age of seven she was taken away from her parents and apprenticed as a maid at a home approximately sixty miles from her birthplace. Her first acknowledgment of a spiritual conscience came shortly thereafter, when she lied about the completion of some household task.

She wrote later in her journal:

> At this awful point, in my early history, the Spirit of God moved in power through my conscience, and told me I was a wretched sinner. On this account so great was the impression, and so strong were the feelings of guilt, that I promised in my heart that I would not tell another lie.

Wrestling with the concept of deity and demon for most of her young life, Jarena later traveled to Philadelphia in search of a job. There, she was mightily transformed by a rousing, impassioned sermon delivered by the Reverend Richard Allen. "That moment, though hundreds were present, I did leap to my feet and declare that God, for Christ's sake, had pardoned the sins of my soul."

Sometime after that powerful spiritual awakening, Jarena Lee felt a calling that both frightened and exhilarated her:

> [T]o my utter surprise there seemed to sound a voice which I thought I distinctly heard, and most certainly understand, which said to me, "Go preach the Gospel!" I immediately replied aloud, "No one will believe me." Again I listened, and again the same voice seemed to say, "Preach the Gospel; I will put words in your mouth, and will turn your enemies to become your friends."

Jarena called for the speaker to make himself known, resulting in the dream that changed her life.

> [M]y mind became so exercised that during the night following I took a text and preached in my sleep. I thought there stood before me a great multitude, while I expounded to them the things of religion. So violent were my exertions and so loud were my exclamations that I awoke from the sound of my own voice.

Jarena, like many others of the time, believed that God communicated through apparitions, voices, and dreams. She was certain that there was a very thin barrier between the concrete and spiritual worlds, and that God could intercede in various ways.

Two days after that dream, Jarena visited Reverend Allen and told him she had received the call. She was destined to preach. God himself had made the request.

Reverend Allen refused to allow the young woman her chance in the pulpit. In the Methodist discipline, he explained, no precedent for women preachers had been set. Jarena argued back in her journal: "If the man may preach, because the Savior died for him, why not the woman? seeing he died for her also? Is he not a whole Savior, instead of a half one?"

But eight years later, during a Sunday service at Bethel, Jarena rose to her feet and launched into a fiery impromptu sermon during which "God made manifest His power in a manner sufficient to show the world that I was called to labor according to my ability. . . . I imagined, that for this indecorum, as I feared it might be called, I should be expelled from the church."

Instead, Allen rose and, according to Jarena, said that she "had called upon him eight years before, asking to be permitted to preach; and that he had put me off; but he now as much as believed that I was called to that work as any of the preachers present."

Lee became a traveling sermonizer, an exhorter who spread the gospel in places few black women had ventured, sharing her love of God with blacks, whites, even Indians. She traveled north to New England and Canada, took steamboats to Delaware and Maryland. She preached in Buffalo and

New York City. She traveled the hundreds of miles any way she could, often on foot. During one year, she traveled more than two thousand miles and delivered 178 sermons.

In an act of extraordinary courage, Lee went into slave states to preach her liberation theology. And she made sure that slaves heard what she had to say. In one passage from her memoirs, she wrote: "Some of the poor slaves came happy in the Lord; walked from 20 to 30, and from that to seventy miles, to worship God." The specter of a free black woman speaking with assurance and spiritual fury amazed and inspired the slaves. They took extraordinary measures to see Lee, even though many had to walk back to be in their slave quarters by morning.

She preached an all-encompassing salvation. To slaves still chained to the South, she preached liberty. Her empowering messages of self-determination were subversive, incendiary. Buoyed by a divine conviction and filled with a singular courage, she entered the den of lions and preached: "The spirit of the Lord God is upon me, because the Lord hath anointed me to preach good tidings unto the meek. He hath sent me to bind up the broken-hearted, to proclaim liberty to the captives, and the opening of the prison to them that are bound."

After twenty-two years on the road, Jarena Lee was growing weary. But her faith held strong. "My money was gone, my health was gone, and I measurably without a home. But I rested on the promises of God."

It didn't matter to Jarena Lee how many voices screamed "No." The one voice that mattered had already said "Yes." She preached with all of her soul—because God himself had made the request.

CHAPTER NINE

PHILADELPHIA, the birthplace of liberty, wasn't heaven—but it was probably the closest a free black American could get.

In the 1820s, it was home to the country's wealthiest black population, and it was held up as the standard of what African Americans could achieve. As he observed the blacks around him, Philadelphian John Watson longed for the olden days:

> Their aspirations and little vanities have been rapidly growing since they got those separate churches, and have received their entire exemption from slavery. Once they submitted to the appellation of servants, blacks or negroes, but now they require to be called coloured people, and among themselves, their common call of salutation is—gentlemen and ladies. Twenty to thirty years ago, they were much humbler, more esteemed in their place, and more useful to themselves and others.

The city's black citizens were in the perfect position to dream. But they couldn't vote. They couldn't send their children to public schools. They were still victims of a numbing prejudice that pervaded every part of their lives. The dream was beginning to dim.

Former overseer Thomas Branagan mirrored the sentiment of many of his white countrymen:

> [I]t is impossible in the nature of things, for the blacks in the North to ever be reconciled to the whites; while hundreds of thousands of their countrymen are groaning, bleeding, and dying, beneath the frowns of despotism, in the South. To suppose they can be reconciled while this is the case, is the first-born of absurdities.

The idea of blacks and whites getting along peaceably while the specter of slavery darkened their path was seen as absurd. So this pie-in-the-sky dream was replaced by a very real fear, a fear that the country's security was threatened by vengeful black freedmen unable to forget the indignities they had suffered as captives.

The Fourth of July was becoming the country's only true national holiday. But free blacks who joined in the annual hoopla risked being driven out by white mobs. During the contention over who had the right to celebrate liberty, well-to-do sailmaker James Forten emerged as one of black Philadelphia's most passionate voices. A veteran of the Revolutionary War, Forten was incensed that any veteran, no matter what his color, would be forbidden to take part in Independence Day festivities:

> It is a well-known fact that black people, upon certain days of publick jubilee, dare not be seen after twelve o'clock in the day. I allude particularly to the FOURTH OF JULY—Is it not wonderful, that the day set apart

for the festival of Liberty, should be abused by the advocates of freedom, in endeavoring to sully what they profess to adore.

Due to a barrage of attacks on their character and ability—indeed, their very humanness—members of the black community turned to themselves for protection. They sensed an unending struggle ahead, where they would have to fight for everything—even the right to their own children.

In the eighteen years since the ban on African labor importation, hundreds of free blacks had been kidnapped into captivity. Many of them were children, considered easy to kidnap and conceal because a couple of years of wretched slave labor often rendered them unrecognizable. A child abducted at eight or nine years of age was a hardened, abused, world-weary slave by the time he reached his teen years. His world-view had been irreparably twisted, a change which served his master well.

In one year alone, sixty children disappeared from Philadelphia. Since southern courts denied the testimony of blacks, whether free or enslaved, their stories of abduction had little chance of being heard or believed.

A young black person living in Philadelphia in the 1820s was extremely vulnerable, constantly exposed to danger. Because housing conditions were mostly cramped and intolerable, children spent a great deal of their time outdoors where they were easy prey for slave catchers. The sight of several black children being hustled down the street elicited no questions. No explanations were warranted. The children just disappeared.

The disappeared children had often lived and worked outside the home. Parents believed their children were offered some measure of protection by the employer. The employers assumed that runaway children had returned to their parents. Since no one was sure of their whereabouts, it was often some time before anyone realized the children were really missing.

Kidnappers often lured children onto ships with a black decoy and the promise of money. Philadelphia was in a recession, and poor children peppered the streets, searching for change. After capture, they would be bound and chained until enough were rounded up for transport.

It had been a long-standing problem. Years earlier, in 1799, Reverend Absalom Jones and a group of noted black Philadelphia citizens had petitioned Congress, describing "a trade . . . practised openly by Citizens of some of the Southern States, upon the waters of Maryland and Delaware," a trade in which free blacks were abducted in Philadelphia and "fettered and hurried into places provided for this most horrid traffic, such as dark cellars and garrets."

While most Philadelphians probably did not approve of the abductions, the city's rapidly growing black population frightened the white majority. The 1820 census recorded 11,891 black residents without taking into consideration thousands of fugitive slaves. In the next ten years, the number of black citizens increased by some 30 percent. To drive blacks from the city, laws were proposed to limit their movements; they were slapped with special taxes. Organizations such as the American Colonization Society increased in popularity.

Although an 1820 law promised twenty-one years' imprisonment and hard labor to anyone convicted of kidnapping, the slickly organized practice soon became routine.

In 1826, planter John W. Hamilton wrote to Philadelphia's mayor with the suspicion that a group of young, newly arrived slaves at his Rocky Spring, Mississippi, plantation were free blacks who had been captured in Philadelphia. One of the boys, Samuel Scomp, begged Hamilton to protect him against further mistreatment. He insisted that the captives had been forced to walk barefoot for a total of six hundred miles and that they were whipped soundly whenever they complained. Another of the boys, Alexander Manlove, exhibited an uncanny knowledge of Philadelphia and showed Hamilton the whip scars on his back.

Hamilton questioned the slave trader, who insisted that the slaves were obtained legally and showed the planter the bill of sale.

Scomp had made a bid for freedom in Indian territory by running away and seeking sanctuary with the Choctaw. But he was returned and beaten with a handsaw, which was merciful compared to the fate of a young companion.

"Joe was lame and frosted in the feet," Scomp told authorities. "[H]e was very weak, and for near three weeks fell frequently as he walked; the weather was very cold in Alabama; about one day before he died he was severely flogged with a cart whip: he died in the wagon."

Scomp was lucky. He and another boy were returned to Philadelphia by Hamilton. Even after the kidnappings were exposed, the victims' identities—according to Mississippi law—had to be established in court before their release. But Mississippi courts allowed only the in-person testimony of whites. The Philadelphia High Constable of police made two trips there in the summer of 1826 but managed to free only three children. One of them, James Daily, died just days after his return of injuries he'd suffered as a slave.

Most of the children remained "disappeared."

Proslavery factions were gaining ground. Due to the rampant growth of the cotton economy, a fairly new idea began to formulate, particularly in the South: Americans did not have to apologize for slavery. Slavery was good. It freed whites from menial labor, and Africans benefited by their contact with white Christian culture.

And just to prove that ignorance was the black man's natural state of being, some whites took the scientific approach.

A generation before, Thomas Jefferson had set forward crude theories regarding black sexuality and the natural inferiority of Africans and their descendants. In 1781 in *Notes on the State of Virginia*—a petite volume analyzing the state's natural resources—he abandoned his scientific musings long enough for a scathing attack on blacks and their myriad defects, which included their odor, inability to communicate intelligently, and their idea of love as animalistic coupling. Never had he heard of a black man who "uttered a thought above the level of plain narration"; all blacks were "in imagination . . . dull, tasteless and anomalous" and "inferior to whites in the endowments of body and mind."

Founding Father Jefferson, one of the most thoughtful and well-read men in the eighteenth century, was clearly seeking an excuse for why he had failed to practice what he preached when it came to the immorality of slavery. His answer was that Africans and African Americans were essentially children, biologically inferior to whites. It was the responsibility of conscientious white men to care for those who simply couldn't care for themselves.

Scientists sought to buttress those ideas by measuring skulls, analyzing physical features, and rooting out diseases particular to blacks. If they couldn't justify slavery on moral grounds, they'd convince the public that it was scientifically predestined and therefore best for all involved.

Philadelphia doctor Charles Caldwell penned two lengthy essays on African inferiority. In his *Thoughts on the Original Unity of the Human Race*, he wrote:

> To the Caucasian race is the world indebted for all the great and important discoveries, inventions and improvements, that have been made in science and the arts, [while the African has remained] Motionless; fixed to a spot, like the rocks and trees, in the midst of which they dwell; each generation pursuing the same time-beaten track. . . . Even century succeeds to century, and the last finds them the same degraded and unimproved beings with the former.

Although Caldwell admitted that Africans *could* be taught by Caucasians, the instruction had to be a lifelong undertaking if it was to be beneficial at all. For once the teaching ended and blacks were left to their own devices, "instead of advancing in knowledge, or even retaining what they have received, their course will be retrograde, until they shall have returned to their original ignorance." How did Caldwell explain a James Forten, a Phillis Wheatley? Mere quirks of nature: "As there are Caucasian imbeciles, so are there some Africans and Indians more highly gifted than others."

The doctor's parade of scientific fallacies quickly gave way to the most savage stereotypes. He decried the African penchant for "gorging themselves, of choice, with human flesh," and stated that "Their intercourse is as loose as that of apes and monkies." But in making the sweeping declaration that "No point of time can be indicated when the Caucasians were real savages," Caldwell conveniently forgot the senseless brutality his race exhibited in the treatment of its slaves.

Julien Joseph Virey first published *Histoire naturelle du genre humain* in Paris in 1801. Unfortunately, the book was reprinted several times, affording Virey's racist rhetoric a larger audience. In 1837, the section of the book regarding blacks was translated into English by J. H. Guenebault and published as *Natural History of the Negro Race.*

Virey's theories were based on the belief that the intelligence and physical beauty of whites made them more civilized than blacks, whose ugly and exaggerated features were a sure sign of savagery. "In our white species," he wrote, "the forehead is projecting, and the mouth retreating, as if we were rather designed to think than to eat; in the negro species, the forehead is retreating, and the mouth projecting, as if he were made rather to eat than to think."

Surgeon and comparative anatomy student Charles White concluded that "in bodily structure and economy," blacks were closer to apes than to Europeans. In 1799, he waxed poetic, asking who but whites could possess

> that nobly arched head, containing such a quantity of brain? Where that variety of features, and fullness of expression; those long, flowing, graceful ringlets; that majestic beard, those rosy cheeks and coral lips? . . . Where, except on the bosom of the European woman, two such plump and snowy white hemispheres, tipt with vermillion?

Psychological attacks culminated in the late 1820s in the work of caricaturist Edward Clay, who satirized black progress on broadsides, then on small, collectible cards.

Clay's caricatures drew heavily from reality. With some fifteen thousand blacks in Philadelphia by 1830, and at least a thousand of them economically prosperous, there were inroads being made into middle-class life. The cartoons, documentation as well as ridicule, used the era's upfront, confrontational humor to batter blacks and their aspirations. The black middle class was depicted as filthy, ignorant, and pretentious.

One cartoon, "Home and Abroad," depicts a couple at home, doing dishes in what is clearly a basement apartment. In the next panel, they are outdoors, dressed to the nines, strutting and behaving as if the street belonged to them.

In the 1830s, the attacks grew even more pointed with the introduction of Jim Crow. Sometimes he was known as Cuff. Snowball. Sambo. Whatever his name, he represented the ugliest of what whites saw in blacks. He was a caricature designed to prove that a black man was not a human being, but a parody of one.

Jim Crow, entertaining on homemade stages, existed to hoof and guffaw for the pleasure of the white working class and extended his appeal to even larger audiences in big-city professional theaters. His white face, blackened by burnt cork, reinforced what most of America wanted to believe—that the slave was a happy-go-lucky type, endlessly jolly, blissful in his subservience. The genre is believed to have originated with one Thomas Dartmouth "Daddy" Rice, who, searching for new performance material, launched into an impersonation of a handicapped black stable hand.

The *New York Tribune* lent credence to the Jim Crow myth:

> Absurd as may seem negro minstrelsy to the refined musician, it is nevertheless beyond doubt that it expresses the peculiar characteristics of the negro as truly as the great masters of Italy represent their more spiritual and profound nationality.

His white eyes rolled and bulged in what was assumed to be a savage rhythm. Clumsy acrobatics were overwrought. The huge drooping clothing and flopping shoes reaffirmed the stereotype of Negro as clueless, carefree child. Then there was the stuttering darky of the plantation, the pretentious, eye-rolling dandy. All objects of ridicule.

This was black man as created by whites, by the whims and prejudices of whoever hid behind the makeup. Consider this *Knickerbocker* review of a minstrel performance by T. D. Rice:

> Entering the theater, we found it crammed, from pit to dome, and the best representative of our American negro that we ever saw, was stretching every mouth in the house to its utmost tension. Such a natural gait!—*such* a laugh!—and such a twitching-up of the arm and shoulder! It was the negro, par excellence. Long live *James Crow,* Esquire!

Not only couldn't the black man in America gain control of his own life, now even the perception of that life was in someone else's hands.

On June 24, 1826, an ill, infirm, and aging Thomas Jefferson declined an invitation to celebrate the fiftieth anniversary of the Declaration of Independence in Washington, D.C.:

> *[O]n the fiftieth anniversary of American Independence, as one of the surviving signers of an instrument pregnant with our own, and the fate of the world . . . it adds sensibly to the sufferings of sickness, to be deprived . . . in the rejoicings of that day.*
>
> *I should, indeed, with peculiar delight, have met and exchanged their congratulations personally with the . . . remnant of that host of worthies . . . and to have enjoyed*

> *with them the consolatory fact that our fellow citizens . . . continue to approve the choice we made.*

In the same letter, Jefferson declared that *"All eyes are opened, or opening, to the rights of man."*

The former president lay on his deathbed in Monticello, stubbornly clinging to life until the Fourth of July—the day he had chosen to die. Although he had hoped to be remembered for the crafting of the Statute of Virginia for Religious Freedom, the establishment of the University of Virginia, and, of course, the Declaration of Independence, Jefferson's legacy also included the two hundred slaves he left behind in Monticello. In eighty-three years of life, the symbol of American democracy had freed only three of them.

One was his bondsman James Hemings, who had traveled with Jefferson to Europe. Jefferson drafted a contract after agreeing to free Hemings, who had been tutored by French chefs to create dishes that pleased his owner's palate. Jefferson seemed most interested in recouping the cost of that training:

> Having been at great expence in having James Hemings taught the art of cookery, desiring to befriend him, and to require from him as little in return as possible, I do hereby promise and declare, that if the said James shall go with me to Monticello in the course of the ensuing winter, when I go to reside there myself, and shall there continue until he shall have taught such persons as I shall place under him for that purpose to be a good cook, this previous condition being performed, he shall be thereupon made free, and I will thereupon execute all proper instruments to make him free.

The date of the contract was September 15, 1793.

Five more slaves found freedom in Jefferson's will. They

were all Hemingses. Many believe they were related to him by marriage and were the children of John Wayles, Jefferson's father-in-law, which made them the half-sisters and half-brothers of Jefferson's late wife, Martha.

Throughout his life, Jefferson orated and wrote beautiful, heartfelt words envisioning equality for all—but, as his position in *Notes on the State of Virginia* attests, that egalitarian veneer barely disguised the spirit of a Negrophobic southern planter whose solution to the country's most pressing problem was avoidance.

Jefferson's death caused the young nation to stop and reflect, it also caused his human property a great deal of anxiety. Since he had made a habit of living beyond his means, it was inevitable that his heirs would liquidate to recover the debt.

> Inventory of the estate of Thomas Jefferson, deceased. Dated seventh day of August, 1826: Negro man, Barnaby, valued at $400. Negro woman, Betty Brown, no value. Critty, $50. Negro woman, Ellen, $300. Negro man, Peter Hemmings [*sic*], $100. Negro Sally Hemmings [*sic*], $50. Negro man, Wormley, $200. Negro woman, Ursula and her young child, $300. Negro woman, Anne and her young child, $350 . . .

More than 130 slaves were sold at auction in one day. To satisfy Jefferson's $100,000 debt—roughly $10 million today—the seams of families came loose.

William Chambers observed a sad, telling game that often went on at slave auctions:

> Conceive the idea of a large shop with two windows, and a door between; no shelving or counters inside; the interior a spacious, dismal apartment. . . . I say, conceive the idea of this dismal-looking place, with nobody in it

> but three negro children. . . . An intensely black little negro, of four or five years of age was standing on the bench, or block, as it is called, with an equally black girl, about a year younger, by his side, whom he was pretending to sell by bids to another black child . . . rehearsing what was likely soon to be their own fate.

By 1830, the slave population of the United States had grown to over 2 million. Slaves had been siphoned into the Deep South and West to grow the cotton which kept Europeans supplied with underwear, dresses, shirts, and bedsheets. Since the cotton gin's invention, over 200,000 slaves in Virginia alone had been torn away from their homes and families. Slavery was no longer a question. It was an answer.

In 1819, when a bill admitting Missouri as a slave state came before the House, all hell broke loose. The admission of Missouri, which lay almost completely north of the Ohio River, would violate the traditional dividing line between North and South, and would upset the balance of free and slave states in the Senate.

Then Maine applied for statehood, and a way was found to break the deadlock. In 1820, Missouri was admitted as a slave state and Maine as a free one, but Congress insisted on banning slavery in all territory north of the southern border of Missouri. The Missouri Compromise temporarily calmed the sectional rift but did nothing to resolve the problem of an immoral system in a society that stressed its morality.

While the institution crumbled in the North—in 1827, New York freed all ten thousand men, women, and children held in bondage—fewer than 3 percent of the nation's 12 million citizens were free blacks.

There were still attempts at progress. On September 15, 1830, an elderly Reverend Richard Allen gathered forty delegates from battered black communities in New York City, Boston, Baltimore, and Wilmington for the first national convention of Free Persons of Colour. The assembly crafted an address which began with a pointed reference to the opening lines of the Declaration of Independence. And they initiated a discussion on acquiring land in Canada as a refuge for free African Americans.

On March 26, 1831, before the group could meet for a second time, Richard Allen died.

The founder of the African Methodist Episcopal Church had spent his life believing that blacks could reach an equal place, and he preached that belief until the end of his life. Blacks, especially those who were enslaved and embittered, had to struggle to hold on to Allen's message.

But in 1829, a Boston used-clothing salesman named David Walker countered growing proslavery sentiment by publishing his *Appeal to the Coloured Citizens of the World, But in Particular and Very Expressly to Those of the United States of America.*

"The Americans say, that we are ungrateful," Walker wrote,

> but I ask them for heaven's sake, what should we be grateful to them for—for murdering our fathers and mothers? Or do they wish us to return thanks to them for chaining and handcuffing us, branding us, cramming fire down our throats, or for keeping us in slavery. . . . They certainly think that we are a gang of fools.

In the passionate pamphlet, Walker warned Americans that they would soon have to pay for the sin of owning human beings.

> They [the whites] know well, if we are *men*—and there is a secret monitor in their hearts which tells them we are—they know, I say, if we *are* men, and see them treating us in the manner they do, that there can be nothing in our hearts but death alone, for them.

David Walker promised the slaves that God would send them a Hannibal.

In 1831, some believed that's exactly what he did.

> While labouring in the field, I discovered drops of blood on the corn as though it were dew from heaven. . . . For as the blood of Christ had been shed on this earth and had ascended to heaven for the salvation of sinners . . . it was plain to me that the Saviour was about to lay down the yoke he had bourne for the sins of men, and the great day of judgment was at hand.
>
> —Nat Turner

Nat Turner was born in 1800, five days before Gabriel was hanged for his attempt at insurrection. It was told that Turner's African mother, unable to bear the thought of surrendering her son to slavery, had to be prevented from murdering him.

Turner came up listening to the canting of white preachers who used religion to keep their slaves at bay. He served his master faithfully, once voluntarily returning to bondage after a successful escape. He said that the Spirit had appeared to him and told him to surrender to his earthly master.

But now the Spirit was back. And surrender was out of the question.

> I heard a loud noise in the heavens, and the Spirit instantly appeared to me and said the Serpent was loos-

> ened, and Christ had laid down the yoke he had borne for the sins of men, and that I should take it on and fight against the Serpent, for the time was fast approaching, when the first should be last and the last should be first.
>
> And immediately . . . the seal was removed from my lips, and I communicated the great work laid out for me to do. . . . I should arise and prepare myself, and slay my enemies with their own weapons.

Nat Turner saw and believed the signs. Visions filled his head regularly—black and white spirits entangled, a blue sun, leaves splotched with blood. And he became God's executor on earth, an insistent death blow against the sins of white men and the evils of the slave system. He believed he was sanctioned by God.

> I saw white spirits and black spirits engaged in battle, and the sun was darkened . . . and I heard a voice saying, "Such is your luck, such you are called to see, and let it come rough or smooth, you must surely bear it."

At midnight on August 21, 1831, on the road to Jerusalem, Virginia, Nat Turner began to kill.

> [A]rmed with a hatchet and accompanied by Will, I entered my master's chamber; it being dark, I could not give a death blow: the hatchet glanced from his head. He sprang from the bed and called his wife; it was his last word.

Unlike Gabriel or Denmark Vesey, Nat Turner had no clear plan to guide him. He had mapped out no route for eluding pursuers. He and a small band of seven slaves simply vowed to kill all the whites.

> [W]e entered and murdered Mrs. Reese in her bed while [she was] sleeping; her son awoke, but it was only to sleep the sleep of death; he had only time to say "Who is that?" and he was no more. . . .
>
> Having murdered Mrs. Waller and ten children, we started for Mr. William Williams'. Having killed him and two little boys that were there; while [we were] engaged in this, Mrs. Williams fled . . . but she was pursued, overtaken . . . after showing her the mangled body of her lifeless husband, she was told to get down and lay by his side, where she was shot dead.

For thirty-six hours, Turner's bloody rampage continued unabated. The rebellion gathered recruits, and soon the murderous army numbered fifty to sixty men. The most trusted fifteen or twenty rode in front, hurtling toward their victims to elicit horror and prevent escape. Sometimes Turner didn't reach a home until the murders had already been committed:

> I sometimes got in sight in time to see the work of death completed, viewed the mangled bodies as they lay in silent satisfaction, and immediately started in quest of other victims.

At least fifty-seven white people lost their lives—men, women, and children bludgeoned, stabbed, disemboweled, beheaded, hacked, and clubbed. Putnam Moore, the young boy who legally owned Nat Turner, was slain in his bed.

By August 23, military from Virginia and federal forces from Fort Monroe as well as detachments from the warships *USS Warren* and *USS Natchez* had been mobilized, and fear took the form of a devastating retaliatory strike. Approximately three thousand white men fought to quash the insurrection, and least a hundred innocent blacks died in their answer to Turner's rampage.

"Nat Turner's insurrection broke out; and the news threw our town into great commotion," wrote Harriet Jacobs.

> I knew the houses were to be searched; and I expected it would be done by country bullies and the poor whites. . . . Every where men, women, and children were whipped till the blood stood in puddles at their feet. Some received five hundred lashes; others were tied hands and feet. . . .
>
> I saw a mob dragging along . . . a respectable old colored minister. They had found a few parcels of shot in his house, which his wife had for years used to balance her scales. For this they were going to shoot him on Court House Green.

Although more than fifty of the insurrectionists were rounded up almost immediately, Turner eluded capture for six weeks. He was finally taken into custody in October.

The unrepentant rebel recounted his horrific agenda to court-appointed lawyer Thomas Gray. The transcript of that confession is chilling, the enduring portrait of a man who believed that he killed with the hand of God.

Nat Turner was hanged on November 11, 1831. Thomas Gray offered up his impressions of the man who sought to end slavery with a sword.

> He is a complete fanatic, or plays his part most admirably. On other subjects he possesses an uncommon share of intelligence, with a mind capable of attaining any thing but warped and perverted by the influence of early impressions. . . . The calm, deliberate composure

with which he spoke of his late deeds and intentions—the expression of his fiend-like face when excited by enthusiasm—still bearing the stains of the blood of helpless innocence about him—clothed with rags and covered with chains, yet daring to raise his manacled hands to heaven, with a spirit soaring above the attributes of man—I looked on him and my blood curdled in my veins.

THE SOULCATCHER

IN THAT BOSTON MARKET on a Thursday in 1853, there were two men, one black, one white, who were as intimately bound, in a way, as brothers, or perhaps it was better to say they were caught in a macabre dance, one that stretched from rural South Carolina to Massachusetts over a period of three long months of hiding, disguises, last-minute escapes, name changes, and tracking leads that led nowhere until it brought them both here to the bustling open-air market perched near the waterfront on a summer afternoon.

They were weary, these two. Hunter and Hunted.

The Hunter paused just at the periphery of the market, breathing in the salt-laced air, looking at the numerous stands filled with freshly baked bread, a variety of vegetables, fish caught earlier that day, and handicrafts—wood carvings, colorful quilts, and hand-sewn leather garments—sold by black and white Bostonians alike. The Negroes, he noticed, including the one he was looking for, had set up their stands toward the rear of the market, separating themselves from the others. A gnarled, little merchant with a Scottish brogue, and wearing a yeoman's cap and burnoose, suddenly pulled at the sleeve of the Hunter's jacket. He pointed with his other hand at boots on the table beside him. Irritated, the Hunter shook loose his arm from the merchant's grasp, then moved on a few paces through the crowded market, tilting down his hat brim a bit to hide his face, and positioned himself to one side of a hanging display of rugs. From there he could see the Negro he wanted but was not himself in plain view. He reached into a pocket sewn inside his ragged, gypsy cloak, felt around his pistol—a Colt .31— and his fingers closed on a folded piece of paper. The Hunter withdrew it. He opened it slowly, as he'd done nearly a hundred times in the last three months in dozens of towns in North Carolina, Virginia, Pennsylvania, and New York, in daylight and dark, when the trail he was following went cold and he sat before a campfire, wondering how long it would be before he would collect his bounty. The paper had been folded and creased so often a few of the words on it were feathery. In the upper right-hand corner he saw the long-dried stain of dark blood—his brother Jeremiah's—and below it this notice:

> RUN away from Charlotte on *Sunday*, a Negro slave named FRANK, well known about the Country as a craftsman, has a scar on one of his Wrists, and has lost one or more of his fore Teeth; he is a very resourceful Fellow, skilled as a smithy and saddle-maker, loves Drink, and is very often in his Cups, but surly and dangerous when sober. Whither he has run to, I cannot say, but I will offer $200 to have him returned to me. He can read and write.
>
> APRIL 2, 1853 JUBAL CATTON

From where he stood, the Hunter had a side view of a black craftsman seated before a table of wood carvings, talking to a nearby old Negress selling fish and a balding black man hawking produce. The Hunter was sure this was Frank. When last he'd seen him—just outside Norfolk—he was wearing Lowell pants and a jerkin. Today he was dressed better in a homespun suit. Under the table, he noticed, there was a flask, which the Negro occasionally lifted to his lips, then slid back out of sight. For a time, the Hunter was content simply to study him. He didn't want to rush. That's what Jeremiah always told him: You move too quick, you'll startle the prey. When the moment's right to move, you'll know. *Now that he nearly had Frank trapped, the Hunter wished his brother could be there, at the market, for the catch. But Jeremiah was back in Charleston. Blind. When Frank bolted from Jubal Catton's farm, he'd stolen his master's Walker .44, and when they found him hiding in a barn, Frank fired at Jeremiah's face from five feet away, missing him—the nigger was a bad shot—but the blast seared his brother's eyes. Yes, thought the Hunter. He wished like hell Jeremiah was here now. They both still wanted that reward. But this runaway had made the hunt personal. During the first month he pursued Frank, his intent was to kill him. Then, as the weeks drew on, he realized slavery was worse than death. It was a little bit of death every day. It was even worse than being blind.*

He would take him back, the Hunter decided. Jeremiah'd want it that way.

The Hunted reached under his table, grabbed the bottle by its neck, then drank just enough to take away the dryness in his throat. He never knew exactly why, but for some reason he'd always fought better drunk than sober. And it looked like he had a fight coming now, though he had thrown away his master's gun and had nothing to defend himself with but his bare hands. He thought, All right, if that's the way it has to be. *He'd seen the white man—his name was Clement Walker—the moment he entered the market, or rather his nerves had responded, as they always did, when a soulcatcher was close by. He could smell them the way a rabbit did a hound. It was the way they looked at colored people, he supposed. Most whites didn't bother to look at you at all, like you were invisible. Or as unimportant as a fence post. Or if they were afraid of you, they'd look away altogether. But not soulcatchers. They wanted to see your face. Match it with a description on a wanted poster. Oh yes,* they *looked. Real hard.*

That was how he'd spotted the Hunter. But he didn't need that sixth sense anymore to recognize Walker. The Hunted rubbed his left shoulder, massaging the spot where the Hunter had months ago left a deep imprint of his incisors—this, during their tussle after he shot at Jeremiah Walker. No question he'd know Clement any*where. The man was in his dreams or—more precisely—his nightmares since he left his master's farm. Not a day passed when Frank didn't look over his shoulder, expecting him to be there, holding a gun in one hand and manacles in the other. It was almost as if he was* inside *Frank now, the embodiment of all his fears.*

His first instinct had been to flee when he saw him, but Lord, he felt tired of running. Of being alone. That he'd not counted on when he ran for freedom: the staggering loneliness. The suspicions. The constant living in fear that he might be taken back to the tortures of slavery at any time. For months, he'd been afraid to speak to anyone. Every white man was a potential enemy. No Negro could be fully trusted either. But along the way he'd been fortunate. More so than many fugitives. He met white ministers who were conductors for the Underground Railroad, men who fronted as his master long enough for him to traverse the states of North Carolina and Virginia; and here, in Boston, he'd found free blacks—the very portrait of Christian kindness and self-sacrifice—willing to risk their own lives to help him. They were deeply religious, these Negroes. Lambs of Jesus, he thought at first. They put him up in their homes, fed him, provided him with clothes and a fresh start. Even helped him pick a new name. Jackson Lee was the one he used now. And he deployed those many skills he'd learned as a slave, plus his own God-given talent, to rebuilding his life from scratch. At least, until now.

Out of the corner of his eye he could see the Hunter moving closer, circling round toward the front of the market, keeping the waterfront at Frank's back, to cut him off if he tried to run. This time the Hunted decided, no. He would stay, dying here among free black people. He'd been to their churches, heard their preachers say no man should fear death because the Son of God conquered that for all time. And no man could be enslaved, they said, if he was prepared to die.

The Hunter stopped in front of his table. He looked over the carvings, picked up one of a horse, and examined it, the faintest of smiles on his lips. "You do right fine work."

"Thank you."

"I once knew a fellah in Charleston was almost as good as you."

"That so?"

"Um-huh." The Hunter put the carving down. "Nigger named Frank. I don't suppose you know his work, do you?"

"No," he shook his head. "Never been to Charleston. Lived here my whole life. You kin ask anybody here 'bout that." He tilted his head toward the balding man, then at the old black woman selling fish. "Ain't that so?"

"Yes, sir." The balding man held out his hand at waist-level, his palm facing down. "I been knowin' Jackson since he was yea-high."

The old woman chimed in, "That's right. He belong to my church."

The Hunter's eyes narrowed, he looked at both of them irritably, said, "I think you two better mind your own damned business," then he swung his gaze back toward the Hunted. "I ain't here to play games with you, Frank."

"My name is Jackson Lee."

"Right, and I'm Andrew Jackson."

Slowly, the Hunter withdrew his pistol. His arm bent, close to his side, he pointed the barrel at the Hunted. "Get up."

Frank sat motionless, looking down the black, one-eyed barrel. "No."

"Then I'll shoot you, nigger. Right here."

"Guess you'll have to do that then."

The old woman said, "Mister! You don't have to do *that!"*

"Naw," the balding man pleaded. "He from round here!"

Frowning, the Hunter took a deep breath. "I told *y'all to shut up and stay out of this! It ain't your affair!"*

In the market there came first one shot, shattering the air. By the time the second exploded, merchants and patrons were screaming, scattering from the waterfront like windblown leaves, tipping over tables that sent potatoes, cabbages, and melons rolling into the street. When the thunderous pistol reports subsided, leaving only a silence, and the susurration of wind off the water, the only figures left in the debris of broken displays and stands were the Hunter—he was sprawled dead beneath a rug he'd pulled to the ground as he fell—and the Hunted. There were also his new friends: The black fish woman. The balding man. Both were members of Boston's chapter of the Liberty Association, devoted to killing bounty hunters on sight. The balding man was Frank's minister. The fish woman was the minister's mother. They were the ones who'd taken him in. Helped him set up his stall in the market. And they were much better shots than he was.

It was good, thought Frank, to have friends—hunters in their own right— like these.

PART FOUR

Judgment Day

ANDREW JACKSON. *Andrew Jackson of Tennessee was the first president elected from America's new "cotton belt." His policies displaced whole nations of Native Americans and paved the way for a new generation of slavery on the western frontier.*

NATIONAL PORTRAIT GALLERY, SMITHSONIAN INSTITUTION/ART RESOURCE, NEW YORK

FREDERICK DOUGLASS, C. 1848. *Fugitive slave and abolitionist Frederick Douglass had another vision of America. Douglass's eloquent firsthand account of the life of a southern slave moved both black and white Americans to join the fight against slavery.*
CHESTER COUNTY HISTORICAL SOCIETY, WEST CHESTER, PENNSYLVANIA

Walker's Appeal, Boston, Massachusetts. *In 1829, David Walker, a fiery used-clothing salesman in Boston, issued one of the most powerful indictments of slavery that the nation had ever heard, calling on the nation to heed its own language of equal rights or be damned in the tide of retribution.*

LIBRARY OF CONGRESS

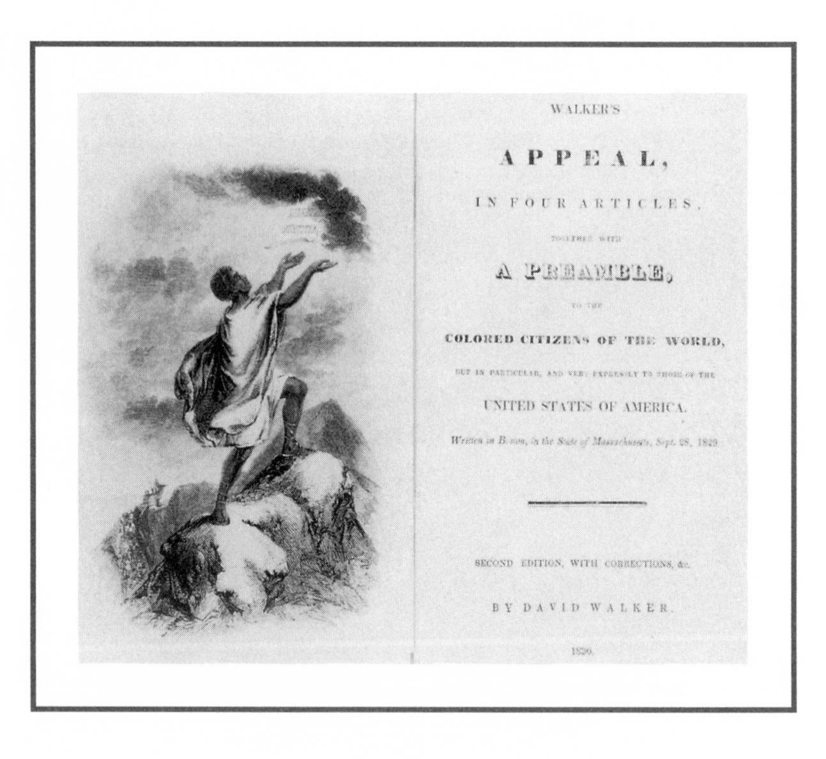

WALKER'S

APPEAL,

IN FOUR ARTICLES,

TOGETHER WITH

A PREAMBLE,

TO THE

COLORED CITIZENS OF THE WORLD,

BUT IN PARTICULAR, AND VERY EXPRESSLY TO THOSE OF THE

UNITED STATES OF AMERICA.

Written in Boston, in the State of Massachusetts, Sept. 28, 1829.

SECOND EDITION, WITH CORRECTIONS, &c.

BY DAVID WALKER.

1830.

LABORERS RETURNING FROM THE FIELD, SOUTH CAROLINA. *Even as Walker was printing his* Appeal, *hundreds of thousands of slaves were being force-marched into ever deepening oppression in the cotton fields of the Deep South and West. By 1861, there were over 4 million slaves in America.*

FANNY KEMBLE. *British actress Fanny Kemble was appalled at the conditions she found on the rice plantation of her husband, one of the richest men in America. Before leaving the South, Kemble painstakingly recorded the tragic circumstances of the slave men and women she met there.*

THE GRANGER COLLECTION, NEW YORK

Harriet Tubman (date unknown). *Harriet Tubman had survived the nightmare that Kemble had written about. After her own escape from slavery, she escorted hundreds to freedom through the Underground Railroad. She is pictured here (far left) with some of the slaves she had helped to free, including family members.*
SOPHIA SMITH COLLECTION, SMITH COLLEGE

COVER OF A PAMPHLET, 1854, TELLING OF THE TRIAL OF ANTHONY BURNS. *Anthony Burns was the most celebrated victim of the Fugitive Slave Act of 1850. The act was part of a legislative compromise that promised the South stronger enforcement of fugitive slave laws in return for allowing California to join the union as a free state.*

THE GRANGER COLLECTION, NEW YORK

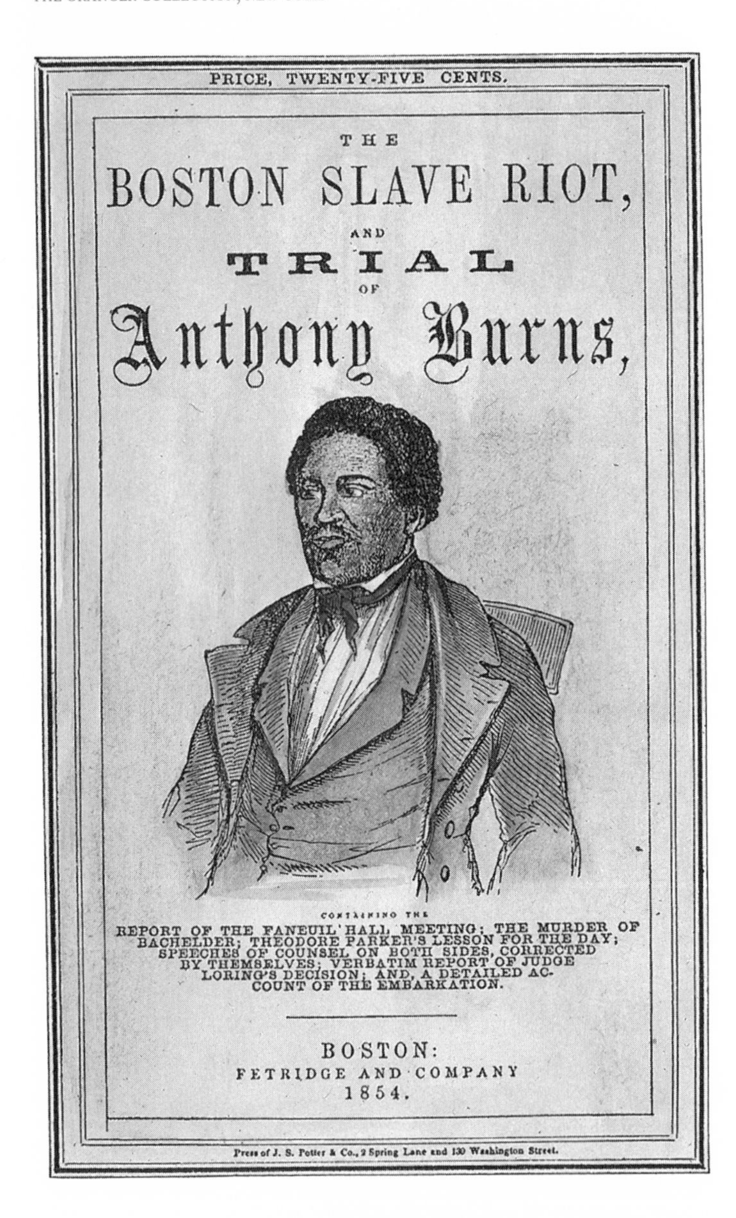

PRICE, TWENTY-FIVE CENTS.
THE
BOSTON SLAVE RIOT,
AND
TRIAL
OF
Anthony Burns,
CONTAINING THE
REPORT OF THE FANEUIL HALL MEETING; THE MURDER OF BACHELDER; THEODORE PARKER'S LESSON FOR THE DAY; SPEECHES OF COUNSEL ON BOTH SIDES, CORRECTED BY THEMSELVES; VERBATIM REPORT OF JUDGE LORING'S DECISION; AND, A DETAILED ACCOUNT OF THE EMBARKATION.
BOSTON:
FETRIDGE AND COMPANY
1854.
Press of J. S. Potter & Co., 2 Spring Lane and 130 Washington Street.

FREE SOIL!

FREE LABOR! FREE SPEECH!

RALLY OF THE PEOPLE!

☞All persons opposed to the Election of TAYLOR or CASS to the Presidency, and to the Extension of Slavery and the Slave Power, are invited to meet at the

LYCEUM HALL, in Dorchester,

MONDAY EV'G, 24TH inst.

AT 7½ O'CLOCK,

To choose Delegates to attend the Free Soil Convention, to be holden at Dedham on the 28th inst., and to organize in order to carry out the Free Soil Movement.

COME ONE! COME ALL!

Hon. STEPHEN C. PHILLIPS,

OF SALEM, AND OTHERS WILL ADDRESS THE MEETING.

DORCHESTER, July 21, 1848.

John G Nazro
Eben. Clapp, jr
Sam'l Downer, jr.
John J. May
Henry Humphreys
Edward Jarvis
Jona. Battles, jr.
Thomas C. Wales
Franklin King
Richard Clapp
Charles Carruth
S S Curtis
J C Lindsley
George C Wales
Winslow Battles
William Trask
Abijah Cotton
James Robinson
Jos T Robinson
Andrew Glover
Elias White
Samuel Hildreth

T P Brown
Wm Henry
Edward Preston
Samuel Thomas
Joseph Gunnison
Prescott Hildreth
Franklin Briggs
Thomas Knapp
Albion Benson
Eben W. Ruggles
Fred'k P Moseley
Oliver Davenport
Wm B Trask
Alfred Clapp
Calvin Bird
John Field, jr
Ira Adams
James Swan
Thomas Beals
John Kneeland
James H Blake
Benj Cushing

Henry Guild
Jona Wheeler
Asahel Glover
J P Cotton
Seth Williams
Ira Foster
Jacob Foster, jr
Lem S Blackman
Stephen Gulliver
Otis Shepard, jr
Henry Richards
Increase S Smith
Wm B Ellis
Ebenezer Bird
Charles Munroe
Wm Richardson
Samuel Tileston
Cyrus Brewer
Asaph Churchill
Joseph Wiswell
John A Tucker
Wm Tucker

Edward Holden
Darius Brewer
Henry Durell
Josiah V Marshall
Wm N Hart
George Clark
J Kendrick
L Nickerson
Wm Bowman
John C Dale
Josiah Webb
Josiah F Twombly
Ira Greeley
Wm T Johnson
Leonard Everett
S J Clapp
Henry Crane
Robt Cunningham
B F Hebard
C P Swan
S W Johnson
M Whittemore

H F Packard
Eben Sanborn
Joseph Hutchinson
Geo A Hall
Sylvest'r H Hebard
John Burt
Zimri Burgess
John Robie
R Hutchinson
Robert Hall
John Stacy
Minott Thayer
Sumner P Ruggles
R F Raley
Wm Bird
John Hawes
Rufus Nason
John W. Legalee
David F Patch
Thos W Pillsbury
Wm Adams
Brooks Crane

P J Bigelow
Josiah Wilder
D B Bartlett
H W Blanchard
John W Means
Eleazer Hill
Henry L Fowles
Luther Spear, jr.
Geo Vinton
Caleb Pillsbury
Chas. Parker
M Leavitt
John Q A Spear
O Putnam Bacon
James H Upham
Chas F Watson
Rufus Gibbs
Wm Gutterson
Alvah Phelps
Nathaniel Bailey
S F Hollis
P Lyman

Giles Randall
J M Johnson
Wm Randall
P Bracken
Frederick Crafts
Orin Jenks
Patrick Morgan
Wm S Allen
John Foster
Peter Salmon
Robert Hussey
Geo Carpenter
P Fenley
James Murphy
Geo Morey
Jos W Kilden
Chas H Halstat
P Maghoran
Jeremiah Deady
Benj Hickman
John Mington
Bennet Allen

Chas C Nichols
J L Bowers
Samuel Mitchell
D W Robinson
H M Goodwin
Benjamin Baker
Thomas Frost
Tully Freeman
James Jenkins
Wm Prescott
Isaiah Royce
E C Pruean
Elisha W Bounce
H G Fittman
George Adams
Samuel Goodwin
Wm Withington
Stephen Baker
James Baker
Geo Ford
Chas A Upham
Thos Bird
Jos S Wilder
Orin Young

H O Hildreth
Chas A Wood
Nathaniel Tolman
Norton Pratt
Wm Cole
Thos A Spencer
Daniel Grover
Josiah W Morse
James B Hill
Wm Harris
Wm Greene
Robert Hill
Joseph Glover
John Moore
Isaac Morse
Isaac Fisk
Wm Hammond
Jonathan Hammond
Thos B Richardson
Wm. F. Snow
Nathan'l H Snow
James Hildreth
Ebenezer Haines
Dr F Leavenworth
Wm P Peaker
Jos Pillsbury
John Hoit

FREE-SOILERS. *As the nation expanded west, a plan evolved to flood new territories with settlers who opposed slavery's expansion but were not necessarily pro-black. The movement became known as "Free Soil."*

COURTESY, AMERICAN ANTIQUARIAN SOCIETY

MINERS IN SPANISH FLAT, CALIFORNIA, 1852. *By the 1850s, both free blacks and slaves were moving into the West. They created communities based on the same hope of freedom and fortune that inspired the whites who worked alongside them in the gold mines of California.*

CALIFORNIA HISTORY ROOM, CALIFORNIA STATE LIBRARY, SACRAMENTO, CALIFORNIA

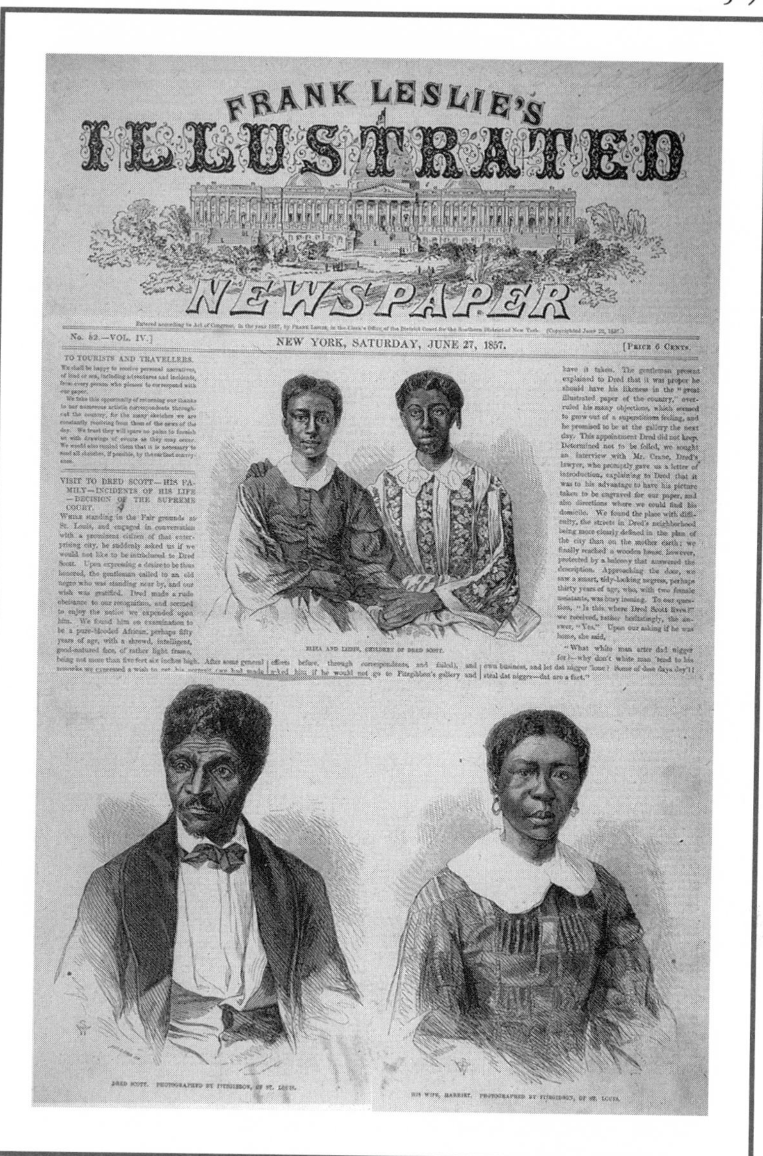

FRANK LESLIE'S ILLUSTRATED NEWSPAPER

No. 82.—VOL. IV.] NEW YORK, SATURDAY, JUNE 27, 1857. [PRICE 6 CENTS.

(Copyrighted June 25, 1857.)

TO TOURISTS AND TRAVELLERS.

We shall be happy to receive personal narratives, of land or sea, including adventures and incidents, from every person who pleases to correspond with our paper.

We take this opportunity of returning our thanks to our numerous artistic correspondents throughout the country, for the many sketches we are constantly receiving from them of the news of the day. We trust they will spare no pains to furnish us with drawings of events as they may occur. We would also remind them that it is necessary to send all sketches, if possible, by the earliest conveyance.

VISIT TO DRED SCOTT—HIS FAMILY—INCIDENTS OF HIS LIFE—DECISION OF THE SUPREME COURT.

While standing in the Fair grounds at St. Louis, and engaged in conversation with a prominent citizen of that enterprising city, he suddenly asked us if we would not like to be introduced to Dred Scott. Upon expressing a desire to be thus honored, the gentleman called to an old negro who was standing near by, and our wish was gratified. Dred made a rude obeisance to our recognition, and seemed to enjoy the notice we expended upon him. We found him on examination to be a pure-blooded African, perhaps fifty years of age, with a shrewd, intelligent, good-natured face, of rather light frame, being not more than five feet six inches high. After some general remarks we expressed a wish to get his portrait (we had made [illegible] efforts before, through correspondents, and failed), and asked him if he would not go to Fitzgibbon's gallery and have it taken. The gentleman present explained to Dred that it was proper he should have his likeness in the "great illustrated paper of the country," overruled his many objections, which seemed to grow out of a superstitious feeling, and he promised to be at the gallery the next day. This appointment Dred did not keep. Determined not to be foiled, we sought an interview with Mr. Crane, Dred's lawyer, who promptly gave us a letter of introduction, explaining to Dred that it was to his advantage to have his picture taken to be engraved for our paper, and also directions where we could find his domicile. We found the place with difficulty, the streets in Dred's neighborhood being more clearly defined in the plan of the city than on the mother earth; we finally reached a wooden house, however, protected by a balcony that answered the description. Approaching the door, we saw a smart, tidy-looking negress, perhaps thirty years of age, who, with two female assistants, was busy ironing. To our question, "Is this where Dred Scott lives?" we received, rather hesitatingly, the answer, "Yes." Upon our asking if he was home, she said,

"What white man arter dat nigger for?—why don't white man 'tend to his own business, and let dat nigger 'lone? Some of dese days dey'll steal dat nigger—dat are a fact."

ELIZA AND LIZZIE, CHILDREN OF DRED SCOTT.

DRED SCOTT. PHOTOGRAPHED BY FITZGIBBON, OF ST. LOUIS.

HIS WIFE, HARRIET. PHOTOGRAPHED BY FITZGIBBON, OF ST. LOUIS.

DRED SCOTT. *In 1857, the Supreme Court gave its answer to black aspirations—slave and free—for full citizenship. "We have come to the decision that the African race," the judge ruled, "[was] not intended to be included in the Constitution for the enjoyment of any personal rights."*

THE GRANGER COLLECTION, NEW YORK

WILLIAM LLOYD GARRISON AT AGE THIRTY, C. 1835. *Garrison was one of a new generation of abolitionists who agitated tirelessly for total and immediate emancipation of America's slaves. The* Liberator, *a militant abolitionist newspaper published by Garrison, would lay the framework for a radical movement opposing slavery.*

HENRY HIGHLAND GARNET. *Unlike Garrison, who advocated nonviolent resistance, abolitionist Henry Highland Garnet saw a different solution to America's problem. In 1843, he urged the slaves to take up arms. "You had far better all die*—die immediately,*" he told them, "than to live to be slaves."*

NATIONAL PORTRAIT GALLERY, SMITHSONIAN INSTITUTION/ART RESOURCE, NEW YORK

PIERCE BUTLER. *By 1859, forces other than abolitionism were conspiring to undo slavery's hold on America. Pierce Butler, one of the richest men in the country, had squandered a fortune built on the labor of black people. To recoup his losses, he auctioned off 429 slaves—at a racetrack in Savannah.*

THE HISTORICAL SOCIETY OF PENNSYLVANIA, PHILADELPHIA

JOHN BROWN. *John Brown could not wait for slavery to die a slow death. In 1859, in Harpers Ferry, Virginia, Brown led twenty-two men, five of them black, on a raid to rid the nation of its cancer. Though the raid was quickly put down, in a little over a year the nation would be at war—and at the heart of the conflict was slavery.*

BOSTON ATHENÆUM

CHAPTER TEN

I was born a slave; but I never knew it till six years of happy childhood had passed away. . . . I never dreamed I was a piece of merchandise. . . . When I was six years old, my mother died; and then, for the first time, I learned by the talk around me, that I was a slave.

—Harriet Jacobs

Dr. James Norcom and his wife owned a great deal of property, and more than fifty slaves. In 1825, twelve-year-old Harriet Jacobs became one of them. That year her mistress, Margaret Horniblow, died, and Harriet was bequeathed—along with "a bureau & work table & their contents"—to Horniblow's three-year-old niece, Mary Matilda Norcom. She was sent to live with the Norcoms in their Edenton, North Carolina, home.

> [O]n my fifteenth year . . . [m]y master began to whisper foul words in my ear. . . . He peopled my young mind with unclean images, such as only a vile monster could think of. . . . He told me I was his property; that I must be subject to his will in all things. My soul revolted against the mean tyranny. But where could I turn for protection? . . . My master met me at every turn . . . swearing by heaven and earth that he would compel me to submit to him.

Many years after Harriet's startling realization regarding the full implications of being born into servitude, she wrote about her experiences as a captive, adding her words to a growing body of narrative reminiscences. In the memoir, she called herself Linda Brent. Her owner, Dr. Norcom, became Dr. Flint.

Harriet's terse, straightforward prose was particularly chilling when she chronicled the cruelty woven so inextricably into the fabric of her life.

> Mrs. Flint, like many southern women, was totally deficient in energy . . . but her nerves were so strong, that she could sit in her easy chair and see a woman whipped, till the blood trickled from every stroke. . . . If dinner was not served at the exact time on that particular Sunday, she would station herself in the kitchen and wait till it was dished, and then spit in all the kettles and pans that had been used . . . to prevent the cook and her children from eking out their meagre fare. . . .
>
> Dr. Flint was an epicure. The cook never sent a dinner to his table without fear and trembling; for if there happened to be a dish not to his liking, he would either order her to be whipped, or . . . cram it down her throat till she choked.

As Harriet approached her teenage years, Norcom began an unrelenting campaign of sexual harassment, eventually insisting that she become his concubine. To discourage him, Harriet began a relationship with a young white lawyer, Samuel Tredwell Sawyer, and gave birth to his two children, Joseph and Louisa.

When she was twenty-one, Norcom, who had already fathered eleven slave children, told Harriet that if she did not agree to concubinage he would ship her away to one of his plantations. She rejected him, and he carried out his threat. But when Harriet discovered that he also planned to make plantation slaves of her children, she took action. "I knew the doom that awaited my fair baby in slavery, and I determined to save her from it, or perish in the attempt."

In 1835, Harriet ran.

Running was a gamble, but the outcome was exactly what Harriet had hoped for. Convinced that she had fled north, Norcom sold the children to their father, who allowed them to reside in town with Harriet's free grandmother.

But Harriet was running out of time and places to hide. She took refuge with a succession of neighbors, but with Norcom so close it was impossible to escape Edenton. Finally she found sanctuary in a tiny crawl space above the shed attached to her grandmother's home.

> Between these boards and the roof was a very small garret. . . . [T]he garret was only nine feet long . . . the highest part three feet high. . . . To this hole I was conveyed. . . . [T]he air was stifling; the darkness total. . . . The rats and mice ran over my bed.

And that is the way Harriet Jacobs passed her days, cramped, freezing, and ill, hiding in a space no larger than that allotted captives on a slave ship. Friends brought her food and slipped it into the tiny space.

> I lived in that dismal hole, almost deprived of light and air, and with no space to move my limbs, for nearly seven years. . . .
>
> Yet I would have chosen this, rather than my lot as a slave.

By the mid–nineteenth century, slavery was the way America breathed.

Indeed, there may have been no America without it. It was an institution with thick, tangled roots, one that even touched the lives of those who had never owned slaves. It was difficult to envision the country without the ceaseless labor of captive black men, women, and children.

Many felt that America and its shame were inseparable. And there were those who didn't see slavery as shameful. In fact, as early as the 1820s, many southerners began to stress what they saw as the positive aspects of the institution. Preachers, politicians, and teachers touted slavery as a venerable and expanding institution.

South Carolina congressman James Henry Hammond, addressing his colleagues in 1836, argued that the institution could *never* be abolished. He cited not moral or legal reasons, but economic ones. He pointed out that there were 2.3 million slaves in the United States with 60,000 being added every year. If they were freed, their owners should, of course, be compensated. Estimating the average worth of each slave at $400, he concluded that to free them would cost the government approximately $34 million a year for the next hundred years.

The figure was mind-boggling, especially in light of the

fact that the total yearly receipts of the federal government were then less than $25 million. England had been able to end slavery in 1808, in part by compensating slaveholders for their slave property. In the United States, many agreed with Hammond that this was impossible.

Slavery's signature was stamped on many of the country's necessities such as rice, tobacco, sugar, and cotton. Slaves also worked in cities, in manufacturing, on the railroads, the docks, and in many other enterprises. With one institution wielding the power to change all others, it became easier to rationalize its wrongs for the sake of the whole.

There were more questions than answers. If the oppressive majority suddenly faced its conscience and freed the slaves, what would the nation do with the millions of newly freed? And, after suffering generations of abuse, what would those freed slaves do to their former oppressors and to a country which readily claimed them as property, but not as men? Fear was a powerful motivation for inaction.

Many white proponents of abolition were in favor of freeing the slaves and sending them elsewhere. Other whites were interested only in the relatively small number of blacks already free and didn't particularly want to link themselves with the destinies of blacks still captive and toiling in the South.

But blacks could not deny the link between the free and the enslaved, nor forget their common heart. The more the country accepted slavery as the status quo, the more fervent and insistent black voices became. In 1827, those voices found a home in *Freedom's Journal,* a pioneering black periodical that declared:

> The civil rights of a people being of the greatest value, it shall ever be our duty to vindicate our brethren when oppressed, and to lay the cure before the publick. We

> shall also urge upon our brethren (who are qualified by the laws of the different states) the expediency of using their elective franchise; and of making an independent use of the same. We wish them not to become tools of party.

The periodical consistently advocated the black cause, encouraged cultural and political progress, and provided information for whites seeking a role in the struggle.

Several whites had already taken on that challenging role. Anthony Benezet, a Huguenot who immigrated to Philadelphia in 1731, published uncompromising antislavery pamphlets, tutored free blacks and slaves in his home (discovering, according to a biographer, that black and white children were equally capable when learning to write and read), and enthusiastically debated widespread beliefs of black inferiority. Along with Benezet, John Woolman—a quiet but fiercely determined abolitionist—pressured the Quakers to prepare the enslaved for eventual emancipation through education and religious instruction.

However, in the late 1820s, David Walker's voice would grow particularly strident, calling forcefully for an immediate end to slavery.

Walker was born legally free in Wilmington, North Carolina, in 1785. In the 1820s, he devoted much time to travel, witnessing firsthand the sorrow wrought by slavery—a son forced to whip his naked mother until she died, a man forced to whip his pregnant wife until the child was lost. "If I remain in this bloody land," Walker concluded, "I will not live long."

By 1828, Walker had defined his purpose. He was destined to break through the surface of the movement toward a more energized radicalism. In the fall, he spoke before the General Colored Association of Massachusetts, stressing that a cohesive, singularly focused community was the first step in any quest for freedom. "Ought we not to form ourselves into a general body to protect, aid, and assist each other to the utmost of our power?" he asked.

Few dared oppose the institution of slavery with the force Walker exhibited in his *Appeal to the Coloured Citizens of the World*. The fiery 1829 pamphlet practically foretold the coming of Nat Turner:

> Let no man of us budge one step. . . . America is more our country than it is the whites. . . . The greatest riches in all America have arisen from our *blood and tears*: and will they drive us from our property and homes? . . . They must look sharp or this very thing will bring swift destruction upon them. Americans have got so fat on our blood and groans, that they have almost forgotten the God of armies. . . .
>
> [T]hey want us for their slaves, and think nothing of murdering us . . . therefore, if there is an *attempt* made by us, kill or be killed . . . and believe this, that it is no more harm for you to kill a man who is trying to kill you, than it is for you to take a drink of water when thirsty.

Walker's soul was etched on every page of the *Appeal*. It was every bit what he believed in, the dogged pursuit of justice that had become his religion. Refusing to merely chronicle despair, he cajoled, urged, protested, warned, lashed out, reflected, and wailed "to awaken in the breasts of my afflicted, degraded and slumbering brethren, a spirit of inquiry and investigation respecting our miseries and wretchedness in this Republican Land of Liberty!!!!!!"

In his *Appeal,* Walker insisted that blacks take an unflinching look at both their oppression and their oppressors. He advocated a staunch solidarity, stressed the importance of religion, and spoke of the value of education. He asked blacks to treasure their link to an African homeland.

The idea of solidarity, especially across lines that sought to separate free from captive, was at the root of Walker's radical stance. His unquestioning love for black people and commitment to their well-being meant that the system scarring their lives had to be overturned. In his eyes, there was no other choice. Walker was also a deeply committed Christian and a believer in the "unalienable rights" cited in the Declaration of Independence:

> [It is] an unshaken and forever immovable *fact,* that your full glory and happiness, as well as all other coloured people under Heaven, shall never be fully consummated, [without] the *entire emancipation of your enslaved brethren all over the world.*

Walker detested the compromise of colonization—he declared that America belonged to whoever helped build it. He took the Declaration's rhetoric of equality and—as many black abolitionists would continue to do—turned it to his own end, effectively chastising a nation of hypocrites and openly challenging the racist status quo. For instance, he insisted black people resist the theories in Thomas Jefferson's 1781 *Notes on the State of Virginia,* which touted black inferiority.

Walker believed deeply in a just and righteous God, and he insisted that God believed in freedom for black people. The liberation of his people was a "glorious and heavenly cause," and any armed uprising to that end was a holy crusade, divinely sanctioned. "If you commence, make sure work," he said. "Do not trifle, for they will not trifle with you."

Walker circulated the *Appeal* by stitching it into the clothing of black sailors who patronized his Boston used clothing shop. The pamphlet soon found its way to the South, where it sparked a flurry of laws forbidding any black person to learn to read. Many southern slaveholders were horrified. When it was rumored that a group of men in Georgia had put a $1,000 price on Walker's head, friends urged him to flee to Canada. But the activist was undaunted:

> I will stand my ground. Somebody must die in this cause. I may be doomed to the stake and the fire, or to the scaffold tree, but it is not in me to falter if I can promote the work of emancipation.

On June 28, 1830, David Walker collapsed and died near his shop in Boston. Many blacks believed he had been poisoned.

He did not know it, but Walker's insistence on immediate emancipation would give birth to a new movement, and David Walker gained a reputation as the man who pushed the abolitionist movement from musings to militancy. In fact, even today in America's black nationalist movement, the idea that blacks must organize amongst themselves and argue for themselves in achieving liberation can be traced to the fiery ideology set forth in the pages of *Walker's Appeal.*

White voices also began to speak out more forcefully against slavery. The most prominent of those voices, William Lloyd Garrison, was one of the movement's focal figures, a man who absolutely infuriated those who opposed his unwavering "freedom now" stance. Like David Walker, his views made him a wanted man. A believer in moral suasion, Garrison worked to end slavery not by political action or violence but by forcing a national awareness of its immorality. In light of his fervent antislavery stance, proslavery advocates were forced to fight back.

Garrison, born in Newburyport, Massachusetts, in 1805, grew up in a tumultuous home, abandoned by a boozing father at the age of three. Although he received little formal education, he taught himself as he worked with a printer, setting type. He dabbled in journalism part-time, becoming the editor of a weekly newspaper in 1825. From there, he tackled reform journalism, a movement that aimed to better society by preaching and pursuing various worthwhile causes in newspapers and magazines.

Soon he met Benjamin Lundy, a newspaper publisher who favored colonization as a solution to the problem of slavery. Garrison, who became acting editor of Lundy's newspaper, the *Genius of Universal Emancipation*, witnessed slavery firsthand in Baltimore. He came to believe that total and immediate emancipation was the only answer. In January 1831, he began publishing the *Liberator*, a fiercely antislavery newspaper.

The statement that introduced the paper's first issue jolted the antislavery movement with its stinging accusations and tough, unapologetic language:

> Assenting to the "self-evident truth" maintained in the American Declaration of Independence, "that all men are created equal, and endowed by their Creator with certain unalienable rights—among which are life, liberty and the pursuit of happiness," I shall strenuously contend for the immediate enfranchisement of our slave population.

Garrison then moved beyond his advocacy of gradual abolition, which he had expressed during a speech in Boston's Park Street Church:

> I seize this opportunity to make a full and unequivocal recantation, and thus publicly to ask pardon of my God, of my country, and of my brethren the poor slaves, for having uttered a sentiment so full of timidity, injustice and absurdity.

The *Liberator* developed a new framework for the antislavery movement. In the early opposition to slavery, especially after the Revolutionary War, gradual emancipation and colonization were seen as working hand in hand. In his writing and in public speeches, Garrison not only condemned colonization, but the very souls of those who favored it.

He also put proslavery factions on the defensive by using incendiary, confrontational language in his relentless barrage of abolitionist argument:

> I do not wish to think, or speak, or write, with moderation. No! No! Tell a man whose house is on fire to give a moderate alarm; tell him to moderately rescue his wife from the hands of the ravisher; tell the mother to gradually extricate her babe from the fire into which it has fallen;—but urge me not to use moderation in a cause like the present. I am in earnest—I will not equivocate—I will not excuse—I will not retreat a single inch—AND I WILL BE HEARD.

He was heard. Enthusiastically supported by black subscribers, the *Liberator* overcame financial troubles to become one of the leading abolitionist publications of the nineteenth century. However, the American Anti-Slavery Society, which Garrison cofounded in 1833, split when he insisted on adding feminism and nonresistance to the agenda and because he refused to take his fight into the political arena.

Garrison believed that the Constitution was a proslavery

document, and anything that supported the institutions of the country—such as voting and holding public office—thus honored the Constitution and supported slavery. Many blacks, including Frederick Douglass, eventually disagreed with Garrison and broke with him over this point.

Black abolitionists and some of their white allies began to speak of a multiracial society in which all Americans were entitled to fair, equal treatment. They petitioned Congress, boycotted products grown by slaves, and slapped abolitionist sentiments on everything from sugar bowls to children's books. They grew more visible, more vocal. They read the Declaration of Independence and the Constitution with new eyes, eyes that saw every man, black and white, under an umbrella of equality.

However, Garrison and his followers scorned the Constitution as an instrument of the devil, publicly burning the document and calling for northern secession. And the forces seeking to silence both black and white abolitionists grew more determined.

In both the North and South, favoring emancipation was a dangerous undertaking. A great number of northerners were tied in to the shipping and processing sides of the highly productive and profitable cotton industry. By the late 1830s, the majority of the world's cotton was grown by slaves in the American South. America's strength in foreign exchange depended almost entirely on cotton. In Europe, southern-grown cotton was the lifeblood of the textile mills.

All these were inescapable facts. Speaking out against slavery struck at the heart of America's livelihood.

In Philadelphia in 1838, the National Anti-Slavery Convention of American Women convened in Pennsylvania Hall, the city's new abolitionist meeting place. Women publicly took the stage, a revolutionary—and, to some, troubling—idea that threatened the accepted social order. Abolitionists told their stories, speaking with conviction and furor. Woman after woman strode to the podium to speak out against the evils of servitude, including fervent white abolitionist Lydia Maria Child, who was profoundly influenced by William Lloyd Garrison. "I am fully aware of the unpopularity of the task I have undertaken," she said, speaking of her vow to end slavery. "But though I expect ridicule and censure, it is not in my nature to fear them."

Other women, both black and white, took the stage. Maria Weston Chapman. Angelina Grimké. Abby Kelley. Philadelphia's leading abolitionist, Lucretia Mott. Incensed at the thought of this interracial cadre of women acting as a very public force, protesters rushed the building.

"The mob had now increased to several thousand and got in the hall by dashing open the doors with their axes," Garrison wrote. "They then set fire to this huge building and in the course of an hour it was a solid wall of flame."

The building had been open only four days. Black and white women were stoned as they left the chaos, their arms linked.

The angry arsonists continued to smell smoke—and blood. Within days of the attack, the city's Shelter for Colored Orphans as well as a small black church in the Northern Liberties were set afire. Abolitionists had long understood that they were risking their lives. There was no place to be safe, not even in the "free" North.

Garrison related this dire prophecy: "These are perilous times, especially for the people of color. Bloody scenes, I fear, are in reserve for our vision."

Those perilous times reached every corner of the country. And those "people of color" included the Native Americans.

Thousands of Cherokee and other native peoples had lived among the whites for decades. But America was a land ravenous for yet more land. Before 1840, 4.5 million Americans crossed the Appalachians into the West and Southwest in one of the most notable migrations in history. Lt. Charles Noland, a U.S. soldier who wrote about the Cherokee removal of 1835, observed: "The white population is flowing in on them in torrents. Georgia and North Carolina pressing them on one side. Tennessee and Alabama on the other. They must emigrate or perish. Fate has decreed it."

In America, land was always the key to prosperity. Burgeoning eastern populations hungered for the lush land inhabited by the Indian tribes within their states. In 1828, a brash frontiersman and planter from Tennesee, Andrew Jackson, was elected president—the first from the "American West" as it existed then—and he promised white Americans the land they coveted.

The new president believed that Indians were only entitled to the land they occupied physically, not the sprawling tribal region they claimed. He was also convinced that they were on American soil and therefore subject to governmental control. Treaties with them had no legal standing.

Jackson would not exterminate the Indians or work to blend them into an already tumultuous societal mix. The preservation of ancestral lands had proved troublesome and was becoming impossible in the South. So Jackson devised what he thought was the most humane and statesmanlike option remaining. He would seize thousands of acres of native ancestral lands in Florida, Alabama, Georgia, and other states, and relocate the Indians to less-desirable land after compensating them for their previous landholdings.

Jackson defended what many white citizens denounced as a cruel act:

> What good man would prefer a country covered with forest and ranged by a few thousand savages to our extensive republic, studded with cities, towns and prosperous farms and filled with all the blessings of liberty, civilization and religion?
>
> The tribes which occupied the . . . eastern states were annihilated or have melted away to make room for the whites. The waves of population and civilization are rolling to the westward.

Some of the tribes "melted away," and lost much of their tradition before they lost their land. Patterning their lives after those of their white neighbors, tribes such as the Cherokee, Creeks, Chocktaw, and Chickasaw had transformed their culture. They adopted the white manner of dress, built missionary schools, and cultivated sizable plantations. Striving to be accepted by their white neighbors, they even had black slaves.

These attempts to be American failed to impress the leaders of the status quo. Georgia senator John Forsyth described the Indians as "a race not admitted to be equal to the rest of the community; treated somewhat like human beings, but not admitted to be freeman; not yet entitled and probably never will be entitled to equal civil and political rights."

Economics was the harsh determining factor. If white men had not craved their land, Indians may have been allowed to live peaceably. But whites, convinced they needed the land to realize America's manifest destiny, had decided to move whatever stood in their way. Their eyes were trained on the West.

The government forced the Indian nations to sign treaties exchanging their ancestral lands for land in the West. Indians were given a certain amount of time to go. After that, those remaining were rounded up and marched or shipped west. Nearly seventeen thousand Cherokees were rounded up in stockades. In 1838, they were marched from Tennessee, North Carolina, Georgia, and Alabama to Indian Territory west of the Mississippi. Many succumbed to starvation, illness, and exposure. The Cherokee called the journey "the road where they cried."

They were not alone in their tears.

This version of civilized progress also included Africans and their descendants. Wrote one white physician:

> While the contact of the white man seems fatal to the Red Indian, whose tribes fall away before the onward march of the frontier-man like snow in the spring, . . . the Negro thrives under the shadow of his white master, falls readily into the position assigned him, and exists and multiplies in increased physical well-being.

Thousands of slaves accompanied white pioneer families west, and slave dealers, called Negro speculators, brought entire black families west to be sold. These slaves cleared virgin territory, erected homes, and carved roads out of the wilderness, much of which had belonged to the Indians.

From 1830 to 1840, in Mississippi alone, the slave population tripled. Established slave markets in major cities guaranteed that slaves would be processed quickly and efficiently.

Speculators brought their captives to the markets by ship or by forced march. As locomotives grew more common in later years, slavery took to the rails.

Jacob Stroyer described the chaos as slaves were taken away by train:

> We arrived at [Clarkson Depot] . . . we heard wailing and shrieks from those in the cars. Louisiana was considered by the slaves as a place of slaughter, so those who were going did not expect to see their friend again . . . but when the cars began to start, and the conductor cried out . . . the colored people cried out with one voice as though the heavens and earth were coming together, and it was so pitiful, that those hard-hearted white men, who had been accustomed to driving slaves all their lives, shed tears like children.

In 1827, a writer for the *Alexandria Gazette* described that city's slave market:

> Here you may behold fathers and brothers leaving behind them the dearest objects of affection and moving slowly along in the mute agony of despair; there a young mother stooping over an infant whose innocent smiles seem but to increase her misery. From some you will hear the burst of bitter lamentation, while from others a loud hysteric laugh breaks forth denoting still deeper agony.

Washington, D.C., the showplace of American government, was home to one of the most notorious and lucrative slave markets in the country.

Dr. Jesse Torrey, who studied the trade extensively, witnessed "a procession of men, women and children, resembling that of a funeral" in the streets of Washington. "They were [slaves] bound together in pairs, some with ropes, and some with iron chains."

Every black person in the vicinity of a slave market was in danger of being captured and sold into servitude.

Many of the slaves were confined in pens. Throughout

Washington and Alexandria, there were secret slave dungeons and cells where kidnapped men and women were held until they could be safely "sold down the river" to the Southwest. The most infamous was Robey's Pen, located right outside the Capitol. As a congressman, Lincoln commented on being able to see Robey's from the Capitol. Here it is described by Edward Strutt Abdy, an English writer visiting in 1835:

> It is surrounded by a wooden paling fourteen or fifteen feet in height, with posts outside to prevent escape, and separated from the building by a space too narrow to admit of a free circulation of air. At a small window above, which was unglazed and exposed alike to the heat of summer and the cold of winter, so trying to the constitution, two or three sable faces appeared, looking out wistfully to wile away the time and catch a refreshing breeze; the weather being extremely hot. In this wretched hovel all colors, except white—both sexes, and all ages, are confined, exposed indiscriminately to the contamination which may be expected in such society and under such seclusion.

Slavery was the lifeblood of Washington, D.C., the city that slave owners controlled. Many of the men who ran the country also ran plantations.

The die had been cast the first moment the struggling new nation had appointed a gentleman slave owner as its first president and real-life hero. Five presidents had been slaveholders, as were the Speakers of the House for twenty-eight of America's first thirty-four years. Many justices of the Supreme Court, ultimate upholders of the law, also held slaves.

Washington, D.C., was where slavery lived. And in 1841, it was where the international slave trade went on trial.

Two years earlier, this report had appeared in the *Washington Globe*:

> Much excitement has been generated in New York for the past several weeks from the report of several pilot boats having seen a clipper-built schooner full of negroes, and in such a condition to lead to the suspicion that they were pirate. Several naval vessels are said to have been dispatched in pursuit of her.

The black sailors who manned the boat were not pirates. They were Mende people, Africans from Sierra Leone, who had been kidnapped into slavery. On board the Spanish slaver *Amistad* was a young captive, Singbe Pieh, a rice planter who had left behind a wife and three children. Abolitionist missionaries would later call him Joseph Cinque. This brooding, dignified son of a Mende headman cringed inwardly as he saw the brutal treatment afforded his countrymen. He grew anxious wondering what ultimate fate awaited them.

And he watched his captors carefully.

Along the Cuban coast, en route to the sugar plantations, Cinque and a fellow captive, Grabeau, plotted a revolt. Using a nail to pick the iron collar locks of their fellow captives, they found boxes of sugarcane knives to aid in their insurrection. After several tense moments of chaos and capture, Cinque and his band of forty rebels had wrenched control of the *Amistad* and killed the ship's captain and the cook.

Cinque ordered Montes, a Spaniard who had once been a sea captain, to sail the ship into the sun, in the opposite direction of the voyage from Africa. Secretly wishing to sabotage the passage, Montes steered in the proper direction during the day and reversed course at night. For two months, the *Amistad* stayed a ragged north and northwest course toward America.

Thunderous storms hampered the voyage, supplies were exhausted, and the blacks grew fearful of losing their lives to a moody and often violent sea.

Montes continued to do what he could to lengthen the voyage while hoping for rescue. He adjusted sails so the ship would travel slowly during the day. But soon Cinque began to suspect that the ship was headed back toward Havana; he spared Montes's life, but ordered that the Spaniard be accompanied at the helm.

At one point in the Caribbean, the owner of a small fishing boat spotted the anguished, knife-wielding blacks aboard the *Amistad;* for seven days, Montes kept the ship in the area, hoping the incident would be reported. Meanwhile, conditions on board grew intolerable. There was no more drinkable water; some blacks consumed the contents of bottles found belowdecks. The medicine in the containers killed them.

Montes was losing hope. There seemed to be no chance of rescue. Several ship captains who sighted the *Amistad* fled at the sight of the desperate Africans waving their sugarcane knives.

By late summer, the *Amistad* approached the end of its voyage—not Africa, but Montauk Point at the end of Long Island. The insurrectionists were taken into custody by a navy brig-of-war and transported to New Haven, Connecticut, to await trial.

The case of the captured Africans raised a troubling, insistent question. Their kidnapping was contrary to the laws of both the United States and Spain, which banned participation in the Atlantic slave trade. Were the passengers of the *Amistad* now free, or were they property to be returned to the Spaniards?

The *Amistad* case was the most important involving slavery up to this time. It became an opportunity for a growing abolitionist movement to take center stage.

Curious whites flocked to the jail to gawk at the caged Africans. Visitors were charged admission for a time. White abolitionists Lewis Tappan and Roger Baldwin led the effort to prepare a legal defense for the Africans and publicized their plight to the nation. Congregations of Connecticut's black churches raised funds for the rebels. Abolitionists succeeded in creating unprecedented interest in the upcoming trial—in New York, the *Commercial Advertiser* called the possible return of the captives to Cuba an "outrageous violation" of "justice and human rights," while the play *The Black Schooner or the Private Slaver "Amistad"* was performed in four theaters, raising more than $5,000. Cinque, leader of the rebellion, became a figurehead for the abolitionist movement.

During their imprisonment, many rebels learned English and wrote pointed and impassioned messages that were reprinted in abolitionist newspapers. Young Ka-le, one of the first to master the language, penned an impassioned letter to the man charged with their defense.

> *Dear friend Mr. [John Quincy] Adams:*
> *. . . What for Americans keep us in prison? Americans. . . . they say we make you free. If they make us free, they tell truth, if they no make us free, they tell lie. . . . we sorry—sorry for Mendi people little, we sorry for America people great deal, because God punish liars. . . .*
>
> *Your friend, Ka-le*

The Africans had won their freedom in the lower courts, and the federal government appealed the decision to the

Supreme Court. Adams's chief argument actually attacked President Van Buren for interfering in the case and ordering the appeal in order to seek favor with slaveholders.

In February of 1841, the case was finally heard by the United States Supreme Court in Washington, D.C. Former president John Quincy Adams had painstakingly prepared his case. Few people believed that the Africans would see justice.

For two days, Adams stood before the court and argued that the free men, women, and children aboard the *Amistad* had been taken illegally from their homeland and slated for passage to Cuba, in clear violation of the outlawed trans-atlantic trade. The Africans were free, he insisted. And they had a perfect right to rebel to preserve that freedom.

"Dear Friend Mr. Adams," Ka-le wrote.

> *I want to write a letter to you because you talk to the grand court. . . . We want you to ask the court what we have done wrong. . . . What for Americans keep us in prison? . . . Some people say Mendi people crazy; Mendi people dolt, because we no talk American language. Merica people talk no Mendi language; Merica people dolt? . . . Mendi people* think, think, think. *All we want is make us free.*

On March 9, 1841, Justice Story of Massachusetts read the court's decision:

> If then, these Negroes are not slaves, but are kidnapped Africans . . . We may lament the dreadful acts by which they asserted their liberty . . . but they cannot be deemed pirates or robbers. Upon the merits of the case, then, there does not seem to us to be any ground for doubt that these Negroes ought to be deemed free.

Ka-le and his countrymen got their wish. No court mindful of the law could find fault with Adams's argument. For a moment in time, blacks were seen by whites around the country as human beings deserving of justice. Through the *Amistad* case, the abolitionists had succeeded in putting slavery before the public. The case of the *Amistad* rebels did not change the status of America's enslaved, but it was a rare moment of hope. And it put the South on notice.

For many, slavery now had the face of a human.

By the first part of the nineteenth century, the money invested in slaves was the largest concentration of capital in America. Much of the resultant wealth was distributed among the planter aristocracy and the mercantile and shipping elite of the North, families whose bloodlines stretched back to the early years of the American colonies.

Since the climate on many of the great southern plantations was harsh and living conditions dismal, many well-to-do planters found a welcome retreat in the North. A number of southern families established residences in Pennsylvania, New York, and Rhode Island.

From the earliest days of the republic, the Butlers were one of the wealthiest families in Philadelphia. In the 1830s, their Georgia plantations at Butler Island and St. Simons, spread over 1,500 acres with more than eight hundred slaves, comprised one of the largest complexes in the country. Major Pierce Butler had helped write the Constitution, had twice served as a United States senator, and had been one of the first planters in Georgia to grow sea island cotton.

His grandsons, Pierce and John, were fabulously wealthy

charmers who loved horseback riding, gambling, and cavorting in Europe. They seemed as close as America could come to aristocracy.

Pierce Butler was the one of the planter elite—men who were powerful, secure, and certain that they were driving the economy for the rest of America.

In 1836, after pursuing her doggedly for some time, Pierce Butler married the internationally popular and headstrong English actress Fanny Kemble. Kemble had gone on stage at nineteen to ease family financial woes, and her marriage to Butler was an escape from that role as provider and a beginning of her dream to be a writer. Immediately after becoming a wife, Fanny turned her American tour proceeds over to her father and quit the stage.

The union of Kemble and Butler forged two divergent traditions and viewpoints. If either had known how this fact would alter the rest of their lives, the marriage might never have taken place. He had hoped for a dutiful, traditional, submissive wife. Fanny looked forward to the aristocratic life she'd live as Mrs. Pierce Butler.

Pierce Butler saw no need to discuss the source of his wealth with his young bride. But many people believed she was naive not to realize her new husband was heir to a fortune in human beings. "When I married Mr. Butler," she wrote in 1839, "I knew nothing of these dreadful possessions of his."

However, her writings indicate that, after learning that her husband, with his brother, had inherited control of the family plantations at Butler Island, she pushed her husband to take her to Georgia to see slavery firsthand:

> Mr. [Butler], in his letter, maintains that they *are* an inferior race . . . "incapable of mental cultural or moral im-

> provement." . . . Mr. [Butler] says that . . . teaching them to read "impairs their value as slaves, for it destroys their contentedness." Nevertheless I go prepared to find much kindness on the part of the masters, much content on that of the slaves.

On the last day of 1838, Frances and Pierce Butler and their two children arrived on Butler Island. The new mistress of the plantation visited the infirmary and knew immediately that she'd have to look elsewhere for the "contented" slaves she'd hoped to find:

> Buried in tattered and filthy blankets . . . here, in their hour of sickness, lay those whose health and strength are spent in unrequited labor for us . . . to buy for us all the luxuries which health can revel in. . . . Here lay women . . . groaning over the anguish of miscarriages—here lay some burning with fever, others . . . aching with rheumatism, upon the hard, cold ground—here they lay like brute beasts. . . . Now pray take notice that this is supposed to be the hospital of an estate where the owners are supposed to be humane and the negroes remarkably well cared for. . . .
>
> Such of these dwellings as I visited today were filthy and wretched in the extreme. . . . Instead of the order, neatness and ingenuity which might convert even these miserable hovels into tolerable residences, there was the careless, reckless, filthy indolence which even the brutes do not exhibit in their lairs and nests.

Word spread quickly in the slave quarters that the mistress of the manor seemed to take a genuine interest in their lives. At first tentatively, and then with more confidence, women brought Fanny Kemble their stories.

> *Nanny* has had three children; two of them are dead. She came to implore that the rule of sending them into the field three weeks after [giving birth] might be altered.
>
> *Leah,* Ceasar's wife, has had three children; three are dead.
>
> *Sophy,* Lewis's wife, is suffering fearfully. She had ten children. Five are dead.
>
> *Sarah,* Stephen's wife; this woman's case and history were alike deplorable. She had had four miscarriages, had brought seven children into the world, five of whom were dead, and was again with child. . . . There was hardly one of these women . . . who might not have been a candidate for a bed in a hospital, and they had come to me after working all day in the fields.

Fanny Kemble had stepped into a nightmare. It was a place where the health of women and their children was of importance only when it threatened to break the rhythm of production. The cycle never stopped. A woman's body was never her own.

Changed almost daily by what she witnessed and learned, Fanny could not ignore the fact that she was raising two young children of her own:

> I do not think that a residence on a slave plantation is likely to be particularly advantageous to a child like my oldest. . . . She said something about a swing, and in less than five minutes headman Frank had erected it for her, and a dozen young slaves were ready to swing little "missis." Think of learning to rule despotically over your fellow creatures before the first lesson of self-government is well spelled over. It makes me tremble.

Fanny Kemble and the Butler Island slaves had at least one common goal in mind, and that was the preservation of their families. That was the one prayer everyone prayed—that the family would stay together. And the slave family, threatened at every turn, went to extraordinary lengths to assure that one measure of contentment and continuance.

Once Pierce Butler, in a fit of generosity, decided to make a gift of a slave, Joe, to up-and-coming planter Roswell King Jr. This would have separated Joe from his wife, Psyche, and their children.

Fanny Kemble wrote:

> I saw Joe, the young man, poor Psyche's husband, raving almost in a state of frenzy, and in a voice broken with sobs and almost inarticulate with passion, reiterating his determination never to leave this plantation . . . never to leave his old father and mother, his poor wife and children, and dashing his hat, which he was wringing like a cloth in his hand, upon the ground, he declared that he would kill himself if he was compelled to follow Mr. K[ing]. . . .
>
> [King] heard that [Joe] had kicked up a fuss about it . . . and said that if the fellow wasn't willing to go with him, he did not wish to be bothered with any niggers down there who were to be troublesome, so he might stay behind.

For African Americans, family created a reality that had nothing to do with those who kept them in bondage or the reality of work. It allowed for love between two like-minded individuals. It allowed a man to be something more than a machine—wrapped in the arms of family, he could be an uncle, a father, a son, a brother. It allowed a mother to nurture her child, to imagine, for a moment, that that child was solely hers. It allowed for community, the one door a slave owner could not open without permission.

The isolated islands were perfect for the forging of community. But even the relatively fortunate Butler slaves were helpless once a white man exerted his will. Roswell King, overseer on the Butler plantation for years, raped Betty, wife of the plantation's head driver. She bore the overseer a son. Sexual violation was the source of far more mixed-race children than the white South ever cared to admit.

Of course, such indignities were commonplace. But Frank, the head driver, was an unusually trusted and dedicated member of the Butler slave family. When Mr. King the overseer was away from the island for any reason, it was Frank who was responsible for the entire plantation and its slaves. He would confer with the overseer during planting, flooding, and cultivation of the rice fields. He was the most powerful black man on the plantation.

But when it came to his own wife, he could not protect her.

"I see that man . . . ," wrote Fanny, "looking, with a countenance of deep thought . . . over the broad river, which is to him as a prison wall. . . . I marvel what the thoughts of such a man may be."

Fanny's poetic musings could not express or change what Betty and Frank had lost. Their marriage, the first link of community, had been violated.

Inevitably, Pierce Butler grew tired of his wife's interest in the slaves. While at Butler Island, she flooded him with petitions from the slaves, asking for more food, clothing, or more rest after childbirth. He urged her to stay away from the slave quarters. She refused. It was a battle of wills, which eventually contributed to the end of their marriage.

> Today . . . I have had a most painful conversation with Mr. [Butler], who has declined receiving any of the people's petitions through me. . . . Whether he is wearied with the number of these prayers and supplications . . . or whether he has been annoyed at the number of pitiful and horrible stories of oppression . . . which cannot by any means, always be done away with by his angry exclamations of . . . "Why do you believe such trash? Don't you know the niggers are d——d liars?," etc., I do not know.

What Fanny Kemble did know was that slavery existed despite any earthly measure she could take to combat it. She would learn much about herself, her husband, the slaves who opened their lives to her. But she could change very little. Slavery would continue to drive a wedge between Fanny and Pierce, and they divorced in 1848. Kemble had underestimated the slave system; to think that she could so easily change it was sad arrogance.

"This is no place for me," concluded Fanny, "since I was not born among slaves and cannot bear to live among them."

CHAPTER ELEVEN

When I started on this hazardous undertaking, I resolved that, come what would, there should be no turning back. "Give me liberty, or give me death," was my motto.

—HARRIET JACOBS,
Incidents in the Life of a Slave Girl

AFTER SEVEN YEARS OF being one of the "disappeared," Harriet Jacobs dared to join the world again. She had eluded her abusive master by folding herself into a crawl space in a building, a space which never allowed her to stand upright. Burdened with a mother's pain, she observed the growth of her children through a peephole and watched almost daily the master who hunted for her and who had sexually threatened her for almost half of her life. He was so close. If she had dared to call out, he would have heard her.

But in 1842, with the help of friends, Harriet's unthinkable ordeal ended. She was smuggled by sea to Philadelphia.

"I never could tell how we reached the wharf," she wrote of her journey's beginning. "My brain was all of a whirl and my limbs tottered under me."

But when Harriet Jacobs encountered freedom, she found the words for it.

> The next morning I was on deck as soon as the day dawned. . . . We watched the reddening sky, and saw the great orb come up out of the water, as it seemed. Soon the waves began to sparkle, and every thing caught the beautiful glow. Before us lay the city of strangers. We had escaped from slavery. . . . But we were alone in the world.

With her desperate flight toward liberty, she joined other slaves who had risked their lives to escape bondage. Most followed the star. They headed north.

Lear Green shipped herself to freedom in a sailor's chest. Henry "Box" Brown also mailed himself free. Maria Weems disguised herself as a boy to escape. Minty was barely seven when she ran away. Later, as Harriet Tubman, she would be pulled again and again to the South as she helped hundreds more escape slavery.

Henry Bibb, his eyes trained on the ultimate prize, ran away from seven masters. In a letter to one of them, William Gatewood, he wrote:

> *You may perhaps think hard of us for running way from slavery, but as to myself, I have but one apology to make for it, which is this: I have only to regret that I did not start at an earlier period. . . .*
>
> *To be compelled to stand by and see you whip and slash my wife without mercy, when I could afford her no*

> *protection, not even by offering myself to suffer the lash in her place, was more than I felt it to be the duty of a slave husband to endure. . . . My infant child was also frequently flogged by Mrs. Gatewood, for crying, until its skin was bruised literally purple. This kind of treatment was what drove me from home and family, to seek a better home for them.*

The flight to freedom was fraught with peril.

Fugitive slave Frederick Augustus Washington Bailey, who would later become known as the fiery black abolitionist Frederick Douglass, told of the fears he and fellow slaves faced as they plotted escape:

> At times we were almost tempted to abandon the enterprise. . . . Upon either side we saw grim death, assuming a variety of horrid shapes. Now it was starvation, causing us, in a strange and friendless land, to eat our own flesh. Now we were contending with the waves and were drowned. Now we were hunted by dogs and overtaken, and torn to pieces by their merciless fangs. . . . after having succeeded in swimming rivers, encountering wild beasts, sleeping in the woods, and suffering hunger, cold, heat, and nakedness, were overtaken by hired kidnappers, who . . . would, perchance, fire upon us, kill some, wound others, and capture all.

If fugitive slaves managed to avoid the vicious dogs trained to track them, brutal slave catchers, and roving patrols of police and vigilantes, there was still the problem of where to turn once they reached free territory. They had to find homes, work, clothing, the practical things that made a life. Those accustomed to the southern climate were ill-prepared to deal with brutal northern winters. Many northerners, while sympathetic to the plight of the fleeing slave, wanted them to keep fleeing. Working-class whites didn't look forward to black competition on the job front.

The natural instinct of runaway slaves was to look for faces mirroring their own.

The black community played an essential role in harboring fugitives and educating them to the realities of their freedom. Vigilance committees circulated information about kidnappers and slave catchers and served as a source for food and medicine. When fugitive slaves were recaptured, the committees would organize rescue parties. This secretive network of abolitionists—both blacks and whites—became known as the Underground Railroad. Workers on the Underground Railroad spirited runaways to points further north and west and provided support for indefatigable fighters like Harriet Tubman.

The abolitionists were so hated by southerners that bounties were placed on their heads. James Henry Hammond minced no words: "I warn abolitionists, ignorant and infatuated barbarians as they are, that if chance shall throw any of them into our hands, they may expect a felon's death."

Abolitionists met Harriet Jacobs in Philadelphia and arranged rail passage to New York. The former slave was dismayed to see how blacks and whites were segregated even in the North: "Colored people were allowed to ride in a filthy box car, behind white people, at the south, but there they were not required to pay for the privilege. It made me sad to find how the North aped the customs of slavery."

Like the South, the North wholeheartedly subscribed to the ideals of democracy, but it was a democracy for whites only. Former slaves who had risked their lives to pull in an unburdened breath still encountered a racism that was keen and insidious.

Fanny Kemble wrote of their painful predicament:

> They are not slaves, indeed, but they are pariah; scorned by the lowest white ruffian in your streets. All hands are extended to thrust them out, all fingers point at their dusky skin, all tongues—the most vulgar as well as the most refined—have learned to turn the very name of their race into an insult.

Blacks who traveled to communities in Boston, Philadelphia, New York, or other "promised lands" found themselves in all-black enclaves where they created institutions, such as churches and orphanages, that were uniquely theirs. But the enclaves were ringed by anxious, resentful whites and racial intolerance, and were haunted by the danger of betrayal.

This intolerant atmosphere greeted young Frederick Bailey, a fugitive from Maryland who found himself wandering the streets of New York.

> [I]mmediately after my arrival in New York, I said I felt like one who had escaped a den of hungry lions. This state of mind, however, very soon subsided; and I was again seized with a feeling of great insecurity and loneliness. . . . There I was in the midst of thousands and yet a perfect stranger; without home and without friends, in the midst of thousands of my own brethren—children of a common Father, and yet I dared not to unfold to any one of them my sad condition. I was afraid to speak to anyone for fear of speaking to the wrong one, and thereby falling into the hands of money-loving kidnap-

> pers, whose business it was to lie in wait for . . . their prey. The motto which I adopted when I started from slavery was this—"Trust no man!"

Bailey was taken under the wing of David Ruggles, head of the New York Committee of Vigilance and a compassionate soul who had come to the rescue of hundreds of runaways. The outspoken Ruggles was fueled by the struggle, much like his predecessor David Walker. Not only did he provide shelter for those newly arrived in New York, he also kept a close eye on the court cases of fugitives who were recaptured, refusing to surrender them to a racist legal system. Over a period of five years, David Ruggles assisted in the escape of more than a thousand slaves. Later, Frederick Douglass would say of him, "He was a whole-souled man, fully imbued with a love of his afflicted and haunted people."

At the time Douglass encountered David Ruggles and the wonders of New York, abolitionism was a key element of the struggle of blacks in the North and abolitionist groups were a permanent and persistent segment of the political landscape. Although blacks had provided many of the movement's most powerful voices, there was an uneasy and uncertain undercurrent to the relationship between black abolitionists and their white counterparts.

While it couldn't be denied that white abolitionists and their families were indefatigable workers who risked their lives and livelihoods to toil for the black cause, their umbrella organizations on both local and national levels were managed by whites and operated from a singularly white perspective. While white resisters spoke fervently of the absolute and unconditional abolishment of slavery, they found the second part of the bargain—granting blacks equality—somewhat harder to fathom. Understandably, this led to tensions between the black and white abolitionists.

However, there *was* common ground. Both sides understood that slavery was morally wrong and believed that God's goodness would not allow it to continue. They agreed that the system was exploitative and cruel. They had no patience for talk of gradual abolishment.

But while white abolitionists focused their attention on a pervasive but somewhat distant evil, blacks were involved on a much more personal level. Although they were calling for the abolishment of an institution, they were also seeking justice for sons, brothers, mothers, daughters, fathers, sisters and grandmothers, uncles. There was very little room for negotiation when it came to the cause of freedom. Abolition would mean the forging of a black community that crossed regional and economic lines—a community with a singular purpose, a common heart. Black abolitionists saw prejudice as the root of slavery and sought to expose it and attack it in northern communities—wherever it showed itself.

The difference between black and white abolitionists was most apparent when the two groups worked closely together. The whites, mindful of their destiny to deliver the underclass, patronized their black coworkers. And the blacks' refusal to fit the image of the humble subservient unnerved many of their white collegues.

One of those who refused to hide his erudition and anger was Frederick Douglass. He traveled north to freedom and, obsessed with the liberation of his still-enslaved brothers and sisters, joined forces with white abolitionist William Lloyd Garrison.

Douglass began to tell his story at abolitionist meetings. Later, he began to write, penning bitter and biting observations on the institution he had escaped. "*Slavery is alike the sin and the shame of the American people,*" he wrote. "It is a blot upon the American name."

Through his writings and oratory, Frederick Douglass became one of the nation's most persistent agitators against "the grand aggregation of human horrors." He openly declared war on the corrupt institution that still held sway over most of his brethren. And he chronicled his experiences as a slave, joining other ex-captives whose narratives offered public testimony that damned the southern propaganda that slaves were content in bondage and well-treated.

These moving and matter-of-fact chronicles of lives spent in slavery became the most controversial literature of the time. It was important for the abolitionist cause that whites with no direct ties to slavery could read what was happening in the hearts and minds of the slaves.

"They say that the negroes were very well contented in . . . slavery," wrote J. Sella Martin.

> [S]uppose it were the fact the black man was contented in bondage, suppose he was contented to see his wife sold on the auction-block or his daughter violated . . . or having his own manhood crushed out of him, I say that is the heaviest condemnation of the institution, that slavery should blot out a man's manhood so as to make him contented to accept this degradation, and such an institution ought to be swept from the face of the earth.

While Douglass's 1845 narrative is perhaps the most famous, many other slaves turned to pen and paper to chronicle their histories. Harriet Jacobs. Solomon Northup. Lewis Hayden. Charles Ball. J. Sella Martin. Josiah Henson recalled this horror:

> I can remember my father one day with his head bloodied and his back lacerated. His right ear had been cut off close to his head and he received a hundred lashes on his back. He had beaten the overseer for a brutal assault on my mother. This was his punishment.

These classic American tales of tribulation and eventual triumph gave black abolitionists a voice that was uniquely theirs, providing them with the powerful and persuasive language that made slavery and its horrors real, in print and in their very presence as speakers and witnesses.

Of course, the narratives infuriated white southerners, who could now read about the many ways their "contented slaves" realized that they were entitled to freedom. Frederick Douglass remembered his early curiosity about the word *abolition*:

> I often found myself regretting my own existence, and wishing myself dead; and but for the hope of being free, I have no doubt but that I should have killed myself, or done something for which I should have been killed. . . . Every little while, I could hear something about the abolitionists. . . . If a slave ran away and succeeded in getting clear, or if a slave killed his master, set fire to a barn, or did any thing very wrong in the mind of a slaveholder, it was spoken of as the fruit of *abolition*. Hearing the word in this connection very often, I set about learning what it meant.

Outspoken fugitive slaves like Frederick Douglass—and the issue of their eventual place in society—spelled change for the abolitionist movement. Up to the mid–nineteenth century, the majority of Garrisonian abolitionists were pacifists who denounced violence as a means to a peaceful end. They were ambivalent about the radical actions of Nat Turner. Slavery was a system built on violence, they reasoned, and it was immoral to try to end it by using violence. Abolitionists believed that people would see the moral wrong in the system and change within themselves to overthrow it.

But racism was written into the very documents that guided the country. There were jobs black people could not hold, places where they couldn't live, schools where they were forbidden to learn. "We don't allow niggers in here" was a common sentiment greeting newly "free" slaves.

"It is not the black man's color which makes him the object of brutal treatment . . . ," wrote Douglass. "While we are servants we are never offensive to the whites. . . . We are then a persecuted people; not because we are *colored,* but because . . . that color has been coupled in the public mind with the degradation of slavery and servitude. In these conditions we are thought to be in our place, and to aspire to anything above them . . . is to commit the provoking sin of *impudence.*

"What *is* a white man that you do so revolt at the idea of making a negro equal to him?" asked Douglass with his own singular logic.

The abolitionists were a very small, extremely unpopular minority in the North. They didn't speak for the majority of whites. And black leaders were speaking in louder, more insistent voices—not just calling for an end to slavery, but advocating the rights inherent in citizenship. These ideas often elicited violent reactions.

A LION AT PENDLETON

Am I sadly cast aside,
On misfortune's rugged tide?
Will the world my pains deride
Forever?

THE WHITE MOB in Pendleton, Indiana, had dragged him from the outdoor platform in the woods, where he was denouncing the evils of slavery, how it dehumanized Christian masters and bondsmen alike—this, after the townspeople had denied him use of the local Baptist church. His voice, a bronze basso profundo, filled the woods, rolling over a crowd that favored parishioners at a camp meeting. Delicate white women in the front seats fainted (as they often did when he spoke), partly because they had never heard a Negro whose oratorical skills outdistanced even those of a Cicero, and partly because of how this remarkable mulatto looked: tall, muscular from a life of field work, ship caulking, and handling coal, he stood before them broad-shouldered, with a striking mane of obsidian hair, appearing for all the world like a lion who'd decided one day to assume the shape of a man. This was the Frederick Douglass they'd read and heard so much about, of whom James Russell Lowell said, "The very look of Douglass was an irresistible logic against the oppression of his race." Oh yes, they fainted dead, these polite, white ladies in Pendleton, because he was Shakespearean in his bearing, more handsome than their husbands, with a voice that ran rill-like in their heads, and who could doubt the desire they felt for him, the fugitive slave who was the best thing that ever happened to the abolitionist movement, overshadowing even William Lloyd Garrison? To be honest, it was better to faint than face the troubling fact that they felt themselves melting in their seats when he turned his penetrating gaze their way.

No doubt the gang of white men who entered the woods noticed how Douglass ensorcelled their women, and for a moment they were mesmerized themselves, staring up in a few unguarded seconds of awe at the lion-become-man, who not only challenged every idea they'd ever believed about Negroes, but called in question their manhood as well. Could they *have survived all he had? Wrestling with his master Thomas Auld's dogs (that were better fed than he was) over bones to feed himself? A whipping every week for six straight months from Mr. Covey, a well-known "negro-breaker" Auld had hired him out to when he was sixteen, and whom, once Douglass had had enough of this treatment, he had fought for two hours straight until the older man gave up, never raising a hand to him again or mentioning this shameful defeat to other white men? Could they have conceived his masterful plans for escaping bondage? Taught themselves (and other slaves) to read? No, they were not—and would never be—*his *equal. And so they fell upon him, there in the woods, tearing down the* *platform after hauling him from it (that took twelve grown men), with him trading two blows for each of theirs, shifting instantly from eloquent oratory to raining punches upon them that broke cartilage and bone until by the sheer weight of their numbers they pinned him down, kicked and pummeled him round his great head, and then at last left when he lost consciousness. They were bruised, bleeding from their noses, and limping, but they were sure the abolitionist nigger from New England was dead.*

Must I dwell in Slavery's night,
And all pleasure take its flight,
Far beyond my feeble sight,
Forever?

He awoke, his head pounding, in the spare bedroom of Neal Hardy, one of his Quaker friends in Pendleton. Experimentally, he tried to sit up, felt a pain—prismatic in its complexity—pierce through his chest, and fell back with a moan onto his pillow, closing his eyes. Was he still alive? He wasn't sure at first. Did he still have all his teeth? Was it night or day? One of his hands, bandaged, was badly throbbing. Although it hurt to raise his arm, he did so, then poked the index finger of his unbandaged hand into his mouth, probing until he was satisfied that, yes, all his teeth were there. He took deep, long breaths just to see if he still could. If he didn't know better, he'd swear from the throbbing ache in his legs and arms that he was back on his pallet in the slave quarters of Edward Covey, who worked his bondsmen in all weather—indeed, worked beside them sometimes so he knew how much effort a chore demanded and if a slave was slacking off—and drove his field hands until they dropped. Or, if they endured his hellish regimen, they turned to drink to dull their minds when their master was not working them or watching them in secret.

Gradually, he opened his eyes again, peering from left to right, taking in a candlestand, a fireplace directly in front of him, and directly to his right Neal Hardy, who sat in a ladder-backed chair, his long face full of sorrow.

Worst of all, must hope grow dim,
And withhold her cheering beam?
Rather let me sleep and dream
Forever!

"Fred," said Hardy, "you've been out a long time. We've been worried."

"Have I? What day is this?"

"Wednesday. It's almost midnight. We brought you to my home straightaway after those hooligans beat you this afternoon."

"Beat me? I barely remember it. I recall a fight, but I thought I was winning. Did I give as good as I got?"

Hardy smiled. "Better, given the odds. But for a little while there I was afraid we were going to lose you. We would *have lost any other man, but thank God you've got the constitution of a horse."*

"A tired horse, I daresay." He struggled to sit up. Hardy quickly moved to his side, helping him as he winced, biting down on his lower lip, his eyes squeezed shut from the pain of changing his posture. "Thank you, Neal. I guess I'd better rest for a few hours before we move on to the next engagement tomorrow. Where is it?"

"Noblesville, but you're not going. I won't allow it."

"What's this now?"

"You heard me. That hand of yours is broken. *And I'm not a doctor, so I pray my wife and I set it correctly. Not only do I want you in bed for the rest of the week, I'd like to have a doctor drop by in the morning to examine you for anything I might have*

missed. For all I know, the blows you took could prove fatal. Here now, look at me. How many fingers am I holding up?"

Actually, he wasn't sure. He squinted, seeing two, but . . . there was a hazy, wavering digit between them that might have been a third.

"I can count, *Neal," he said, trying to dodge the examination. "And I* must *be in Noblesville tomorrow evening. I've been beaten before—you know that—at the hands of drunken slaveholders and other mobs drunk with hatred. They've not stopped me yet."*

"No, they haven't. But I *am. For a week at least." Hardy felt the orator's brow with his fingers, frowned at its warmth, then stepped toward the bedroom door. "We are not finished with Frederick Douglass. We need him too dearly to allow him to push himself into an early grave. I'll be just outside this door. Try to rest.* I *plan to. I'm too exhausted to even unhitch the horses until morning—"*

"Am I a prisoner then?"

"A guest! You've been on the road speaking for over a month now, traveling to five towns a week! That beating you took may be a good thing. It may be a blessing, God's way of telling you to slow down, for heaven's sake, in order to preserve yourself until this fight is over!" He paused, his voice and eyes softening. "Please do as I say. If anything happens to you, our cause will be severly impaired."

"As you wish. I'll rest."

"Good . . . and good night."

Something still my heart surveys,
Groping through this dreary maze;
It is Hope?—then burn and blaze
Forever!

He lay awake for hours, his body burning with injuries so varied, ranging from mild aches and tender spots to outright agony in his broken hand, that he spent close to an hour marveling at just how badly white men had hurt him this time. Perhaps Neal Hardy was right. Since his escape to New Bedford in 1838 when he was twenty years old, since changing his name from Frederick Augustus Bailey to Frederick Johnson and at last to Frederick Douglass (an abolitionist friend, Nathan Johnson, suggested "Douglass" after reading Lady of the Lake, *and he settled into that new incarnation), since the day the Massachusetts Anti-Slavery Society discovered his gifts and engaged him as a lecturer, he had not rested. Nor had he wanted to. How could his spirit sleep as long as a single black man or woman was in chains? But was he too wounded this time? Yes, he ached from chin to calves, but despite Hardy's obvious compassion and concern for his health, it annoyed him a little whenever white men told him what to do. He'd had quite enough of their hostile—or benign—advice when he was in bondage. If they could not truly understand all he'd endured or had not walked a mile in his boots (when he had boots, which was seldom during his childhood), then how could they recommend* any*thing to him. And besides, most of the time their advice was wrong. Like the Massachusetts Anti-Slavery Society, which initially asked him only to describe his victimization as a slave, not launch into a devastating critique of the country as a whole—*that, *they told him, was the province of white men like the society's William Collins or the venerated Garrison.* Stay in your place *is what they were telling him,* We know best. *Well, they had not. Only he knew what was best for Douglass. They warned him against publishing an undisguised narrative on his life, insisting that such a document would reveal that he was Frederick Bailey, a runaway slave, and bring the slave* *catchers to his door. He'd thought,* Damn the slave catchers, *and planned one day to release his account of his life anyway, and if it brought him even greater fame than white freedom fighters or black ones, would that cause tension within the movement? If so, very well. He had no time for the petty reactions of lesser men, black or white.*

Leave me not a wretch confined,
Altogether lame and blind—
Unto gross despair consigned,
Forever!

Yet perhaps—just perhaps—he should stay abed long enough to heal a little. If he needed convalescence it would give him time to write. His thoughts began to drift to possible subjects and alighted on the class of forty slaves he once taught to read on Sundays at the home of a free colored man. He was breaking the law, doing that. How might he describe them when time permitted him to turn to the narrative he hoped to compose? . . .

They were noble souls; they not only possessed loving hearts, but brave ones. We were linked and interlinked with each other. . . . I believe we would have died for each other. We never undertook to do anything, of any importance, without a mutual consultation. . . . We were one. . . . When I think that these precious souls are to-day shut up in the prison-house of slavery, my feelings overcome me, and I am almost ready to ask, "Does a righteous God govern the universe? and for what does he hold the thunders in his right hand, if not to smite the oppressor, and deliver the spoiled out of the hand of the spoiler?

He sat bolt upright in bed, the sudden move sending pain through his back. But, no! He must not rest. They were still in bondage, those others, suffering like the slave in George Moses Horton's tragic poem. Waiting for him . . .

> Heaven! in whom can I confide?
> Canst thou not for all provide?
> Condescend to be my guide
> Forever!

*With an effort that brought beads of glistening sweat to his forehead, he climbed down from the bed, swinging his feet over the side first, then standing. The room spun. He steadied himself by gripping the ladder-backed chair with his good hand. (*Would the injured one, *he wondered,* ever heal?*) His clothes were on the chair. Slowly, he pulled them on with one hand. Given his injuries, dressing took an hour. When he was fully clothed, he padded quietly to the bedroom door, opened it cautiously, and found Hardy just outside the room, where he'd promised to be, but sleeping, his arms crossed over his chest and head tilted forward.*

He tipped past him, exited through the house's rear door, and made his way to Hardy's carriage. The horses were still hitched to it, hardly a situation his host would have allowed under normal circumstances, but Lord knew they'd had an extraordinary day in Pendleton. He pulled himself up onto the seat. He took the reins in his left hand, snapped them, and geed the horses out onto the dark road. If he drove through the night and morning surely he would be in Noblesville in time for his next speech: yet another nail driven into slavery's casket. And if his death delivered his loved ones to freedom one *day sooner, then so be it. Hardy, he supposed, would be upset when he awakened, discovering him and his horses gone. But this Quaker friend would know where to find him. Possibly he would follow him to Noblesville, arriving just toward the end of his engagement—a little late, as white men fighting oppression often were. And perhaps he would understand why his guest left. If Hardy did not, more's the pity, for, as he drove the horses on through the darkness, he did not have a spare moment to explain. Or to wait for white men—even the good ones—to catch up to him.*

And when this transient life shall end,
Oh, may some kind, eternal friend,
Bid me from servitude ascend,
Forever!

Abolitionism was the enemy. Douglass told of being chased by mobs in small midwestern towns; he was attacked at a meeting in Pendleton, Indiana, and it was in this fight that Douglass broke his right hand. White abolitionist newspaper editor Elijah Lovejoy was killed as he defended his press in Illinois. As this violence slapped pacifists awake and black abolitionists espoused a more radical agenda, many abolitionists embraced a radical philosophy to end slavery any way they could.

Another former fugitive, Henry Highland Garnet of Maryland, believed that bloodshed was inevitable.

A New York Presbyterian minister, Garnet delivered the principal address at the National Convention of Colored Citizens in Buffalo in 1843. The audience sat in excited anticipation, knowing the speech—"An Address to the Slaves of the United States of America"—would be controversial. Garnet, an opponent of pacifists like Garrison and even the more radical Douglass, had long espoused violent resistance as an answer to slavery. In many ways, his views evoked the spirit of David Walker.

"Think of the undying glory that hangs around the ancient name of Africa," Garnet told the crowd,

> and forget not that you are native born American citizens, and as such, you are justly entitled to all the rights that are granted to the freest. Think how many tears you have poured out upon the soil which you have cultivated with unrequited toil and enriched with your blood; and then go to your lordly enslavers, and tell them plainly, that you are *determined to be free.*
>
> . . . Do this, and forever after cease to toil for the heartless tyrants, who give you no other reward but stripes and abuse. If they then commence the work of

> death, they, and not you, will be responsible for the consequences. You had far better all die—*die immediately*, than live slaves, and entail your wretchedness upon your posterity . . . there is not much hope of redemption without the shedding of blood. If you must bleed, let it all come at once—rather *die freemen, than to live to be slaves.*

Garnet lauded the heroics of Nat Turner, Denmark Vesey, Joseph Cinque. He warned blacks that waiting on white abolitionists would be their undoing. He reminded them that they were 4 million strong. It was a call to battle addressed to blacks, and blacks only. Several times during the speech, he stressed that a revolution without the sword would be no revolution at all.

Garnet's impassioned speech was the focal point of the convention—not only because of its confrontational content, but because convention delegates would have to vote whether or not to support the "Address" as their own document. To do so would mean that they recommended Garnet's course of action. Frederick Douglass protested the undercurrent of physical force in the speech. After voting three times, the convention decided not to support the "Address" as their own. At one point, only one vote separated yea and nay.

The urgency of Garnet's message matched the urgency many blacks felt as slavery expanded into new territories, bringing all the poisons of prejudice along with it. In 1836, Arkansas entered the union as a slave state; in 1845, Texas and Florida joined that growing list. And three years before the outbreak of war in the Southwest, Garnet had warned that "the propagators of American slavery are spending their blood and treasure" to take over the heart of Mexico.

Mexico and the great Southwest beckoned, ripe for the exploitation of black labor. The war against Mexico, beginning in 1846, was sparked by American expansionist policy and by the southerners' desire for more places to grow cotton. By the time the battle ended two years later, America had acquired more than half of Mexico's territory, and in that territory the quarrel over "slave or free" began anew.

Whites arriving from Europe quickly learned to look upon free blacks as interlopers. In 1846, after suggesting that blacks leave the country and vowing not to hire or trade with them, a group of German settlers in Ohio came to this conclusion: "We will resist the settlement of blacks and Mulattoes in this country to the full extent of our means, the bayonet not excepted."

And men like Frederick Douglass remained in the thick of things, thundering against the status quo. At the October 1847 National Colored Convention in Troy, New York, Douglass introduced the following resolutions:

> Resolved, that our only hope for peaceful emancipation in this land is based on a firm, devoted and unceasing assertion of our rights and a full, free and determined exposure of our multiplied wrongs.
>
> Resolved, that in the language of inspired wisdom, there shall be no peace to the wicked, and that this guilty nation shall have no peace, and that we will do all we can to agitate! *Agitate!* AGITATE!!! till our rights are restored and our brethren are redeemed from their cruel chains.

Later that year, he published the first issue of the *North Star*:

> We solemnly dedicate the "NORTH STAR" to the cause of our long oppressed and plundered fellow countrymen. . . . It shall fearlessly assert your rights, faithfully proclaim your wrongs, and earnestly demand for you instant and even-handed justice. Giving no quarter to

> slavery at the South, it will hold no truce with oppressors at the North. . . . Every effort to injure or degrade you or your cause . . . shall find in it a constant, unswerving and inflexible foe.

As the *Appeal* had been the soul of David Walker, the *North Star* was the soul of Frederick Douglass. It was, in its time, the voice of black America.

And black America's voice was rising to a roar. Congress was openly debating whether land acquired in the Mexican conflict would turn to slavery. Northern states forbade black participation in the political process. In the South, continued restrictions on free blacks were designed to force them back into captivity. Times were desperate.

In 1849, during a speech in Boston's Faneuil Hall, Douglass voiced that desperation, declaring that he would "welcome the news that the slaves had risen and that the sable arms which have been engaged in beautifying and adorning the South were engaged in spreading death and destruction there."

In January 1848, the world was changed by the discovery of dull yellow flakes in a millstream in the territory of California. It was the start of the California Gold Rush.

Only months later, the first of twelve thousand wagons were daring the moody Missouri River, Indian attacks, and starvation in a relentless trek to California and promises of fortune. Every water route to California was clogged with rickety makeshift vessels commandeered by decidedly amateur sailors. Farmers sold their farms, laborers abandoned their jobs, and preachers walked away from their pulpits to head west. It was rumored that anyone with a wash pan and shovel could sift out fifty dollars of pure gold in one day.

Some slaves moved west with their masters to help coax the precious metal from the goldfields. Slavery was conquering new territory.

The gradual and inevitable western expansion of slavery was a dynamic social and economic force that changed the face of the country. Like a predator that couldn't be sated, slavery moved into Mississippi. Alabama. It crossed the Mississippi River into Louisiana. It moved into the Southwest. And by the end of the 1840s, fueled by the lure of gold, it reached America's other shore.

During the long, often perilous journey to California, slaves prayed that freedom awaited them. Instead, they were exploited and deceived. Many, like Alvin Coffey of Missouri, found the road to freedom cluttered with obstacles:

> On the morning of the fifteenth [of October] we went to dry-digging mining. We dug and dug till the first of November, at night it commenced raining and rained and snowed pretty much all the winter. We had a tent but it barely kept us all dry. . . .
>
> I worked 13 months for [Dr. Bassett] in California. I saved him $5500 in gold dust. I saved $616 of my own money in gold dust. . . . He kept my money, and when we got up to Missouri, he sold me for a thousand more.

Coffey was forced to return to California and dig gold for his new master, eventually paying out $7,000 for freedom for himself and his family. Many slaves sent money home to buy those they loved out of bondage.

In 1850, Californians, to prevent the permanent establishment of slavery in their territory, petitioned Congress to join the union as a free state. California had already drafted a constitution prohibiting slavery, ratified with more than twelve thousand yes votes to only eight hundred noes. The people had already chosen a governor and governing body. All that remained was official admission to the union.

Southern slaveholders immediately opposed the move. If they were to be an integral part of the country's future and maintain their disproportionate strength in the country's government, slavery had to continue its drive west. There was also a strong desire for new land and free enterprise.

The persistent threat posed by abolitionist forces had to be squelched. And if California was declared a free state, western expansion would be effectively thwarted, and the dream of an invincible republic of slaveholders, stretching from ocean to ocean, would die before it was realized.

Eventually California was granted its request. Zachary Taylor, a tough soldier and the new president of the United States, saw no need to coddle the South; and although a slaveholder himself, he vowed to put down any moves toward secession with federal troops.

In a very direct way, black people were made to pay for the Compromise of 1850, the act which welcomed California into the union. The compromise contained one extraordinary and particularly painful provision, an amendment to the 1793 Act Respecting Fugitives from Justice, and Persons Escaping from the Service of Their Masters.

A stringent new fugitive slave law.

Under this law, any person—black or white—could be deputized to help capture and return a runaway slave. Refusing to participate in the recapture of the fugitive would result in imprisonment and fine. And the only testimony allowed was the testimony of the person who claimed to own the alleged fugitive. The commissioner would judge the truth of the story, and in the overwhelming majority of cases, the person would be returned to slavery. The captive had no rights, no voice, no possible way to have his or her story considered. The extraordinary cynicism undergirding the new law was revealed in the fee system: federal commissioners received $10 for each person sent into slavery, but only $5 for each person set free.

The Fugitive Slave Act radicalized many whites by making them directly involved in the maintenance of slavery. It was an impingement on white civil rights and was a primary cause of so many white abolitionists suddenly becoming as confrontational as the black ones.

In New York, fugitive Harriet Jacobs, desperately trying to build a free world for her children, learned that Dr. Norcom, encouraged by the new law, had sent slave catchers to track her down.

"It was the beginning of a reign of terror to the colored population," she wrote.

> Many families, who had lived in the city for twenty years, fled from it now. . . .
>
> I seldom venture into the streets. . . . I went as much as possible by back streets and by-ways. A disgrace to a city calling itself free. . . . All that winter I lived in a state of anxiety.

Not all blacks retreated in fear. Abolitionist Martin Delany declared:

> If any man approaches [my] house in search of a slave—I care not who he may be, whether constable, or sheriff, magistrate or even judge of the Supreme Court—nay let it be President Millard Fillmore surrounded by his cabinet and his bodyguard . . . if he crosses the threshold of my door, and I do not lay him a lifeless corpse at my feet, I hope the grave may refuse my body a resting place, and righteous heaven, my spirit a home. O, no! He cannot enter that house and we both live.

THE MAYOR'S TALE

ONCE UPON A TIME in a nation not very old the people of a large, northeastern city awoke one morning and discovered to their surprise (though they should have seen it coming) that something had changed in their lives.

The city's Mayor like many others went to sleep the night before, curled beneath the warm covers beside his Wife, feeling as he drifted off to sleep that all was well in the world. Their two children rested comfortably down the hallway in the great, three-story house; they were doing well at their studies, according to the tutor he'd hired for them, and it was likely both boys—then ages eight and twelve—would easily be accepted at the nation's oldest and most prestigious college when the time came for them to apply. His investments were performing better than expected, given the country's delicate political situation (but when, after all, was politics not a delicate matter?). Added to which, he'd worked hard all throughout 1850 to beat his competitors in neighboring cities along the eastern seaboard for a few lucrative contracts that would further industrialize his own city, which would assure his reelection, and he was meeting with representatives of those companies in the morning. Furthermore, his Wife of twenty years seemed pleased with her personal affairs, the charity work she and her friends did each weekend, and particularly with her abolitionist activities. He, being a progressive man, supported fully this cause of Negro manumission, both in his role as Mayor and, even more importantly, in his home, where he employed five free Negroes as servants. Indeed, he had cheered on and publicly supported the recent Compromise that abolished the slave trade in the District of Columbia. He treated his black help royally, or so the Mayor believed, and he overlooked what everyone in his social circle agreed were inherent and unfortunate deficiencies in colored people. These shortcomings, after all, were not their *fault, but rather the unjust distribution of talent, beauty, and intelligence by Nature, so that those more generously endowed by Providence were duty bound to help them. Without white men, the Negro would be lost. They were like children in their dependency. The Mayor paid his servants handsomely and on time, was lavish with tips, inquired frequently into their health and well-being, told them repeatedly they were an important part of his family, and he proudly pointed them out when his friends, business associates, and political colleagues dined with his family or dropped by. And, as if that were not enough, the Mayor had a lovely, new mistress—a young singer of thirty (which was half his age), who gave him good reason to look forward to those weekends his Wife and her friends were away.*

Yes, all was well—as well as a civilized man might expect—in the world on Wednesday, January 1, 1851.

Thursday, however, was quite another story. When he opened his eyes and stretched, having slept well—the sleep of the just, he'd say—the Mayor felt as rested as he did on Saturday, the day he normally slept in. But this wasn't the weekend. Or was it? For a moment he wasn't sure. He shook his Wife's shoulder, rousing her awake, and she said, "Why are you still here? Aren't you supposed to be at City Hall?" Like Immanuel Kant, the Mayor preferred his life "to be like the most regular of regular verbs." So he was at first bewildered, then upset, by this disruption of his schedule. He stumbled from bed, his bare feet landing on a floor so cold its chill went through him like a shock, squeezed a whoop from his lips, and sent him hopping around the room for his slippers. He found his wire-rim spectacles on a nightstand, then shivering so badly his teeth chattered, he bent over to better see the small, wooden clock. It was quarter past eleven. He'd slept all morning, missing at least five appointments.

And all the fireplaces were dark and cold.

The Mayor rang for his butler, Henry, who always awoke him and had each fireplace blazing by 5 A.M. *No answer. He rang again, waiting and watching his breath steam the bedroom air as if he were standing outside on the ice-cold street. "Please get him to light the fireplaces* now*!" wailed his Wife. "I'm not leaving this bed until the house is warm! And tell the maid I'm* hungry*!" The Mayor sighed and said, "Yes, dear, I . . . I will. Henry must be sick this morning—he's never been remiss in his duties before, you know." He hurried to dress himself, and found to his great dismay that not only had his personal servant failed to wake him, but Henry had not prepared or set out his clothing for the day either. Because he was so late and had no idea where Henry put his freshly pressed linen, the Mayor grumbled and pulled on his wrinkled shirt from the day before (On the front was a red soup stain from a lunch he'd taken at his club, but he couldn't worry about that now), his uncreased trousers, his coat, then hurried downstairs and through the frigid hallways of his many-roomed house, calling for their servants. Again, there was no answer. In the kitchen, in the chambers set aside for their live-in help, and in* *the livery stable there was only silence. And not a black face to be found. Moreover, the horses had not been groomed. Or fed. His carriage was not ready. He would have to travel, he realized, the five miles to City Hall under his own locomotion!*

Not being accustomed to walking, it took the Mayor two hours to traverse the distance between his home and office. He stopped to rest often, puffing, placing his hand against a wall, his heart racing and empty stomach growling. And what he saw—or rather didn't see—along the way to work startled him. There were no black people. It wasn't as if he looked for them every day. No, most of the time they blended into the background of his city, as unnoticeable as trees or weather vanes or lampposts—or maybe like the inner workings of a finely tuned watch. Obviously, no one paid attention to a timepiece's hidden mechanism until it ceased to work. But now, along the five-mile stretch between his home and City Hall, he saw chaos. Coal had not been delivered to homes, and this was the dead of winter! Barges had not been unloaded in the harbor. Fresh bread had not been delivered from bakeries. Roadwork lay unfinished, as if the fingers of God had plucked its dusky crews off the face of the earth. No windows were washed. No snow was shoveled. It was as if his city had run out of its primary source of power, coal. (A terrible pun, he knew, but on this awful day it seemed appropriate.) He wondered aloud as he galumphed down the nearly empty streets, "What in heaven's name is going on?" No carriages, driven by black coachmen, bore white passengers to and from the offices where they conducted the country's crucial business, domestic and international. Indeed, half the offices he saw were closed.

It was, therefore, a befuddled and disheveled Mayor who finally reached City Hall by 2 P.M. and slumped heavily behind his desk, wondering if his heart might fail him once and for all after his morning's exertions. Everything he'd accomplished this morning (which wasn't much) had taken two—perhaps three—times longer to do. His secretary, a young man named Daniel, looked very sad that Thursday. He told the Mayor the people with whom he'd missed appointments were furious. Two entrepreneurs of enormous wealth and influence who'd traveled a great distance to see him—one a railroad man, the other a maritime merchant—felt insulted by what they called Hizzoner's "malfeasance" and planned to cancel further discussions of their proposed contracts and in the future only do business with other cities.

"No!" whispered the Mayor.

His secretary said, "I'm afraid so, sir. Your political rivals will make great capital of this. Your reelection is only months away, and you promised in the last campaign to improve commerce, shipping, and transportation."

"I know *what I promised, damn it!" The Mayor pounded his desk. "But it's not my fault! Nothing's been normal today!" He leaned back in his seat, red-faced, and began pulling at his fingers. "All the Negroes are gone. Have you noticed that? What on earth happened to them?"*

"What you *agreed to, I guess," said his secretary.*

"Me*? What are you babbling about, man? Talk sense! I never told the Negroes to go away! Have you been drinking?"*

"No, sir. I'm quite sober, insofar as it appears we both will be out of a job by November. I'm referring to the Compromise in Congress, which you fully endorsed."

"What does that *have to do with our Negroes being gone?"*

Quietly, his secretary stepped from the Mayor's office to his own room, then returned after less than a minute with a copy of a newspaper from the day before. "Perhaps you should read this. Please read it carefully, *sir. Meanwhile, if you don't mind, I'd like to repair to my office in order to finish sending out copies of my résumé to potential, future employers. And I have a dreadful headache today . . ."*

His secretary departed, leaving the Mayor more baffled than before. He opened the day-old newspaper, and there it was, the complex Compromise. In it, California became the thirty-first state. New Mexico and Utah were to be organized as territories and residents could decide for themselves whether to be free or slave. The slave trade was ended in D.C., and—Wait! *He looked closer, bringing the paper closer to his eyes in order to read some changes in the Fugitive Slave Act of 1793. Vaguely, he recalled this item, but hadn't attended closely to its details. Under the amendment, federal commissioners were granted the power to issue warrants for runaway slaves. They could form posses to capture fugitive blacks. They could fine citizens if they refused to help in returning Negroes to their former masters, who had to do nothing more than submit an affidavit in court. The blacks were denied a jury trial. They could not testify to defend themselves. Slowly, he put the newspaper down. His man Henry . . . their cook . . . their three other servants and perhaps* all *the coloreds in his city were runaways. No doubt they'd changed their names. And once they learned of the amendment to the Fugitive Slave Act, they'd fled en masse during the night, probably to Canada. Who could blame them? And* he *had endorsed this disaster?*

Gloomily, the Mayor left City Hall. Night was coming on . . . and streetlamps were unlit. He plodded on, realizing that until now he'd not seen how dependent the life of the city—and his own fortune—was on blacks. They were interwoven, albeit invisibly, into the fabric of everything; and, like the dangling string on a sweater which, if pulled, unraveled the entire garment, so too their removal caused everything—high and low, private and personal—to collapse. Without sealing the deal on those contracts, he would lose his office. He was certain of that now. His own businesses would suffer. My God, he might even lose his mistress and be left with only his Wife, who sometimes could be a shrew! Miserably, he tramped back home in the snow, which seeped into his shoes and dampened his feet so thoroughly he felt his toes had frozen in one solid block of flesh by the time he reached his front door, coughing, his nose burning and running badly, because—yes—he'd picked up a nasty cold.

The house was colder and darker than before. If anything, he only wanted a little sympathy now from his Wife. He did not see her downstairs. So, blowing his nose into his handkerchief, he climbed the steep stairs to their bedroom, dripping all the way. "Dear," he said, opening the door, "I have some bad news . . ."

"Well," she crabbed, "you can save whatever it is until you find dinner for us. I haven't eaten all day. I'm starving*! And so are the children!"*

It dawned on him that she had not left their bed all day. "You couldn't find something for yourself in the kitchen?"

"Nothing's prepared! I haven't had to cook in years! You know that. I want you to go out right now and find us something to eat."

"Now?"

"Yes, now.*"*

Slump-shouldered, feeling euchered, the Mayor went back outside, walking two miles in the darkness, with fresh snow beginning to fall, flaking on his shoulders. An hour later he arrived at the building that housed his club, thinking perhaps there they would wrap four plates of food, which he could carry home to his family. He tried the door. It was locked. Inside no lights were on whatsoever. Then he saw a sign in the ground-floor window. NO WAITERS OR COOKS TODAY. *He stared blankly, helplessly, at the words. His mouth wobbled.* Of course, *he thought,* Of course . . .

And then Hizzoner broke down and wept in the snow.

Soon after the passage of the Fugitive Slave Act, Frederick Douglass, in Rochester, New York, was asked to help celebrate the country's seventy-sixth birthday. The black leader was insulted and angered by the request.

> This Fourth of July is *yours,* not *mine.* . . . Do you mean, citizens, to mock me, by asking me to speak today? . . . What, to the American slave, is your Fourth of July? . . . a sham; your boasted liberty, an unholy license . . . your shouts of liberty and equality, hollow mockery; your prayers and hymns . . . and solemnity, are to him, mere bombast, fraud, deception, impiety and hypocrisy. . . . There is not a nation on the earth guilty of practices more shocking and bloody than are the people of the United States, at this very hour.

Between 1850 and 1860, an estimated twenty thousand black Americans fled from the northern states, migrating to Canada. Pittsburgh newspapers reported that all the city's Negro waiters had fled under the cover of darkness. Then there were those who steadfastly refused to run, standing their ground, boldly declaring themselves free. Some joined forces with white sympathizers to directly confront slave hunters. In Boston, black people formed the League of Freedom; in Chicago, they set up the Liberty Association.

In September of 1851, the confrontations took a bloody turn.

Negroes who settled in Lancaster County, Pennsylvania, bordering Maryland, often opened their homes to fugitive slaves and conspired to turn away those who came looking for them. When Maryland slave owner Edward Gorsuch tracked four escaped slaves to Christiana, Pennsylvania, and the home of William Parker, he expected no trouble recovering the property he had come for. After all, it was now the law that a United States deputy marshal was by his side. But standing with Parker were white and black townspeople who had been rehearsing for such an emergency.

Parker described the exchange that led to tragedy:

> I met them at the landing, and asked, "Who are you?"
>
> The leader, Kline, replied, "I am the United States marshal."
>
> I then told him to take another step, and I would break his neck.
>
> He said again, "I am the United States marshal."
>
> I told him I did not care for him nor the United States. . . .
>
> "Yes," said Kline, "I have heard many a negro talk as big as you, and then have taken him, and I'll take you."
>
> "You have not taken me yet," I replied; "and if you undertake it, you will have your name recorded in history."

The slave hunters, determined not to leave empty-handed, were soon surrounded by armed local residents. Shots rang out. When the smoke cleared, Edward Gorsuch was dead, and the fugitives, along with their protectors, had fled.

Thirty-one blacks and five whites were rounded up and arrested, although only one person—a white man—was brought to trial and acquitted. The repercussions of the incident went far beyond Pennsylvania's borders. The rebels were praised for their heroic stance, and their treatment was cause for critical commentary. It was noted that the whites involved were released on bail while the blacks languished in jail.

The Fugitive Slave Act guaranteed that it was only a matter of time before a showdown between abolitionist forces and the federal government. When an escaped slave named Anthony Burns was captured in Boston in 1854, the time had come.

Following the violence in Pennsylvania, as well as several other incidents like it across the North, President Franklin Pierce moved to enforce the act with the full power of the federal government. If he wanted to prove to the South that he was deadly serious, Boston—the focal point of the abolitionist movement—was the perfect place to do it.

On two occasions, abolitionist mobs in the city had stormed the courthouse to liberate captive slaves. Many southerners were demanding that the federal government investigate this apparent lawlessness. They had a constitutional right to their property.

As news of Anthony Burns's arrest spread through Boston, both black and white abolitionists sprang into action.

> *Dr. W. Higginson:*
> *Last night a man was arrested here as a fugitive. We have called a public meeting at Faneuil Hall for tomorrow (Friday). Give all the notice you can. The friends here are wide awake and unanimous. Vigilance Committee meets this afternoon. Come strong. In Haste Yours,*
> *Samuel May Jr.*

Hundreds of whites gathered at the city's Faneuil Hall, while incensed black citizens came together in the basement of Tremont Temple. The whites engaged in spirited debate, weighed their options, and searched for the most effective course of action. In the midst of their meanderings, word came that the blacks were attacking the courthouse. The discussion was abandoned as they too set out to free Anthony Burns.

Reverend Thomas Wentworth Higginson, a leader of the attack, said:

> [W]e hammered away at the southwest door of the Court-House. . . . [I]t began to give way. . . . There was room for but one to pass in. I glanced instinctively at my Black ally. He did not even look at me, but sprang in first. . . . We found ourselves inside, face to face with six or eight policemen, who laid about them with their clubs, driving us to the wall and hammering away at our heads.
>
> I did not know . . . till next morning . . . that, just as the door sprang open, a shot had been fired, and that one of the marshal's deputies, a man named Batchelder, had been killed.

Following James Batchelder's death, federal authorities, U.S. Marines, and local militia flooded the streets of Boston. But black abolitionists were unrepentant. Frederick Douglass remarked:

> For a *white* man to defend his friend unto blood is praiseworthy, but for a *black* man to do precisely the same thing is a crime.
>
> We hold that when Batchelder undertook to play the bloodhound, he forfeited his right to live.

Unwilling to surrender one of their own, hundreds of Negroes from the areas around Boston surrounded the courthouse on the day following the killing. William J. Watkins, assistant editor of Douglass's paper, the *North Star*, defended the violence:

> A colored man is living quietly in Boston, one mile from Bunker Hill Monument. He is a free man, for God created him. He stamped His image upon him. Slavery has well nigh murdered him. He has contrived to break loose from its iron grasp. He is pursued by his murderers. The hall of justice has become a den of thieves. A man leaves the honorable occupation of driving horses, and consents, for a "consideration," to be appointed Deputy Marshal, consents to be invested with power to rob him of his God-given rights. The miserable hireling is shot in the attempt. Is that man a murderer who sent the well-directed bullet through his stony heart?

Tension escalated, especially after the failure of an attempt to purchase Burns's freedom, organized by Twelfth Baptist Church pastor Leonard Grimes and others. The attempts to save the fugitive, by force or compromise, affected even the most apathetic northerners. Massachusetts resident Amos Lawrence described the impact of the case on stiff, staid Boston: "We went to bed one night old fashioned, conservative, Compromise Union Whigs and waked up stark mad Abolitionists."

The hearing dragged into the following week, until, on June 2, 1854, Judge Edward G. Loring ordered Burns's return to Virginia. All the while, the fugitive's would-be saviors maintained a vigil outside the courthouse. Black waiters refused to serve the soldiers occupying the town. During the trial, free blacks had perjured themselves in an attempt to free Burns.

A Lynn, Massachusetts, resident wrote in the *Liberator:*

> Through that long week of agony, the vicinity of the slave pen was thronged by colored men and women, watching from dawn till eve, and some of them the long night through, patiently awaiting . . . the fate of their poor brother in bonds; seeking in every way in their power to show their sympathy for him, and hoping and praying, to the last moment, for his deliverance from the hand of the kidnapper.

"Our worst fears are realized," said abolitionist Charlotte Forten.

> The decision was against poor Burns. . . . Today Massachusetts has again been disgraced; again has she showed her submissions to the Slave Power . . . and this by express orders of a government which proudly boasts of being the freest in the world.

In the end, Anthony Burns was led through streets cleared and guarded by members of the state militia. He was accompanied by a military escort fit for royalty—the National Boston Lancers, the U.S. infantry, the Marines, volunteer guards, and a loaded six-pound cannon. Windows were draped in black; many flags were hung "union down." The message on a coffin in the street was THE FUNERAL OF LIBERTY. Stunned residents lined Burns's passage to the waterfront; there he boarded a cutter, headed for the South and servitude.

Later, Grimes raised the money to buy Burns out of slavery, and the freedman became a minister himself.

But for two weeks an escaped slave had been the focal point of a uniquely American drama, bringing growing regional tensions into keen relief. In nine days, he had cost the federal government many thousands of dollars, one riot, and one life. The president had made his case, but not even slaveholders were sure it had been worth the price.

Anthony Burns's official return to slavery did little to prove the ability of the Fugitive Slave Act to unite the country, pacify the South, or pave the way for the smooth future return of escaped slaves. In fact, throughout the northern states, determination to defy the law grew more heated.

What did white southerners make of the government's victory? The Richmond, Virginia, *Enquirer,* although supportive of the federal government's action, noted the high price tag of the Burns case and pointed out that southern taxes helped pay the cost. Could the South handle that heavy a burden for a sole refugee when it was northerners who essentially caused the problem?

A South Carolinian, temporarily in residence at Harvard, saw no advantages for the South in the Fugitive Slave Act:

> Can any one fail to perceive that the very boast of its enforcement proves the great fear there was, even in their own minds, of its possibility? Can any reflecting Southern man read the facts of this case, and not see, with such associates and rulers, that he verges towards the brink of a horrible and bottomless abyss of infamy and misery?

MURDEROUS THOUGHTS

ALL RIGHT, YOU CAN *interview me if you wish, but there's really not much to say. I think that white bier you see swinging over the street, just above our heads, with the legend* THE FUNERAL OF LIBERTY *says it all. Or over there—do you see it?—the union flag hanging upside down? Or there, on those shopkeepers' windows? They're draped in black because today we have collectively committed suicide in Boston. That's why you've got twenty thousand people out here today. We are dead. We are mourning* ourselves *as much as we are the decision that went against Anthony Burns. By returning that colored man to his master we have thoroughly undone the Revolution. We are not who we say we are. There's nothing left, I'm telling you, but lies and hypocrisy. And so I feel ashamed to wear this uniform. What's that? Yes, I resigned this morning as captain of the watch. Until this trial—this mockery of justice—came along, I was damned proud to be a Marine. My grandfather was with General Washington at Valley Forge. I grew up hearing stories every night at the dinner table about how the*

Tree of Liberty is watered with the blood of patriots. That's Jefferson, in case you didn't know, and from the time I was a boy I have believed that sentiment, sir, with all my heart and soul. I cut my teeth on the words of Thomas Paine. On his belief that our Revolution, our freedom, was worth protecting with my life, if need be. I was a soldier. My daily bread was duty and obedience to the nation I served. So yes, I suppose it seems odd that I disobeyed a direct order from my commanding officer to escort Burns from his jail in the courthouse in order for this *contingent of men to march him back into bondage. But it's* not *odd, I'm saying. You can quote me on that. My refusal to be a party to the enslavement of another human being is of a piece with my grandfather's resistance to British oppression during the war. There's the rub! D'you see what we've become? By holding the Negroes in slavery* we *are the very enemy we fought in 1776. As a patriot to the* principle, *if not this wretched Government that intensified the Fugitive Slave Act four years ago, I have chosen to leave the military that has been my life. Now tell me again, what newspaper did you say you represent?"*

"Disappointed? Why yes, I suppose you can say that. I've been here in Boston for the last month on business. What is my business? Tobacco. My home is Charleston, and what that means is that I know a great deal more about Negroes and their needs than do you northerners. I've watched this trial, you know, for the last nine days. By my *calculations, the cost of returning this runaway to his owner is a riot, the life of one U.S. marshal, and $50,000, which must be taken from the public treasury. No doubt the North will find a new way to tax the South to pay for the expenses. From my hotel window I saw the abolitionists when they stormed the southwest door of the courthouse, determined to break out this nigra Burns and set him free. I was watching too when it was over*

and the body of that marshal's deputy was brought outside. What I *wish to know is why no one has called that criminal action by its proper name:* treason. *It is blatantly against recent legislation, and the Constitution, to harbor or abet a fugitive nigra. He is property, first and foremost. If you were in that courthouse on the last day of the trial, as I was, you would have seen the recognition in Burns's eyes when his master appeared—it was the look of a craven, guilty animal cornered at last. But was* anyone *here, in this city, at all pleased that the rightful goods of an honest man were restored? That today the law is being enforced? Hardly. And* that *is why I am illy pleased. Nay, disgusted. If this tenuous union is to prevail, which I doubt increasingly every day I am in Boston, then you Yankees* must *honor the customs and way of life in the southern states. You must—I put it to you, sir—stop this rape of* our *rights. Oh, you don't agree with me? Then consider these facts: since declaring independence, the United States has acquired 2,373,046 square miles of territory from which it has excluded the South. But it is the slavery question that stings us most. On this the North has been irrational. You—and your agitators for Negro manumission who now control the Government—force the South to choose between abolition or secession. We have no* say *in this Government. None a'tall! As John C. Calhoun put it, what was once a constitutional federal republic has been subverted and transformed into one that is as absolutist as that of the Autocrat of Russia. Can you see the South's position?* My *position? I do not want my businesses destroyed. My liberties rescinded. Or to see an inferior race released upon the South to wreak havoc with all that is genteel, civilized, and sanctioned by the Almighty. But that is what is happening day after day, and it will result—mark my words—in the dissolution of the union. No, if you knew the Negro better, you would not have such a long face today. But enough! This insufferable Government will be the ruin of us all . . ."*

"Aye, guv'nor, I think it's a pitiful sight! All those soldiers and a cannon just to send one poor black devil back into slavery? Sweet, merciful Heaven, what's to become of us! What'd ye say? That's right I owns this bakery behind us. Worked on ships twelve years afore I could buy it. And it was me put black drapery in the window this morning. Sure now, I worked beside coloreds, unloadin' boats when they come in, and far as I can see they're no diff'rent than other blokes here in Boston. I'd wager a few are better *citizens. They have to be. Some of 'em are fugitives, sure enough. They run here to get away from their bloody owners, find wives and husbands, and start families. And what's this new law say? I'll tell ye! It says a man kin be torn away from his rightful wife and wee li'l ones, put in chains like that fellah Burns, and taken back to a life of torture. Anyone kin see why this city is under martial law. No self-respectin' Christian can just stand by and watch the Devil at work right outside his door. No, guv'nor, if we don't right this wrong—and bloody soon—we all deserve to burn in hell."*

"You want to know about that *night? Fine, then, I'll tell you, but only if your newspaper prints* exactly *what I say. And* as *I say it. After Anthony was captured and locked away in the courthouse, a public meeting to discuss his plight was called at Faneuil Hall. The time was seven o'clock.* I *should have been on my way to work at the hotel. I'm a waiter, and a damned good one, but I saw the notice of what they were doing to this black man. I couldn't carry on as if everything was normal, now could I? So I went to the*

meeting at Faneuil Hall. I sat for an hour listening to the city's important colored and white men debating the question of what to do about poor Anthony's imprisonment. You know, it's always this way when whites and Boston's officially chosen black spokesmen are brought together to confront the evils of oppression. Nothing happens but talk. Guilty whites bare their souls. They listen, oh so sympathetically, to handpicked representatives of the Negro community narrate a litany of abuses they've endured since childhood. And nothing gets done! I hate those meetings. I've been to dozens of them, and after every one the whites feel so much better about themselves because they spent an evening with their darker brothers, and the official Negroes—oh, let me tell you!—they use those meetings to emotionally blackmail white people, wringing concessions out of them for their own personal advancement. I left in disgust with a friend of mine, another waiter, who informed me that only a few blocks away another gathering of only blacks was about to take place to decide what to do about Anthony. We went there straightaway. The room held about ten men and women. There wasn't a Negro spokesman anywhere to be seen. The talk was over in ten minutes, I tell you! For what was there, after all, to discuss? A man was being enslaved. We had to free him. Period. Fifteen minutes after my friend and I arrived, we were all out on the street, moving on the courthouse, battering at its door. When word of our attack reached Faneuil Hall—where they were still talking, trying to determine what to do—the hall emptied, and they joined us in our assault. As you know, we were beaten back by the guards, and driven away, but not before that marshal's deputy was killed. No, I cannot tell you how he died. But when he did, that was all the excuse the authorities needed for bringing in eight companies of militia and the United States Marines. The sight of them on the streets makes me sick. They are arrogant! Worse, they tell me that the Government is a willing accomplice in this crime against Anthony Burns. Would that I could do *something! You know, blacks comprise almost the entire class of waiters here in Boston. We took a vow—all of us—to refuse to serve* any *of the soldiers who have taken over this city. It's a small thing, I know. But during this crisis even meager acts of resistance are better than none at all. And whose side, pray, are* you *on?"*

"You want my *opinion of this affair? Mine? Do you know who I am? For your information, I am a mystic, a Transcendentalist, and a natural philosopher. I have been imprisoned by this Government for refusing to pay my poll tax, the reason being that I knew it was applied to the support of slavery. I have spoken with John Brown. I am, you should know, an advocate of civil disobedience. And you still want to quote me? Very well. Write this down, young man:* My thoughts are murder to the State today. *Little by little, week by week, I have watched the American government lose its integrity. Now it endeavors to make all of us agents of injustice. One can no longer be associated with it except in disgrace. Look around you right now. D'you see that detachment of lancers marching in front of Anthony Burns? They are unthinking* machines *of the State, serving it with their bodies, and they command no more respect from me than men of straw or a lump of dirt. And over there, in the courthouse, we have legislators, politicians, and lawyers who serve the State with their heads, though they rarely make any moral distinctions, and thus are as likely to serve the Devil, without intending it, as God. All of them tools of the State, not men, and the slave Government that is their master has on this day forced them to commit a crime against humanity. My advice to all Anthony Burns's friends who call themselves abolitionists is that they should effectually withdraw their support, both in person and property, from the Government of first*

Massachusetts, then the United States. They must see that the only social obligation any of us have is to do at any time what we know is right. They must be willing to go to prison for their beliefs, just as Anthony Burns is now being led to a lifelong prison sentence; they must, I am saying, get it into their heads, once and for all, that any State that can do to a man what we have done today must be torn down, destroyed, and let the Devil take the hindmost. Then, when this stain on our souls has been scrubbed away through Revolution, perhaps men and women of God, blacks and whites, can rebuild America with wood less crooked than that used by the Founders. Did you get all that? Even the part about Government officials? Good. Now please excuse me. I must return to my room for a time to write down all the details I can remember of this monstrous day. One of the most important things we can do, young man, is never forget . . ."

> It seems strange to me now . . . why the people of the South were so determined in bringing their slaves into Kansas, knowing as they must have, the fight that was going on to keep them out. But they persisted.
>
> —Annie Gilkeson

The next great confrontation over slavery, in 1854, was in the heartland. Conflicting definitions of freedom collided and led to a battle that compromised the country's heart and its future.

Ironically, the crisis began with a plan to bring the country together—a railroad connecting the East to California. Since savvy Illinois senator Stephen A. Douglas wanted that transcontinental railroad to slice through Chicago, he introduced a bill to divide the Great Plains into two territories, Kansas and Nebraska, bringing American law and government to the railroad's proposed right-of-way and encouraging settlement on land that had once been promised to the Indian tribes "as long as grass shall grow and water run." The bill also provided that the residents of Kansas and Nebraska would vote on whether their respective territories would be slave or free. The bill went through three versions, intense debate, and only narrowly passed in the House.

Its passage effectively repealed the Missouri Compromise, which for three decades had maintained a tenuous balance of political power between North and South. As part of the 1820 edict, Congress had drawn a line across the continent limiting the expansion of slavery.

The Kansas-Nebraska Act passed in 1854. Frederick Douglass called it a breach of honor. The *New York Times* declared that "the repeal of the Missouri Compromise has done more than any other event of the last ten years to strengthen anti-slavery sentiment." Nebraska was so far north there was no doubt it would vote for free soil. But Kansas, which bordered the slave state of Missouri, was up for grabs.

That summer, the opposing forces began converging on Kansas. What started out as an election to determine whether the territory would be slave or free turned into a bloody rehearsal for civil war.

New York senator William H. Seward drew an unmistakable line in the sand: "Come on, then, gentlemen of the Slave States; since there is no escaping your challenge, I accept it in behalf of the cause of freedom. We will engage in competition for the virgin soil of Kansas, and God give the victory to the side that is stronger in numbers as it is in right."

In South Carolina and other states, visiting Englishman T. H. Gladstone "witnessed extraordinary meetings at which addresses of incredible violence were delivered on the necessity of 'forcing slavery into Kansas,' and 'driving back at the point of the bayonet the nigger-stealing scum poured down by northern fanatics.'"

White northerners braced for battle. Most of them heading for Kansas opposed the institution of slavery, but that didn't mean they sided with abolitionists. They were Free-Soilers, advocating free states for free white men. These workers were intrigued by the possibility of moving west and owning their own land, their own businesses. And they wanted access to all of the land—unencumbered by slaves and slave owners, and without competition from free blacks.

"Opposing slavery and hating its victims has become a very common form of Abolitionism," wrote Frederick Douglass. "They meet colored men on their thresholds, and say, 'we care not how temperate and industrious you may be . . . we want none of you here.' This is a government of white men."

That's exactly what many of the Free-Soilers wanted. Most states denied African Americans the right to vote, to raise their voices in a courtroom, to enter into a binding contract. So white Kansas settlers adopted two widely variant points of view. Some favored slavery, some advocated free soil. But most were in agreement on one thing—free blacks had no place in either of the territories.

One of the most powerful organizations set up by slavery's opponents was the New England Emigrant Aid Company, which counted among its members many influential northerners. A charter for the group was prepared by Eli Thayer, a representative in the Massachusetts legislature. His intention? To flood Kansas with freemen. And to make money in the process.

A New England Emigrant Aid Company committee which suggested that twenty thousand Massachusetts residents a year be transported to Kansas also lured stockholders with the promise of "an investment which promises large returns at no distant day." Investors were encouraged to buy land and sell it at a profit. Circulars were distributed touting the benefits of the region, including the quality of the soil, absence of marshes and swamps, hefty supplies of timber, attractive varieties of produce, and the fact that lots would be donated to new settlers. By the summer of 1854, the first of Thayer's settlers founded the town of Lawrence, Kansas.

Edward Bridgeman, a native of Northampton, Massachusetts, was twenty-two years old in 1856 when he set out for Kansas. Once he arrived, he became embroiled in the heated battle for the state's soul, which he described in letters to his cousin Sidney:

> *In some small towns parties of Alabamians, Georgians and Missourians are continually plundering clothes yards, horses and cattle and anything they can lay hold of. Last Thursday, news came from [the town of] Lawrence that she was in the hands of Ruffians and that they had demolished the free State Hotel, and destroyed the two printing presses.*

Lawrence, Kansas, had been a free-soil town. As an immigrant to Kansas and a self-appointed advocate of the slaves, John Brown declared himself its avenger. But, as Frederick Douglass wrote, the religiously fervent Brown "never lost sight of what he called his greater work—the liberation of all the slaves in the United States."

Brown, a fifty-six-year-old rebel with an uncompromising hatred of slavery, believed he'd been sanctioned by God to break the back of the institution. Having abandoned an earlier hostility to violence, Douglass and other abolitionists helped Brown amass revolvers, rifles, and military broadswords for what the rebel called his "particular business."

Brown had written to Douglass of "malignant spirits" and "fiends cloaked in human form" who had made laws like the Kansas-Nebraska Act. No one—judges, police, or the preachers who defended the law—escaped his ire.

When the news came that Lawrence was being destroyed, Brown and his sons were enraged. The old man vowed to strike back against proslavery settlers, admitting that it would involve "some killing."

On May 24, 1856, Brown and his allies killed five members of a proslavery faction on the Pottawatomie Creek.

"[W]e heard that five men had been killed by Free State men," Edward Bridgeman wrote his cousin.

> *The men were butchered—ears cut off and the bodies thrown into the river. The murdered men (Proslavery) had thrown out threats and insults, yet the act was barbarous and inhuman whoever committed by. . . . The War seems to have commenced in real earnest.*
>
> *Since yesterday I have learned that those men who committed those murders were a party of Browns. . . .*

The attacks and counterattacks in Lawrence and along the Pottawatomie sparked "Bleeding Kansas"—bitter, open warfare, a guerrilla battle on the plains that was strikingly similar to the Civil War to come. More than fifty men lost their lives in the conflict before Kansas voted itself free. White men squared off with other white men, each convinced that their vision of the future was the right one. But men like John Brown who truly believed that slavery was morally wrong were rare; neither the proslavery nor free-soil visions held a place for free African Americans.

"The horrors wrought by his iron hand cannot be contemplated without a shudder," said Frederick Douglass, "but it is the shudder which one feels at the execution of a murderer. . . . To call out a murderer at midnight, and without a note of warning, judge or jury, run him through with a sword is a terrible remedy for a terrible malady."

William Lloyd Garrison seized the opportunity to comment on the changing climate in the country:

> [T]he sympathy and admiration now so widely felt for [Brown] prove how marvelous has been the change affected in public opinion during the thirty years of moral agitation—a change so great indeed, that whereas, ten years since, there were thousands who could not endure my lightest word of rebuke of the South, they can now

> easily swallow John Brown whole and his rifle into the bargain. In firing his gun, he has merely told us what time of day it is. It is high noon, thank God!

And there was yet another showdown.

Abolitionists like Garrison held no illusions about the Constitution being anything other than a proslavery document. For some seventy years, it bound North and South together and recognized slavery as part of the American fabric without ever using the word.

"There is much declamation about the sacredness of the compact which was formed between the free and slave states on the adoption of the Constitution," said Garrison. "Yes, we recognize the compact, but with feelings of shame and indignation; and it will be held in everlasting infamy by the friends of justice and humanity throughout the world."

Impatient with the lack of progress under Garrison's leadership, black activists began promoting the Constitution as a "glorious liberty document." Douglass declared:

> [T]he constitution of the United States—inaugurated to "form a more perfect union, establish justice . . . promote the general welfare and secure the blessings of liberty"—could not well have been designed at the same time to maintain and perpetuate a system of rapine and murder like slavery; especially as not one word can be found in the constitution to authorize such a belief.

The chief reason Douglass and other black abolitionists opposed Garrison's interpretation of the Constitution was that if Garrison was right and the Constitution was proslavery, then he was also right in his call for northern states to leave the union. But, the black abolitionists reasoned, how could they leave the union on some political principle and abandon enslaved African Americans to their bondage?

It made sense for black abolitionists to interpret the Constitution for their own purposes. But what did the writers of the nation's guiding documents really intend?—and did they intend it for everyone?

In 1857, the United States Supreme Court ruled on a case that many hoped would heal the divisions and determine the future of the black race in the country. Of course, it was simply the latest in a seemingly endless line of cases, each of which supposedly held "the answer" to a question long ago rendered unanswerable.

Dred Scott, born into slavery around 1795, was the property of the Blows, a Virginia family who relocated to St. Louis in 1827. In 1833, Scott was sold to army surgeon Dr. John Emerson. The following year Dr. Emerson was transferred to Rock Island in Illinois, where slavery was forbidden by state law. Dred Scott was with him until they returned to Missouri in 1838. He had lived on free northern soil for five years. He was entitled to his freedom. There was reason to be hopeful. Seven previous cases brought on the same grounds in Missouri had freed the slave plaintiffs.

In 1852, the state's highest court ruled that Missouri law dictated Scott's status. He was, and would remain, a slave. The case might have been forgotten had it not been for the chaos in the adjoining territory of Kansas, the battle between free-soil and proslavery factions.

Dred Scott's case went all the way to the Supreme Court, guaranteeing that it would have national impact. Chief Justice for the Court was Roger B. Taney—the same Taney who had presided sixteen years earlier when the court had freed the *Amistad* mutineers. A resident of Maryland, he had many years before freed his own slaves. And as a young barrister, he had argued that slavery was a blot on our national character. As attorney general for Andrew Jackson, Taney had already written an opinion paper that explained why black people were not citizens of the country. Now eighty years old, Taney was about to decide the most famous slavery case in the nation's history, one that would eclipse the *Amistad* decision in its impact on white and black Americans.

His decision would profoundly affect the future of slavery and the status of black people in America. On March 6, 1857, the decision came down.

> We have come to the conclusion that the African race who came to this country, whether free or slave, were not intended to be included in the Constitution for the enjoyment of any personal rights of benefits. . . . [T]he court is of the opinion that . . . Dred Scott was not a citizen of Missouri within the meaning of the Constitution of the United States and not entitled as such to sue in its courts.

Taney went on to say that the nation's founders believed that Negroes were "beings of an inferior order, and altogether unfit to associate with the white race, either in social or political relations; and so far inferior that they had no rights which the white man was bound to respect."

By a five-to-two majority, the Supreme Court of the United States ruled that Scott, a slave, had never been a citizen. The message was clear. If you were a black in America in the mid–nineteenth century, there was absolutely no way to define your future. It was no longer a simple case of being free or enslaved—it was a man's skin color, not his place in the social hierarchy, which determined his citizenship and share in the democracy. America was a white man's country, which, Taney ruled, was exactly what the Founding Fathers intended. *No* Negro had rights.

The decision confirmed the entire experience of black people since the founding of the nation. Only now the humiliation was official. The court had also ruled that Congress had no right to ban slavery anywhere in the United States. There was no place to hide.

Wherever and whenever possible, incensed blacks flocked to meetings; some engaged in more flagrant acts of civil disobedience or made plans to emigrate. It was a time of desperation, a time when eyes were finally opened to painful realities.

Frederick Douglass clung to hope even as he grieved over the decision:

> We are now told . . . that the day is lost—all lost—and that we might as well give up the struggle. The highest authority has spoken. The voice of the Supreme Court has gone out over the troubled waves of the National Conscience. . . . [But] my hopes were never brighter than now.
>
> I have no fear that the National Conscience will be put to sleep by such an open, glaring, and scandalous tissue of lies.

But the decision directly challenged Douglass's notion that the Constitution was an antislavery document. Instead, Taney's decision rendered it firmly proslavery.

The tireless black activist was dismayed but not deterred. "The Supreme Court of the United States is not the only power in this world . . . ," he said. "Judge Taney can do many things, but he cannot perform impossibilities. He cannot bale out the ocean, annihilate the firm old earth, or pluck the silvery star of liberty from our Northern sky."

CHAPTER TWELVE

Dear husband,
I want you to buy me as soon as possible, for if you do not get me somebody else will. . . . Dear husband, you [know] not the trouble I see. . . . It is said Master is in want of monney. If so, I know not what time he may sell me, an then all my bright hops of the futer are blasted, for there has ben one bright hope to cheer me in all my troubles, that is to be with you—for if I thought I shoul never see you this earth would have no charms for me. Do all you can for me, witch I have no doubt you will.

Your affectionate wife,
Harriet Newby

HARRIET NEWBY penned that earnest plea in August of 1859. Dangerfield Newby was determined not to lose her and their six children, still enslaved in Brentville, Virginia. He had no money to buy them out of servitude. If they were sold farther south, odds were he would never see them again. Slavery would devour them.

Newby, a free man, knew he had only one choice. Only thirty miles away, that insistent and consummate abolitionist, John Brown, was assembling a small army to liberate the black people of Virginia. Newby would join Brown and other abolitionists in a raid on the federal arsenal in the sleepy hamlet of Harpers Ferry, Virginia; they would commandeer the weapons housed there and use them to spark slave uprisings throughout the state. Brown hoped that the raid—a direct blow against the federal government—would finally force the country to confront the sin of slavery.

By the summer of 1859, Brown was a fugitive, concealing his identity, hiding out near Harpers Ferry, and making no secret of his distaste for the federal government. When President James Buchanan put a $250 bounty on his head, Brown responded by placing a $2.50 bounty on James Buchanan.

Some skeptics in the black community doubted the viability of Brown's plot and thought that such a blatant slap at the face of white America would endanger the lives of black people everywhere. But it was hard to question his commitment, since he had risked his life and taken lives in the struggle for Kansas, and he continued to be active in the Underground Railroad in Ohio.

The Underground Railroad was a loosely organized network of safe houses, guides, and financiers who worked to steal slaves out of servitude in the South and take them north to freedom, setting up escape routes all the way to Canada. Many of those who worked on the Railroad risked their lives and their own freedom as they rescued fugitives from northern jails and courtrooms.

The most active operator on the Underground Railroad

was Harriet Tubman. After gaining her own freedom, she returned to the South at least nineteen times to rescue her own family and more than three hundred other captives. Her success brought her notoriety in the South, where slaveholders put a price of $40,000 on her head.

Tubman first met John Brown in 1858. She called him Captain. He called her the General.

Tubman was enthusiastic about Brown's plan to liberate slaves, even suggesting that July 4 would be a perfect day for the insurrection. She introduced him to the leaders of the black community in Chatham, Ontario, a vital terminus for the Underground Railroad and an area that had lured many dissatisfied blacks from the United States.

In Chatham in 1858, Brown sought money, weapons, and volunteers for his guerrilla war. He told potential recruits that he had studied the Roman Wars, the battlefield at Waterloo, the Haitian slave rebellion. He insisted that slaves in the South were just waiting for a spark to ignite an insurrection. Fresh from the melee in Kansas, John Brown was prepared to engage the slaveholding South in a war and set up a free state in the Appalachians—a state that would have its own constitution and state flag. His Provisional Constitution declared:

> Slavery, throughout its entire existence in the United States, is . . . an unjustifiable war of one portion of its citizens upon another . . . in utter disregard and violation of those eternal and self-evident truths set forth in our Declaration of Independence.
>
> Therefore, we . . . the oppressed people who, by a recent decision of the Supreme Court, are declared to have no rights which the white man is bound to respect . . . do . . . ordain and establish for ourselves the following Provisional Constitution.

While those who signed the Provisional Constitution approved of its ideals, many still doubted the wisdom of Brown's planned raid. There was always the chance that the old man was indeed an instrument of God, but he could have also been delusional.

Frederick Douglass, who had known Brown for more than a decade, admired the rebel as a man of action. In fact, much of the Provisional Constitution had been drawn up while Brown was a guest for a month in the winter of 1858 at the home of the black activist. So when Brown wrote to his friend to request his help, Douglass was ready. But he didn't know that Brown's strategy had changed significantly.

Brown's earlier plans involved manning forts in the Allegheny Mountains, bordering Maryland and Virginia. From these forts, the guerrillas would raid farms and plantations, taking some black fugitives into the mountains, while others stayed behind to fight. Others would be funneled north through the Underground Railroad into Canada. Brown predicted that the attacks and organized escapes would bring about the economic collapse of slavery in the region.

Brown's previous successes had been in raids on Missouri farms, small confrontations along creeks in Kansas. Harpers Ferry was a small town sixty miles from Washington—a small town where craftsmen made guns for the government. But in August of 1859, when Douglass heard the details of Brown's plan to attack the federal arsenal, he was frightened by the recklessness of the plot. This was more than a war on slaveholders—this was an attack on the U.S. government itself.

The two met in secret at an old stone quarry in Chambersburg, Pennsylvania, twenty-five miles north of Harpers Ferry.

Douglass chronicled the moment: "[H]e put his arms around me . . . and said 'Come with me, Douglass, I will defend you with my life. I want you for a special purpose. When I strike the bees will begin to swarm and I shall want you to help hive them.'"

Douglass warned Brown that the direct attack on the government was bound to fail:

> I told him, and these were my words, that he was going into a perfect steel trap and that once in he would never get out alive. . . .
>
> [W]e spent the most of Saturday and a part of Sunday in this debate—Brown for Harpers Ferry, and I against it—he for striking a blow which should instantly rouse the country, and I for the policy of gradually drawing off the slaves to the mountains, as at first suggested and proposed by him.

But Brown was possessed, believing himself the ordained savior of thousands. He had no patience for Douglass's brand of truth. And ill health eventually forced Harriet Tubman to miss the insurrection, although she may also have seen the wisdom in leaving Brown to his own schemes. Brown had wanted a notable presence from the black community, but time was running out.

The meeting in Chambersburg was the last time Brown and Douglass would see each other.

There were those who readily signed on for John Brown's drastic measure. Printer Osborne Anderson from Chatham, Canada. Aaron Stevens, said to have an explosive temper. Quaker brothers Barclay and Edwin Coppoc. Lewis Leary, whose Irish grandfather and free black great-great-grandfather had fought against the British in the Revolutionary War. Leary's college-educated nephew John A. Copeland Jr., who had already risked his life to rescue a runaway slave from Kentucky bounty hunters. The Thompson brothers, William and Dauphin. Dangerfield Newby, whose wife was about to be sold to a slave buyer from Louisiana, and his six children scattered.

Shields Green, introduced to Brown by Frederick Douglass, faced a difficult choice. Would he rejoin Douglass in Rochester or join Brown's spirited, if lonely, army? "I asked Green what he had decided to do," said Douglass, "and was surprised by his coolly saying in his broken way, 'I b'leve I'll go wid de ole man.'"

Eventually, Brown settled for an army of twenty-two people—seventeen white, five black. Among them were three of his sons—Owen, Oliver, and Watson, all veterans of the melee in Kansas.

Osborne Anderson survived to document the fateful day:

> On Sunday morning, October 16th, Captain Brown arose earlier than usual, and called his men down to worship. He read a chapter from the Bible . . . and then offered up a fervent prayer to God to assist in the liberation of the bondsmen in that slaveholding land. Every man there assembled seemed to respond from the depths of his soul.

Before setting out to the Ferry, according to Anderson, Brown said:

> "And now, gentlemen, let me impress this one thing upon your minds. You all know how dear life is to you, and how dear your life is to your friends. And in remembering that, consider that the lives of others are as

> dear to them as yours are to you. Do not, therefore, take the life of any one, if you can possibly avoid it; but if it is necessary to take life in order to save your own, then make sure work of it. . . ."
>
> At eight o'clock on Sunday evening, Captain Brown said, "Men, get your arms; we will proceed to the Ferry." The company marched along as solemnly as a funeral procession, till we got to the bridge, when everything was ready for the taking of the town.

At first, the guerrillas moved with the precision of a military unit. In the woods, two men cut the telegraph lines. Another group crossed the bridge and captured the town's night watchman. Dangerfield Newby guarded Shenandoah Bridge. In town, the old man captured the armory and led his rebels up the street to take the Hall's Rifle Works. The little army soon held all of their prime military targets, including weapons and munitions belonging to the federal government that were worth between $1 million and $2 million. Brown's men barricaded the railroad bridge and stopped the express train coming in from Wheeling. Now, with no functioning telegraph office in Harpers Ferry, there was no way word of the revolt could pass down the line.

At first, Brown's strategy seemed to work. No shots were fired during the taking of the musket factory, the arsenal, and the rifle works. A squad dispatched pikes to neighboring plantations for men willing to join the battle. But Brown, perhaps overwhelmed at the thought of his real or imagined destiny, did not move through the town fast enough. He was convinced that once slaves heard of the insurrection they would begin pouring in from Maryland and Virginia.

When the night watchman's relief came for the beginning of his shift, Brown's men opened fire and wounded him. The train engineer headed down the track, and the rebels fired on the train. The station's baggage master—a free black man named Hayward Shepard—appeared on the railroad trestle and, in the dark, he was shot and killed.

The Lutheran church began tolling the alarm. Riders galloped to other villages shouting, "Insurrection at Harpers Ferry!" For some unknown reason, Brown allowed the detained train to leave, effectively spreading news of the rebellion to Monacacy and Frederick, Maryland. Telegraph operators transmitted the alarm to Baltimore, and from there to Richmond and Washington. Since Nat Turner's bloody rebellion, southerners had feared this kind of uprising. Only now, blacks were being armed and abetted by whites from the North.

"[A]s the sun arose the panic spread like wild-fire," said Osborne Anderson. "Men, women and children could be seen leaving their homes in every direction . . . impelled by a sudden fear. . . . The judgment-day could not have presented more terror in its awful and certain prospective punishment."

By eleven the next morning, a full-scale war was raging. Farmers and militiamen had flooded the town, pinning down Brown's men at the rifle works and at the fire-engine house. Rebels trapped at outposts away from the security of the firehouse were stalked, shot down, and mutilated.

"Of the men shot on the rocks, when Kagi's party were compelled to take to the river," said Osborne Anderson, "some were slaves, and they suffered death before they would desert their companions, and their bodies fell into the waves beneath."

Anderson also described a particularly wrenching moment: "Dangerfield Newby, one of our colored men, was shot through the head by a person who took aim at him from a brick store window, on the opposite side of the street, and who was there for purpose of firing upon us. . . . Newby was shot twice; at the first fire, he fell on his side and returned it; as he lay, a second shot was fired, and the ball entered his head."

When Newby's body was discovered, his wife Harriet's love letters were nestled in his pocket. One of the townspeople had cut off his ears for a souvenir.

In an attempt to end the standoff, Brown sent two men out with a flag of truce. They were gunned down by the mob. Thirty-six hours after John Brown and his solemn, fiercely dedicated allies marched on the town, the raid was over.

President Buchanan—acting on reports that seven hundred whites and Negroes had invaded Harpers Ferry—ordered in three artillery companies and some ninety U.S. Marines under the command of Brevet Colonel Robert E. Lee. The forces rushed the firehouse, where at least ten of Brown's twenty-two men were dead or dying. The dead included the ringleader's sons Oliver and Watson.

John Brown, Shields Green, and John Copeland were captured, and would have their day in court.

Osborne Anderson blamed Brown for the failed coup. "It was no part of the original plan to hold on to the Ferry, or to parley with prisoners," he said. "But by so doing, time was afforded to carry the news of its capture . . . and forces were thrown into the place, which surrounded us."

It was, as Douglass had warned, a "perfect steel trap." Brown's decision to delay and not flee the arsenal was his downfall. Some felt that he could have succeeded, but instead he saw the raid as a crusade, a route to martyrdom.

Brown's bold fight for black freedom frightened and angered southern slaveholders. They were now certain that a northern conspiracy existed. It shocked whites that white men were willing to die to end racial slavery. White involvement made Harpers Ferry disturbingly different from uprisings led by Gabriel, Denmark Vesey, and Nat Turner.

In his address to the Virginia court on November 2, 1859, John Brown attempted to conceal the truth of his plan. Perhaps it was to protect his coconspirators:

> I never did intend murder, or treason or the destruction of property, or to excite or incite slaves to rebellion, or to make insurrection . . . [but] had I so interfered in behalf of the rich . . . every man in this court would have deemed it an act worthy of reward rather than punishment.

On December 2, John Brown rode his coffin to the gallows. Bells pealed in tribute in many northern cities, and Brown—the restless white man with the piercing eyes and a score to settle—was extolled as a martyr in black communities. Said antislavery activist Frances Ellen Watkins:

> In the name of the young girl sold from the warm clasp of a mother's arms . . . in the name of the slave mother, her heart rocked to and fro by the agony of her mournful separations—I thank you. . . . You have rocked the bloody Bastile; and I hope that from your sad fate great good may arise to the cause of freedom.

John Copeland could not be charged with treason as the white rebels were since, technically, he was not a citizen. But that didn't mean he couldn't die in the name of freedom. He and Shields Green were convicted of murder and insurrection and sentenced to death. Before he died, Johnny Copeland wanted everyone to know what he was dying for.

"My fate, so far as man can seal it, is sealed," he wrote his family,

> *but let not this fact occasion you any misery; for remember the cause in which I was engaged,* remember it was a holy cause, *one in which men in every way better than I am have suffered & died. Remember that if I must die, I die in trying to liberate a few of my poor and oppressed people from a condition of servitude against which God in his word has hurled his most bitter denunciations, a cause in which men, who though removed from its direct injurious effects by the color of their faces have already lost their lives, and more yet must meet the fate which man has decided I must meet.*
>
> *Goodbye Mother & Father, Goodbye brothers and sisters, and by the assistance of God, meet me in heaven.*

That same year, Pierce Butler, the dashing young man who wanted for nothing, had lost practically everything. The Butler family mansion was gone, sold to pacify creditors. His enterprising wife, Fanny Kemble, was gone after a scandalous, very public divorce in 1848. Butler remained an avid market speculator; he also gambled voraciously, reportedly losing as much as $25,000 on a single hand of cards. Even before the financial panic of 1857, he was deeply in debt, and his estate in the hands of trustees. After the market crash, it was rumored that he had run through an inherited fortune of some $700,000 and was looking for a way to save his own skin.

After liquidating Butler's properties in Philadelphia, trustees for the Butler estate traveled to Georgia to assess the family's human property.

"Allotment A" was Pierce Butler's share of the slaves at Butler Island and St. Simons. "Allotment A" contained 429 living, breathing men, women, and children. Their total market value was estimated to be more than $260,000.

Throughout Georgia and the rest of the South, there was talk of dissolving the union. Some proponents of slavery, fearing that the institution would be rejected in the West, touted the invasion and annexation of Cuba as a solution. So high was the demand for captive labor, there was even talk of once again legalizing the importation of slaves from Africa.

Some slaveholders were growing cocky.

In 1857, the same year Dred Scott discovered that, for him, at least, there was no real meaning to the term *free soil,* America was suffering from a case of industrial and financial overconfidence. Overzealous building of railroads and overspeculation of lands to the west brought on a financial panic which caused more than five thousand businesses to fail.

A master in need of money was a dangerous master to have. Considering their master's dire financial straits, the enslaved residents of Butler Island may have felt a price weighing on their heads. Or perhaps they believed that a slave community such as theirs—where the roots of family ran long and deep—would go on forever.

If that was the hope they clung to, Pierce Butler proved them wrong.

Ads for the auction appeared:

> FOR SALE—LONG COTTON AND RICE NEGROES . . . A NUMBER OF GOOD MECHANICS AND SERVANTS, WILL BE SOLD ON 2ND AND 3RD OF MARCH NEXT . . .

Immediately, the unprecedented event was the talk of the region. Pierce Butler's personal and financial life was publicly dissected and criticized, and armchair financiers speculated as to the amount of money the sale of the slaves would bring.

In February, 429 men, women, and children were loaded onto railroad cars and carried north to Savannah's Ten Broeck racetrack. Husbands and wives. Sisters and brothers. Elderly parents. Infants, some only days old. The destruction of community, the tearing apart of families was legal, socially acceptable, justified in churches and the halls of government.

The last of the fated crew reached the auction point five days before the sale. Once arrived, they were housed in sheds that usually held horses and the carriages of moneyed track patrons. Mr. Joseph Bryan—Negro broker, auctioneer, and manager of the sale—was charged with the slaves' well-being, which meant keeping them in salable condition until March 2.

For days before the sale, slave speculators from all across the South filled Savannah's hotels and rooming houses, sniffing the air for a good deal. Bryan's office was packed with the keenly curious and those who wondered if their securities would be acceptable when the time came to buy. Mortimer Neal Thomson, who disguised himself as a slave speculator to write an exhaustive chronicle of the sale for the *New York Tribune,* wrote: "The buyers were generally of a rough breed, slangy, profane and bearish, being for the most part from the back river and swamp plantations, where the elegancies of polite life are not, perhaps, developed to their fullest extent."

Thomson overheard a group of potential buyers "conversing on the fruitful subject of managing refractory 'niggers.'" One particularly brutish man had this to say:

> "You may say what you like about managing niggers; I'm a driver myself, and I've had some experience, and I ought to know. You can manage ordinary niggers by

> lickin' 'em, and givin' 'em a taste of the hot iron once in awhile when they're extra ugly; but if a nigger really sets himself up against me, I can't never have any patience with him. I just get my pistol and shoot him right down; and that's the best way."

Some of the slaves could be sold into that version of hell. And many eyes were on Pierce Butler, the man who set the tragedy in motion.

Sidney George Fisher, socialite, Philadelphia associate, and faithful chronicler of all things Butler, wrote: "Pierce Butler has gone to Georgia to be present at the sale of his Negroes. It is highly honorable to him that he did all he could to prevent the sale, offering to make any personal sacrifice to avoid it."

Fisher, who also noted that Butler would walk away with a fortune of $200,000 to $300,000 and keep the family's country retreat, Butler Place, once the auction was completed, then turned his pen to the plight of the slaves. What he wrote mirrored the viewpoint of many of those who knew and respected Pierce Butler:

> Families will not be separated, that is to say, husbands & wives, parents & young children. But brothers & sisters of mature age, parents & children of mature age, all other relations & the ties of home & long association will be violently severed. It will be a hard thing for Butler to witness and it is a monstrous thing to do.
>
> Yet it is done every day in the South. It is among the many frightful consequences of slavery and contradicts our civilization, our Christianity, our Republicanism. Can such a system endure, is it consistent with humanity, with moral progress? These are difficult questions,

> and still more difficult is it to say, what can be done? The Negroes of the South must be slaves or the South will be Africanized. Slavery is better for them and for us than such a result.

The story eventually written by Mortimer Thomson—complete with drama, pathos, and twists of fate that couldn't have been predicted—answered Fisher's larger, more insistent question: "Is such a system consistent with humanity, with moral progress?"

In all of the word pictures painted by the observant Thomson, the answer was no.

> Who can tell how closely intertwined are a band of four hundred persons, living isolated from all the world besides? Do they not naturally become one great family, each man a brother unto each?
>
> It is true they were sold "in families"; but let us see: a man and his wife were called a "family," their parents and kindred were not taken into account; the man and wife might be sold to the pine woods of North Carolina, their brothers and sisters be scattered through the cotton fields of Alabama and the rice swamps of Louisiana, while the parents might be left on the old plantation to wear out their weary lives in heavy grief, and lay their heads in far-off graves, over which their children might never weep.

On the first morning of the sale, Pierce Butler appeared among his slaves. He took great care to speak with each of them, and the slaves responded respectfully, even affectionately, despite the fact that Butler was directly responsible for their dire predicament:

> The men obsequiously pulled off their hats and made that indescribable sliding hitch with the foot which passes with a negro for a bow; and the women each dropped the quick curtsy, which they seldom vouchsafe to any other than their legitimate master and mistress. Occasionally, to a very old or favorite servant, Mr. Butler would extend his gloved hand, which mark of condescension was instantly hailed with grins of delight from all the sable witnesses.

Pierce Butler, for all his aristocratic posturing, was selling human beings to ensure a life of luxury.

During the two days of the sale, a violent rain drenched Savannah, the racecourse, the speculators, the buyers, the slaves. Regional attendance at the auction site was lower than expected, but those who had traveled long distances to buy were there in force.

> The wind howled outside and through the open side of the building, the driving rain came pouring in; the bar downstairs ceased for a short time its brisk trade; the buyers lit fresh cigars, got ready their catalogues and pencils, and the first lot of human chattels was led upon the stand, not by a white man, but by a sleek mulatto, himself a slave, and who seems to regard the selling of his brethren, in which he so glibly assists, as a capital joke.

The slaves were led into the racecourse's grandstand, a room measuring one hundred feet long by twenty feet wide. The miserable weather and cramped conditions under which they'd been housed had taken a toll. They looked exhausted, moved listlessly. Clutching their bits of baggage, they stood before the probing eyes of potential masters, waiting to be called upon the block and sold to the highest bidder.

Buyers were to bid one price for an entire "family" lot. Slave patriarchs sought out planters who seemed compassionate and begged them to bid for them and their families. A list of slave sales appeared in the auction catalog:

> 111—Anson, 49: rice—ruptured, one eye.
> 112—Violet, 55; rice hand.
> Sold for $250 each.

Or $500 for the pair.

> 113—Allen Jeffrey, 46: rice hand and sawyer in steam mill.
> 114—Sikey, 43; rice hand.
> 115—Watty, 5; infirm legs.
> Sold for $520 each.

$1,560 for a couple and their child.

> 345—Dorcas, 17, prime woman.
> 346—Joe, 3 months.
> Sold for $1,200 each.

A new young mother and her baby. $2,400.

> On the faces of all was an expression of heavy grief; some appeared to be resigned to the hard stroke of Fortune that had torn them from their homes, and were sadly trying to make the best of it; some sat brooding moodily over their sorrows, their chins resting on their hands, their eyes staring vacantly, and their bodies rocking to and fro, with a restless motion that was never stilled; few wept, the place was too public and the driv-

ers too near, though some occasionally turned aside to give way to a few quiet tears.

All the while it rained. For generations, those two fateful days would be known as "the weeping time," a time when a community as old as the nation itself was dismantled to pay the debts of a single man. And the heavens couldn't stop crying.

On March 2 and 3, 429 men, women, and children were sold. The highest price paid for a single man was $1,750, for a single woman $1,250. The highest price paid for a family was $6,180 for Sally Walker and her five children. A few of the lot originally announced available were too sick to journey to Savannah. Headman Frank and his wife, Betty, were considered of no value—too old for sale.

When the last family to be sold stepped down from the auction block, the rain stopped. Once the sale was over, Mr. Bryan, the broker, provided champagne; corks popped and everyone toasted the good fortune of the buyers and the bad fortune of the slaves, many of whom had already departed with their new masters. The auction netted $303,850.

Leaving the racetrack, Mortimer Neal Thomson spotted a crowd of blacks gathered around a white man.

> That man was Pierce M. Butler, of the free City of Philadelphia, who was solacing the wounded hearts of the people he had sold from their firesides and their homes, by doling out to them small change at the rate of a dollar a head. To every negro he had sold, who presented his claim for the paltry pittance, he gave the munificent stipend of one whole dollar, in specie; he being provided with two canvas bags of 25 cent pieces, fresh from the mint, to give an additional glitter to his generosity.

It was the last chance for mothers to embrace their grown children, for brothers to look into each other's eyes, for unmarried lovers to swear undying devotion. The rain had stopped, but the weeping continued.

That night many ships and trains leaving the region held a sad and dispirited cargo—slaves torn from the only lives they had ever known. Headed not toward freedom, but toward servitude. Again.

> [T]he stars shone out as brightly as if such things had never been, the blushing fruit-trees poured their fragrance on the evening air, and the scene was as calmly sweet and quiet as if Man had never marred the glorious beauties of Earth by deeds of cruelty and wrong.

One year after John Brown encountered his destiny, Abraham Lincoln was elected president of the United States. A Republican, he was determined to keep slavery out of the new western territories. He was also opposed to the concept of full citizenship for black Americans. He promised slaveholders that their profitable institution would continue to exist, but that it would not move into the West.

South Carolina felt that Lincoln's election was a sign to leave the union, and ultimately eleven out of fifteen southern states followed suit. Lincoln took office on March 4, 1861. Five weeks later, the North and South were at war.

"Mr. Joe Walton said when he went to war, they could eat breakfast at home, go and whup the North, and be back for dinner," said ex-slave Hannah Crasson. "He went away, and it was four long years before he come back to dinner. The table was sure set a long time."

It may have begun as an attempt to save the union, but before it was over the Civil War had become an abolitionist war. More than 200,000 free black men and runaway slaves fought for the Union cause. In the end, 617,000 Americans died, more than in the two World Wars, Korea, and Vietnam combined. When this bloody conflict was over, slavery was dead.

The Constitution was amended to guarantee citizenship, and the abolitionist vision of freedom was now the same as the American vision. At last, the country was emancipated.

The wretched institution may have been dead, but it died a long, slow death. Many slaves, burdened by shackles that couldn't be seen, didn't know how to wear freedom. And they couldn't really be sure freedom was theirs. There was no one moment when the grand declaration came down. No great liberating hand swept the savanna, no booming voice jolted the slaves from their all-consuming tasks with the long-awaited words, "You are now free."

All there was was some faraway document, out of sight, out of reach, that said "Neither slavery nor involuntary servitude . . . shall exist within the United States, or any place subject to their jurisdiction."

From the first day that North and South tangled in battle, there were slaves who believed that they would automatically be free once the Yankees were in their region. But the situation was never so clearly defined. Since military maneuvers were often chaotic and subject to last-minute decisions and numerous revisions, a consistent and meaningful Union presence could not be counted on. The former slaves were on an emotional ride with devastating lows and exhilarating peaks.

Ambrose Douglass, a former slave in North Carolina, expressed the confusion of captives who were free, and then not free.

> I guess we musta celebrated 'Mancipation about twelve times in Harnett County. Every time a bunch of No'th-ern sojers would come through they would tell us we was free and we'd begin celebratin'. Before we would get through somebody else would tell us to go back to work, and we would go. Some of us wanted to jine up with the army, but didn't know who was goin' to win and didn't take no chances.

There were also slave owners who opted not to take chances. Some steadfastly ignored the Emancipation Proclamation issued by President Lincoln in 1863 while others claimed never to have heard of it. Then there were those slaves not covered in its provisions.

The first priority of a battle-weary army was not the liberating of slaves. Troops that needed to abandon one territory for another did just that, much to the dismay of blacks who had depended on them to define their status. Slaves who suspected that they were free weren't always willing to confront a master without Yankee support. "Didn't do to say you was free," remembered a former Alabama slave. "When de war was over if a nigger say he was free, dey shot him down. I didn't say anythin', but one day I run away."

Many slaves went back to work as if nothing had changed, assured by Confederate scouts that the Yankees had no authority to set them free. Freedom was dictated by individual masters, by precarious military strategizing, and by sundry interpretations of the proclamation. Only when the city of Richmond fell to the Yankees, signaling the final crumbling of the Confederacy, did many slaves consider themselves free.

Once again, former slave Ambrose Douglass decided not

to push his luck: "I was 21 when freedom finally came, and that time I didn't take no chances on 'em taking it back again. I lit out for Florida."

Still, there were those who wouldn't believe their good fortune until they heard it from their masters. They felt compelled to get the official word from those who had oppressed and exploited them, or simply to see the truth reflected in the changed behavior of their owners. One Virginia slave, working in the field when a fellow slave told her the news, ran seven miles to her mistress's house, shouting jubilee all the way. When she confronted her former owner, the white woman burst into tears. Only then was the slave certain that she was free.

Once the word of true freedom spread, the resultant celebrations rattled the heavens. When slaves heard of what they called "the surrender," they raised their voices in song and danced with an abandon they had never known. In Charleston, more than four thousand blacks, fueled by the support of ten thousand black onlookers, took over the streets. Everywhere there were black people, there was jubilation. And the black community—so long splintered into North and South, free and not free—became one.

Entwined in the rhythm of that freedom song were the perceptive musings of Olaudah Equiano, the questions of the child Broteer, and the sweet probing rhymes of Phillis Wheatley. That ode of unleashed joy celebrated the unquestioning fury of Denmark Vesey, Gabriel, Nat Turner, and John Brown. Each joyous lyric told the story of visionaries Richard Allen, David Walker, and Jarena Lee.

The newly liberated slaves sang for themselves, for their new country, and for the thousands upon thousands of

Africans ripped from the clutches of home. They sang for those who surrendered to the water during passage, for those who refused to eat, for those who died chained below the decks of a creaking ship. And they sang for the survivors, who lived through the indignities of torn families, numbing labor, and the dreaded auction block.

No song ever held so much.

Even today, every strong bloodline carries with it a song sung of Emancipation Day, a story passed down to the children of the children of the children of slaves.

Many Americans who fled during the war came back to the counties where they had been slaves. Like their former masters, they faced the difficult challenge of life in a new land. It would be more difficult than they ever imagined. Yet they began.

Dear Mrs. Cheney,

I felt I would like to write to you a line from my old home. I am sitting under the old roof twelve feet from the spot where I suffered all the crushing weight of slavery. thank God the bitter cup is drained of its last dreg. there is no more need of hiding places. . . .

I cannot tell you how I feel in this place. the change is so great I can hardly take it all in. I was born here. . . . I have hunted up all the old people, done what I could for them. . . . many of them I have known from Childhood. . . .

I never saw such a state of excitement. . . .

My love to Miss Daisy. I send her some jassmine blossoms. tell her they bear the fragrance of freedom.

Yours Truly,
H Jacobs

They began.

During all my slave life I never lost sight of freedom. It was always on my heart; it came to me like a solemn thought, and often circumstances much stimulated the desire to be free and raised great expectation of it. . . . We always called "freedom" "possum," so as to keep the white people from knowing what we were talking about. We all understood it . . . and now all my children are good scholars; one is a minister, one has charge of an academy; I have a good house of seven rooms, and eleven acres of land about it, besides a farm of 320 acres in the country.

—Ambrose Headen, 1878

They began.

We has a right to the land where we are located. For why? I tell you. Our wives, our children, our husbands, has been sold over and over again to purchase the lands we now locates upon; for that reason we have a divine right to the land. . . . And den didn't we clear the land, and raise de crops of corn, of cotton, of tobacco, of rice, of sugar, of everything?

—Freedman Bayley Wyat, Philadelphia 1867

They persevered.

We feel that there is some happiness yet in store for us; our countrymen are repenting of the great sin they have committed against us for centuries, and the good time is coming when the colored American will be recognized as one of the free institutions of the land; when it will no longer be a disgrace to own that we have African blood in our veins.

—Philip Bell, editor, *The Pacific Appeal*

They dreamed.

Sir, old things are passing away, all things are becoming new. Now a black man has rights, under this government, which every white man, here and everywhere, is bound to respect. The damnable doctrine of the detestable Taney is no longer the doctrine of the country. The Slave Power no longer rules at Washington. The slaveholders and their miserable allies are biting the dust.

—Robert Purvis, May 1863

They dreamed.

Colored Men! Fellow Citizens of America! AWAKE TO ACTION!! . . . Lay claim to every available opportunity of amassing property, increasing wealth, becoming stockholders, merchants and mechanics, that our foothold may be strengthened upon the soil of our native land. Let us, en masse, make rapid strides in literary culture and moral improvement, ever remembering that domestic happiness depends, in a great measure, upon moral impetus . . . as taxpayers, and loyal subjects of a Free Republican Government, let us contend lawfully, rightfully and perseveringly for our political rights, in common with other men, who cannot boast of greater loyalty, and whom the Painter slighted when giving out the sable hue.

We have feasted on celebrations enough to go on and do a little more work. . . . *No shouting yet! Go on and complete the victory!*

—*Christian Recorder,* March 25, 1865

They held fast to the dream.

> The chance is now given you to end in a day the bondage of centuries, and to rise in one bound from social degradation to the place of common equality with all other varieties of men . . . this is our golden opportunity. Let us accept it, and forever wipe out the dark reproaches unsparingly hurled against us by our enemies. Let us win for ourselves the gratitude of our country, and the best blessings of our posterity through all time.
>
> —Frederick Douglass

And through that time, in that time, they became us. Free. Forever searching for freedom.

NOTES

Prologue

2 "Before the white man": Samuel Sulemana Fuseini, interviewed by Orlando Bagwell and Susan Bellows, Salaga, Ghana, January 1996.

7 "The gold mines were seven": Edward Reynolds, *Stand the Storm: A History of the Atlantic Slave Trade* (London: Allison & Busby, 1985), 8.

10 "got into his possession": Elizabeth Donnan, *Documents Illustrative of the History of the Slave Trade to America*, vol. 1 (Washington, D.C.: Carnegie Institution, 1930), 46.

11 "These people are all black": Roland Sanders, *Lost Tribes and Promised Lands: The Origins of American Racism* (Boston: Little, Brown & Co., 1978), 217.

11 "Reveal to us": Mary C. Fuller, *Voyages in Print: English Travel to America, 1576–1624* (New York: Cambridge University Press, 1995), 63.

PART ONE
Chapter One

29 *"It was at last"*: Judith M. Gutman, *The Colonial Venture: An Autobiography of the American Colonies from Their Beginnings to 1763* (New York: Basic Books, 1966), 25.

29 "first to preach": Forrest Wood, *The Arrogance of Faith: Christianity and Race in America from the Colonial Era to the Twentieth Century* (New York: Alfred A. Knopf, 1990), 18.

31 "I never saw": Mary C. Fuller, *Voyage in Print: English Travel to America, 1576–1624* (New York: Cambridge University Press, 1995), 69–70. The spelling in this quote has been modernized.

31 "propagating the Christian religion": Wood, *Arrogance of Faith*, 18.

32 "The fourth day": Lyon Gardiner Tyler, ed., *Narratives of Early Virginia, 1606–1625* (New York: Barnes & Noble, 1966), 21.

32 "Nay, so great": Ibid., 295.

33 "stinking suffumigation": James I, *A Counter-Blaste to Tobacco* (Emmaus, Pa.: Miniature Books, Rodale Press, 1954), 12.

35 *"Loving Father"*: Paul Lauter, ed., *The Heath Anthology of American Literature* (Lexington, Mass.: D. C. Heath, 1990), 173–74.

36 "About the last of August": Tyler, *Narratives of Early Virginia*, 337.

38 "Antonio a Negro": Virginia M. Meyer and John Frederick Dorman, eds., *Adventurers of Purse and Person, Virginia 1607–1624/5*, 3d ed. (Alexandria, Va.: Order of First Families of Virginia, 1607–1624/5, 1987), 241.

38 "now I know myne owne ground": T. H. Breen and Stephen Innes, *"Myne Owne Ground": Race and Freedom on Virginia's Eastern Shore, 1640–1676* (New York: Oxford University Press, 1980), 6.

41 "The said three servants": "Decisions of the Virginia General Court," *Virginia Magazine of History and Biography* 5, no. 3 (1898): 236.

43 "have bine inhabitants in Virginia:" Northampton County Deeds, Wills, Etc., 1651–1654 (Circuit Court of Northampton County, Va.), file 161.

44 "written under the said": J. Douglas Deal, *Race and Class in Colonial Virginia: Indians, Englishmen, and Africans on the Eastern Shore during the Seventeenth Century* (New York: Garland Publishing, 1993), 227.

45 "terrible transformation": Peter Wood, interviewed by Orlando Bagwell, May 21, 1996.

47 "It is the first principle": Ronald Segal, *The Black Diaspora* (New York: Farrar, Straus, & Giroux, 1995), 23.

48 "All servants imported": William W. Hening, *The Statutes at Large: Being a Collection of All the Laws of Virginia, from the First Session of the Legislature in the Year 1619* (Charlottesville: Published for the Jamestown Foundation of the Commonwealth of Virginia by the University Press of Virginia, 1969).

Chapter Two

60 *"Who are we looking for"*: Ibo verse, as recited by Chinua Achebe in interview with Orlando Bagwell, May 23, 1996.

60 "I believe there are a few events in my life": Olaudah Equiano, *The Interesting Narrative and Other Writings* (New York: Penguin Books, 1995), 31.

61 "In one of the most remote": Ibid., 32.

61 "I was the youngest": Ibid., 46.

61 "When the grown people": Ibid., 46–47.

61 "One day, when": Ibid., 47.

61 "The next day proved": Ibid., 48.

62 "Concerning the trade": A. Van Dantzig, trans. and ed., *The Dutch and the Guinea Coast 1674–1742: A Collection of Documents from the General State Archive at the Hague* (Accra: Ghana Academy of Arts and Sciences, 1978), 112.

63 "There is great reason": Alexander Falconbridge, *An Account of the Slave Trade on the Coast of Africa* (New York: AMS Press, 1973), 13–14.

63 "The Igbo recognized": Edward Reynolds, *Stand the Storm: A History of the Atlantic Slave Trade* (London: Allison & Busby, 1985), 37.

64 "DECEMBER 29, 1724": Anthony Benezet, *Some Historical Account of Guinea: Its Situation, Produce, and General Disposition of Its Inhabitants* (London: J. Phillips, 1788), 99.

65 "I have found no place": Nicholas Owen, *Journal of a Slave-Dealer*, ed. Eveline Martin (London: George Routledge & Sons, 1930), 97–98, 105.

66 "We call them Oye-Eboe": Equiano, *The Interesting Narrative*, 37.

66 "At last I came": Ibid., 54.

67 "Their way of bringing": Elizabeth Donnan, *Documents Illustrative of the History of the Slave Trade to America*, vol. 2 (Washington, D.C.: Carnegie Institution, 1931), 395.

67 "The first object": Equiano, *The Interesting Narrative*, 55.

68 "can easily hold": Madeleine Burnside, *Spirits of the Passage: The Transatlantic Slave Trade in the Seventeenth Century*, ed. Rosemarie Robotham (New York: Simon & Schuster, 1997), 103.

68 "*When these slaves come to Fida*": Elizabeth Donnan, *Documents Illustrative of the History of the Slave Trade to America*, vol. 1 (Washington, D.C.: Carnegie Institution, 1930), 441–42.

69 "It matters not": Falconbridge, *An Account of the Slave Trade*, 18.

69 "They cannot believe": Isidor Paiewonsky, *Eyewitness Accounts of Slavery in the Danish West Indies: Also Graphic Tales of Other Slave Happenings on Ships and Plantations* (New York: Fordham University Press, 1989), 21.

70 "When I looked round": Equiano, *The Interesting Narrative*, 55.

70 "The men negroes": Falconbridge, *An Account of the Slave Trade*, 19–20.

72 "Some wet and blowing": Ibid., 24–25.

72 "By this means": Ibid., 28.

73 "I was soon put down": Equiano, *The Interesting Narrative*, 56.

73 "We have likewise seen": Donnan, *Documents*, vol. 1, 402–3.
74 "Often did I think": Equiano, *The Interesting Narrative*, 58.
74 "By the favour of": John Newton, *The Journal of a Slave Trader, 1750–1754, with Newton's Thoughts upon the African Slave Trade*, ed. Bernard Martin and Mark Spurrel (London: Epworth Press, 1962), 71.
75 "We stood in arms": Steven Mintz, ed., *African American Voices: The Life Cycle of Slavery* (St. James, N.Y.: Brandywine Press, 1993), 49–50.
75 "sick, beaten for being lazy": Newton, *Journal*, xiv.
75 "We are for the most part": Ibid., xiv.
75 "The three greatest blessings": Ibid., xii.
76 "Thus I was brought": Ibid., 70.
76 "I think I should have quitted": Ibid., 99.

Chapter Three

77 "A CHOICE CARGO": Slave Advertisement, May 6, 1780s, Library of Congress.
78 "SLAVES REMARKABLY HEALTHY": Broadside for Sale of Slaves, Charlestown, March 18, 1769, American Antiquarian Society, Worcester, Mass.
78 "*Permit us now to inform you*": Michael Mullin, ed., *American Negro Slavery: A Documentary History* (Columbia: University of South Carolina Press, 1976), 51.
79 "At last we came in sight": Olaudah Equiano, *The Interesting Narrative and Other Writings* (New York: Penguin Books, 1995), 59–61.
83 "[Rice] is the most unhealthy": Charles Joyner, *Remember Me: Slave Life in Coastal Georgia* (Atlanta: Georgia Humanities Council, 1989), 7.
84 "RUNAWAY . . . TWO NEGRO MEN": Peter H. Wood, *Black Majority: Negroes in Colonial South Carolina from 1670 through the Stono Rebellion* (New York: W. W. Norton & Co., 1975), 243.
84 "HERCULES": Ibid., 247.
84 "TOM": Ibid., 247.

85 "All Negroes, Mollatoes and Indians": Marion E. Sirmans, *Colonial South Carolina: A Political History, 1663–1763* (Chapel Hill: Published for the Institute of Early American History at Williamsburg, Va., by the University of North Carolina Press, 1966), 65.

86 "I had seen a black woman slave": Equiano, *The Interesting Narrative*, 62–63.

87 "8 FEBRUARY 1709": Mullin, *American Negro Slavery*, 99–100.

88 "Their numbers increase": Wood, *Black Majority*, 224.

90 "A poor slavewoman": Francis Le Jau, *The Carolina Chronicle of Dr. Francis Le Jay, 1706–1717*, ed. Frank J. Klingberg (Berkeley: University of California Press, 1956), 55.

90 "Mr. D. told me": Equiano, *The Interesting Narrative*, 104–5.

92 "I have had of late": Le Jau, *Carolina Chronicle*, 108.

93 "secret poisonings": Vincent Harding, *There Is a River: The Black Struggle for Freedom in America* (New York: Harcourt Brace Jovanovich, 1992), 33.

93 "The Spanish are receiving": Wood, *Black Majority*, 304–5.

94 "It is shocking to human nature": *The Darien Petition against Introducing Negroe Slaves into the Province of Georgia, 1738–1739* (Darien, Ga.: Ashantilly Press, 1984).

96 "They increased every Minute": Mullin, *American Negro Slavery*, 85.

106 "The Negroes were soon routed": Ibid., 85–86.

110 *"[Sir] . . . the horrible executions"*: T. Wood Clarke, "The Negro Plot of 1741," *On New York History*, April, 1944, 179–80.

112 "Is not the slave trade": Equiano, *The Interesting Narrative*, 110–11.

PART TWO
Chapter Four

129 *"I remember this place"*: *Five Black Lives: The Autobiographies of Venture Smith, James Mars, William Grimes, the Reverend G. W. Offley, and James L. Smith* (Middletown, Conn.: Wesleyan University Press, 1971), 4–5.

130 "The army of the enemy": Ibid., 6–8.
130 "on account of him": *Five Black Lives,* 10.
131 "It is a great deal better": Bernard Bailyn, *Voyagers to the West: A Passage in the Peopling of America on the Eve of the Revolution* (New York: Alfred A. Knopf, 1986), 172.
131 "was pretty much employed": *Five Black Lives,* 12.
131 "came up to me": Ibid., 12.
132 "I, Augustine Washington": Worthington Chauncy Ford, ed., *The Wills of George Washington and his Immediate Ancestors* (Brooklyn, N.Y.: Historical Printing Club, 1891), 41–52.
133 "defective education": James T. Flexner, *George Washington: The Forge of Experience, 1732–1735* (Boston: Little, Brown & Co., 1962), 24.
133 *"I will take six"*: George Washington, *The Writings of George Washington from the Original Manuscript Sources,* 1745–1799, ed. John C. Fitzpatrick, vol. 29 (Washington D.C.: United States Government Printing Office, 1931–44), 56.
134 "promised not to betray": *Five Black Lives,* 13.
136 "When I was most sorely oppressed": Harriet Jacobs, *Incidents in the Life of a Slave Girl: Written by Herself,* ed. Jean Fagan Yellin (Cambridge, Mass.: Harvard University Press, 1987), 62.
136 "When I entered the house": *Five Black Lives,* 14.
136 "When my master returned": Ibid., 15.
137 "I continued to wear": Ibid., 16.
138 "I left Colonel Smith": Ibid., 18–19.
139 "I lived a bad life": David George, "An Account of the Life of David George," in *The Baptist Annual Register: Including Sketches of the State of Religion among Different Denominations of Good Men at Home and Abroad,* vol. 1, ed. John Rippon (London: 1790/1793), 473–84.
140 "Our master's name was Chapel": Ibid.
140 "[A] man of my own color": Ibid.
140 "I went to a fwamp": Ibid.
141 "The custom of the country": Allan Kulikoff, *Tobacco and Slaves: The Development of Southern Cultures in the Chesapeake,*

1680–1800 (Chapel Hill: Published for the Institute of Early American History and Culture, Williamsburg, Va., by University of North Carolina Press, 1986), 382.

142 "In four years": *Five Black Lives*, 18

142 "shunned all kind of luxuries": Ibid., 20.

143 *"Should you, my lord"*: William H. Robinson, ed. *Critical Essays on Phillis Wheatley* (Boston: G. K. Hall, 1982), 31.

143 "Aunt Wheatley was in want": William H. Robinson, *Phillis Wheatley in the Black American Beginnings* (Detroit: Broadside Press, 1975), 13.

144 "singular genius": Ibid., 24.

144 *"I have lately met"*: Ibid., 18.

152 "Richard Nisbet . . . Bernard Romans": Ibid., 25.

152 "Religion, indeed, has produced a Phillis Wheatley": Sidney Kaplan and Emma Nogrady Kaplan, *The Black Presence in the Era of the American Revolution*, rev. ed. (Amherst, Mass.: University of Massachusetts Press, 1989), 189.

153 "Petitions were sent to the Massachusetts Colonial Assembly": "Slave Petitions to Massachusetts General Court," January 6, 1773, and "Petitions of Africans Living in Boston," April 20, 1773, in *A Documentary History of the Negro People in the United States*, ed. Herbert Aptheker (New York: Citadel Press, 1990), 5–9.

Chapter Five

156 "[N]ow will these Americans": Edmund S. Morgan and Helen M. Morgan, *The Stamp Act Crisis: Prologue to Revolution* (Chapel Hill, N.C.: Published for the Institute of Early American History and Culture at Williamsburg, Va., by the University of North Carolina Press, 1953), 67.

157 "I speak it with grief": Bernard Bailyn, *The Ideological Origins of the American Revolution* (Cambridge, Mass.: Belknap Press of Harvard University Press, 1967), 233.

157 "[We are] the most abject sort of slaves": Ibid., 233.

157 "What have the unhappy Africans": Ibid., 243.
157 "[Y]e trifling patriots": Ibid., 240.
158 "a motley rabble": Sidney Kaplan and Emma Nogrady Kaplan, *The Black Presence in the Era of the American Revolution*, rev. ed. (Amherst, Mass.: University of Massachusetts Press, 1989), 8.
160 "They dare not fire": Ibid., 7.
160 "killed on the spot": Ibid., 8.
160 "On that night": Lerone Bennett, *Before the Mayflower: A History of the Negro in America, 1619–1964,* rev. ed. (Baltimore: Penguin Books, 1970), 61.
160 "Who set the example": Ibid., 19.
161 "The die is cast": John Hope Franklin and Alfred A. Moss Jr., *From Slavery to Freedom,* 7th ed. (New York: McGraw-Hill, 1994), 70.
161 "[I]n every human Breast": Deirdre Mullane, ed., *Crossing the Danger Water: Four Hundred Years of African-American Writing* (New York: Anchor Books, 1993), 46.
162 "Among the foremost of the leaders": Kaplan, *Black Presence,* 21.
163 "And I do hereby further declare": Lord Dunmore's Proclamation, Library of Virginia, Richmond, Virginia.
163 "Negroes are double": Peter H. Wood, "Impatient of Oppression: Black Freedom Struggle on the Eve of White Independence," *Southern Exposure* 12, no. 6 (November/December, 1984): 12.
164 "If that man is not crushed": Ibid., 15.
164 "Hell itself": Margaret Wheeler Willard, ed., *Letters on the American Revolution,* 1774–1776 (Boston: Houghton Mifflin Co., 1925), 231–34.
165 "Stay you d——d white bitch": *Virginia Gazette,* December 29, 1775, in Benjamin Quarles, *The Negro in the American Revolution* (New York: W. W. Norton & Co., 1961), 31.
165 "melancholy account": John Adams, *The Works of John Adams:*

Second President of the United States, With a Life of the Author, Notes, and Illustrations by His Grandson Charles Francis Adams (Boston: Little, Brown & Co., 1850), 428.

166 "It is an awful business": Wood, "Impatient of Oppression," 16.

167 "had not a fever crept": Quarles, *The Negro in the American Revolution*, 30.

169 "He has waged cruel war": Willard Sterne Randall, *Thomas Jefferson: A Life* (New York: HarperPerennial, 1994), 276–78.

169 "As all are of one species": Ruth Bogin, "Liberty Further Extended: A 1776 Antislavery Manuscript by Lemuel Haynes," *The William and Mary Quarterly*, 3d ser., 40 (January 1983): 92.

177 "I wish most sincerely there was not a slave": Kaplan, *Black Presence*, 15.

178 "every NEGROE who shall desert": Sylvia Frey, *Water from the Rock: Black Resistance in a Revolutionary Age* (Princeton, N.J.: Princeton University Press, 1991), 113.

179 "a very bad man": Boston King, "Memoirs of the Life of Boston King, a Black Preacher, Written by Himself, During His Residence at Kingswood-School," *The (Arminian) Methodist Magazine* (London) 21 (March, April, May, June 1798): 268.

179 "They received me readily": Ibid., 107.

180 "expected every moment to fall": Ibid., 109.

180 "the happiness of liberty": Ibid., 107.

Chapter Six

181 *"Three pounds reward"*: Graham Russell Hodges and Alan Edward Brown, eds., *"Pretends to Be Free": Runaway Slave Advertisements from Colonial and Revolutionary New York and New Jersey* (New York: Garland Publishing, Inc., 1994), 185.

182 "about fifty negroes": *New Jersey Journal*, July 15, 1797, *Documents Relating to the Revolutionary History of the State of New Jersey*, vol. 3 (Trenton: John L. Murphy Publishing Co., 1901–1917), 504.

184 "Cornwallis destroyed": Thomas Jefferson, *The Papers of*

Thomas Jefferson, vol. 13, March 7 to October 1788, ed. Julian P. Boyd (Princeton, N.J.: Princeton University Press, 1956), 363.

186 "But Madam never again": Catherine Sedgwick, "Slavery in New England," *Bentley's Miscellany* 34 (1853): 418.

188 "Anytime while I was a slave,": Ibid., 420.

189 "[Mum Bett] was prepared for them": Richard E. Welch, Jr., "Mumbet and Judge Sedgwick, A Footnote to the Early History of Massachusetts Justice," *Boston Bar Journal* (January 1964): 15.

189 "I Elizabeth Freeman of Stockbridge": Elizabeth Freeman's Will, October 18, 1829, The Elizabeth Freeman Collection, Stockbridge Public Library, Stockbridge, Massachusetts.

190 "She was born a slave": Sidney Kaplan and Emma Nogrady Kaplan, *The Black Presence in the Era of the American Revolution*, rev. ed. (Amherst, Mass.: University of Massachusetts Press, 1989), 247.

190 "OCTOBER 16, 1781": Robert J. Tilden, trans. and ed., "The Doehla Journal," *The William and Mary Quarterly*, 2d ser., 22 (July 1942): 250–51.

191 "I have more than once witnessed": James T. Flexner, *George Washington in the American Revolution, 1775–1783* (Boston: Little, Brown & Co., 1968), 455.

191 "We drove back to the enemy": Johann von Ewald, *Diary of the American War: A Hessian Journal*, trans. and ed. Joseph P. Tustin (New Haven: Yale University Press, 1979), 335.

191 "turned adrift": Joseph Plumb Martin, *Private Yankee Doodle: Being a Narrative of Some of the Adventures, Dangers, and Sufferings of a Revolutionary Soldier*, ed. George E. Scheer (Boston: Little, Brown & Co., 1962), 241.

192 "Many Negroes and mulattos": George Washington, *The Writings of George Washington from the Original Manuscript Sources, 1745–1799*, ed. John C. Fitzpatrick, vol. 23 (Washington, D.C.: United States Government Printing Office, 1931–44), 264–65.

193 "Peace was restored": Boston King, "Memoirs of the Life of Boston King, a Black Preacher, Written by Himself, During his Residence at Kingswood-School," *The (Arminian) Methodist Magazine* (London) 21 (March, April, May, June 1798): 157.
194 "a dishonorable Violation": Benjamin Quarles, *The Negro in the American Revolution* (New York: W. W. Norton & Co., 1961), 168.
195 "Fine boy, stout wench": Graham Russell Hodges, ed., *The Black Loyalist Directory: African Americans in Exile after the American Revolution* (New York: Garland Publishing, with the New England Historic Genealogical Society, 1996).
196 "[I]ndeed the slaves about Baltimore": King, "Memoirs," 110.
196 "I thought I was not worthy": Ibid., 110.
197 "thought I heard a voice": Ibid., 209.
197 "I found my mind drawn out": Ibid., 209.
198 "All . . . was desolation": Sylvia Frey, *Water from the Rock: Black Resistance in a Revolutionary Age* (Princeton, N.J.: Princeton University Press, 1991), 207.
198 "This cursed war": Ibid., 206.
198 "Not the vestiges": Ibid., 206.
201 "The constitution that is submitted": John Ferling, *The First of Men: A Life of George Washington* (Knoxville: University of Tennessee Press, 1988), 361.
201 "Yet, in the aggregate": Ibid., 362.
201 "No mention was made": John P. Kaminski, ed., *A Necessary Evil? Slavery and the Debate over the Constitution* vol. II (Madison, Wis.: Madison House, 1995), 117.
202 "Nothing but the rooting out": Ibid., 244.
202 "I can only say": Ibid., 276.
203 "I wish I could liberate": Ibid., 244–45.
203 "It will probably be asked": Thomas Jefferson, *Notes on the State of Virginia* (Richmond, Va.: J. W. Randolph, 1853), 149.
204 "Our Washington is no more": Barry Schwartz, *George Washington: The Making of an American Symbol* (New York: Free Press, 1987), 91.

204 "Upon the decrease": Ferling, *The First of Men*, 502–3.

212 "I am now sixty-nine years old": *Five Black Lives: The Autobiographies of Venture Smith, James Mars, William Grimes, the Reverend G. W. Offley, and James L. Smith* (Middletown, Conn.: Wesleyan University Press, 1971), 24.

PART THREE
Chapter Seven

229 *"The first command"*: Benjamin Rush, *Letters of Benjamin Rush*, ed. L. H. Butterfield, vol. 2 (Princeton, N.J.: Princeton University Press, 1951), 627.

230 "Can the liberties": Thomas Jefferson, *Notes on the State of Virginia* (Richmond, Va.: J. W. Randolph, 1853), 174.

231 "I tremble for my country": Ibid., 174.

232 "I was awakened": Richard Allen, *The Life Experience and Gospel Labors of the Rt. Rev. Richard Allen* (New York: Abingdon Press, 1960), 15.

232 "One preacher's fiery sermon": Ibid., 17.

233 "I preached in the commons": Ibid., 24.

234 "so general as to embrace all": Gary Nash, *Forging Freedom: The Formation of Philadelphia's Black Community* (Cambridge, Mass.: Harvard University Press, 1988), 113.

235 "We expected to take the seats": Allen, *Life Experience*, 25.

235 "As I was the first proposer": Ibid., 28.

236 "a day to be remembered": Nash, *Forging Freedom*, 121.

236 "SEPTEMBER 2, 1793": Elizabeth Drinker, *Extracts from the Journal of Elizabeth Drinker, from 1759 to 1807 A.D.*, ed. Henry Biddle (Philadelphia: J. B. Lippincott, 1889), 192–94.

237 "The week before last": Thomas Jefferson to Col. David Humphreys, September 11, 1793, André de Coppet Collection, Princeton University, 428.

238 "[T]he meek and humble Jesus": Richard Allen and Absalom Jones, *A Narrative of the Proceedings of the Black People During the Late Awful Calamity in Philadelphia in the Year 1793* (Philadelphia: Independence National Historical Park, 1993), 26.

238 "[W]e think, that when a physician": Ibid., 5.
238 *"You can not immagin"*: Isaac Heston to John Todd, September 19, 1793, Independence National Historical Park Collection, Philadelphia.
247 "The great demand for nurses": Mathew Carey, *A Short Account of the Malignant Fever, Nov. 14, 1793* (Philadelphia: Printed for the Author, 1793), 77.
248 "separate from our white brethren": Nash, *Forging Freedom,* 130.
249 "To keep millions in ignorance": Ethan A. Andrews, *Slavery and the Domestic Slave Trade in the United States* (Boston: Light & Stearns, 1836), 198–99.
250 "The god who created the sun": C. L. R. James, *The Black Jacobins* (New York: Vintage Books, 1963), 87.
251 "a wall of fire": Robert Debs Heinl Jr. and Nancy Gordon Heinl, *Written in Blood: The Story of the Haitian People, 1492–1971* (Boston: Houghton Mifflin Co., 1978), 44.
252 "The City presents": Ibid., 46.
252 "One of them expired": Ibid., 46.
253 "From the summit": Althea de Puech Parham, *My Odyssey: Experiences of a Young Refugee from Two Revolutions, by a Creole of Saint Domingue* (Baton Rouge: Louisiana State University Press, 1959), 91.
254 "The negroes are about to rise": Douglas R. Egerton, *Gabriel's Rebellion* (Chapel Hill: University of North Carolina Press, 1993), 57.
254 "All the whites were to be massacred": Willie Lee Rose, ed., *A Documentary History of Slavery in North America* (New York: Oxford University Press, 1976), 114.
255 "1,000 men was": Ibid., 109–10.
255 "Death or Liberty": Egerton, *Gabriel's Rebellion,* 109.
256 "I have nothing": Robert Sutcliff, *Travels in Some Parts of North America in the Years 1804, 1805, & 1806* (Philadelphia: B & T Kite, 1812), 50.
256 *"There is a strong sentiment"*: Thomas Jefferson, *The Writings*

of Thomas Jefferson, vol. 7, ed. Paul Leicester Ford (New York: G. P. Putman's Sons, 1896), 457–58.

257 "[O]ne cannot go to bed": Jesse Torrey, *A Portraiture of Domestic Slavery in the United States* (St. Clair Shores, Mich.: Scholarly Press, 1970), 12–13.

258 "I told him I had not": Letter from Tobias Lear to James Madison, Cape Frangois, July 17, 1801 in James Madison, *The Papers of James Madison,* Secretary of State Series, vol. 1, ed. Robert J. Brugger (Charlottesville, Va.: University Press of Virginia, 1986).

265 "[W]e shall be the murderers": Jefferson, *Writings,* 168.

265 "Remember that this soil": Stephen Alexis, *Black Liberator: The Life of Toussaint Louverture,* trans. William Stirling (New York: Macmillan Co., 1949), 181.

Chapter Eight

267 "As the state of Virginia": Jeanette Mirsky and Allan Nevins, *The World of Eli Whitney* (New York: Macmillan Co., 1952), 75.

268 "Has the machine": Ibid., 75.

268 "That with this Ginn": Thomas Jefferson, *The Papers of Thomas Jefferson,* vol. 26, ed. John Catanzariti (Princeton, N.J.: Princeton University Press, 1995), 334.

269 "The spirit of the master": Thomas Jefferson, *Notes on the State of Virginia* (Richmond, Va.: J. W. Randolph, 1853), 175.

270 "Let the first of January": Absalom Jones, *A Thanksgiving Sermon, Preached January 1, 1808, in St. Thomas's, or the African Episcopal Church, Philadelphia, on Account of the Abolition of the African Slave Trade, on that Day, by the Congress of the United States* (Philadelphia: Rhistoric Publications, 1969), 19–20.

270 "ordered me to cross": Charles Ball, *Slavery in the United States: A Narrative of the Life and Adventures of Charles Ball, a Black Man* (Detroit, Mich.: Negro History Press, 1970), 24.

271 "To sell cotton": Joseph Ingraham, *The South-west, by a Yankee* (New York: Harper & Brothers, 1835), 91.

272 "resolved to sell my father": Ball, *Slavery in the United States,* 10–11.

272 "We all lay down": Charles Ball, *Fifty Years in Chains* (New York: Dover Publications, 1970), 38–39.

272 "get another wife": Ball, *Fifty Years in Chains,* 36.

273 "She knew that *some*": Harriet Jacobs, *Incidents in the Life of a Slave Girl, Written by Herself,* ed. Jean Fagan Yellin (Cambridge, Mass.: Harvard University Press, 1987), 16.

277 "It has been a subject": Isaac Brown, *The Biography of the Rev. Robert Finley* (New York: Arno Press, 1969), 106–7.

278 "free people of color": Ibid, 115–116.

279 "[A]nd there was not one sole": Paul Cuffe, *Captain Paul Cuffe's Logs and Letters, 1808–1817,* ed. Rosalind Cobb Wiggins (Washington, D.C.: Harvard University Press, 1996), 502.

279 "Whereas our ancestors": Steve Klots, *Richard Allen* (Broomall, Pa.: Chelsea House, 1991), 77.

287 "Jack Pritchard called": *Slave Insurrections: Selected Documents* (Detroit: Negro Universities Press, 1970), 37.

288 "I was one night met at Vesey's": Ibid., 35.

289 "Denmark Vesey . . . It is difficult": John Lofton, *Denmark Vesey's Revolt: The Slave Plot that Lit a Fuse to Fort Sumter* (Kent, Ohio: Kent State University Press, 1983), 161.

289 "In the prosecution": Willie Lee Rose, ed., *A Documentary History of Slavery in North America* (New York: Oxford University Press, 1976), 121.

291 "At this awful point": Jarena Lee, *Religious Experience and Journal of Mrs. Jarena Lee: Giving an Account of Her Call to Preach the Gospel* (Philadelphia: Printed and published for the author, 1849), 3.

291 "That moment": Ibid., 5.

291 "[T]o my utter surprise": Ibid., 10.

291 "[M]y mind became so exercised": Ibid., 10–11.

292 "If the man may preach": Ibid., 11.

292 "God made manifest": Ibid., 17.

292 "had called upon him": Ibid., 17.

293 "Some of the poor slaves": Ibid., 39.
293 "The spirit of the Lord": Ibid., 78, quoting from Isaiah, Chapter 61, Verse 1.
293 "My money was gone": Lee, *Religious Experience*, 61.

Chapter Nine

294 "Their aspirations": Hugh Honour, *The Image of the Black in Western Art*, vol. 4, part 2, general editor, Ladislaw Bugner (Houston, Tex.: Menil Foundation, 1989), 59.
295 "[I]t is impossible": Thomas Branagan, *Serious Remonstrances, Addressed to the Citizens of the Northern States, and Their Representatives* (Philadelphia: Thomas J. Stiles, 1805), 39.
295 "It is a well-known fact": "Letter 4" in James Forten, *Letters from a Man of Colour, on a Late Bill before the Senate of Pennsylvania* (Pennsylvania: s.n., 1813), 8.
297 "a trade practised openly": Julie Winch, "The Underground Railroad," *The Pennsylvania Magazine* 3, no. 1 (January 1987): 6.
298 "Joe was lame": Enoch Lewis, ed., *The African Observer*, May 1827 (Philadelphia: Published by the editor, 1828), 37.
299 "uttered a thought": Thomas Jefferson, *Notes on the State of Virginia* (Richmond, Va.: J. W. Randolph, 1853), 150–51.
300 "To the Caucasian race": Charles Caldwell, *Thoughts on the Original Unity of the Human Race* (New York: E. Bliss, 1830), 136–37.
300 "instead of advancing": Ibid., 139–40.
300 "As there are Caucasian imbeciles": Ibid., 140.
300 "gorging themselves": Ibid., 141.
301 "In our white species": Honour, *Image of the Black*, 18.
301 "that nobly arched head": Ibid., 18.
302 "Absurd as may seem": Annemarie Bean, James V. Hatch, and Brooks McNamara, eds., *Inside the Minstrel Mask: Readings in Nineteenth-Century Blackface Minstrelsy* (Hanover, N.H.: Wesleyan University Press, 1996), 3.
303 "Entering the theater": Gary D. Engle, ed., *The Grotesque Essence: Plays from the American Minstrel Stage* (Baton Rouge: Louisiana State University Press, 1978), xiv.

303 *"[O]n the fiftieth anniversary"*: Thomas Jefferson, *The Writings of Thomas Jefferson,* vol. 10, ed. Paul Leicester Ford (New York: G. P. Putnam's Sons, 1899), 390–91.

304 "Having been at great expence": Thomas Jefferson, *The Papers of Thomas Jefferson,* vol. 27, ed. John Catanzariti (Princeton, N.J.: Princeton University Press, 1995), 119–20.

305 "Inventory of the estate": Inventory of Estate of Thomas Jefferson, Monticello.

305 "Conceive the idea": Willie Lee Rose, ed., *A Documentary History of Slavery in North America* (New York: Oxford University Press, 1976), 143–44.

307 "The Americans say": David Walker, *David Walker's Appeal* (New York: Hill & Wang, 1965), 56.

307 "They [the whites] know well": Ibid., 61.

307 "While labouring in the field": William F. Cheek, *Black Resistance before the Civil War* (Beverly Hills, Calif.: Glencoe Press, 1970), 120–21.

308 "I heard a loud noise": Ibid., 121.

309 "I saw white spirits": Ibid., 120.

309 "[A]rmed with a hatchet": Ibid., 122.

310 "[W]e entered and murdered": Ibid., 123.

310 "Having murdered Mrs. Waller": Ibid., 124.

310 "I sometimes got in sight": Ibid., 124.

311 "Nat Turner's insurrection broke out": Eric Foner, ed., *Nat Turner,* Great Lives Observed (Englewood Cliffs, N.J.: Prentice-Hall, 1971), 69.

311 "I saw a mob dragging": Ibid., 71.

311 "He is a complete fanatic": Cheek, *Black Resistance,* 128.

PART FOUR
Chapter Ten

335 *"I was born a slave"*: Harriet Jacobs, *Incidents in the Life of a Slave Girl: Written by Herself,* ed. Jean Fagan Yellin (Cambridge, Mass.: Harvard University Press, 1987), 5–6.

335 "a bureau & work table": Ibid., 213.

336 "[O]n my fifteenth year": Ibid., 27–28.
336 "Mrs. Flint, like many": Ibid., 12.
337 "I knew the doom": Ibid., 90.
337 "Between these boards": Ibid., 114.
338 "I lived in that dismal hole": Ibid., 114.
338 "Yet I would have chosen": Ibid., 148.
339 "The civil rights of a people": Martin E. Dann, ed., *The Black Press, 1827–1890* (New York: G. P. Putnam's Sons, 1971), 35.
340 "If I remain in this bloody land": Vincent Harding, *There Is a River: The Black Struggle for Freedom in America* (New York: Harcourt Brace Jovanovich, 1992), 81.
341 "Ought we not to form": Ibid., 84.
341 "Let no man of us budge": David Walker, *David Walker's Appeal* (New York: Hill & Wang, 1995), 65.
341 "[T]hey want us for their slaves": Ibid., 25–26.
341 "to awaken in the breasts": Ibid., 2.
342 "[It is] an unshaken": Ibid., 29.
342 "glorious and heavenly cause": Ibid., 12.
343 "If you commence": Ibid., 25.
343 "I will stand my ground": Harding, *There Is a River*, 93.
344 "Assenting to the 'self-evident'": George M. Fredrickson, ed., *William Lloyd Garrison* (Englewood Cliffs, N.J.: Prentice-Hall, 1968), 23.
345 "I do not wish to think": Walter M. Merrill, *Against Wind and Tide: A Biography of William Lloyd Garrison* (Cambridge, Mass.: Harvard University Press, 1963), 45.
347 "I am fully aware": Lydia Maria Child, *An Appeal in Favor of that Class of Americans Called Africans* (Boston: Allen & Ticknor, 1833), 5.
347 "The mob had now increased": William Lloyd Garrison to Sarah Benson, May 19, 1838, Garrison Papers, Anti-Slavery Collection, Boston Public Library.
347 "These are perilous times": Ibid.
348 "The white population is flowing": Lt. Charles Fenton Mercer Noland, *Noland's Cherokee Diary: A U.S. Soldier's Story from*

Inside the Cherokee Nation, ed. Mildred E. Whitmire (Spartanburg, S.C.: Reprint Company, 1990), 6.

349 "What good man": Louis Filler and Allen Guttman, eds., *The Removal of the Cherokee Nation: Manifest Destiny or National Dishonor?* (Boston: D. C. Heath & Co., 1967), 51.

349 "a race not admitted": Theda Purdue and Michael D. Green, eds., *The Cherokee Removal: A Brief History with Documents* (Boston: Bedford Books of St. Martin's Press, 1995).

350 "While the contact of the white man": George M. Fredrickson, *The Black Image in the White Mind: The Debate on Afro-American Character and Destiny, 1817–1914* (New York: Harper & Row, 1971), 78.

351 "We arrived at [Clarkson Depot]": Jacob Stroyer, *My Life in the South* (Salem, Mass.: Newcomb & Gauss, 1898), 40–41.

351 "Here you may behold": *Alexandria (Virginia) Gazette*, June 22, 1827.

351 "a procession of men": Jesse Torrey, *American Slave Trade* (London: J. M. Cobbett, 1822), 55–56, 96–97.

352 "It is surrounded by": Edward Srutt Abdy, *Journal of a Residence and Tour in the United States of North America*, vol. 2 (London: John Murray, 1835), 96–97.

353 "Much excitement": *The Washington Globe*, August 31, 1839.

355 "outrageous violation": Howard Jones, *Mutiny on the Amistad* (New York: Oxford University Press, 1987), 156.

355 *"What for Americans keep us in prison?"*: John W. Blassingame, ed., *Slave Testimony: Two Centuries of Letters, Speeches, Interviews, and Autobiographies* (Baton Rouge: Louisiana State University Press, 1989), 33–34.

356 *"I want to write a letter"*: Ibid., 33–34.

356 "If then, these Negroes": Deirdre Mullane, ed., *Crossing the Danger Water: Four Hundred Years of African-American Writing* (New York: Anchor Books, 1993), 105.

358 "When I married Mr. Butler": Frances Anne Kemble, *Journal of a Residence on a Georgian Plantation in 1838–1839*, ed. John A. Scott (New York: Alfred A. Knopf, 1961), 138.

358 "Mr. B[utler], in his letter, maintains": Ibid., 4–5.
359 "Buried in tattered": Ibid., 70.
359 "Such of these dwellings": Ibid., 68.
360 "*Nanny* has had three children": Ibid., 230–31.
360 "I do not think that a residence": Ibid., 93.
361 "I saw Joe": Ibid., 136.
361 "[King] heard that [Joe]": Ibid., 138.
362 "I see that man": Ibid., 81.
363 "Today . . . I have had": Ibid., 210.
363 "This is no place for me": Ibid., 211.

Chapter Eleven

364 *"When I started"*: Harriet Jacobs, *Incidents in the Life of a Slave Girl: Written by Herself*, ed. Jean Fagan Yellin (Cambridge, Mass.: Harvard University Press, 1987), 99.
365 "I never could": Ibid., 156.
365 "The next morning": Ibid., 158.
365 *"You may perhaps think"*: John W. Blassingame, ed., *Slave Testimony: Two Centuries of Letters, Speeches, Interviews, and Autobiographies* (Baton Rouge: Louisiana State University Press, 1989), 49.
366 "At times we were almost tempted": Frederick Douglass, *The Life and Times of Frederick Douglass* (New York: Collier Books, 1962), 161–62.
367 "I warn abolitionists": Eugene Genovese, *The Slaveholders' Dilemma: Freedom and Progress in Southern Conservative Thought, 1820–1860* (Columbia, S.C.: University of South Carolina Press, 1992), 93.
367 "Colored people were allowed": Jacobs, *Incidents*, 162–63.
368 "They are not slaves": Frances Anne Kemble, *Journal of a Residence on a Georgia Plantation in 1838–1839* (New York: Alfred A. Knopf, 1961), 7.
368 "[I]mmediately after my arrival": Frederick Douglass, *Narrative of the Life of Frederick Douglass, an American Slave*, ed. Houstin A. Baker Jr. (New York: Penguin Group, 1982), 143–44.

369 "He was a whole-souled man": Vincent Harding, *There Is a River: The Black Struggle for Freedom in America* (New York: Harcourt Brace Jovanovich, 1992), 123–24.

371 *"Slavery is alike": The Life and Writings of Frederick Douglass:* vol. 2, *Pre–Civil War Decade, 1850–1860,* ed. Philip S. Foner (New York: International Publishers, 1950), 47.

371 "They say that the negroes": Peter C. Ripley, ed., *Witness for Freedom: African American Voices on Race, Slavery, and Emancipation* (Chapel Hill: University of North Carolina Press, 1993), 80–81.

372 "I can remember my father": Josiah Henson, *The Life of Josiah Henson, Formerly a Slave, Now an Inhabitant of Canada, as Narrated by Himself* (Boston: A. D. Phelps, 1849), 1–2.

372 "I often found myself": Douglass, *Narrative,* 85.

373 "It is not the black man's color": *The Life and Writings of Frederick Douglass,* vol. 2, 128–30.

383 "Think of the undying glory": Peter C. Ripley, *The Black Abolitionist Papers,* vol. 3, *The United States, 1830–1846* (Chapel Hill: University of North Carolina Press, 1991), 408–9.

384 "the propagators of American slavery": Harding, *There Is a River,* 150.

385 "We will resist the settlement": Leon Litwack, *North of Slavery: The Negro in the Free States* (Chicago: University of Chicago Press, 1961), 167.

385 "Resolved, that our only hope": Harding, *There Is a River,* 146.

385 "We solemnly dedicate": "To Our Oppressed Countrymen," *The North Star* 1, no. 1, December 3, 1847.

386 "welcome the news": *The Life and Writings of Frederick Douglass,* vol. 1, *The Early Years: 1817–1849,* ed. Philip S. Foner (New York: International Publishers, 1950), 398–99.

387 "On the morning": *The Society of California Pioneers, Autobiographies,* vol. 1, 46.

389 "It was the beginning of a reign of terror": Jacobs, *Incidents,* 191.

389 "If any man approaches": Harding, *There Is a River,* 159.
397 "This Fourth of July": *The Life and Writings of Frederick Douglass,* vol. 2, 189, 192.
398 "I met them at the landing": William Loren Katz, *Eyewitness: A Living Documentary of the African American Contribution to American History* (New York: Simon & Schuster, 1967), 193.
399 *"Dr. W. Higginson"*: Samuel May to W. Higginson, May 25, 1854, Rare Books Department, Boston Public Library, Ms #B.1.22 (4).
400 "[W]e hammered away": Katz, *Eyewitness,* 195.
400 "For a *white* man": *The Life and Writings of Frederick Douglass,* vol. 2, 288.
401 "A colored man is living": Ripley, *Witness for Freedom,* 183.
401 "We went to bed one night": William H. Pease and Jane H. Pease, *The Fugitive Slave Law and Anthony Burns: A Problem in Law Enforcement* (Philadelphia: J. B. Lippincott Co., 1975), 43.
402 "Through that long week": *Liberator,* July 7, 1854.
402 "Our worst fears": Charlotte Forten Grimké, *The Journals of Charlotte Forten Grimké,* ed. Brenda Stevenson (New York: Oxford University Press, 1988), 65–66.
403 "Can any one fail": Pease, *The Fugitive Slave Law and Anthony Burns,* 52.
411 "It seems strange": Joanna Stratton, *Pioneer Women: Voices from the Kansas Frontier* (New York: Simon & Schuster, 1981), 237.
412 "Come on, then, gentlemen": James A. Rawley, *Race and Politics: "Bleeding Kansas" and the Coming of the Civil War* (Lincoln: University of Nebraska Press, 1969), 80.
412 "witnessed extraordinary meetings": Elmer Le Roy Craik, *Southern Interest in Territorial Kansas, 1854–1858,* vol. 15 (Lawrence: Kansas State Historical Society, 1922), 347.
412 "Opposing slavery and hating": *The Life and Writings of Frederick Douglass,* vol. 2, 387.
413 "an investment which promises": "Missouri's Pro-Slavery

Fight for Kansas, 1854–1855" in *Missouri Historical Review* 48 (1953–1954): 226.

414 *"In some small towns"*: *The Mississippi Valley Historical Review* 6, no. 4 (1919–1920): 557–58.

414 "never lost sight": Frederick Douglass, *Narrative of the Life of Frederick Douglass, an American Slave; My Bondage and My Freedom; Life and Times*, ed. Henry Louis Gates Jr. (New York: Library of America, 1994), 743.

414 "malignant spirits": Stephen Oates, *To Purge This Land with Blood: A Biography of John Brown*, 2nd ed. (Amherst, Mass.: University of Massachusetts Press, 1984), 79.

414 *"[W]e heard that"*: *The Mississippi Valley Historical Review* 6, no. 4 (1919–1920): 559.

415 "The horrors wrought": Frederick Douglass, *The Life and Times of Frederick Douglass*, 303.

415 "[T]he sympathy and admiration": J. Saunders Redding, *They Came in Chains: Americans from Africa* (Philadelphia: Lippincott, 1973), 125.

416 "There is much declamation": George M. Fredrickson, ed., *William Lloyd Garrison* (Englewood Cliffs, N.J.: Prentice-Hall, 1968), 141.

416 "[T]he constitution of the United States": Frederick Douglass, *My Bondage and My Freedom* (New York: Dover, 1969), 397.

418 "We have come to the conclusion": Don E. Fehrenbacher, *The Dred Scott Case: Its Significance in American Law and Politics* (New York: Oxford University Press, 1978), 364.

418 "beings of an inferior order": Richard Kluger, *Simple Justice: The History of Brown v. Board of Education and Black America's Struggle for Equality* (New York: Alfred A. Knopf, 1976), 39.

419 "We are now told": *The Life and Writings of Frederick Douglass*, vol. 2, 410–11.

419 "The Supreme Court of the United States": Ibid., 411.

Chapter Twelve

420 *"Dear husband"*: John W. Blassingame, ed., *Slave Testimony: Two Centuries of Letters, Speeches, Interviews, and Autobiographies* (Baton Rouge: Louisiana State University Press, 1989), 118–19.

422 "Slavery, throughout its entire existence": Stephen B. Oates, *To Purge This Land with Blood: A Biography of John Brown*, 2nd ed. (Amherst, Mass.: University of Massachusetts Press, 1984), 245.

424 "[H]e put his arms": Frederick Douglass, *Life and Times of Frederick Douglass* (New York: Collier Books, 1962), 320.

424 "I told him": Ibid., 319–20.

425 "I asked Green": Ibid., 320.

425 "On Sunday morning": Osborne Perry Anderson, *A Voice from Harper's Ferry* (Boston: Printed for the Author, 1861), 28.

425 "And now, gentlemen": Ibid., 28–29.

426 "At eight o'clock": Ibid., 31.

427 "[A]s the sun arose": Ibid., 36–37.

427 "Of the men shot": Ibid., 60.

427 "Dangerfield Newby": Ibid., 40.

428 "It was no part of the original plan": Ibid., 38.

429 "I never did intend murder": Address of John Brown to the Virginia Court on November 2, 1859, Oberlin College Archives, Oberlin, Ohio.

429 "In the name of the young girl": Frances Ellen Watkins Harper, *A Brighter Coming Day: A Frances Ellen Watkins Harper Reader*, ed. Frances Smith Foster (New York: Feminist Press at the City University of New York, 1990), 49.

430 *"My fate, so far as man can seal it"*: John Copeland to his parents, November 26, 1859, Oberlin College Archives, Oberlin, Ohio.

431 "FOR SALE": Malcolm Bell Jr., *Major Butler's Legacy: Five Generations of a Slaveholding Family* (Athens: University of Georgia Press, 1987), 328.

432 "The buyers were generally": Q. K. Philander Doesticks [aka Mortimer Neal Thomson], *What Became of the Slaves on a Georgia Plantation? Great Auction Sale of Slaves, at Savannah, Georgia, March 2nd & 3rd, 1859. A Sequel to Mrs. Kemble's Journal* (n.p., 1863), 4. Originally published as an article in the *New York Daily Tribune*, March 9, 1859.

432 "You may say what you like": Ibid., 13.

433 "Pierce Butler has gone": Bell, *Major Butler's Legacy*, 325.

433 "Families will not be separated": Ibid., 325.

434 "Who can tell how closely": Doesticks, *What Became of the Slaves*, 5.

435 "The men obsequiously": Ibid., 11.

435 "The wind howled": Ibid., 11.

436 "111—Anson": Ibid., 12.

436 "On the faces of all": Ibid., 7.

437 "That man was Pierce M. Butler": Ibid., 20.

438 "[T]he stars shone": Ibid., 20.

438 "Mr. Joe Walton said": James Mellon, ed., *Bullwhip Days: The Slaves Remember, An Oral History* (New York: Weidenfeld & Nicolson, 1988), 339.

440 "I guess we musta celebrated": Leon Litwack, *Been in the Storm So Long: The Aftermath of Slavery* (New York: Vintage Books, 1980), 173.

440 "Didn't do to say": Ibid., 175–76.

441 "I was 21": Ibid., 177.

442 *"Dear Mrs. Cheney"*: Harriet Jacobs, *Incidents in the Life of a Slave Girl, Written by Herself*, ed. Jean Fagan Yellin (Cambridge, Mass.: Harvard University Press, 1987), 249–50.

443 "During all my slave life": John W. Blassingame, *Slave Testimony: Two Centuries of Letters, Speeches, Interviews, and Autobiographies* (Baton Rouge: Louisiana State University Press, 1977), 744.

443 "We has a right": Eric Foner, *Reconstruction: America's Unfinished Revolution, 1863–1877* (New York: Harper & Row, 1988), 105.

443 "We feel that there is": James M. McPherson, *The Negro's Civil War: How American Negroes Felt and Acted During the War for the Union* (New York: Vintage Books, 1967), 309.
444 "Sir, old things are passing": Ibid., 309.
444 "Colored Men!": Ibid., 290.
445 "The chance is now given": Frederick Douglass, *Narrative of the Life of Frederick Douglass, an American Slave; My Bondage and My Freedom; Life and Times*, ed. Henry Louis Gates Jr. (New York: Library of America, 1994), 780.

Acknowledgments

This book is a companion to the four-part documentary series *Africans in America* produced by WGBH Boston for public television. So many people have given their talent, vision, hard work, and dedication to the creation of this book that it is impossible adequately to thank them all.

Karen Johnson, executive director of publishing and product merchandising at WGBH, believed from the beginning in the idea of combining a narrative nonfiction text with fictional stories inspired by the history as a way to enter and understand sometimes difficult subject matter, and she worked hard to secure the author team who could bring this notion to fruition. She also provided valuable advice and support all along the way.

Throughout the project, Nancy Lattanzio, the senior editor for WGBH Publishing, was a tireless leader and guide through a complicated production process. Her attention to the day-to-day details as well as her vision of the big picture allowed us all to contribute and participate as a coordinated and collaborative creative team. Her unwavering desire that every detail receive the utmost attention and care made an ambitious idea also seem doable, the journey of this book pleasurable and satisfying.

We cannot thank Patricia Smith and Charles Johnson enough for the passion and creativity they produced on these pages. Patricia's prose brought to life both the poignancy and pain and the unflagging spirit of resistance that laces through this history. Charles Johnson dived into the history and the fictional possibilities it suggests and found ways to open doors in our minds. His inventiveness never ceases to amaze us. His insight into the complexities of human nature challenges us. We owe an enormous debt of gratitude and admiration to them both.

Steve Fayer, scriptwriter for the television series, has given so much to this book. He read every word of every draft and sent us back to check and recheck facts and interpretations. He suggested new avenues to explore and encouraged us to peel away our preconceptions to find more complex truths, urging us always to let the history speak for itself. If any errors have found their way into this text, it is certainly not for lack of vigilance on Steve's part. He has been the book's chief guide, a crucial collaborator.

Jane Isay, our editor at Harcourt Brace, has been a staunch believer in the book from the beginning. She has carried it on her capable shoulders with an inimitable mix of intelligence, humor, and persuasiveness, patiently cajoling and rewarding us at all the right times. She has been an extraordinary partner in the creation of the book and has made a wonderful place for it at Harcourt.

The television program producers, Susan Bellows, Noland Walker, Jacquie Jones, and Llew Smith, have shared two very precious commodities with us—their ideas and their time. This book has been the direct beneficiary of their research and creativity, and it is indebted to them for so willingly taking the time—time they didn't have—to discuss, read, and critique chapters.

On that same note, we owe a huge debt of thanks to the many talented associate producers, researchers, and production people on the series for somehow fitting critical research and fact checking for the book into their already demanding schedules. Patricia Garcia-Rios, Megan Gelstein, Catherine Benedict, Aimee Sands, Abby Whitlow, and Franziska Blome were all there when we needed them, which was very often! Ann Bennett, Leslie Norman, and Karen Carroll also provided crucial support.

For additional assistance with the manuscript we are grateful to our academic readers Professor Peter Wood, Duke University; Gary Nash, University of California at Los Angeles; and David Blight, University of Massachusetts. Thanks to all of them, whose candor and expertise we depended on.

In addition, a special thanks goes to senior producer Susan Bellows for her help with an endless stream of queries and her crucial role in coordinating overall book and series efforts. Thanks also to producer Jacquie Jones for taking on the job of writing captions. Her unique perspective has added a whole other dimension to the book.

Our photo researcher, Debby Paddock, has done a superb job responding to crazy deadlines and requests to locate an ever-shifting list of difficult-to-find images. Her poise, dedication, and professionalism made it possible to get the job done.

Olivia Parker has created beautiful and compelling art for the book's jacket and for the series, distilling many levels of mood and meaning and translating them into collage.

Many more behind-the-scenes people have all in some way gone a few extra miles to make this book possible. At WGBH we'd like to acknowledge Marita Rivero, executive in charge of production; Alison Kennedy, graphic designer for the TV series and its ancillary materials; Jeffery Garmel, WGBH attorney; Karen Barss; Lisa Gregory; Beth Kirsch; Judy Matthews; Bara Levin; and Naomi Cummings. At Harcourt Brace, we thank David Hough, our more-than-patient managing editor, whose flexible attitude was key; Lorie Stoopack, whose capable presence we counted on; advertising manager Dori Weintraub, marketing manager Jennifer Holiday, and publicist Lynn Goldberg, whose professionalism was matched only by their enthusiasm; Vaughn Andrews; copyeditor Rachel Myers, for her truly outstanding efforts; book designer Linda Lockowitz; and publisher Dan Farley. Special thanks also to Ruth Davis and Miriam Powers.

Our sincerest appreciation goes also to Steve Axelrod, our devoted agent of many years.

We would also like to thank the television series funders for their support. A separate list of funders follows below.

A bold idea always has a beginning. The idea for a documentary television series on the history of slavery in this nation began in the editorial room of the *American Experience* and was developed and relentlessly pursued by Judy Crichton and her staff, Margaret Drain, Llew Smith, and Peter Cook, more than ten years ago. It is a long journey from idea to completion in the world of documentary filmmaking and PBS programming. We thank and salute the foresight and determination of those with the *American Experience* who believed then and now in the power and the importance of remembering the past.

—Orlando N. Bagwell
Executive Producer
Africans in America

SERIES FUNDERS

Major funding for *Africans in America* was provided by the National Endowment for the Humanities. National sponsorship was provided by Bankers Trust and the Fannie Mae Foundation. Additional funding was provided by the Ford Foundation, The John D. and Catherine T. MacArthur Foundation, The Rockefeller Foundation, Stratford Foundation, the Corporation for Public Broadcasting, and public television viewers.

Africans in America is a production of WGBH Boston.

INDEX

Note: Italic page numbers indicate photographs and related captions. Fictional accounts are indicated by the word *story* in parentheses.